LESSONS FROM RESTRUCTURING EXPERIENCES

SUNY Series, Restructuring and School Change

H. Dickson Corbett and Betty Lou Whitford, Editors

LESSONS FROM RESTRUCTURING EXPERIENCES

STORIES OF CHANGE
IN PROFESSIONAL DEVELOPMENT SCHOOLS

EDITED BY
NANCY E. HOFFMAN, W. MICHAEL REED,
AND GWEN SOCOL ROSENBLUTH

STATE UNIVERSITY OF NEW YORK PRESS

Published by
State University of New York Press, Albany

For information, address State University of New York Press,
State University Plaza, Albany, N.Y. 12246

Production by M. R. Mulholland
Marketing by Theresa A. Swierzowski

Library of Congress Cataloging-in-Publication Data

Lessons from restructuring experiences : stories of change in
    professional development schools / edited by Nancy E. Hoffman, W.
    Michael Reed, and Gwen Socol Rosenbluth.
        p.   cm. — (SUNY series, restructuring and school change)
    Includes bibliographical references and index.
    ISBN 0-7914-3407-9 (hc : acid free). — ISBN 0-7914-3408-7 (pb :
acid free)
    1. Laboratory schools—United States.   2. College-school
cooperation—United States.   3. Educational change—United States.
4. School improvement programs—United States.   5. Action research
in education—United States.   I. Hoffman, Nancy E., 1952-
II. Reed, W. Michael.   III. Rosenbluth, Gwen Socol, 1940-
IV. Series.
LB2154.A3L47   1997
370'.711—dc20   96-34720
                                                              CIP

10 9 8 7 6 5 4 3 2 1

CONTENTS

Part III. The Outcomes of Restructuring: Problems and Possibilities

INTRODUCTION

"Stories have the power to direct and change our lives."

—Nel Noddings (1991, 157)

School restructuring is a complex, difficult, and highly contextual process. Even in school communities that are solidly committed to reform, members are likely to discover that the journey to systemic change is a long and arduous one. Those who initiate and participate in restructuring may seek recipes for achieving their goals and assurances about outcomes, but the reality is that there are no algorithms for effective restructuring and no up-front guarantees about results.

Despite the complicated, site-specific nature of substantive educational reform, experts suggest that we must move beyond "first-order" changes (those that simply help us do what we already do more efficiently and effectively) if we are to create the schools we need for the future. America's educators appear ready to accept this challenge. The results of *Instructor's* recent National Teacher Survey portray a teaching force committed to substantive school reform ("Teachers Want Change," 1993). Despite their interest in change, educators will need help in finding their way through the maze of issues encountered when they attempt school restructuring. Fullan, perhaps more effectively than anyone else, has tried to provide helpful guidance for those who take on the work of educational change; however, despite his success in this regard and despite the importance he attaches to second-order change, he chose not to address restructuring in *The New Meaning of Educational Change.*

> I will not take on here the big question of restructuring. . . . We are still at the early stages of restructuring experiments, which should serve to help clarify the concept and debug how it might best be implemented. (Fullan 1991, 87–88)

Professional development schools are one of the approaches being used to foster school restructuring but the approach is unique in that it focuses on simultaneous restructuring of schools and teacher preparation, thus requiring ongoing school-university collaboration. The history of prior school-university collaborations has been described as a "long and happy saga . . . 'a glowing picture of non-events' in which 'the glow of advertising exaggerate[s] the radiance of the product.'" (Ross 1995, 195) Can professional development schools be any different? Can the "reality approach the rhetoric?" (Ross 1995, 195)

Some publications that focus on restructuring through the use of professional development schools have appeared, most notably Darling-Hammond's *Professional Development Schools: Schools for Developing a Profession* (1994). These publications help clarify the meaning of second-order change in schools and the concept of professional development schools and, in that regard, they are quite helpful to those interested in exploring this approach to reform. However, there is a need for works featuring first-person accounts that can inform others by illuminating the processes and results of professional development school work. The stories of those who have first-hand experience with such work are a valuable resource for anyone considering restructuring and may help those who are new to the process to "go the distance" and to reach their goals. As Carter (1993) noted, stories are central to teachers' knowledge and are "especially useful devices for dealing with situation, conflict or obstacle, motive, and causality. . . . to impose order and coherence on the stream of experience and work out the meaning of incidents and events in the real world" (7).

Lessons from Restructuring Experiences: Stories of Change in Professional Development Schools is intended to fill this need for narrative accounts of change. The book was conceived, written, and edited collaboratively by participants in the Benedum Collaborative, an eight-year-old restructuring partnership between West Virginia University and four county school systems in north-central West Virginia. Using the professional development school (PDS) idea as their starting place, the Benedum Collaborative participants set out to achieve significant change in a diverse group of public schools.

West Virginia University, a partner in the Benedum Collaborative, is a member of the Holmes Group, a national consortium of universities committed to education reform. The Benedum Collaborative has made significant, substantive progress in implementing the consortium's professional development schools (PDS) concept. West Virginia University collaborated with the Holmes Group to conduct one of eight state case studies on the contexts of educational change, which will soon be released. In addition to participation in the Holmes Group, The Benedum Collaborative is a participant in the National Center for Restructuring Education, Schools, and Teaching (NCREST), a network for the nation's restructuring community. Its affiliates are a group of reform projects with proven track records in school change.

The Benedum Collaborative's professional development schools (PDSs) host dozens of visitors each year from various regions in the United States. The school teachers and administrators and university personnel who make these site visits come to learn the what, why, and how of PDS facilitated restructuring from those who are actually living it. *Lessons from Restructuring Experiences: Stories of Change in Professional Development Schools* provides in print what these visitors gain in person—an enhanced understanding of the complex but achievable nature of second-order school change and helpful guidance on initiating and sustaining a collaborative restructuring effort using the PDS model. This understanding is conveyed through the personal experiences of participants in school change. In their own words, teachers, administrators, and university faculty share their varied stories and explain what their experiences with school change have meant to them. They describe the values that fuel their reform efforts, the significant events in their journey toward change, and the exciting possibilities for themselves and their students that have been discovered along the way.

The book is divided into three units. The chapters in the first unit, *Working Together to Restructure in Professional Development Schools*, are designed to help readers construct an overall understanding of the concepts and processes of restructuring and collaboration that are important in professional development school work. The second unit, *Stories of Professional Development School Change*, features stories of various aspects of change resulting from school restructuring in The Benedum Collaborative. The chapters of the third unit, *The Outcomes of Restructuring: Problems and Possibilities*, address the complexities of assessing the outcomes of restructuring in both school and university settings.

We intend that this book inform a variety of audiences. It might serve as a primary text in courses focused on issues of school reform/restructuring, educational change, or educational collaboration/partnerships. The volume could serve well as a supplemental text in courses on such topics as school leadership, elementary or secondary curriculum, curriculum development, contemporary trends in curriculum/teaching, teacher empowerment, professionalism in teaching, teacher-as-leader, or school organization. Administrators or teachers who are considering initiating or are in the midst of a restructuring effort should find the book extremely helpful. It will be a valuable professional reference for university and school personnel and others interested in educational reform and school change.

Although the work we describe was done in West Virginia, its value is not limited to our small state. Our experiences in implementing the professional development school model of reform in "regular" schools and a "regular" higher education institution are universal. The children, teachers, and university faculty involved in this effort face the same issues that educators face across this country—issues of confidence, uncertainty, inequity, expectations, and ethics. Questions about the role teachers should play in school leadership, questions about the value of personal, practical knowledge, and questions about the future abound here and everywhere else. School reform done with "regular" schools in West Virginia or anywhere else can inform the practice of others interested in school reform.

In the midst of reform, it is encouraging to hear firsthand accounts of others' experiences. Such stories are a reminder that restructuring that improves the education of children and the professional lives of educators really can be done. We hope this book will be a source of guidance and encouragement for others as they undertake the formidable task of restructuring.

References

Carter, K. (1993). The place of story in the study of teaching and teacher education. *Educational Researcher* 22(1): 5–12, 18.

Darling-Hammond, L. (1994). *Professional development schools: Schools for developing a profession.* New York: Teachers College Press.

Fullan, M. G. (1991). *The new meaning of educational change.* New York: Teachers College Press.

Noddings, N. (1991). Stories in dialogue: Caring and interpersonal reasoning. In C. Witherall and N. Noddings, eds. *Stories lives tell: Narrative and dialogue in education,* pp. 57–170. New York: Teachers College Press.

Teachers Want Change (1993). *Instructor* 102(5): 34–41.

PART I

WORKING TOGETHER TO RESTRUCTURE IN PROFESSIONAL DEVELOPMENT SCHOOLS

OVERVIEW OF PART I

Fullan (1993) describes productive educational change as "uncontrollably complex" (19), suggesting that there is no recipe for effective change and ". . . the solution lies in better ways of thinking about, and dealing with, inherently unpredictable processes" (19). After six years of experience in a complex, multi-site professional development school (PDS) restructuring effort, the authors of this book agree. This book does not offer recipes for restructuring. It does offer insights gained from several years of productive experience in restructuring—insights that will help readers think about this complex process.

Part I of this book is intended to give the reader some ways to think about the contexts, processes, frustrations, and rewards of productive educational change, setting the stage for the subsequent stories of particular PDSs' restructuring efforts and their outcomes. Chapter 1 addresses the literature on reform and teacher professionalism. Chapter 2 addresses the literature on collaboration, focusing on collaboration between universities and K–12 schools. In Chapter 3, the reader is introduced to a particular restructuring effort, the Benedum Collaborative, which has employed the professional development school model in a collaborative restructuring effort. The chapters in Part I might be read in their entirety before reading the remainder of the book, or they might be read selectively, with Chapter 3 serving as a reference for readers perusing the change stories in Part II.

In Chapter 1, Dempsey examines the purposes of educational reform, with particular emphasis on the nature of teacher professionalism. Exploring the implications of reform for teachers, students, and society, he provides readers with a background on professinalism that will inform their reading of the remainder of the book.

In Chapter 2, Shive examines the literature on collaboration between schools and universities in the context of educational reform. He notes the many, and often conflicting, definitions of collaboration, the forms collaboration may take, and the assumptions in which it is grounded. The primary role of culture is examined, as are the challenges and benefits of collaborative work, and the keys to successful collaboration. Readers will find that the chapter's review of the literature on collaboration provides a useful background for reading the chapters in the second part of the book, which explore the initiation and impact of collaborative restructuring in the multiple PDS sites of this particular change effort.

In Chapter 3, Steel and Hoffman provide readers with information about the context of the West Virginia restructuring effort that is the focus of the book, the Benedum Collaborative. Mindful of Fullan's emphasis on the importance of context and history in change efforts, the chapter begins with a history of the Benedum Project, describing its origins, goals, scope, and critical events since the Project's inception in 1988. In the second section of the chapter, the authors provide "biographies" of the six public schools whose professional development school work is depicted in the book. Some readers will wish to read this chapter in its entirety for background. Other readers will prefer to read only the first section, referring to the individual school "biographies" as they begin a chapter that tells a story of change in that school.

Readers completing Part I should have an understanding of the context of restructuring, both as it is depicted in the literature and as it has been experienced by those initiating the Benedum Project—an understanding that will enrich readers' appreciation of the stories of PDS reform in Part II, the outcomes of restructuring in Part III, and the challenges of PDS reform in any context.

1

THE NATURE OF PROFESSIONALISM IN THE CONTEXT OF SCHOOL REFORM

VAN DEMPSEY

Introduction

A theme in the school reform movement has been the call by educators and reformers alike for the professionalization of teaching. What follows in this chapter deals with this theme, and it is useful to describe the context surrounding professionalism in teaching. Efforts to professionalize teaching have become embedded in the plethora of other efforts to improve schools and the education of children. In professional development school initiatives the lines between these efforts tend to overlap and become indistinct. At the same time that educators and reformers began calling for the development of teaching as a profession, the general public was calling for broader and dramatic overhauling of schools. The early and mid-1980s saw the proliferation of commission reports detailing what by the close of the 1980s Sarason referred to as "the predictable failure of school reform" (1990). This predictable and continued failure, according to Sarason, was due to the "intractability" of schools. Raywid offers this explanation:

> Schools are notoriously difficult to change. One major reason is their interconnectedness. Indeed schools are very much like jigsaw puzzles; everything is connected to everything else. It is impossible to modify any one piece without also altering those pieces connected to it—which in turn can require changing successively larger rings of pieces increasingly further from where one began. (1990, 141)

The response to the outcry of the commission reports, as voiced in *A Nation at Risk* (1983), and the need to address fundamental changes in the "puzzle" of schooling was called "restructuring."

Reform is basically about changing the organization and governance of schools in order to encourage school improvement. Reform efforts are intended to change the "rules, roles and relationships" that are the structure in and around schools (Wilson 1971). Elmore discusses ideas around which reform efforts have been organized, including "empowerment of teachers, students and parents to play a more influential role in determining what schools do," "holding schools more accountable for the results they produce with students," and "orienting schools and the people who work in them toward serious, sustained engagement in academic learning" which includes "teaching for understanding" that in turn requires "very different knowledge and skills on the part of educators and very different conditions of work in schools" (1990, 5–9).

One facet of this reform effort has been the attempt to move teaching from at worst an occupation and at best a semi-profession to a full-fledged profession recognized by the public as such. Part of this work has been to change the nature of schools as suggested above, and professional development schools have been one initiative in that direction. The Holmes Group and NCREST (National Center for Restructuring Education, Schools, and Teaching) are two national organizations that have been leaders in this approach to reform. Both groups have proposed visions of what schools would look like under PDS ideals, and both groups' proposals help to describe the kind of work that teachers would do that would, in these organizations' eyes, be deemed professional (NCREST 1993; The Holmes Group 1990). Central to each group's recommendations is the idea that in order for schools to be more valuable institutions for children in their learning and educational well-being, they have to become different kinds of places for the adults who work in them. Both reform groups argue for school cultures that promote and sustain professional renewal and growth. This process includes a particular focus on teachers and principals who see themselves as critical and reflective practitioners, and as professionals who construct, work from, and act on a knowledge base generated out of the contextual life of schooling.

The following discussion is based on several premises. First, there is an ongoing and concerted effort to make teaching more like a profession in the public eye. Second, the efforts to professionalize teaching have been problematic at best and have had little impact at worst. Third, part of the difficulty in the professionalization of teaching is the misappropriation of models of professionalism that have been abstracted from other professions, namely medicine. Fourth, and most importantly, because of the unique, highly contextual nature of the work of teachers, discussions of teaching as a profession should begin with that context and with the daily lives of teachers. Such discussion would be a critical component in school reform.

Top-down, outside-in efforts at professionalization have at their base the assumption that if teaching is treated like vocations that have been successfully professionalized—medicine being the most noted—then it, too, will become a profession. Much of what has been written focuses on how teaching has failed in the quest to achieve the status and rewards commensurate with being a profession, and how it might, like medicine before it, become a profession.

The Critique of Teaching as a Non-Profession

The current lack of public confidence in education as well as other professions is not a new phenomenon, and even the much-emulated medical profession has a mixed history. Oliver Wendell Holmes commented in 1869 that "if the whole materia medica, as now used, could be sunk to the bottom of the sea, it would be all the better for mankind—and all the worse for the fishes" (Numbers 1988, 55). With the same disgust for the medical profession, one of its members stated in the mid-1850s:

> It is very well understood among college boys . . . that after a man has failed in scholarship, failed in writing, failed in speaking, failed in every purpose for which he entered college; after he has dropped down from class to class; after he has been kicked out of college, there is one unfailing city of refuge—the profession of medicine. (Numbers 1988, 58)

In an age when medicine, in spite of persistent problems in areas such as cost escalation and malpractice, continues to rank supreme among professions in this country, it is hard to imagine the depths of social disrespect from which it has risen. It is equally difficult to imagine that education, currently the target of criticism such as medicine suffered a century ago, might ever even approach the professional status and privilege that medicine attained in the first half of this century.

A Nation At Risk (1983), in paralleling the tenor of Holmes's critique above, sharply criticized the occupation of teaching for "being drawn from the bottom quarter of graduating high school and college students," for suffering from training in a "curriculum [that] is weighted heavily with courses in 'educational methods' at the expense of courses in subjects to be taught," for unacceptably low salaries, for lack of autonomy, and for staffing the most important courses in school with people unqualified to fulfill those positions. This landmark statement on public education and the 1986 publication of *A Nation Prepared: Teachers for the Twenty First Century* by the Carnegie Foundation highlighted the perilous nature of teaching as a "profession" in this country. Efforts since 1983 have too often focused on applying external models of professionalism to teaching, models that typically disregard the contexts and organizational environments in which teaching occurs. Our effort here is to refocus on that context, and on the relationship of the development of teacher professionalism with professional development schools.

The point is not to argue that models of professionalism that have worked in other contexts such as medicine fail entirely to speak to teaching. An examination of the history of professions in general, and the history of medicine in particular, contextually could speak rather profoundly to the professionalization of teaching. But that is different from adoption and application of models that have worked in other contexts.

Professionalization is not about oft-cited characteristics of collegial control, client centeredness, and scientific knowledge, but about shared experiences between those who are to fulfill professional roles and those for whom professional roles are filled. Professionalism is about shared experiences between professionals and clients, professionals and knowledge, professionals and colleagues, and professionals and the public, which ultimately grants symbolic authority to a profession. The professionalization of teaching is not about recruitment and retention, improvement in entrance requirements, and improvements in a body of knowledge. *Teacher professionalism* is something unique to the act of teaching. Teacher professionalism is born in and exists in the drama of teaching. It is an artifact of teaching, not a status applied to it. And it is an artifact broadly created and defined by teachers, students, administrators, policymakers, and anyone who participates in the construction of what we call a "teacher." This is in opposition to teacher professionalism defined as new people, new requirements, and new knowledge; instead it is defined as new understandings and new appreciations of the shared experiences in the lives of teachers.

Those shared experiences of teachers are the basis of the discussions of professional development schools that follow in this book, and the lives of teachers to be presented are the essence of the new forms of teacher professionalism that could lie at the heart of not only teaching but school reform and restructuring in general. The experiences that follow—of changing perspectives on what it means to be a teacher, on the changing relationships between teacher practice and professional preparation programs, and on the new relationships between teachers, between teachers and students, between teachers and school administrators, and other relationships—provide the context out of which teacher professionalism can be constructed and understood.

Problems with Theories of Professionalism

In his analysis of problems involving the definition of the teaching "profession," Kimball (1988) states that recent literature promoting strengthening and improving the occupation of teaching can be reduced to three general categories: 1) recruitment and retention of "good" individuals by the profession,

2) improvement in the entrance requirements of the profession, and 3) improvements in the body of knowledge for the profession as well as training in that knowledge (Kimball 1988, 5). Noddings, citing some of the same concerns as Kimball, argues that the Carnegie proposals, as well as those by the Holmes Group, reduce to three themes: standards of practice controlled by the profession, abolishing the undergraduate teaching degree, and establishing "positions of advancement for teachers" (Noddings 1989, 19–20).

In *A Nation Prepared: Teachers for the Twenty First Century* (1986), the Carnegie Task Force on Teaching As a Profession tackled the issue that Kimball proposed as a roadblock to professionalism for education. The Task Force proposed that we:

> Restructure schools to provide a professional environment for teachers, freeing them to decide how best to meet state and local goals for children while holding them accountable for student progress. (55)

These commentaries speak of "professional" in the abstract as a value that exists outside and prior to the occupation and as a goal toward which it should be striving. The concept of "professional" has been established for and can be applied to the teaching occupation. The task is to alter the working conditions of teaching such that they meet the professional model. Cooper (1988, 47) states that the problems in and of teaching have been well documented and that teachers have actually begun to own this "blueprint" of their failures "as if they had written it themselves." She continues, "They have become passive and dependent in pursuit of their own voices."

As an alternative to the imposition described above, it might prove useful to examine closely those ideas upon which "professionalism" rests, and review them in light of the unique conditions of the teacher workplace and educational needs. Reform movements and the literature produced by them, while tinkering with the possibilities of school reorganization, have held the notion of professionalism constant. Reification of the literature on professionalism, coupled with the scarcity of literature about the everyday lives of teachers, has left the relationship between the concept of professionalism and the teacher workplace problematic.

Teaching as a "Profession"

Accepting the argument that there is no abstract model of professionalism that can legitimately be imposed on teaching, educational reform pointing toward the professionalization of teaching has no ready-made standard by which to measure success. The usual calls for raising teaching to the status of other professions such as medicine become less credible.

> [People] take for granted that this is what medicine and law are really like
> and that occupations striving to become professions have only to work
> hard enough, become more and more like this symbol until they finally
> achieve professional status themselves. (Becker 1970, 98)

Even under the assumption that an ideal definition of profession could be
applied, it is foolhardy for educational reformers to aim at such an ideal. The
concepts or attributes that embody "professional" in medical terms were
developed for and within medicine. To assume that such attributes are directly
transferable to teaching might hinder reforms for teaching rather than help.
There are several reasons for this concern. First, while medicine as a profession
requires the public's *acceptance* of it as a profession, it hardly requires public
control (as is attested by recent attempts at medical reform). Clearly "public"
education implies a far greater role for society in terms of control than does
medicine. Not only does each of the states hold implied constitutional authority
over education (and thus teachers) as power reserved to the states in the federal
Constitution, the federal government wields its authority through the granting
and denial of categorical aid to education, and local education agencies wield
theirs through administrative detail (Spring 1989). On this issue alone, the public
exercises ubiquitous control over education well beyond that exercised over
medicine. And as the last decade of reforms can attest, legislators, policy
makers, and administrators do not hesitate to exercise that control over
education.

Education is also unique among the occupations in terms of the familiarity
the public has with schooling. Practically speaking, the entire population of the
country more than six years old has had some (and generally a great deal of)
experience with schools and teachers. This creates a license for "lay preaching"
about schools and teachers because the public sees their beliefs about schools
and experiences to be all there is to school. This perception of institutionalization (Meyer and Rowan 1983) exists more strongly in education than possibly
any other occupation. The public exerts great pressure in terms of what teaching
is believed to be and expected to be.

But the uniqueness of teaching as an occupation aiming to become a
profession entails more than degree of public control. Sykes (1989, 263–267)
points out several "teaching circumstances" that make education unique among
professions or those occupations attempting to achieve professional status: 1)
Teaching is a public monopoly featuring conscripted clients. 2) Teaching is a
mass profession (considerably larger than medicine). 3) Teaching is heavily
unionized. 4) Teaching is a feminized occupation delivered to low status clients
serving an "equivocal" mission. 5) There is no awe of teaching practice. 6)
Teaching is a combination of special and ordinary knowledge. 7) There are no
texts, artifacts, or celebrated cases of teaching. 8) The liberal arts serve as

entitlement (privilege to become) and a performance standard (knowledge base to do) for teaching. Sykes (1989, 267) summarizes the unique character of the teaching occupation by commenting, "Teaching cannot in any crude way emulate other fields. Too much about teaching is unique; its special circumstances are judgmental, not peripheral." Sykes also argues that attempts to embody the ideal attributes of profession may, in fact, be detrimental to value issues for teaching and teachers. First, the quest for technical knowledge may compromise the sense of caring and compassion associated with human services. Second, the professional attempt to be objective may distance the professional from the client, and violate the democratic ideal of schooling. Third, "professionalism may be incompatible with equity goals" (Sykes 1987, 21).

Arguments such as Sykes's point to the notion that teachers face a unique struggle in gaining the stature granted to other professions. Schon has argued that much of what we generally label as professional practice suffers from a lack of regard for "complexity, uncertainty, instability, uniqueness, and value conflicts" (Schon 1983, 14). Schon argues, in a new vision of what constitutes professionalism, that what we cannot say and do not know about professional practice is as important as what we think we do know and can say vis-à-vis "professional knowledge." It is this lack of understanding that has not only highlighted the question of what a profession is, but also has even raised doubts about what the roles and abilities of professionals are. This lack of understanding of knowledge and practice lends doubt to current definitions of what it means to be a professional, and of professionalism:

> [A]s we have come to see with increasing clarity . . . the problems of real world practice do not present themselves to practitioners as well formed structures. Indeed, they tend not to present themselves as problems at all but as messy, indeterminate zones of practice. (Schon 1987, 4)

Hargreaves, in a discussion of teaching quality, has translated Schon's concern with the practical indeterminancy of professionals in general into teaching in particular. He argues that quality of teaching is more than a matter of competency; it is a matter of ". . . teachers actively interpreting, making sense of, and adjusting to, the demands and requirements their conditions of work place upon them" (1988, 211). Hargreaves (1994) reinforces these same points as critical in understanding the nature of teaching and how professionalism is constructed in the "situations that teachers understand best" (4), at the "grassroots of the profession," and from the perspectives of "those who work at the frontlines of our classrooms" (11). Munby, in a discussion of metaphors in teacher practice, supports this issue of uniqueness and indeterminancy of teaching. He argues that the unique circumstances and constructions of teaching are "fundamental to how teachers act" (1987, 378). Grundy, in a critique of

professionalism as a fixed model, argues that such unpredictability and uncertainty are the "hallmarks of professional practice, and teaching practice" (1989,
85). Finally, Lieberman and Miller argue that teaching practices are "highly personal, if not idiosyncratic," and are "forged in the dailiness of work . . . " (1990,
153–154). And overgeneralization about professionalism would tend to ignore
the "flesh and blood of teaching" (156).

Cooper (1988) argues that discussions of reform in teaching have become
distant from the day to day lives and culture of teaching. In a discussion of how
we have "diverged" from actual practice, Cooper describes how we might
reacquaint ourselves with the realities of the occupation. In one divergence, she
argues that reformers treat teaching culture as something that can be created for
and laid over teachers. Cooper contends that cultures are born, grow, and exist in
history, (1988, 47). Second, Cooper asks, "Whose culture is it anyway?"
Harkening back to the Carnegie Report, Cooper states that if teachers must
accept someone else's "blueprint" for professionalism, they will not have
generated a culture but "received" one. Third, Cooper states that by accepting
schools as "living organism" (47), we can more easily see professional overlays
as inappropriate, and can take advantage of the idiographic nature of teaching as
opportunity for reform. Fourth, in similar vein to Sykes's comment on caring
and compassion mentioned earlier, Cooper argues:

> The milieu of schools is written in the lives of children as well as pro-
> fessionals. Yet the lore on school professional culture ignores the client.
> The notion of service, the personal nature of the relationship to youngsters
> and families, the caring and bonding context of the event are embarrass-
> ingly absent. Have we extracted the least admired characteristics of the
> professional models, characteristics that divert teachers from their core
> tasks with children? (1988, p.48)

Thus far I have argued the following points. One, professionalizing
teaching has been part of the reform agenda in education. Two, exactly what
constitutes professionalism in its broadest sense is problematic. Three, applica-
bility of professionalism as defined by other professions is problematic due to the
unique and idiographic nature of teaching. Considering the possibility of variable
definitions and of context-specific definitions, those who seek to professionalize
teaching might need to call "profession" as a concept into question. Part of the
effort to make teaching a profession should include developing a concept of
"profession" that takes into consideration the unique conditions of teaching. As
Grundy suggests, "In many ways 'professionalism' is a tired old concept which
could well be left behind. What is needed is a fresh way of looking at teachers'
work and human action through which educators can move 'beyond

professionalism'" (1989, 79). One "fresh way" is to define profession in context; to ground the definition in the work that teachers do.

My problem with attempts by reformers to professionalize teaching is not that education is not worthy of the benefits of professional stature (as we know them), but that to mimic ideal types of professions or traits embodied in other occupations might be unsuitable for teaching. In order to arrive at a workable notion of what is professional for teaching, we must ground the definition in the work that teachers do. To do so would face up to what Hargreaves describes as "people striving for purpose and meaning in circumstances that are usually much less than ideal and which call for constant adjustment, adoption and redefinition" (1988, 216).

Even if those who advocate the professionalization of teaching could determine an ideal definition at which to aim, it is not certain that the target would be appropriate for teaching. Given Friedson's argument, any analysis of what professionalism means for teaching should focus on what is particular to teaching, not what is generalizable to "professionalism" as a fixed ideal. Jackson (1987), in a critique of the Holmes Group's suggestions that teacher education focus on technical skills and clinical needs, argues that medicine provides an inappropriate model for teacher professionalization:

> Those who point to the medical profession as a standard for teachers to emulate doubtless think they are doing teachers a good torn by making the comparison. Here is an enviable goal to which teachers might well aspire, they probably reason. What they fail to realize is that the comparison is ultimately degrading to teachers. It is so not only because the goal is so ridiculously out of reach in social and economic terms as to be almost cruel in the making but also because the analogy fails to consider all that is unique and ennobling about the teacher's work. (Jackson 1987, 388)

Jackson subsequently argues that educators can generate exciting reforms for teacher professionalism, but to do so would require less attention to "our dreams of a science of education" (1987, 388). He also suggests that our alternatives exist in the everyday lives of teachers.

Toward a New Construction of Teacher Professionalism

How do we go about the task of moving toward a definition of teacher professionalism such that we center on the unique nature of the work of teachers? If we professionalize teaching solely to gain greater economic reward for teachers with little connection to the improvement of education, we take two giant steps back by taking one small step (or stumble) forward. Inherent in plans to "strengthen" teaching through the three themes as presented above, our goal has become professionalizing for professionalism's sake, not for education's sake. Such plans also reflect the subtle distinction between professionalizing and professionalism. Professionalization efforts are concerned with building claims to rewards that the public generally gives to occupations as professions. That requires, as Becker argues above, taking on the characteristics of already recognized professions. Soder argues this case well:

> Make teaching a "real profession" (like medicine), and all will be well the argument runs. That is to say, status discrepancy [the difference between the way an occupation perceives its value and the public perceives the occupation's value] will be reduced, with teachers getting that which they believe they deserve. (1990, 53)

First attempts toward a construction of teacher professionalism can begin from the notion that teacher professionalism consists of shared experiences—and understandings of shared experiences—in the activity of schooling. In their everyday lives, teachers articulate what they do "professionally." Their actions and interactions with students register the trademarks of teacher professionalism continuously. The concept of teacher professionalism exists as the privilege of the shared experiences generated in school. As Carr argues:

> Because teaching is a purposive activity . . . it cannot be learned or understood in isolation from the social context in which it occurs. Since teaching is essentially a social practice, the conceptual schemes governing a teacher's "way of seeing and doing" are derived from tradition and deeply imbedded in the institutional settings in which teachers work. (1989, 12)

These shared experiences generate the "contextual knowledge" on which teachers base their practice. These experiences include those teachers have with children, with colleagues, and with the public (or should have with the public), and their own reflections on that contextual knowledge. Teacher professionalism exists where all these relationships come together in the generation of knowledge and practice. Professionalism, in this sense, is not about new knowledge and new people injected into the arena of teaching. Instead, it is defined by relationships and the understanding of relationships for teaching.

Given these shared experiences, discussions about moving toward a theory of teacher professionalism should center on the issue of contextual knowledge and the role contextual knowledge plays in service to students. Subsequently, discussions of teacher professionalism should center on the ability of teachers to represent that context to the public in terms of teaching's symbolic status. For the sake of clarity I will attempt to explain each of these areas separately as they relate to teacher professionalism, but I believe that in practice they are exceedingly difficult to separate. In practice they may be inseparable; each one's role in the generation of contextual knowledge cannot be singled out from the others.

Teacher Professionalism, Knowledge, and Service

In order to move toward a conception of teacher professionalism, we will first have to come to terms with professionalism's usual need for a "scientific" body of knowledge in which to base practice. Such a body of knowledge for teaching, as a century of research attests, is not only difficult to define, but antithetical to the idiographic nature of teaching experiences. Professionalization efforts to date have emphasized not only the existence of such a credible knowledge base for teaching, but expansion of it. Both of these are accentuated at the expense of a different, possibly much vaster "body of knowledge," and a potentially much more significant one—what we do not know about teaching. The knowledge base important for teaching is that which is created in context, and it is that knowledge that can help us understand the shared experiences of teaching. Goodlad speaks to this same issue when he discusses the "richly layered context" of teaching he discovered in his own research (1990, 19). As he comments:

> Arguments for a profession of teaching in schools must arise out of the special layered context of the work, the complexity of this context, and the special knowledge, skills, and personal characteristics required for the burden of judgment. (1990, 6)

First of all, the knowledge ''base" for teaching is the shared experience of teaching. And it may be uniquely so, for definitions of professionalism at least, in that it is based in uncertainty. McDonald argues:

> I want to call special attention to two thematic threads. . . . One is that the experience of teaching involves a struggle for complex, and ultimately tenuous, control. A second is that as a result of this struggle there is an inevitable and morally legitimate tension between teachers and students. I believe that this struggle and its tensions are at the heart of . . . the uncertainty of teaching, its messy practicality, which theorists generally sidestep. Most theory about teaching . . . supposes that teaching is at best simply the rational application of means to given ends. (1986, 377)

Contrary to "scientific," in the more widely used sense of the term, accepting the idiographic nature of teacher knowledge means basing knowledge of practice not in what can be abstracted, but in what cannot. This suggests that knowledge most important in teaching is not scientific at all, at least not traditionally speaking. Teaching's bodies of knowledge "based" in practice would accept uncertainty as a foundation for teacher knowledge, and make "teachers' intimate knowledge of uncertainty and its central and creative role in practice . . . as much a cornerstone of theory as it is a reality in the classroom" (McDonald 1986, 37).

Given this highly context specific body of knowledge, the source of knowledge of practice becomes teachers themselves, and what knowledge their contextual voices can offer. This body of knowledge, by definition, would be accessible nowhere else. The key question for the knowledge base of teacher professionalism, as posed by McDonald, would become, "how to frame a portrayal of teaching that is true at once to its banality and its mystery" (1986, 363).

A knowledge base for teacher professionalism would need to differ from more general theories of professionalism in that in professions, practice is justified through knowledge. Boreham (1983) argues that professional practice sometimes maintains more jurisdiction than can always be justified given the level of knowledge and skill claimed by professions and professionals. Given this argument, some professional jurisdiction would be illegitimate, in as much as knowledge is key to that jurisdiction. But an important assumption in Boreham's argument is that knowledge justifies practice.

In moving toward a theory of teacher professionalism, the reverse may actually be more appropriate. We would alternatively start with a justification for knowledge in practice, rather than practice in knowledge, or at least a recognition that the two happen concurrently. In moving toward a theory of teacher professionalism, it might be useful to work from the perspective that both processes occur, paying special attention to the justification of knowledge in practice. To do so would pay proper respect to the uncertainty of knowledge in teaching, in that "knowledge" would be contextual. This approach would also guide teacher professionalism toward what teachers do in the immediacy of their contexts, as well as what teachers "know" in the more traditional use of the term. This perspective would highlight and celebrate the uncertainty of teacher knowledge, and defend its "inherently provisional" (McDonald 1986, 363) nature against accusations of being "unscientific."

Finally, Boreham argues that in discussions of professional knowledge, the question arises as to how expertise gets organized as knowledge and how knowledge gets organized as work:

> During the processes of professional socialization organized systems of attitudes and values surrounding the application of professional knowledge are constructed. Knowledge becomes institutionalized as expertise. (1983, 696)

Questions need to be addressed concerning, first, the process through which the work activities of professional occupations come to be established as legitimate derivations of "recognized knowledge" and, second, how their development and utilization becomes organized and controlled. More generally, as Boreham puts it, the key issue is how knowledge gets organized as work.

Again, because of the uncertainty of teacher knowledge, it may be useful in working toward a theory of teacher professionalism to reverse these two questions as well. One, how do we institutionalize expertise as knowledge? Two, how does work get organized as knowledge? Singly, how do we comprehend teacher knowledge in the context in which that knowledge is generated and in which it has meaning?

Efforts based in a vision of professionalization as tantamount to filling the ranks of teaching with "better and brighter" people and subjecting them to more "rigorous" training in a more "scientific" body of knowledge give little attention to the context in which teachers—professional or not—work. Such efforts, while not inherently unimportant or unnecessary in the overall process of teacher professionalization, ignore teaching contexts, students, and the relationships between teachers and students (outside the ability to expose students to more "intelligent" teachers).

Noddings, in her work on caring, offers both disheartening and heartening critiques of the role of professionalism in teaching. She argues (1984) that to move toward an ethic of caring in education, teaching must be deprofessionalized. She also argues (1989) that as teaching progresses (or fails to progress) toward professional status, we must come to grips with the connection between professionalization and better education for children. First of all, it may be jumping the gun to assume that education can be deprofessionalized. That implies that teaching is a profession, and that is debatable, if not false. Secondly, if those who work for the professionalization of teaching fail to come to grips with the issue of client needs—in this case the education of children—then professionalization efforts are probably doomed to failure. In her question "What is the connection between professionalization and better education for school children?" Noddings has proposed the issue on which the professionalization of teaching will and should be judged and ultimately will succeed or fail (i.e., the relationship between teachers and students). It is also the question that lies at the essence and success of the professional development school concept.

The issue of "caring" offers a fresh perspective on how we might look at the issue of professionalism in general and the professionalization of teaching in particular. Caring invites us to look at professionalism not as a sterile organizational phenomenon, but as an artifact of relationships between human beings. Caring also provides us with new ground on which to examine just what the "knowledge base" of teaching is. The truly important knowledge that is produced in good teaching—and caring teaching—may be that knowledge that we do not know, and cannot know, unless we are in the context in which it is created—the interaction between students and teachers. Caring as a perspective requires that we move our thinking on teacher professionalism "toward relational modes and a new emphasis on professional/client relationships" (Noddings 1989, 2).

Caring offers opportunities for discourse on the professionalization of teaching by providing a route to what Smyth (1987) calls the "deconstruction of relationships," and a better understanding of the relationships and interactions that occur in schools. A consideration of caring might also plant discussions of the professionalization of teaching in what teachers do, rather than in the currently rampant discussions of what teachers do not do.

Teaching requires connections between students and teachers, an intimacy. Such connections cultivate an interdependency between student and teacher, or as Gilligan says, "a view of self and other as interdependent and of relationships as networks created and sustained by attention and response" (1988, 8). Gilligan goes on to comment on the importance of caring:

> Being dependent, then, no longer means being helpless, powerless, and without control; rather, it signifies a conviction that one is able to have an effect on others, as well as the recognition that the interdependence of attachment empowers both the self and the other, not one person at the other's expense. The activities of care—being there, listening, the willingness to help, and the ability to understand—take on a moral dimension, reflecting the injunction to pay attention and not turn away from need. (16)

Teaching relies upon the generation of experiences that allows students to trust that teachers will be nurturing. The ability of the teacher to involve himself or herself in the child's world and in the child's success measures to some degree the existence of caring in the experiences that students and teachers share. Noddings claims that "the test of caring" partly lies in "whether the free pursuit of his projects is partly a result of the completion of my caring in him" (1987, 337).

Attention, response, and communication—both physical and verbal come together in the construction of an atmosphere of care. This care exists in the experiences teachers share with their students, and they "know" it "through the experience of engagement with others" (Gilligan 1988, 17). This knowledge of care, constructed in the shared experiences of teachers and students, offers insight into a realm of teachers' knowledge rarely discussed in professionalization efforts, or in educational reform at all. This knowledge originates, develops, and emerges in the context of the experiences students and teachers share. And this knowledge can only be fully understood in the context of these experiences.

Belenky et al. (1986), in a discussion of women's ways of knowing about their worlds and experiences, offer "constructed knowledge" as one perspective of women's knowing. They refer to constructed knowledge as, "a position in which women view all knowledge as contextual, [and] experience themselves as creators of knowledge, and value both subjective and objective strategies for knowing" (15). Belenky et al. also describe "connected knowing" (1986, 101) as that form of knowing that rests upon an orientation toward relationships and conversation. Belenky et al. expand their discussion on knowing from work by Gilligan (1982) and Lyons (1983). Whereas Gilligan and Lyons speak of relationships between people, Belenky et al. include relationships between people and ideas or between knowers and known (Belenky et al. 1986, 102). This expanded definition reflects care as knowledge both constructed and connected—cultivated in the shared experiences of students and teachers. "Connected knowing builds on the subjectivists' conviction that the most trustworthy knowledge comes from personal experience rather than the pronouncements of authorities." "Truth" becomes that knowledge ". . . that is personal, particular, and grounded in firsthand experiences" (Belenky et al. 1986, 112–113; 113).

In the perspectives represented by Belenky et al., Gilligan, and Noddings, empathy plays a vital role in establishing care, and enhancing shared experiences between students and teachers. For teachers, coming to an understanding of the emotional, social, and psychological location of students enhances these shared experiences, in essence by sharing the students' locations. Connected knowers "learn how to get out from behind their own eyes, and use . . . the lens of another person" (Belenky et al. 1986, 115).

In constructed knowledge and connected knowing, "All knowledge is constructed, and the knower is an intimate part of the known" (Belenky et al. 1986, 137). Conversely, and appropriately, the known is a part of the knower and resides there. In the case of care for teachers, it resides as well with the students and in the experiences between teachers and students. And it places what teachers construct as knowledge on an important level:

To see that all knowledge is a construction and that truth is a matter of the context in which it is imbedded is to greatly expand the possibilities of how to think about anything, even those things we consider to be the most elementary and obvious. Theories become not truth but models for approximating experience. (Belenky et al. 1986, 138)

Understanding and accepting the role that constructed knowledge and connected knowing play in teacher knowledge accords a "richness" to teachers' knowledge, and raises the value of their contribution to the "knowledge base" of teaching. If we can accept the importance of the shared experiences of teachers, students, and others who have roles in schools in a meaningful way and we respect, those experiences as the source of teachers' constructed knowledge and connected knowing, then we remove some of the more "scientifically" based barriers to knowledge production and teacher empowerment. Teachers then, to some extent (and I believe to a great extent), can begin empowering themselves through the valuing of their contextual experiences and constructed knowledge.

To encourage this process and enhance the professionalization of teaching, we must rethink our definitions of professionalism, particularly from the standpoint of what we consider to be a "knowledge base" and how we expose fledgling teachers to a knowledge base. We must look to alternative perspectives of valuable teacher knowledge, professional-client relationships based on that knowledge, and resist embedding ourselves "in technical language and elitist hierarchies" simply for the sake of being "professional" (Pickle 1990, 73–74), and in the process, "going over the heads of those whom we teach" (Noddings 1986, 503) in the name of reform. This requires that those who wish to professionalize teaching resist the imposition of predominant models of professionalism, particularly those borrowed from medicine, where scientific methods distance professionals from clients (Gilligan and Pollock 1988; Noddings 1989). It also means that constructed teacher knowledge buttresses the knowledge base of teaching.

Fenstermacher, in his critique of professionalization efforts, claims that "the first characteristic of [the] uniqueness" of teaching as an aspiring profession is "the demand that the best practitioners remain closest to the learners" (1990, 146). He also makes the following argument:

> If those who argue for the professionalization of teaching have medicine and law as models for the transformation, serious difficulties for teaching lie ahead. The capacity of the teacher for moral development is seriously impaired by the kind of professionalization that is so rooted in expertise and skilled practice that it increases the distance between teacher and student, hides needed knowledge from the student, and places the student in the role of passive recipient of skilled treatment. (1990, 138)

As Noddings has suggested, education in many ways reflects issues that have arisen in law, nursing, and theology as models of human caring make their way into those arenas. Yet those models are yet to manifest themselves in any meaningful way in education. It may very well be that an important contribution that the discourse on caring can offer to the professionalization of teaching is to steer discussions in directions they might not have otherwise gone. What does it mean to be "professional" from the context of care? What do professional-client relationships mean from the context of care? The most significant role that caring plays in professionalization efforts in teaching may be to suggest to us that we rethink the theoretical underpinnings of professionalism in general by looking at the everyday lives of people in particular. Noddings suggests that, "We rarely ask how things might be changed so that teachers can accomplish the work they see as teaching, nor do we ask what this work is . . . " (1986, 502)

Teacher Professionalism and Teacher Politics

Meyer and Rowan (1983) argue quite articulately that in order for organizations to survive, they must "institutionalize" the norms and expectations of the society in which they operate. This "isomorphic" relationship between organizations and society invests society in the organization.

Boreham makes a similar argument in saying that organizations must be understood within the total social context in which they operate:

> Organizations are structural facticities but they represent only part of the wider structural facticity which constitutes the totality. Organizations are thus structural elements of a wider structure which they reflect and from which they derive their existence. (1983, 706)

Boreham goes on to argue that authority for professions is not just a matter of attaining legislative licensure and protection/insulation through state certification. For professions, authority is as much a matter of social and broad political acceptance as legislative acceptance (1983). Indeed, political acceptance, narrowly defined as state licensure, is not enough. The attainment of professional stature requires a more widespread and authentic sociopolitical acceptance.

Boreham's argument implies that at least part of the authority vested in professions originates not necessarily in what professions do, but in what society perceives professions to do. For vocations attempting to professionalize, such as teaching, this point cannot be treated lightly. Teaching has to pay particular attention to the symbols it offers the public considering the current negative status granted to teaching by the public.

Starr (1982) states that "power of the professions primarily originates in dependence upon their knowledge and competence" (4). When dealing with professions, the public tends to defer to this knowledge and competence, and we are left to conclude that society does not consider to be knowledgeable and competent those arenas to which it will not defer, or at least accept into the fold of professions.

Starr's analysis, because it comes from a *critical* perspective on the rise of the medical profession, offers lessons to which those who wish to make teaching a profession might attend. Starr places the development of medical professional authority in three contexts. One, Starr places medicine as a profession in its historical context, examining the actions, ideals, and interests involved in that history. Two, he places medicine in a social and political context quite broader than medicine itself. Third, he places the rise of the medical profession's authority in the context of moving from the establishment of cultural authority (I will refer to this later) to market authority and power. This cultural authority cannot be understood outside the context of political economy, nor can medicine's political economic value be understood outside medicine's cultural authority (Starr 1982, 7–9).

When Starr speaks of authority, he branches into two types of authority, cultural authority and social authority. Social authority involves the giving of orders, rules, and regulations. Cultural authority, on the other hand, "entails the construction of reality through definitions of fact and value." Social authority resides in social actors, but cultural authority may reside in social actors, documents (religious texts, for example), standards of reference, scientific publications, and law (13). Significantly different from commands, cultural authority "also refers to the probability that particular definitions of reality and judgements of meaning and value will prevail as valid and true" (13).

Starr moves on from cultural authority to argue that professional authority becomes a type of "dependency condition" (15) where clients acquiesce to the competence of the professional, and this acquiescence is based in cultural authority. And part of the strength of this cultural authority, and clients' submission to it, originates in the professions' ability to develop and instill the belief in society that such submission is important. Starr points out that historically speaking, this trust is a relatively recent phenomenon for medicine, arising in this century. "Authority signifies the possession of a special status or claim that compels trust, and medicine lacked that compelling claim in nineteenth century America" (1982, 17). Prior to attaining that trust, society vested its trust in particular individuals rather than in medicine in general. Medical authority was personal authority and personally won. But by the middle of this century, that trust and authority had become general and a trust in the medical profession as well as individual doctors (19).

This discussion of sociopolitical authority and cultural authority brings to teacher professionalism an important component. If teaching is to professionalize, teaching as a vocation in this country will have to come to grips with where it is located in the psyche of authority in the American public. And this process will require an examination of teaching's political sense both inside teaching and out in the public.

Optimistically, this examination would reveal a level of professional autonomy that teachers may already have but do not articulate to each other or the public very well. To present itself to the public in a way that would cause the public to grant teaching symbolic status, teaching should rely on the very traits that so far have kept it from becoming a profession, its contextual knowledge base and the contextual nature of teaching.

Teachers would need to celebrate, for public consumption, the unique nature of the contextual base of teacher knowledge. This nature takes on a quite ironic character here, given that school is one of our most common cultural experiences. This ubiquity only adds strength to the contextual knowledge base, because it reinforces the notion that the knowledge exists in the experiences of schooling. And the best we can do is carry memories of those experiences away with us, the connection and construction of knowledge being left to another generation of teachers and children.

This necessitates getting the public "in" schools where they can come to a better understanding of the "legitimate complexity" (Soder 1990, 63) of teaching. Having the public "in" schools carries a literal and figurative meaning. Literally, of course, the public may be physically present in schools. Figuratively, the public can be brought into schools through teachers' articulation of what they do in their everyday lives. This requires on the part of teachers an opening up of themselves, an invitation to the public.

Teacher Professionalism and Professional Development Schools

Any attempts at transforming teaching into a profession will have to come to grips with the importance of the contextual nature of teacher knowledge. This contextuality is critical on two counts. One, the truly important knowledge upon which teachers base their practice on a day to day basis is generated in the shared experiences of schooling. Two, because this knowledge is contextual, and not "scientifically" derived, it fails the test of rigor associated with the knowledge base of other professions such as medicine. This failure demeans the status of teaching relative to ideal types of definitions.

For teacher professionalism as a unique situation, we must begin to ask not what knowledge privileges teaching, but how knowledge accords practitioners the ability to carry out their tasks. For teachers, this would seem to be, at least in part, the contextually constructed knowledge of their shared experiences of school.

By what process do we move teaching toward professionalism? The stories and lives presented in this volume suggest that we do so by turning our eyes toward teaching as a moral endeavor, what Fenstermacher defines as, "human action undertaken in regard to other human beings" (1990, 133). Fenstermacher argues that much of the same literature on the professionalization of teaching that I have critiqued here ignores the moral nature of teaching. "It is as if the moral dimensions of teaching were lost, forgotten about, or—to put the best possible light on the matter—simply taken for granted" (1990, 131–132).

The everyday lives of teachers give rise to the contextually constructed knowledge in which so much of teaching is based. As Carr states:

Once the language of teaching is construed as an ethical form of discourse, the division between professional knowledge and professional practice begins to break down. Professional knowledge no longer appears as an externally produced body of value-free theoretical knowledge but as that implicitly accepted body of value-laden knowledge which teachers use to make sense of their practice. On this view, teachers develop professionally by reflecting critically on their own tacit practical knowledge rather than by applying theoretical knowledge produced by academic experts. (1989, 11)

The knowledge that is most important for teaching, the contextually based knowledge of the shared experiences that go on in classrooms and schools, gives to teaching a status that scientific knowledge, rigorous training, and the best and brightest people do not give it in and of themselves. The direction that we should move in making teaching a profession is to highlight the human relationships where teachers ground their everyday lives as professionals.

Noddings, in her call to examine the relationship between professionalism and better education for children, has in essence raised the connection between teacher professionalism and professional development schools. These questions are nested in the claims for the power of context presented in this chapter, and the chapters to come nest questions about the nature of professionalism in the lives of educators in professional development schools. The educators to be discussed have lived experiences that reflect the power of context, constructed knowledge, relationships in schools, and how they are born out and enhanced in professional development schools. These experiences include discussions of new structures in schools, the exercise of constructing professional knowledge and of putting that knowledge to use in classrooms, schools and professional preparation programs, and of celebrating the uniqueness of the lives of teachers. Themes that cut across these stories reflect many of the issues embedded in teacher professionalism as discussed here—interdependence, connection, relationships, empathy, and understanding.

References

Becker, H. S. (1970). *Sociological work: Method and substance*. Chicago: Aldine Publishing Company.

Belenky, M. F., Clinchy, B. M., Goldberger, N. R., and Tarule, J. M. (1986). *Women's ways of knowing: The development of self, voice, and mind*. New York: Basic Books, Inc.

Boreham, P. (1983). Indetermination: Professional knowledge, organization, and control. *Sociological Review 31*: 693–718.

Carnegie Forum on Education and the Economy. (1986). *A nation prepared: Teachers for the twenty-first century.*

Carr, W. (1989). Introduction: Understanding quality in teaching. In Wilfred Carr, ed., *Quality teaching: Arguments for a reflective profession*, pp. 1–20. Philadelphia: The Falmer Press.

Cooper, M. (1988). Whose culture is it anyway?. In Ann Lieberman, Ed., *Building a professional culture in schools*, pp. 45–54. New York: Teachers College Press.

Elmore. R. and Associates (1991). *Restructuring schools: The next generation of school reform*. San Francisco: Jossey Bass.

Fenstermacher, Gary D. (1990). Some moral considerations on teaching as a profession. In John I. Goodlad, Roger Soder, and Kenneth A. Sirotnik, eds., *The moral dimensions of teaching*, pp. 130–151. San Francisco: Jossey Bass.

Friedson, Eliot (1982). The theory of professions: State of the art. In R. Dingwall and P. Lewis, eds., *The sociology of the professions: Lawyers, doctors, and others*, pp. 19–37. New York: St. Martin's Press.

Friedson, Eliot (1986). *Professional powers: A study of the institutionalization of formal knowledge*. Chicago: University of Chicago Press.

Gilligan, Carol (1988). Remapping the moral domain: New images of self in relationships. In Carol Gilligan, Janie Victoria Ward, and Jill McLean Taylor, with Betty Bardige, eds., *Mapping the moral domain: A contribution of women's thinking to psychological theory and education*, pp. 3–20. Cambridge, Mass.: Harvard University Press.

Gilligan, Carol (1982). *In a different voice: Psychological theory and women's development*. Cambridge, Mass.: Harvard University Press.

Gilligan, Carol and Pollack, Susan (1988). The vulnerable and invulnerable physician. In Carol Gilligan, Janie Victoria Ward, and Jill MCLean Taylor, with Fetty Bardige, eds., *Mapping the moral domain: A contribution of women's thinking to psychological theory and education*, pp. 245–262. Cambridge, Mass.: Harvard University Press.

Goode, William J. (1969). The theoretical limits of professionalization. In Amitai Etzioni, ed., *The semi-professions and their organization*, pp. 266–312. New York: The Free Press.

Goodlad, John I. (1990). The occupation of teaching in schools. In John I. Goodlad, Roger Soder, and Kenneth A. Sirotnik, eds., *The moral dimensions of teaching*, pp. 3–34. San Francisco: Jossey Bass.

Grundy, Shirley (1989). Beyond Professionalism. In Wilfred Carr, ed., *Quality in teaching: Arguments for a reflective profession*, pp. 79–99. Philadelphia: The Falmer Press.

Hargreaves, Andy (1994). *Changing Teachers, changing times: Teachers' work and culture in the postmodern age.* New York: Teachers College Press.

Hargreaves, Andy (1988). Teaching quality: A sociological analysis. *Journal of Curriculum Studies 20*: 211–231.

Jackson, Philip W. (1987). Facing our ignorance. *Teachers' College Record 88*: 384–389.

Kimball, Bruce A. (1988). The problems of teacher authority in light of the structural analysis of professions. *Educational Theory 38*: 1–9.

Larson, Magali Sarfatti (1977). *The rise of professionalism: A sociological analysis.* Berkeley: University of California Press.

Lieberman, Ann and Miller, Lynne (1990). The Social Realities of Teaching. In Ann Lieberman, ed., *Schools as collaborative cultures: Creating the future now*, pp. 153–163. New York: The Falmer Press.

Lyons, Nona (1983). Two perspectives on self, relationships, and morality. Harvard *Education Review 53*: 125–145.

McDonald, Joseph P. (1986). Raising the teacher's voice and the ironic role of theory. *Harvard Educational Review 56*: 355–378.

Meyer, John W. and Rowan, Brian (1983). Institutionalized organizations: Formal structure as myth and ceremony. In John W. Meyer and Richard W. Scott, eds., *Organizational environments: Ritual and rationality*, pp. 21–44. Beverly Hills, Cal.: Sage Publications.

Munby, Hugh (1987). Metaphors and teachers' knowledge. *Research In the teaching of English 21*, 377–397.

Noddings, Nel (1989). *Developing models of caring in the professions.* Paper presented at the annual meeting of the American Educational Research Association, San Francisco. (ERIC Document Reproduction Service No. ED 308 594)

Noddings, Nel (1987). An ethic of caring. In Joseph L. Devitis, ed., Women, culture, and morality, pp. 333–372. New York: Peter Lang.

Noddings, Nel (1986). Fidelity in teaching, teacher education, and research for teaching. *Harvard Educational Review 56*: 496–510.

Noddings, Nel (1984). *Caring: A feminine approach to ethics and moral education.* Berkeley: University of California Press.

Pickle, Judy Gebhardt (1990). Toward the reconstruction of teacher professionalism. *Educational Foundations 4*: 73–87.

Raywid, M. (1990). The evolving effort to improve schools: Pseudo-reform, incremental reform, and restructuring. *Phi Delta Kappan*: 139–143.

Sarason, S. (1990). *The predictable failure of school reform.* San Francisco: Jossey Bass.

Schon, Donald A. (1983). *The reflectice practitioner: How professionals think in action.* New York: Basic Books.

Schon, Donald A. (1987). *Educating the reflective practitioner.* San Francisco: Jossey Bass Inc.

Srnyth, John (1987). Transforming teaching through intellectualizing the work of teachers. In John Smyth, ed., *Educating teachers: Changing the nature of pedagogical knowledge*, pp. 155–168. Philadelphia: The Falmer Press.

Soder, Roger (1990). The rhetoric of teacher professionalism. In John I. Goodlad, Roger Soder, and Kenneth A. Sirotnik, eds., *The moral dimensions of teaching*, pp. 35–86. San Francisco: The Falmer Press.

Spring, Joel (1989). *American education: An introduction to social and political aspects.* New York: Longrnan, Inc.

Starr, Paul (1982). *The social transformation of American medicine.* New York: Basic Books, Inc.

Sykes, Gary (1987). Reckoning With the Spectre. *Educational Researcher 16*: 19–21.

Sykes, Gary (1989). Teaching and professionalism: A cautionary perspective. In Lois Weis, Philip G. Altbach, Gail P. Kelly, Hugh G. Petrie, Sheila Slaughter, eds., *Crisis in teaching: Perspectives on current reform*, pp. 253–273. Albany, New York: State University of New York Press.

Tomorrow's schools: Principles for the design of professional development schools. (1990). The Holmes Group, Inc.

United States National Commission On Excellence in Education, (1983). *A Nation At Risk: The Report of the National Commission on Excellence in Education.* Washington, D.C.: US Government Printing Office.

Vision statement: Professional development schools network purposes, commitments, and enabling conditions for professional development schools. (1993, Spring). Resources for Restructuring. National Center for Restructuring Education, Schools, and Teaching.

Wilson, E. (1971). *Sociology: Rules, roles and relationships.* Homewood, Ill.: The Dorsey Press.

2

COLLABORATION BETWEEN K–12 SCHOOLS AND UNIVERSITIES

JERRALD SHIVE

Collaborate: 1. To work together, esp. in a joint intellectual effort.
2. To cooperate reasonably, as with an enemy occupying one's country.

—*The American Heritage Dictionary*, Second College Edition.

Collaboration between colleges and universities and K–12 schools has frequently resembled an enemy attempting to occupy someone else's country. Public schools traditionally represent a foreign country to many university professors; and, likewise, the university is traditionally a place of second-class citizenship for public school teachers. In part this is because schools and colleges and universities have totally different cultures. Collaboration requires learning entirely new roles, norms of behavior, patterns of social organization, and cultural priorities. Additionally, the term, collaboration, has been misused to represent programs that are carried out jointly but under rules clearly established and dictated by one of the partners. The recognition that education, birth through adulthood, is the joint responsibility of all educators because they hold a common stake in the enterprise has come very slowly. Even where the recognition exists, the cultural adaptations required to make it work may be very difficult.

Definitions of Collaboration

Collaboration has been defined in a number of ways. Conoley (1989) defines it simply as "joint responsibility and action to accomplish a task" (245). Fullan (1993) describes collaboration as a symbiotic relationship between universities and schools. Schlechty and Whitford (1988) define it as "an organic relationship with each part fulfilling unique functions, sometimes in a semiautonomous fashion, but with the purpose of serving the body as a whole" (191–192). Thus, collaborations are seen as being more than a temporary arrangement where institutions come together long enough to achieve certain results. Likewise, a collaboration involves more than a network, a group, or arrangement designed to share information but not designed to bring about change (Goodlad 1988). The parties in a collaboration come together for the common good, and both sides provide institutional support. According to Fullan, "alliances, partnerships, consortia and collaborations all connote joint agreements and action over a period of time in which all parties learn to work differently and achieve qualitatively different results" (93). Watson and Fullan (1992) suggest that collaboration is necessary "where parties have a shared interest in solving a problem that none of them can solve alone" (215). The schools and the universities carry out a vision that they share, but that neither can execute by themselves. In this way, collaborations "adjust old forms to new realities" (Pine and Keane 1990, 21). Essentially, they take old structures and beliefs and create new ways to attack problems. Whitford, Schlechty, and Shelor (1987) emphasize the joint nature of collaboration, defining it as working on ideas or issues that belong to both institutions. Conoley, too, emphasizes the "joint responsibility and action to complete a task" (245). To others, the focus of collaboration is on the style of interaction among the participants. Friend and Cook (1992) define collaboration as a "style for direct interaction between at least two coequal parties voluntarily engaged in shared decision-making as they work toward a common goal" (5). According to Clark (1988), an essential feature of a collaboration is the "extent to which the relating agencies function as equals, and in so doing are willing to give up some of their autonomy" (38). In this regard, Lasley, Matczynski, and Williams (1992) note that collaborative partnerships are characterized by low-role certainty, high-work intensity, and personal and institutional interdependence. But to some, it is primarily Fullan's emphasis on results that defines collaboration, rather than the joint nature of the activity. Schrage (1990), for example, defines collaboration as the "process of shared creation; two or more individuals with complementary skills interacting to create a shared understanding that none had previously possessed or could have come to on their own" (40). Although Schrage is referring to collaboration among professional colleagues, the observation holds for institutional collaboration as well. Thus, collaboration may be defined in terms of producing unique results as well as in terms of how an activity is occurring.

Forms of Collaboration

Researchers have noted that there is a wide variety of forms of collaborative partnerships between schools and universities (The Regional Laboratory for Educational Improvement of the Northeast & Islands 1987; Smith 1992). For example, professional development of teachers and university faculty may provide a focus for collaboration. Research, particularly applied research in the classroom, is also a fertile area for collaborations. Curriculum reform in selected subject areas is a third form of collaboration. The collaboration may be in subject areas such as science, social studies, reading, and writing. Collaboration also occurs in somewhat more topical areas such as applications of technology, improving rural education, work force preparation, and improving graduation rates. In teacher education, the focus of a collaboration may be on such things as improving field-based instruction, developing instructional models, developing programs based on specific principles (e.g., outcomes-based or competency-based learning or humanistic education), applying school effectiveness research, or increasing cultural diversity (Smith 1992). Teacher study groups, peer observation, case conferences, program evaluation and documentation, trying out new practices, teacher resource centers, and participation in outside events and organizations are other different ways to collaborate (Lieberman and Miller 1990). When collaborations are very broadly conceived, they may focus on such things as developing a full-service school that integrates knowledge and activities from a variety of human service fields, disciplines, and agencies and brings them to bear on improving the mental, physical, emotional, and social well-being of children in a school (Dryfoos 1994).

Another broadly conceived collaboration is the professional development school (PDS). Goodlad (1984) has argued that teacher preparing institutions must join with school districts in identifying and subsequently working with schools to be designated as key and demonstration schools" (316). Typically, the PDS serves as an exemplary site for the preparation of teachers as well as a school that is engaged in its own reform agenda. In this way, the teacher education program is afforded a site of excellence for teacher education clinical experiences while the school has the advantage of developing and implementing its own reforms. Both the school and the university engage in teacher preparation reform and school reform as well, and both are engaged in the improvement of teaching and learning (Goodlad 1988).

According to the Holmes Group (1990), PDSs should be organized as communities of learning. Darling-Hammond (1994) states that PDSs "aim to provide new models of teacher education and development by serving as exemplars of practice, builders of knowledge, and vehicles for communicating professional understandings among teacher educators, novices, and veteran teachers" (1). As Darling-Hammond notes, both the schools and the teacher education programs become centers for educational renewal and reform. Knowledge informs practice, and theory is no longer separated from its context. The PDS represents a collaboration that can lead to new ways of thinking about learning and teaching. According to Fear and Edwards (1995), PDSs provide an opportunity for collaboration that is participatory, reflective, and conducive to the building of a more democratic community. Such a view reflects the attempt at West Virginia University to develop a community of learners that incorporates new perceptions about how schools and the college function together and is committed to the improvement of teaching and learning.

The National Network for Educational Renewal, headquartered at the University of Washington and initiated by Goodlad, is one group of colleges and universities that are partnered with schools in their local areas to achieve a range of reforms including integrating theory and practice in the preparation of teachers. The National Center for Restructuring Education, Schools and Teaching (NCREST) is another collaboration of schools and universities that has implemented both school and teacher education reform. The Holmes Group (1986, 1990, and 1995) has been an active supporter and advocate of professional development schools. Some literature on professional development schools also exists that considers characteristics, impact on teacher preparation, impact on the broader profession and the relationship of PDS to school reform (Darling-Hammond 1994; Levine 1992).

Assumptions Supporting Collaboration

Collaborations or partnerships operate based upon a number of assumptions. One assumption is that education is a "community responsibility" (The Regional Laboratory for Educational Improvement of the Northeast & Islands 1987, 118). Fullan (1993) states that partnerships among a variety of stakeholders are "another essential ingredient for learning individuals and learning organizations" (96). He also emphasizes the need to "find new allies and build new kinds of connections to the communities of which they are a part" (94). He concludes that schools and universities need each other in order to be successful and that if "ever there was a symbiotic relationship that makes complete sense it is the collaboration of universities and school systems in the initial and ongoing development of educators" (120–121). Griffin (1989) emphasizes the need for collaboration in carrying out teacher education programs. He says that a systematic collaboration is needed between university and school faculty in order that they may come together "to learn from one another such that the various components of our prospective teachers' professional preparation are . . . smoothly and powerfully reinforcing . . . " (286). Fullan concludes that working together "potentially can provide the coherence, coordination, and persistence essential to teacher and school development" (96). Pine and Keane (1990) also emphasize that schools and universities are bound in a common enterprise and that they need each other for curriculum development, inservice preparation, sharing experiences and resources, continuous renewal, and renewed emphasis on quality teaching. Darling-Hammond (1994) makes a similar argument for coherent and consistent progress in all areas of school and teacher education reform. However the assumption is stated, it amounts to saying that all stakeholders in education are responsible for the success or failure of education at all levels, whether K–12 or postsecondary or specifically in teacher preparation. Collaboration means that the players combine to carry out their common interests in improving the quality of life in educational institutions and programs.

Collaborations are based on a particular set of values and beliefs concerning inquiry and its relationship to teaching and learning. Rather than assuming a linear and hierarchical relationship between knowledge and practice, the collaboration literature assumes that research and practice can be integrated (Levine 1992). A collaborative view enables practice to inform knowledge and places value on experience. In a collaborative approach, it is logical that we might ask teachers to define "how things might be changed so that teachers can accomplish the work they see as teaching" (Noddings 1986, 502). Inquiry and research also take on a different significance in dealing with problems of classroom practice. The less hierarchical orientation assumed in collaboration recognizes the value of the "tacit practical knowledge" teachers construct in the context of their every day lives and the more "scientifically" derived "theoretical knowledge produced by academic experts" (Carr 1989, 11).

Teacher education is also assumed to be a career-long continuum and teacher development is assumed to go hand in hand with school development (Watson and Fullan 1992). A collaborative view of knowledge construction respects the richness of practicing teachers' contextual knowledge and greatly enhances their perceived contribution to preservice teacher education programs. Teacher development is assumed to be the path by which changes in schools can both actually happen and be of the highest quality. A collaborative view recognizes that interdependence, relationships, and context are critical aspects of the teaching profession; therefore, a collaborative approach entwines professional development with the lived experiences of teachers.

Finally, according to Watson and Fullan (1992), collaborations do not happen by accident, good will, or establishing ad hoc projects. This means that strong collaborations are planned, intentional, long-term, and aimed at solving real problems. To begin with other assumptions is to doom a collaborative relationship to failure.

Collaborations Merge Cultures

Goodlad (1993) acknowledges the earlier point that the necessary joining of the cultures of the university and the schools can present many challenges. Nonetheless, Schlechty and Whitford (1988) argue that creating a common culture cannot be a byproduct of a collaboration but, rather, its primary goal. Slater et al. (1995) point out that in the case where a new organization is being invented (such as a PDS), fundamental changes in the parent organizations are required and the work is "both daunting and devoid of guidelines" (12). Goodlad and Sirotnik (1988) also urge that both universities and schools recognize and preserve those unique things that they bring to a partnership. For these reasons, too, Rudduck (1992) emphasizes that the partners must give up their traditional mythologies about each other and learn to respect each other's strengths. Lieberman (1992) also emphasizes that one of the first tasks must be for the university faculty to gain legitimacy in the schools. The schools and school districts, on the one hand, and the universities, on the other, will be skeptical of each other and will find it necessary to develop new modes of work to carry out the collaboration.

The Holmes Group (1986) also observes that few precedents exist for managing the complex jobs that "swim in limbo between the agencies" (19). For example, new roles such as project directors, coordinators, adjunct professorships for school faculty, or university faculty liaisons to schools may be designated. These individuals may be in charge of brokering resources, maintaining communication, teaching courses, or assigning and monitoring students in clinical experiences. Little exists in the literature to define roles and responsibilities for these complex kinds of positions. Trubowitz (1990) does suggest that persons familiar with both the school and university cultures should be selected as university liaisons to work with schools. In the Benedum Collaborative at WVU, the liaisons are University faculty members who act as brokers between the schools and the University, facilitators of professional development, and consultants as appropriate on a variety of curriculum and organizational issues. Liaisons may also, as their roles become more defined, be responsible for practica and internship supervision in their respective schools.

The university culture presents a challenge. One of the most persistent problems in establishing successful collaborations is that comfortable habits and the autonomy of departments and individuals in the university are interrupted (King and Galluzo 1992). Faculty members in the university tend to want to protect their isolation—it is both comfortable and protective of their disciplines and departments. Fullan and Stiegelbauer (1991) also note that it cannot be assumed that collaboration is good and autonomy is bad. Isolation may be autonomy for some university or school faculty; collaboration may be viewed as another term for a conspiracy. Groups are also more subject to faddism and "group think" than are individuals, and groups may exercise considerable pressure toward conformity and consensus (Fullan 1993). Anticipation of problems may also be done more effectively by an individual than by a group; for these reasons, Fullan recommends a healthy respect for individuals and personal visions as sources of renewal in inquiry-oriented organizations.

Both schools and faculty, however, can be isolated from the mainstream (Lieberman and Miller 1990). Collaborations enable them to reach out for support, challenge, and legitimacy in their activities. Isolation is also a problem because it can place limits on inquiry (Fullan 1993). Isolation limits the solutions to problems to the experiences of one individual while collaboration enables educators to better deal with complex educational problems. Neufeld (1992) also observes that collaborations require teachers to forsake the role of lone practitioners and become members of collaborative teams. According to Fullan "internal connections (within oneself and within one's organization) and external connections (to others and to the environment) must co-exist in dynamic interplay" in renewing organizations. Among other things, this means that professors and both novice and practicing professionals (teachers and administrators) need preparation and training in recognizing, supporting, assuming, and carrying out new roles and responsibilities, in organizational theory, and in school culture. The creation of collaborative experiences in professional development schools has been a focus of our reform efforts. Later in the book, case studies illustrate the evolution and the impact of collaborative environments for novice and practicing teachers.

The cultures of the schools, including the history of innovation and change, the norms of behavior, and the faculty roles, are quite different from that of the university. Participants in the collaboration must understand the concerns and the attitudes of the school faculty toward the university (Lieberman 1992). For example, school faculty are likely to have experienced university faculty serving as experts, or appearing briefly in schools and disappearing when a project is complete. The strong role of "historical" experiences in our own collaborations is particularly evident in the cases that examine the changing roles of school principals (Chapter 6) and the evolution of Teacher Education Centers (Chapter 10).

School cultures are also complex because conditions vary among levels of schools, individual schools at the same level, and school districts. However, Lieberman (1992) suggests that conflicts may exist not because the organizations of schools and universities are so different but because they are so similar. Both are bureaucracies with established decision patterns, and both will guard their own turf. Sarason (1990), in discussing the generalization that schools are a creation and reflection of the larger society, concludes that schools will accommodate in ways that require little or no change and that, in this respect, they are similar to other traditional complex organizations, including universities. According to Schlechty (1990), to change an organization's structure, one must also change its culture. Not only do rules, roles, and relationships have to change, but also values, beliefs, and knowledge. Neufeld (1992) also notes that traditional collaborations may require little organizational change on the part of participants because authority relationships and roles remain relatively unchanged. Even when a school restructures, it does not necessarily reculture (Fullan 1993). That is, changes in administrative or program structures may leave the basic culture of the school untouched; therefore, no real change in teaching or learning occurs.

PDSs, "in contrast, require changes in roles, role relations, ideas about teaching practice and teacher education, and the allocation of authority" (Neufeld 1992, 136–137). Thus, more complex collaborations such as these are more difficult to achieve because they require fundamental changes in the participating organizations. This accounts for Rudduck's (1992) observation that achieving cultural coherence and significance is slow and that one challenge in the change process is finding ways to keep up the momentum. At West Virginia University, the Benedum Collaborative has now entered the stage of seeking "institutionalization," and substantial time and energy are being devoted to establishing new roles, responsibilities, funding patterns, and relationships that will enable the Collaborative to endure over time. Trubowitz (1990) also suggests the importance of both schools and the university avoiding the blaming cycle when reforms are slow or perhaps do not initially work at all. He notes that some resistance is inevitable and that incremental change is what can be expected and worked toward.

Finally, Fullan (1993) states that "learning organizations will have to be able to form and reform a variety of alliances simultaneously and over time" (97). Thus, collaborations may appear, achieve their goals, perhaps reform, while other collaborations are also starting up or ending. In this regard, while it is true that collaborations take a long time to develop, they can disappear over-night when people leave (Little 1987; in Fullan and Stiegelbauer 1991). Thus, collaborations can be fragile if, for example, key individuals in leadership positions leave the relationship.

Keys to Success

John Goodlad (1988), whose experience and research on the institutional partnership concept is probably the most extensive, notes that history is very "short on examples of carefully crafted agreements and programs accompanied by . . . individual and institutional commitment on both sides" (12). He further notes that school-university partnerships are a largely untried and, therefore, an unstudied phenomenon. Although the literature indicates that there has been some change in that situation since 1988, the change appears not to be very large in terms of numbers, nor have the paths to collaboration been well documented. Winitzky, Stoddart, and O'Keefe (1992) also make the observation that the literature that has accumulated to guide partnerships is quite limited (123). According to Watson and Fullan (1992), much of the literature consists of descriptions of case studies of individual partnerships. Nevertheless, there appear to be some characteristics that have been rather universally identified by working collaborations as necessary ingredients if a collaborative effort is to be successful.

Goodlad and Sirotnik (1988) identify sufficient selflessness on the part of each partner to assure satisfaction of self interests as a key feature of a collaboration. Ward and Pascarelli (1987) identify four principles of effective collaboration, including participants' parity. Friend and Cook (1992), in discussing collaborations among individuals, suggest that contributions must be equally valued. Conoley (1989) emphasizes that the collaborative approach is enhanced by an openness to trying suggestions offered by others. Smith and Auger (1985–86) and Pine and Keane (1990) also emphasize mutuality, respect, and trust. Rosaen and Hoekwater (1990) agree that developing interpersonal and working relationships is an important criterion for success.

Of course, collaborations are aimed at solving problems and achieving selected goals. Lieberman (1992) concludes that the vision must be broad and must allow for participants to create meaning. Friend and Cook (1992) emphasize the importance of mutual goals that are specific enough and important enough to command attention. Pine and Keane (1990) also emphasize that there must be a specific purpose and a focus on action, and that the purpose must be consistent with the mission of all of the partners. Goodlad (1988) suggests that the agenda or problem to be solved should be worthy of a partnership. The agenda should not just represent the latest fad or popular concern about education.

Conoley (1989) observes that the collaborative approach is enhanced by a willingness to stay involved in difficult situations and to assume responsibility for problem resolution. Pine and Keane (1990) also discuss what they refer to as "personal maturity," or the willingness to reflect and consider renewal. Ward and Pascarelli (1987) call for a focus on persistent and important school-based programs.

Responsibility for achieving objectives must also be assigned based on knowledge and skill (Ward and Pascarelli 1987). Darling-Hammond (1994) notes that participants must be honest in assessing the skills that exist and the skills that are needed by the participants in the collaboration in order to achieve their goals. Rosaen and Hoekwater (1990) also emphasize a common knowledge base as being important to the problem-solving process. The more theoretical approach of the university and the pragmatic approach of the schools must be merged to deal with identified problems (Robinson and Darling-Hammond 1994).

Collaboration cannot be mandated if it is to be successful (Friend and Cook 1992). Lieberman (1992) and Winitzky, Stoddart, and O'Keefe (1992) have also found that a bottom-up strategy, with teachers being an integral part of the change process, is necessary for success. Those who implement the reforms should also be those who develop them. Consistent with that conclusion, Lieberman has also found that leadership in a collaboration must be based on knowledge and commitment, as opposed to being based on position in an administrative hierarchy.

In summary, the participants must share a parity in their relationship. This key to success is also variously stated as selflessness, trust, and mutuality. Secondly, there must be a clear purpose, vision, or goals. A problem-solving perspective permeates this criterion. It follows then that participants must accurately assess their knowledge and skills in order to effectively solve problems and achieve goals. Finally, a collaboration should be bottom-up and voluntary. The structure for carrying out the collaboration should be determined by the participants and not imposed by some existing structure.

Challenges in Establishing Collaborations

Darling-Hammond (1994) and the Holmes Group (1986) note that there are few incentives to undertake the work of developing collaborations such as PDSs. Further, universities and schools are quite dissimilar with respect to their reward systems. University faculty are rewarded for research while school faculty have more than enough to do in preparing for and carrying out instruction. In addition, teacher education has a low status in universities (Darling-Hammond; Goodlad, Soder, and Sirotnik 1990), and professional development is not adequately valued by schools. As a result, powerful forces are in place in both schools and universities that will work against attempts at collaborative efforts.

Leadership is also critical. Clark (1988) notes that "boundary-spanners," individuals who are comfortable in both the school and the university environment, tend to be the best leaders. Lieberman (1992) agrees that the director or leader must be "bicultural." As Chapter 6 illustrates, principals of professional development schools may find themselves spanning boundaries between collaborative, restructuring school faculties and more traditional school districts.

In addition to determining leadership, other issues related to determining and carrying out an effective governance structure have been identified by a number of authors as being significant strategies (Lieberman 1992; Sirotnik 1988; Watson and Fullan 1992). For example, resources must be allocated, ideas must be communicated, and decisions must be made. Also, although the leadership for the collaboration cannot be imposed from the top, a commitment from top leadership in the schools and university is essential (Darling-Hammond 1994). Lieberman and Watson and Fullan also believe that goals and structure should be emergent. They should rise out of the activities rather than being predetermined.

Financing is also important (Darling-Hammond 1994; Lieberman 1992; Trubowitz 1990). Levine (1992) believes that all parties must contribute resources that are valuable to achieving the shared goal. Although outside funding to support the partnership or collaborative effort is helpful, the collaborative process can be short-circuited by the arrival of a grant (Darling-

Hammond). When a grant runs out, it also challenges the institutions in the collaboration to pick up the costs necessary to continue the effort. Further, Cooper (1988) notes that higher education missionaries to the lower schools sustain relationships as long as the grant lasts, and then they are gone. The general lack of financial support for teacher education in the university and for the schools in a particular state or locality can also present a formidable obstacle to implementation. However, Lasley, Matczynski, and Williams (1992) suggest that financially difficult times such as exist at present, with institutions facing diminishing funds and resources, may provide incentives for collaboration and the combining and sharing of resources. According to Darling-Hammond, the state may be the funding hope for universities and schools wanting to establish PDS collaborations because the states could recognize PDSs as part of the educational infrastructure and allocate funds to them in the same way they do to other educational agencies.

Lieberman (1992) notes that some collaborative efforts operate essentially outside the core activities of both the schools and the university. In those instances, the collaboration is likely to be viewed as temporary and vulnerable to change because it does not represent a permanent commitment by the institution. This is particularly true with collaborations that may be viewed as "add-ons" as opposed to institutionalized programs that are integral to the activities of the university and schools. In another chapter in this text, Hawthorne refers to the "re-centering" in ethos, beliefs, and values that is both necessary and beneficial to the university as a part of the collaborative process. This speaks to perhaps the greatest challenge in collaboration, the "re-culturing" of both the schools and the university.

Dealing with time is also critical (Coombs and Hansen 1990; Darling-Hammond 1994; Trubowitz 1990). Robinson and Darling-Hammond (1994) note that schools and school faculty are captives of the clock and the calendar. Teachers feel the constraints of teaching, planning for instruction, grading papers, and performing other duties. Yet time is needed by faculty from both the schools and the university to plan and conduct collaborative activities as well as to spend time interacting in as many professional ways as possible. Time is in short supply. Schlechty and Whitford (1988) emphasize that time also allows for the breakdown of stereotypes that exist in both cultures. Thus, time is sometimes recognized as the most valuable resource in attempting to carry out any collaboration (Friend and Cook 1992; Slater et al. 1995).

The significance of culture has already been discussed. Coombs and Hansen (1990) recognize the tenacity of tradition with regard to changing teaching, student teaching, and professional development as a potentially significant problem. Any collaboration faces the difficulty of changing past approaches to activities and problems as well as dealing with institutional cultures.

Benefits of Collaboration

The benefits of collaborations accrue to all of the participants, but not necessarily to equal degrees. The benefits include professional educators beginning to view themselves as members of collegial teams (Levine 1992). Teachers, both preprofessional and practicing, are no longer isolated from one another but view themselves as professional partners. Fullan and Stiegelbauer (1991) conclude that collaborative cultures help reduce professional isolation and promote the provision of support. Opportunities for both formal and informal interaction among and between school and university faculty increase in a collaborative environment, according to Sandholtz and Merseth (1992).

Secondly, Darling-Hammond (1994) notes that all participants learn in a collaboration. Learning may take the form of better understanding their own and other institutions, shared decision making, the nature of mentoring, and new perspectives on teaching. It may also be that teachers learn how to make more informed decisions as members of very complex learning environments. Lieberman and Miller (1990) describe this change as the "building of a culture of support for inquiry" (107–108). Teachers and university faculty are engaged in a process of mutual problem solving and research. The necessary conditions for the culture to be inclusive of the values and beliefs around the concept of the teacher as a researcher are carried out by everyone in the collaboration and supported by those in positions of leadership. A climate of inquiry pervades the daily lives of all of the participants in the collaboration. According to Sarason (1990), students will be effective as collaborators and continuous learners when teachers have these same characteristics.

The codification and sharing of successful practices is a benefit recognized by Fullan and Stiegelbauer (1991). They observe that contributing ideas to others and seeking better ideas is the cornerstone of collaborative cultures. Teachers also feel an increased sense of efficacy after participating in a collaborative professional development school environment, according to Sandholtz and Merseth (1992). Teachers feel that they know more and have a renewed sense of their own competence. As reported by teachers in a Benedum professional development school: "We decide. We have self-direction. There is teacher empowerment." The chapter in this text that speaks to teacher outcomes in professional development schools associated with West Virginia University also finds, among other things, improved teaching for at-risk students, improvements in curriculum, and improved understandings in areas such as assessment and learning styles. Without the partnership with the University, the achievement of these outcomes would have been much less likely.

One outcome of collaboration at West Virginia University has been the development of a radically different teacher education program. The program results in each student's earning a bachelors degree in a content area and a masters degree in education. It features limited enrollments, faculty mentors, student cohorts, evaluation by portfolio assessment, applied research projects, and six consecutive semesters in professional development school practica or internships. Thirteen professional development school faculties have collaborated in the planning and implementation of the program. Goodlad (1993) suggests that any teacher education program that is created or conducted without the collaboration of surrounding schools is defective. Darling-Hammond (1994) also emphasizes that "professionalism starts from the proposition that thoughtful and ethical use of knowledge must inform practice" (4). Practicing and novice teachers and professors can learn together to make informed decisions about complex school problems. The importance of integrating theory and practice, recognizing the importance of teacher experience, bringing inquiry and research to bear on learning in actual classroom environments, and providing for the mutual restructuring of schools and colleges of education have already been discussed. The knowledge base from which teaching operates is enriched as teachers and teacher educators work together and redefine the act of teaching (Darling-Hammond). The partners also have the considerable advantage of utilizing all of their combined skills to understand their own progress and achievements (Rudduck 1992). Structures and strategies can be developed to enhance teaching and learning and to understand how both practice and research contribute to education. The collaborative environment also provides a "safe place" for experimentation and mutual learning that otherwise might not exist for either teachers or university faculty. Therefore, a broader range of solutions may be generated. Teachers also feel an increased ownership and commitment to program goals because they have a personal investment in achieving them.

In addition to personal renewal, the full consideration of solutions and their alternatives results in institutional renewal (Goodlad 1988). As Goodlad points out, institutions do not stand still; they renew or they decline. Therefore, collaborations can provide injections of new knowledge necessary for the institutions in a partnership to grow. Darling-Hammond (1994) also emphasizes that PDSs as collaborations carry implications for how one views the profession. As the characterizations of learning, teaching, and educational organizations change, the profession itself is renewed. New kinds of knowledge are generated that enrich schooling at all levels. A primary objective of the PDS is the sharing of knowledge about teaching and learning, and improvements in how professionals at all levels approach both. The consideration of alternative beliefs related to any inquiry renews both the individuals engaged in the inquiry and the institutions of which they are a part.

There are also more serendipitous benefits. For example, collaborations not specifically aimed at curriculum development may also generate curriculum change. Collaborations that focus on professional development, teacher preparation, or action research are very likely to carry curriculum implications

(Darling-Hammond 1994). Likewise, either intentionally or unintentionally, new faculty roles and responsibilities are created. As noted earlier, clinical faculty or liaisons or adjunct faculty positions may be created that will allow and encourage university and school faculty to merge their responsibilities. Button, Ponticelli, and Johnson (1996), for example, recognize the important role of liaisons in asking questions about practice and working with teachers to solve problems. At West Virginia University, a number of college faculty who work as liaisons are meeting monthly to explore and define their new roles. In the meantime, they serve as knowledge brokers, problem solvers, action research facilitators, and occasionally as clinical experience supervisors in the professional development schools. They are essentially site-based resources for school improvement, professional development, action research, and the merging of theory and practice.

There are also extrinsic rewards to teachers in terms of pay, power, and status (Sandholtz and Merseth 1992). As teachers are involved in collaborative decision making, they carry that norm of behavior over to other activities in the school. The status of teachers is also enhanced as they engage in activities including decision making with regard to curriculum, grant writing, research, or teacher preparation in collaboration with university faculty. To the extent that the schools or the university are able to find funds to release faculty to participate in planning meetings, collaborations may also result in some extra pay or time away from normal activities. The value of time as the scarcest resource for faculty has already been discussed, and release time is a recognition that time is money. For example, the school districts whose teachers participate in planning or policy meetings as a part of the Benedum Collaborative are reimbursed for substitute teachers in order that PDS faculty may involve themselves more completely in Collaborative activities.

As was discussed earlier, collaborations provide a context for the profes-sional studies being conducted in, for example, a teacher preparation program. Zeichner (1992) has found that traditional clinical experiences focus on teachers' reflections on their own teaching and their own students and that the social conditions in the schools are largely ignored. According to Zeichner, novice teachers must be prepared "to enter teaching ready and able to participate in the shaping of the context in which they will work" (298). Participation in collaborations such as the PDS emphasizes the importance of understanding and working within a context, a culture, and that teaching and learning and students cannot be culled out in order that schooling can take place in a sterile environ-ment. Values, beliefs, norms of behavior, and attitudes pervade the environment of the school. The PDS thus becomes a living laboratory to be used by novice and practicing teachers in order to understand the impact of culture on schooling.

Sirotnik and Goodlad (1988) judge the cup of potential for productive partnerships to be half-full. They also believe that schools, colleges, and departments of education in institutions of higher education should be preserved to the extent that they devote "substantial attention . . . to thought and action in collaboration with school-based educators" (xii). According to Clark (1988), partnerships must contribute to the simultaneous reform and renewal of both schools and universities. Meanwhile, public pressure for educational reform has probably never been greater. It may be possible that educational partnerships and collaborations can be one significant piece of the actions necessary to move all of education to more productive levels.

References

Button, K., Ponticelli, J., and Johnson, M. J. (1996). Enabling school-university collaborative research: Lessons learned in professional development schools. *Journal of Teacher Education 47*(1): 16–20.

Carr, W. (1989). Introduction: Understanding quality in teaching. In W. Carr, ed., *Quality teaching: Arguments for a reflective profession*, 1–20. Philadelphia: Falmer Press.

Clark, R. W. (1988). School-university relationships: An interpretive review. In K. A. Sirotnik, and J. I. Goodlad, *School-university partnerships in action: Concepts, cases, and concerns*. New York: Teachers College Press.

Conoley, J. C. (1989). Professional communication and collaboration among educators. In M. C. Reynolds,ed., *Knowledge base for the beginning teacher*. New York: Pergamon Press.

Coombs, C. G. and Hansen, J. M. (1990). Lessons learned. *Educational Horizons 8*(4): 214–216.

Cooper, M. (1988). Whose culture is it, anyway? In A. Lieberman, ed., *Building a professional culture in schools*. New York: Teachers College Press.

Darling-Hammond, L. (1994). Developing professional development schools: Early lessons, challenge, and promise. In L. Darling-Hammond, ed., *Professional development schools: Schools for developing a profession*. New York: Teachers College Press.

Dryfoos, J. G. (1994). *Full-service schools: A revolution in health and social services for children, youth, and families*. San Francisco: Jossey Bass.

Friend, M. and Cook, L. (1992). *Interactions: Collaboration skills for school professionals*. New York: Longman.

Fullan, M. (1993). *Change forces: Probing the depths of educational reform*. Bristol, PA: Falmer Press.

Fullan, M. G. and Stiegelbauer, S. (1991). *The meaning of educational change*. New York: Teachers College Press.

Goodlad, J. I. (1984). *A place called school: Prospects for the future.* New York: McGraw-Hill.

Goodlad, J. I. (1988). School-university partnerships for educational renewal: Rationale and concepts. In K. A. Sirotnik and J. I. Goodlad, eds., *School-university partnerships in action: Concepts, cases, and concerns.* New York: Teachers College Press.

Goodlad, J. I. (1993). School-university partnerships and partner schools. *Educational Policy 7*(1): 24-39.

Goodlad, J. I. and Sirotnik, K. A. (1988). The future of school-university partnerships. In K. A. Sirotnik and J. I. Goodlad, eds., *School-university partnerships in action: Concepts, cases, and concerns.* New York: Teachers College Press.

Goodlad, J. I., Soder, R., and Sirotnik, K. A. (1990). *Places where teachers are taught.* San Francisco: Jossey-Bass.

Griffin, G. A. (1989). Coda: The knowledge-driven school. In M. A. Reynolds, ed., *Knowledge base for the beginning teacher.* New York: Pergamon Press.

Holmes Group (1986). *Tomorrow's Teachers.* East Lansing: Author.

Holmes Group (1990). *Tomorrow's Schools: Principles for the design of professional development schools.* East Lansing: Author.

Holmes Group (1995). *Tomorrow's schools of education.* East Lansing: Author.

King, R. A. and Galluzo, G. R. (1992). Redesigning university curricula and teacher preparation through cross disciplinary collaboration. *Journal of Research and Development in Education 25*(4): 195–203.

Lasley, T. J., Matczynski, T. J.,and Williams, J. A. (1992). Collaborative and non-collaborative partnership structures in teacher education. *Journal of Teacher Education 43*(4): 257–261.

Levine, M. (1992). *Professional practice schools: Linking teacher education and school reform.* New York: Teachers College Press.

Lieberman, A. (1992). School/university collaboration: A view from the inside. *Phi Delta Kappan,* 147–155.

Lieberman, A. and Miller, L. (1990). Teacher development in professional practice schools. *Teachers College Record 92*(1): 106–122.

Neufeld, B. (1992). Professional practice schools in context: New mixtures of institutional authority. In Levine, M., ed., *Professional practice schools: Linking teacher education and school reform.* New York: Teachers College Press.

Noddings, N. (1986). Fidelity in teaching, teacher education, and research for teaching. *Harvard Educational Review 56*: 496–510.

Pine, G. J. and Keane, W. G. (1990). School-university partnerships: Lessons learned. *Record* (Fall-Winter): 19–25.

Regional Laboratory for Educational Improvement of the Northeast & Islands, and National Staff Development Council (1987). *Continuing to learn: A guidebook for teacher development.* Andover, Mass. and Oxford, Ohio: Authors.

Robinson, S. P. and Darling-Hammond, L. (1994). Change for collaboration and collaboration for change: Transforming teaching through school-university partnerships. In L. Darling-Hammond, ed., *Professional development schools: Schools for a developing profession.* New York: Teachers College Press.

Rosaen, C. L. and Hoekwater, E. (1990). Collaboration: Empowering educators to take charge. *Contemporary Education 61*: 144–151.

Rudduck, J. (1992). Universities in partnership with schools and school systems. In M. Fullan, M. and A. Hargreaves, eds., *Teacher development and educational change.* Washington, D.C.: Falmer Press.

Sandholtz, J. H. and Merseth, K. K. (1992). Collaborating teachers in a professional development school: Inducements and contributions. *Journal of Teacher Education 43*(4): 308–317.

Sarason, S. (1990). *The predictable failure of educational reform.* San Francisco: Jossey Bass.

Schlechty, P. (1990). *Schools for the 21st century: Leadership imperatives for educational reform.* San Francisco: Jossey Bass.

Schlechty, P .C. and Whitford, B. L. (1988). Shared problems and shared vision: Organic collaboration. In K. A. Sirotnik and J. I. Goodlad, *School-university partnerships in action: Concepts, cases, and concerns.* New York: Teachers College Press.

Schrage, M. (1990). *Shared minds.* New York: Random House.

Sirotnik, K. A. (1988). The meaning and conduct of inquiry in school-university partnerships. In K. A. Sirotnik, and J. I. Goodlad, eds., *School-university partnerships in action: Concepts, cases, and concerns.* New York: Teachers College Press.

Sirotnik, K. A. and Goodlad, J. I. (1988). *School-university partnerships in action: Concepts, cases, and concerns.* New York: Teachers College Press.

Slater, J., Zaragoza, N., Slater, F., and Skaruppa, C. (1995). Sustaining and integrating constructivist school/university collaboration. Paper presented at the annual meeting of the American Educational Research Association, San Francisco.

Smith, S. D. (1992). Professional partnerships and educational change. *Journal of Teacher Education 43*(4): 243–256.

Smith, S. D. and Auger, K. (1985–86). Conflict or cooperation? Keys to success in partnerships in teacher education. *Action in Teacher Education 7*(4): 1–9.

Trubowitz, S. (1990). What works and what gets in the way. *Educational Horizons 68*(4): 213–214.

Ward, B. A. and Pascarelli, J. I. (1987). Networking for school improvement. In J .I. Goodlad ed., *The ecology of school renewal.* Chicago: University of Chicago Press.

Watson, N. and Fullan, M. (1992). Beyond school district-university partnerships. In M. Fullan and A. Hargreaves, eds., *Teacher development and educational change.* Washington, D.C.: The Falmer Press.

Whitford, B. L., Schlechty, P .C., and Shelor, L. G. (1987). Sustaining action research through collaboration: Inquiries for invention. *Peabody Journal of Education 64*: 151–169.

Winitzky, N., Stoddart, T., and O'Keefe, P. (1992). Great expectations: Emergent professional development schools. *Journal of Teacher Education 43*(1): 3–18.

Zeichner, K. (1992). Rethinking the practicum in the professional development school. *Journal of Teacher Education 43*(4): 296–307.

3

THE BENEDUM COLLABORATIVE: THE STORY OF AN EDUCATIONAL REFORM EFFORT

SARAH STEEL AND NANCY E. HOFFMAN

An understanding of history and context are critical to analyzing or effecting any educational change; therefore, this chapter reviews the history and context of the Benedum Collaborative. The chapter provides an introduction to the complex and ongoing educational change effort initiated by West Virginia University and public schools in north-central West Virginia. After describing the origin and evolution of this collaborative reform effort, the chapter presents individual "biographies" of the six original Benedum Collaborative professional development schools. Readers will find the history portion of the chapter a useful overall introduction to this reform effort. The "biographies" may be read as an introduction to the remainder of the book or for background as the narrative accounts of change in the second section of the book are read.

In the mid-1980s, as West Virginia University completed a long-range planning process, the improvement of teacher education and public education became one of five University-wide strategic initiatives. This focus on educational improvement was reflected in the University's decision to join the Holmes Group in the spring of 1986. Education faculty began to envision the direction of Holmes reform at WVU and concluded that any redesign efforts should be collaborative, inclusive of practitioners and faculty from across the University, and focused on both the product and the process of reform. Three goals based on the work of the Holmes Group were articulated: to make teacher education more intellectually sound, to establish professional development schools, and to develop collaborative structures and processes that would make changes last. Attention to both collaborative processes and products, in the form of a redesigned teacher education program and professional development schools, became important facets of the design of subsequent reform work.

The efforts of education faculty, arts and sciences faculty, and public school representatives produced a major grant proposal which sought support for the redesign of undergraduate teacher education programs and the establishment of professional development schools (PDS). This proposal was funded by the Claude Worthington Benedum Foundation of Pittsburgh, Pennsylvania, in 1989. Using the Tyler model for curriculum development, eight teams were formed: society, pedagogy, students, liberal studies, teaching disciplines, philosophy of education, psychology of learning, and professional development schools. These multidisciplinary teams were composed of higher education and public school representatives. Major work on the redesign of teacher education and the development of professional development schools began in the fall of 1989.

The initial Benedum Collaborative proposal included the following description of professional development schools:

> The professional development schools that we will establish in the proposed project will provide better clinical experiences in the preparation programs of the University, better planned and more supportive programs to introduce new professionals to the schools, more effective professional renewal for practitioners in the schools, increased knowledge about teaching and learning through joint research, and as a net result, better instruction for students. (54)

The proposal also committed the Collaborative to working with professional development schools which differed by level, region, and characteristics. In other words, PDSs would not be limited to schools with a track record of excellence. During the 1989–1990 academic year, the professional development school team initiated discussions about the PDS concept. Since the PDS concept was not well defined at that time, defining what we meant by professional development school was a very important component of our effort. The PDS team's consultations with other reform efforts, readings, explorations, and reflections eventually produced the "PDS Belief Statements" that would guide the initiation and development of the professional development schools we were committed to select. These Belief Statements, presented here, have been central to virtually all aspects of our PDS work since that time.

All in a professional development school are learners. The focus of a professional development school is learning. Students, teachers, administrators, and parents are all learners in a professional development school. Students will have the opportunity to be active learners in an environment that provides for individual needs and abilities. Teachers and administrators will share ideas and opportunities for professional development, including using and contributing to current research. This can occur in the school site as we reflect upon what we know from practice, as well as in collaboration with West Virginia University faculty. Parents and the community will learn from the activities in a professional development school through their involvement with the professional development school site.

All in a professional development school have the opportunity for success. The members of a professional development school will design and implement activities and programs and develop a climate that promotes and recognizes success for all. The school community (which includes students, teachers, administrators, and parents) should be provided with opportunities for growth and challenge. All members of a professional development school community expect to be successful.

The organization of a professional development school encourages all to be empowered. The interactions and organization of a professional development school will initiate and support the empowerment of all members of the school community. A shared decision-making approach will be used in all aspects of school life; ideas will be valued and all will be encouraged and supported in taking risks. Open communication among all groups involved in the school community is necessary for this to occur.

A professional development school fosters an environment of mutual respect. In a professional development school, all respect self, the school community, and the global community. A professional development school will provide experiences that foster appreciation of cultural and human diversity and will promote self-esteem in the entire community.

A professional development school promotes curriculum and instruction that evolves from continual review and that reflects the school's vision. In a professional development school, the best of practice and the best of research guide review and revision of curriculum and instruction.

In December 1989, all public schools in the four counties surrounding West Virginia University were invited to apply to become professional development schools. Interested schools completed applications which addressed their histories, strengths and needs, visions for the future, and the commitment of the faculty and larger school community to participate in the collaborative PDS process. An ad hoc selection team composed of University and public school faculty chose six professional development schools: three elementary schools, one junior high school, and two senior high schools. The selections were announced in late February 1990—just as the state experienced its only state-wide teachers' strike. This strike and the concerns that motivated it delayed PDS start-up efforts. Late in the 1989–1990 school year, the new PDSs began to form site steering committees to govern their work. At the end of the year, the Cross Site Steering Committee (CSSC) was formed to collaboratively govern PDS work and facilitate discussion of issues faced in all sites. The CSSC was composed of University representatives and two representatives from each PDS—the principal and the site steering committee chair.

For the next two years, PDS and teacher education reform teams worked through the academic year and met in summer retreats to pull their work together. This integrative summer work produced two documents, *Novice Teacher Characteristics* and *Characteristics of Effective Teacher Preparation*, that established outcomes for the redesigned teacher preparation program.

The 1990–1991 academic year was a time of great change. The Dean who had initiated our reform efforts left WVU and the search process for a new dean began. As PDS sites began their first year of professional development school work, the Cross Site Steering Committee (CSSC) asked each site to articulate a tentative mission statement. This was intended to give sites a sense of common direction as they began to consider change. The CSSC also established processes for requesting funding for professional development and pilot projects related to PDS mission statements. Most sites explored the new role with small initiatives, but one site, Morgantown High, took a different approach. The University president, Neil Bucklew, an alumnus of the school, worked with them to develop a long-range strategic plan. Their success with strategic planning was very important because it later led to the development of strategic plans in all sites.

During their second full year, PDS sites developed strategic plans and initiated a number of professional development efforts. Using Morgantown High's work as a pilot, the CSSC designed a long-range strategic planning process which each site completed. The resulting strategic plans formed the basis for internal and external grant proposals and professional development. PDS teachers studied grantsmanship, clinical supervision and peer coaching, critical thinking, and a number of other areas related to their strategic plans in within-site and cross-site groups. During this year, collaborative research was linked more closely with PDS work. Internal grants required formal evaluation components and a competitive research mini-grant program was established to support University and public school collaboration on research efforts.

An important connection between PDS work and teacher education redesign was also initiated in 1992, when the faculty at Suncrest Primary collaborated with WVU to design a pilot Teacher Education Center (TEC) in which cohorts of elementary education majors completed their field experiences at the school. The University supervisor role was filled by a Suncrest faculty member released half-time from classroom teaching to supervise University students. In the fall of 1993, a similar arrangement was established at Morgantown High. These TECs have provided contexts for field testing many of the organizational patterns being considered for the redesigned teacher education program.

During the two-year period required to complete all the program approvals for the redesigned teacher education program (1992 through 1994), teacher education teams fleshed out syllabi, developed specific standards and procedures for admission and retention, and completed the myriad of tasks associated with implementing a very innovative program. Professional development schools continued the individual reform efforts described in the PDS "biographies" and began to consider the need to select additional PDS sites. Using a revised application process designed by the CSSC, a second round of invitations to become a PDS was sent to all public schools in the region. In the spring of 1994, eight additional PDS sites were selected and another cycle of development began. Work with this second generation of PDSs has been informed and enriched by the experiences of the original six sites.

To help readers understand the complexity of an individualized, multi-site change effort and the diversity of the six original PDS sites, which are the focus of this book, the next section of this chapter provides a "biography" of the PDS process in each of the original six sites. The professional development schools are diverse in a number of ways which include their size, socioeconomic status, academic traditions, faculty stability, location, and history of change and collaboration. Table 3.1 which presents each school's demographics and highlights of their PDS work is followed by narrative biographies for each school. This background will provide readers with a context for the stories of change presented in the second section of the book.

Suncrest Primary School

"When you drive up to our school, it is not very impressive . . . It looks like a fairly typical . . . West Virginia school. . . . It's what's happening here in the school and the hallways. . . . Teaching values and respectability and honoring each other's learning styles and honoring each other's backgrounds and being understanding of each other . . . "

—Susanne Lynch, principal, Suncrest Primary

Background

Suncrest Primary is a small neighborhood elementary school that houses approximately 200 children in Head Start through third grade. Built in 1939, it stands on the site of a one-room neighborhood school. Suncrest Primary's community has a tradition of being very involved in the life of the school. Every year approximately sixty percent of the families work in some volunteer activity at the school. Parents have been instrumental in enhancing Suncrest's computer technology as well as in organizing a series of "exploratories," parent-led hands-on sessions for students in areas of the parents' interest or expertise. Parents also organize periodic brown bag lunch presentations and evening sessions where faculty members share information on topics suggested through parent surveys

TABLE 3.1

Description of Key PDS Characteristics

SCHOOL NAME & INFORMATION	Grafton High	East Dale Elementary	Central Elementary
Driving Time to WVU Miles	45 minutes 29 miles	25 minutes 20 miles	15 minutes 3 miles
No. of Teachers No. of Administrators	42 2	39 2	10 1
No. of Students	760 (Grades 9-12)	639 (Kindergarten - Grade 6)	114 (Kindergarten - Grade 6)
Year Became a PDS	1990	1990	1990
Socio-economic Indicator	42% free/reduced meals	45% free/reduced meals	68% free/reduced meals
Ethnicity	99.25% Caucasian 0.25% Asian 0.25% African American 0.25% Indian	99.91% Caucasian .01% Asian .08% African American .01% Asian	57% Caucasian 21% Asian 14% African American 21% Asian 8% Other * 32% of students speak English as a second language
Average Faculty Years of Experience	16.9	13.9	13.6
Faculty with Master's Degree or more	66%	56%	55%

TABLE 3.1 (*continued*)

Description of Key PDS Characteristics

SCHOOL NAME & INFORMATION	Grafton High	East Dale Elementary	Central Elementary
School-wide vision	Grafton High School is a school that fosters a positive attitude toward lifelong learning and where staff and students can reach their highest potential.	As we enter the 21st century, East Dale is the nucleus of the learning environment that encompasses our continually changing world. Through collaboration we plan to integrate Core knowledge and critical thinking to develop the whole learner.	The Central School community will be involved with the education of the whole child to develop the ability for all to live and work individually and cooperatively in a changing world.
Themes	1) Positive attitude 2) Academic success 3) Self-improvement	1) Motivation 2) Collaboration 3) Education	1) Self esteem 2) Professional growth 3) Intellectual use of academic skills 4) Communications 5) Develop a Central School community
Connections	*Peer Coaching:* Hosted an on-site peer coaching graduate course collaboratively taught by a WVU professor in educational administration and a Grafton High School English teacher	*Beyond the School Day:* Collaboratively developed, with both WVU and a PDS high school, community outreach programs that extend science and math learning beyond the school day, such as "Night Under the Stars" and "In Search of an Adventure"	*WVU/Central Reading Course:* Developed a reading course for pre-student teachers that directly benefits Central students and is taught on-site by both WVU and Central faculty

TABLE 3.1 (*continued*)

Description of Key PDS Characteristics

SCHOOL NAME & INFORMATION	Grafton High	East Dale Elementary	Central Elementary
Innovations	*JTPA Grant*: Researched extensively programs for disadvantaged students which culminated in a major JTPA grant for extended counseling services and other programs for their substantial at-risk student population	*S/M/T*: Developed a K-6 integrated science/math curriculum that capitalizes on a state-of-the art Science/Math/Technology Lab	*Student as Authors*: Created a K-6 project that involves Central Elementary students in writing, illustrating, copywriting, publishing and marketing their own multi-lingual books
Future Directions	*Schedule Restructuring*: Examining new schedule options at a variety of high schools, including one high school in the PDS network	*Core Knowledge (thematic units) or Art Focus*: Building all-school thematic units based in topics that emerge from Core Knowledge literature with particular emphasis on the arts.	*Hypermedia*: Extending the Student As Author Project so as to access student-authored books through multi-lingual interactive computer technology

TABLE 3.1 (*continued*)

Description of Key PDS Characteristics

SCHOOL NAME & INFORMATION	Morgantown High	Suncrest Primary	Valley/W. Preston Jr. High
Driving Time to WVU Miles	15 minutes 4 miles	5 minutes 2 miles	30 minutes 20 miles
No. of Teachers No. of Administrators	72 3	11 1	16 1
No. of Students	1,335 (Grades 10-12)	221 (Pre-Kindergarten - Grade 3)	253 (Grades 7-9)
Year Became a PDS	1990	1990	1990
Socio-economic INdicator	8% free/reduced meals	5% free/reduced meals	48.8% free/reduced meals
Ethnicity	95.8% Caucasian 2.1% African American 1.9% Asian/Pacific Islander 0.2% Hispanic	88.21% Caucasian 8.49% Asian/Pacific Islander 2.83% African American 0.47% Hispanic	100% Caucasian
Average Faculty Years of Experience	17.4	18.5	14.9
Faculty with Master's Degre or more	83%	100%	41.18%

TABLE 3.1 (*continued*)

Description of Key PDS Characteristics

SCHOOL NAME & INFORMATION	Morgantown High	Suncrest Primary	Valley/W. Preston Jr. High
School-wide vision	To become a school of the 21st Century.	The Suncrest School Community is a place where individual differences are identified and valued, where varying needs are met, and where each person's potential to learn and grow is realized. All members of the school community are actively engaged in developing their abilities as life-long learners. Suncrest Primary will provide an example of the best of classroom practice and a forum for effective preservice field experiences.	The West Preston School Community is dedicated to providing an environment of mutual trust conducive to the continuing development of life-long learners
Themes	1) Critical thinking 2) Professional development 3) Restructuring 4) Student success 5) Technological enhancement	1) Developmentally appropriate curriculum 2) Individual differences 3) Teacher education center 4) Life-long learning	1) Motivation 2) Communication 3) Self-Esteem 4) Critical thinking 5) Independence and responsibility 6) Interaction
Connections	*Teacher Education Center:* Established a two-semester field experience for teams of WVU teacher education students in a variety of disciplines who are supervised half-time by a member of the MHS faculty	*Teacher Education Center:* Provided a continuum of school-based field experiences for a team of WVU teacher education students by establishing a Teacher Education Center that is supervised by a half-time Suncrest Primary teacher	*Appalachian Literature and Crafts Courses:* Designed and offered courses that directly addressed the cultural heritage of students

TABLE 3.1 (*continued*)

Description of Key PDS Characteristics

SCHOOL NAME & INFORMATION	Morgantown High	Suncrest Primary	Valley/W. Preston Jr. High
Innovations	*Schedule Restructuring:* Initiated an innovative schedule that preserves traditional course length while providing extended periods (90 minutes) of instruction on alternating days	*4-MAT:* Implemented, through thematic units, an integrated curriculum approach to learning based on Bernice McCarthy's analysis of different learning styles and right brain/left brain research	*Foxfire Education:* Implemented a grant proposal, designed and received by eighth grade students, that supported an instructional unit centering on learning about the history and culture of West Virginia through actual experiences
Future Directions	*Integrated Curriculum:* Building on prior more focused curricular initiatives (humanities curriculum, integrated math curriculum, integrated science curriculum) MHS is planning an integration of instruction across all disciplines	*Integrating the Arts:* Using the arts across the curriculum as a vehicle for extending the classroom application of right brain/left brain theory	Withdrew from the Benedum Collaborative in 1993

created and administered by this group. The school community at large communicates via a school-wide newsletter with standing columns from teachers, the principal, and the parent groups.

Suncrest Primary's full-time teaching staff is highly qualified, stable and experienced, most of the teachers having taught at Suncrest for more than ten years. The teaching staff is professionally active on county, regional, and state level curriculum committees. Suncrest's principal, considered a state as well as local educational leader, has close to twenty years of administrative experience. With two teachers per grade level, cooperative teaching within the grade levels has been the norm at Suncrest.

Many of Suncrest Primary's students come from families with parents who are professionals. On the Comprehensive Test of Basic Skills (CTBS), typically ninety percent of Suncrest students score in the average to gifted range. Ten percent of the students score near or below the fortieth percentile on this test. Attendance at Suncrest averages near ninety-five percent, with attendance being problematic for only two percent of the student population. Approximately five percent of Suncrest students qualify to receive free or reduced lunch.

Strategic Plan

As part of Suncrest Primary's PDS work a school-wide strategic plan was developed in 1992. The faculty, with input from the larger school community, created a plan that includes a school motto, a clear vision statement, related themes and goals, and action plans to guide their progress toward these goals.

Motto. We Learn . . . We Care . . . We Share . . .

Vision Statement. The Suncrest School Community is a place where individual differences are identified and valued, where varying needs are met, and where each person's potential to learn and grow is realized. All members of the Suncrest Primary School Community are actively engaged in developing their abilities as life-long learners. We envision that Suncrest Primary School will provide an example of the best of classroom practice and a forum for effective preservice field experiences.

Themes. Plan and implement a developmentally-appropriate curriculum; Expand the variety of instructional approaches to address individual differences; Continue to develop and expand the Teacher Education Center; Encourage life-long learning for all members of the Suncrest Primary School Community.

Highlights. Suncrest Primary's Teacher Education Center represents a unique contribution to the redesign of West Virginia University's teacher preparation program. It was Suncrest Primary teachers working in collaboration with WVU faculty who designed the pilot that was to become a model for clinical placement for preservice teachers in the new program. This innovative model, called a Teacher Education Center, is described in detail in Chapter 10.

Designing curriculum and instruction that address children's various learning styles has become the centerpiece of Suncrest's school reform work. After an intensive study of learning styles research, Suncrest faculty focused on the work of Bernice McCarthy. Her 4MAT system provides instructional approaches that address learning styles and hemisphericity (right and left brain tendencies). Faculty have built a large repertoire of "4MAT" interdisciplinary units, which have become the backbone of their curriculum. Suncrest has recently begun to collaborate with University faculty and parents to integrate the fine arts into these thematic units.

"Suncrest was like a home away from home for our son. The staff was concerned about our whole child–not just interested in teaching him reading, writing, and arithmetic. They modeled the kind of growing, caring adult I hope he'll grow up to be."

—Clay Pytlik, parent, Suncrest Primary

Central Elementary School

"Central: Pathway to life-long learning through challenge, encouragement, multi-culturalism, and fun."

—Sally Reilly, teacher, Central Elementary

Background

Central Elementary School is a small K–6 school located in the heart of downtown Morgantown. It is within easy walking distance of the Arts and Science campus of West Virginia University and is the neighborhood school for many international families who live in university housing. The student population at Central makes it unique in the region. About thirty-six percent of Central's 120 students speak English as a second language. These children typically come from ten to twenty different countries and will be in the United States for a limited time. Central also serves all of the county's elementary-aged hearing-impaired children. These children are, for the most part, mainstreamed into the regular classroom. Additionally, approximately one-third of the student population come from single-parent families. Because seventy-eight percent of Central students qualify for free or reduced lunch, the school has been classified as a Chapter 1 school, which means that all Central students have access to Chapter 1 services. The unique characteristics of Central's student population have provided a focus for much of the PDS work done at the school.

Central's faculty has experienced a great deal of turnover since it was named a PDS. Of the seven grade levels, five are currently taught by teachers who are new to the school. The part-time principal, Chapter 1 teacher, teacher of the hearing-impaired, and teachers in grades two and three have been at the school for an average of fifteen years. Those most actively involved in PDS work come from this group.

Strategic Plan

Central engaged in strategic planning in 1992, developing a plan focused on serving their diverse student population and school community.

Motto. The World Begins With Us

Vision Statement. The Central School community will be involved with the education of the whole child to develop the ability for all to live and work individually and cooperatively in a changing world.

Themes. Self-esteem; professional growth; intellectual use of academic skills; communications; develop a Central School community.

Highlights. Central faculty instituted a "Students-as-Authors" program to build students' self-esteem and increase students' language proficiency. This project provides opportunities for children to write, illustrate, and publish their own stories in both English and their native languages. The project also involves the parents of Central's large LEP (Limited English Proficiency) population by inviting them to participate in translating their children's stories. The project has proven to successfully impact the self-esteem of Central students.

While the Central faculty has explored a variety of more traditional forms of professional development, participation in the Literacy Discussion Group (LDG) has proven to be a very meaningful professional development initiative. The LDG was created by Central's Chapter 1 teacher and a professor in Reading at WVU. One outcome of this group's work has been the complete redesign of an elementary reading methods course for preservice teachers (see Chapter 10). The support and expertise of the LDG has also allowed some Central teachers to move from a very traditional approach to language instruction to a whole language approach through collaborative planning and action research.

"Central School is a school for the children of the world. All the children from all countries never feel alone. If we don't know English, the teachers do everything to improve it. Every teacher cares about us!"

—Student, Central Elementary

Grafton High School

"In the past few years, we have become more aware of our teaching performance and the school community as a whole. I examine my teaching and my interactions with others much more than before."

—Lisa Lucas, teacher, Grafton High School

Background

Grafton High School (GHS) is the only high school in Taylor County, a rural county with a population of approximately 15,000. This consolidated high school which houses over seven hundred ninth through twelfth graders is located about twenty-five miles from West Virginia University, down a curving country road. The area's economy offers very few job opportunities for GHS graduates since the community has an unemployment rate of more than ten percent. With the departure of a major employer and the decline in coal mining, Taylor County has experienced an out-flux of jobs and population. Today the largest employers in the area are the local schools, the West Virginia Department of Health and Human Services, and the local hospital.

In addition to the minimal economic base, Grafton High has one of the highest dropout rates in the state, a high teenage pregnancy rate, and very low scores on achievement tests. A significant number of GHS students exhibit drug/alcohol problems, low self-esteem, and lack of motivation. Relatively few students come from intact, two-parent families.

This rural, impoverished context offers major challenges to the faculty at Grafton High School. This stable faculty is comprised of experienced teachers, sixty percent of whom hold masters degrees. When developing a strategic plan for their PDS work, the faculty decided that their focus had to be on finding ways to help the large at-risk student population succeed.

Strategic Plan

Vision Statement. Grafton High School is a school that fosters a positive attitude toward lifelong learning, where staff and students can reach their highest potential.

Themes. Positive attitude; academic success; self-improvement.

Highlights. Grafton High School has focused much of their PDS work on addressing the needs of their large at-risk student population. An initial activity was the formation of an At-Risk Committee which researched strategies for dealing effectively with at-risk students, developed a substantial professional library on the topic, attended a national at-risk conference, and provided staff development programs for the entire GHS faculty. The staff development focused on motivating at-risk students, improving teaching for student success, and integrating a variety of models of teaching to create a positive learning environment for all students.

The outcome of this committee's work was a school-wide effort to develop research-based initiatives that would address the dropout/at-risk problem at GHS. One of these initiatives was the "Buddy System," a mentoring program in which faculty members are paired with potential dropouts to make positive contacts on a regular basis. The Buddy System has been very successful at Grafton High. Participants experience less failure, their grades improve, and the dropout rate has decreased.

Another effort to help at-risk students is a Students With Stress program developed in collaboration with WVU's Counseling and Guidance Department. In this program WVU students organize self-help groups for GHS students. These groups meet over a period of several weeks, focusing on strategies to help deal with the many stresses in students' lives.

Another successful initiative that not only addressed the needs of at-risk students but benefitted all students is GHS's "Consultative/Collaborative Model for Regular and Special Education." In this model, part of a regional effort to help students receiving special services, academic area teachers and special educators team teach courses to heterogeneous groups. This allows all students to benefit from the content specialist's expertise and the pedagogical expertise of the special educator.

A PDS course on grant writing ultimately resulted in Grafton High's being awarded a Jobs Training Partnership Act (JTPA) grant. Through this grant, GHS was able to fund an additional counselor. The program was so successful that since the funding cycle ended, Taylor County has continued to fund the position—a major commitment when resources are so limited.

"Another great thing about going here is that most of the teachers care about you. If you're upset they'll ask you what's wrong and try to help. It means a lot to know that a teacher cares about you and that you're not just a number to them."

—Student, Grafton High School

Morgantown High School

"Some of the teachers that had been here for a while realized that we needed a change, that all of us needed to change. We needed a shot in the arm, and I think this [becoming a PDS] really provided it."

—Earl Straight, teacher, Morgantown High School.

Background

Morgantown High School (MHS), in Monongalia County, was built in 1927. The campus-style facility, located within walking distance of downtown Morgantown, serves about 1400 students in grades ten through twelve. The campus is currently being renovated and expanded to accommodate the ninth grade, which will be added in about two years. In the 1980s it was named a West Virginia Exemplary School.

MHS has traditionally offered an academically-oriented program including nine Advanced Placement courses, honors courses, and opportunities for early entry into WVU. Vocational education is offered through a program that releases students half-days to attend the local Technical Education Center. A variety of special education programs are offered at the school. Many extra-curricular activities, including a rich tradition in men's and women's athletics and instrumental music, are available at MHS.

While the school's facility is outdated in many ways, they have procured state-of-the-art technology, including CD ROM, laser discs, multimedia, and seven networked computer labs, two of which have access to Internet. Teachers have received extensive training and the instructional technology has been integrated into all disciplines.

MHS's student population is quite diverse. Most students are bussed into the school from outlying rural areas. Almost one-third of the students have parents in professional careers while most of the remaining two-thirds are from blue-collar backgrounds. Nearly one-third of the students are from low-income households and qualify for free or reduced lunch. The student population at MHS is overwhelmingly Caucasian with small percentages of students from African American, Asian/Pacific Islander, or Hispanic families. Graduates attend institutions of higher education in large numbers. MHS averages twelve National Merit Semi-Finalists per year and a significant number of its graduates are consistently accepted by very prestigious colleges, universities, and military academies. However, there is a concern among the faculty about a growing number of students that are not motivated, not doing homework and make-up work, not preparing for exams, and not exhibiting pride in their school. This group of students provides an important challenge to the school.

Strategic Plan

Strategic planning for Benedum Collaborative PDSs began at MHS. When the faculty realized that they needed to develop a strategic plan to help focus their PDS work, they sought the help of the president of West Virginia University, an alumnus of MHS, who shared his expertise in strategic planning.

Vision. To become a school of the twenty-first century.

Vision Statement. Our school community is committed to implementing a process of innovation and change that will result in the creation of a school that can effectively prepare our students to deal with the rapidly changing world of the twenty-first century.

Themes. Critical thinking; professional development; restructuring; student success; technological enhancement.

Highlights. An emphasis on professional development pervades the work done at MHS. In addition to on-site courses focused on strategic planning themes, the school has designed and produced three major professional conferences. The first conference was called the September Snow Day. Students were allowed to remain at home while faculty members attended sessions geared to school-wide professional development. That summer, faculty again met at a Restructuring Institute where they expanded their study of issues related to restructuring. The following year, Snow Day II was held. This third school-wide conference helped solidify the school's adoption of a ninety-minute, odd-even day, block schedule.

Teams of MHS teachers have developed integrated curricula as part of their PDS work. One team has initiated a mastery math curriculum that integrates geometry and algebra, emphasizes hands-on activities, and provides summer classes for students who need extra time to master the math unit objectives or who need supplemental work in topics essential to success in subsequent courses. A second team of teachers collaborated with a WVU chemistry professor to completely redesign the chemistry curriculum. The usual macroscale approach to chemistry instruction has been replaced with microscale chemistry. Students now work with microscale equipment and mere drops of chemicals. This redesign has resulted in: (1) greater flexibility in incorporating lab activities into the curriculum, and (2) quick, easy mini-labs that enable students to use critical thinking strategies more often to discover scientific relationships for themselves. A third team of teachers developed a new interdisciplinary American humanities curriculum that integrates English, social studies, art, and music curricula for tenth and eleventh grade honor students. This interdisciplinary course, called Linking the Humanities, schedules students in back to back English and social studies courses. A multimedia computer lab was integrated into the eleventh grade course so that students could create a year-long project developed collaboratively by using the computer application *Linkway Live!*, a multi-media program in which students created text, pictures, and digitized photos and sound. These curricular, teaching, and schedule innovations grow from the school's strategic planning process.

> "If you walk down any three of the hallways at any day after school, you will see at least five or six doors open with teachers helping students. They can leave at 3:15, but they don't."
>
> —Brooke Phillips, student, Morgantown High School

East Dale Elementary School

> "Dream big and don't be afraid to take risks to reach your goal."
>
> —Donna Peduto, teacher, East Dale Elementary

Background

East Dale Elementary School is a rural, K–6 elementary school serving approximately 600 children in Marion County, West Virginia. Located on the northern end of Fairmont, about twenty miles from West Virginia University, the school's service area is large. The school serves approximately twenty-five percent of Marion County, a rural area with rugged terrain and small, isolated communities located on mountain ridges and river valleys.

The facility, built on ten acres in 1971, was designed as an open school with large instructional areas surrounding the library media center. A state-of-the-art Science, Math, and Technology Lab was added in 1991, supported by a school-wide capital funds drive and by grants, including a $400,000 Eisenhower Grant. The kindergarten classes are housed in an older building nearby.

East Dale draws both rural and suburban children who come from medium to low income families. The school's draw area has a high rate of unemployment and is generally isolated with little access to the world via technology. The student body is predominantly Caucasian with less than ten percent coming from African American or Asian backgrounds. Eighteen percent of the children receive special education services.

For the past ten years, East Dale Elementary has achieved local, state and national recognition for innovative programs, student achievement, community involvement, and community-wide programming. East Dale has been selected as a West Virginia Exemplary School and a National School of Excellence. East Dale's principal of fifteen years, Janet Crescenzi, was named both the West Virginia and the National Principal of the Year in 1986.

Strategic plan

East Dale's strategic plan, developed in 1992, has as its main goal the school's becoming the nucleus of a learning environment encompassing the world and providing educational opportunities for students, parents, and community members, enabling them to become productive citizens of society. It envisions the school as the hub of the community, offering accessible facilities and opportunities, and serving as a focal point for change.

Motto. Motivate, educate, and collaborate.

Vision Statement. As we enter the twenty-first century, East Dale School is the nucleus of the learning environment that encompasses our continually changing world. Through collaboration with higher education, the community, the teaching staff, and students, we plan to integrate Core Knowledge and critical thinking to develop the whole learner. Our goal is to motivate our students to value education and become responsible decision makers and life-long learners.

Themes. Motivation; collaboration; education

Highlights. After reflecting on school-wide measures of student achievement, East Dale targeted the areas of science and math for its early PDS work. Student test scores showed a deficit in these areas, especially for female students. To address this deficit, East Dale began exploring ways to enhance the math/science curriculum. The culmination of this work was the creation of the Science/Math/ Technology (SMT) Lab (see Chapter 8). East Dale teachers have developed an integrated math and science curriculum in which students build critical thinking skills.

Integrating the Core Knowledge program into East Dale's curriculum has been another curricular initiative. This program was chosen to help students gain a common core of shared knowledge, defined in terms of specific content that builds grade by grade. To do this, East Dale has organized across-grade level thematic instructional units around particular core knowledge ideas. The faculty has also begun to integrate fine arts into these units.

"The teachers here were always trying new ideas. They got as excited as we did!"

—East Dale student

Valley Junior High/ West Preston Junior High

"Working with other PDSs and being part of a PDS gave each of us the opportunity to realize our potential. Even though we are not a PDS any more, the knowledge and skills that we gained will be with us forever. It was worth the effort."

—Rhonda Jenkins, teacher, West Preston

Background

In 1990, Valley Junior High became a PDS. Valley was located in Arthurdale, a historical resettlement community in rural Preston County, West Virginia. The junior high facility included two of the six original buildings of the Arthurdale Community School, which was built in the 1930s as the center of the community life in Arthurdale, the first New Deal Homestead farm project. Eleanor Roosevelt personally selected Elsie Clapp, a progressive educator from Columbia University, to direct the school.

Valley served approximately 200 seventh and eighth graders from the rural communities of Arthurdale, Reedsville, and Masontown and the surrounding area which is sparsely populated. Eighty-two percent of the students lived outside any town limits. Because of distance and/or lack of transportation, many students did not have access to educational resources outside the school.

Students came mainly from farming and mining communities, and only twenty percent of the parents had graduated from a four-year college.

Valley's faculty was comprised of twelve full-time and three part-time teachers. One-third of these teachers had earned masters degrees and most of them had about ten years teaching experience. Half of the faculty had grown up in Preston County and had attended the schools there. Valley's faculty hoped that working with WVU as a PDS would open up the academic resources of the University to both the faculty and the students.

In 1992, Valley Junior High consolidated with West Preston Junior High and moved into a different facility in Masontown, West Virginia, about five miles away. This change marked the beginning of reduced involvement of the school as a PDS. One faculty member, Rhonda Jenkins, who made this change with the school, shared her insights as to why the school made the decision to withdraw from their commitment to being a PDS. She felt one factor in their leaving the PDS community was a feeling that they had not been successful in building authentic connections between the institutions of school and university. While their goal in becoming a PDS was to access the resources of WVU, the partnerships that would have facilitated that were never fully developed. Jenkins said, "If we had made some of those connections early on, it might have made a difference." However, she felt that consolidation was the primary factor in the school's decision to withdraw. Others, noting that a number of connections had been established with WVU, have attributed the school's withdrawal from PDS to personnel changes that reduced the cadre of teacher leaders, to difficulties in implementing shared decision making, and to a perceived lack of county support for the school's efforts. All agree, however, that the enormous changes in community, staff, and direction caused by the consolidation were major factors in the school's decision to withdraw.

All the school's early PDS work focused on their connection to the Arthurdale community. More than a school, Valley was a community center. West Preston Junior High, on the other hand, had a more traditional junior high culture. Leaving Arthurdale meant losing the focus of their PDS work. With the consolidation of the two schools, many new faculty members joined the staff. These new faculty members had not been part of the decision to become a PDS, and, therefore, did not feel the same degree of commitment the original faculty did. They had not had the opportunity to build an investment in the collaboration with the University. While several members of the Valley faculty had experienced some real growth through their relationship with WVU and had seen how that relationship could benefit their students, the new faculty struggling to form a new organization perceived the obligations of PDS work as too much of a burden. Requirements such as developing a strategic plan or redesigning a proposal became overwhelming to the new school, and the school's commitment to PDS gradually disappeared. The school formally withdraw from PDS in the spring of 1993.

Strategic Plan

From 1990 to 1992, Valley Junior High's school community was involved in a variety of PDS work. Although at this time the school had not developed a formal strategic plan, they had written a long-range building focus. This document stated their intention to involve students in the democratic learning processes of the Foxfire approach to education. It also described the school's focus on helping students to explore their cultural heritage.

Guided by this document, the school community became involved in work centered around their heritage and the historic community of Arthurdale. For example, Valley students designed and drafted a grant proposal centered on using the Foxfire approach to learn about the history and culture of West Virginia—a project in keeping with the progressive educational philosophy upon which the school had been founded. In another initiative, a Valley teacher collaborated with West Virginia authors to offer a course in Appalachian literature. As part of this course, two WVU professors participated in a West Virginia Author Day at Valley, sharing their experiences as authors to encourage writing among students. Another project Valley undertook as a PDS was the development of an Appalachian Folk Arts and Crafts course for students. The purpose of the course was to introduce and allow students to participate in the arts and crafts that are part of their cultural heritage. Local craftsman guided students in their exploration of these arts. Valley's library media specialist, a leader in the school's PDS efforts, worked with students to organize a West Virginia annex to their library media center. Along with materials purchased by the school, students' work was included in this collection, which became well used by the entire school community.

This early PDS work by members of the Valley Junior High School community was grounded not only in their rich mountain heritage, but also in their philosophy of student-centered learning and curriculum. All their PDS work was focused directly on their students and the local community.

After Valley consolidated to form West Preston Junior High in the fall of 1992, the new, larger school community developed a formal strategic plan, although there seemed to be little consensus that the plan actually represented a school-wide mission. In effect, this planning effort was the school's final experience as a PDS and indicates a departure from the original focus of their PDS work. In the spring of 1993, the school formally withdrew from the PDS collaboration.

Vision Statement. The West Preston school community is dedicated to providing an environment of mutual trust conducive to the continuing development of life-long learners.

Themes. Motivation, communication, self-esteem, critical thinking, independence and responsibility, and interaction.

Conclusion

When we began this reform effort, the professional development school concept was relatively undefined. We invented the concept as we went, a process one of the teachers calls "inventing the airplane while you're flying it." We are struck by the congruence of the PDS Belief Statements we developed in 1989 and current definitions of PDS. While the specific foci of professional development schools still vary among change efforts, the National Center for Restructuring Education, Schools, and Teaching (NCREST) recently developed a statement that conveys the current consensus about the concept of professional development schools:

> A professional development school is both a place and an idea. Professional development schools are collaborative school/University partnerships that provide models of exemplary practice for students and their families, and they provide exemplary programs for the preparation, induction, and professional development of prospective, novice, and experienced teachers. Professional development schools are characterized, in part, by inquiry, documentation, and dissemination of new knowledge, developed through the collaborative partnership, toward the improvement of educational services to children and families. They are committed to the transformation of both school and University structures and practices on behalf of improved teaching and learning. (Vision Statement 1993, 3)

The president of the Holmes Group, Judith Lanier, recently expressed a similar understanding of the nature and purpose of Professional Development Schools:

> Not simply schools that would be good places for preparing future teachers, PDSs are places for responsible, enduring innovation in education. And they are not simply places for restructuring schools— "fixing them so we get them right this time." Rather, they are places of ongoing invention and discovery; places where school and University faculty together carry on the applied study and demonstration of good practice and policy the profession needs to improve learning for young students and prospective educators. (Darling-Hammond 1994, ix)

The experiences that we have had in "inventing while flying" over the past eight years have led us to write this book. We believe the stories we have to tell about our experiences with the change process can aid others in defining their own efforts to create lasting change using the professional development school model. We have chosen to share our stories as narratives because, like teachers everywhere, we know that stories are a powerful way to communicate the culture that has evolved in the collaborative reform effort known as the Benedum Collaborative. As Tom Hart, principal of Morgantown High, puts it, "We may not be able to generate a road map for other reform efforts, but I believe our stories may help others set a direction. We can't tell others the exact exits or side streets they should take, but we can help them choose the interstate they will travel."

References

Darling-Hammond, L. (1994). *Professional development schools: Schools for developing a profession.* New York: Teachers College Press.

National Center for Restructuring Education, Schools, and Teaching (NCREST). (1994). Vision statement: Professional development schools network. *PDS Network News* 1(1), New York: Professional Development School Network, National Center for Restructuring Education, Schools, and Teaching, Teachers College, Columbia.

PART II

STORIES OF PROFESSIONAL DEVELOPMENT SCHOOL CHANGE

∾∾❖∾∾

OVERVIEW OF PART II

People have used stories for centuries to pass on their culture, their values, and their experiences. Stories are particularly effective in capturing knowledge that grows from experience (Carter 1993). We noticed several years ago that stories had become part of our change effort. When we asked educators (public school and university faculty) to share what they were learning from their collaborative work, they told us stories. When they remembered difficult meetings, they recalled them as stories. And those stories were powerful—we understood what restructuring was like for them. Visitors who come to the professional development schools have a chance to hear the stories about reform and, more than anything else, the stories captivate them and help them understand the changes in school life and culture that come with genuine reform.

Part II of this book has grown from the stories Benedum Collaborative participants tell about their experiences with school change. The seven chapters tell stories of change in people, schools, and relationships. What changes when teachers become action researchers? How do major school changes happen? If schools and the University make major changes in their relationship, what happens? What does it mean to be the principal of a restructuring professional development school? Readers will hear these stories in the voices of those who are participating in the change process. If readers want more background on individual schools as they read this part of the book, they may find it helpful to refer to the PDS "biographies" in Chapter 3.

In Chapter 4, Steel, Jenkins, and Colebank depict the impact of the Benedum Collaborative on the lives of two rural teachers. Colebank, who teaches English at Grafton High School, and Jenkins, who is currently the librarian at West Preston Junior High School (the only PDS to withdraw from the Collaborative), share their experiences as classroom teachers who have become leaders in their schools. They describe changes in their schools and classrooms, changes in students' experiences, and offer some advice to others who are considering restructuring.

In Chapter 5, Reed, Ayersman, and Hoffman describe the experiences of classroom teachers conducting action research in several PDSs. Using field notes, survey data, and follow-up interviews, they describe the changes in teachers over a year of studying, conducting, and reporting action research. The teachers' action research studies are summarized, and the authors conclude with suggestions for fostering teacher research.

In Chapter 6, Dempsey, Hart, and Lynch collaborate to share the experiences of Tom Hart, principal of the largest PDS, Morgantown High School, and Susanne Lynch, principal of the smallest PDS, Suncrest Primary School. These principals discuss their approach to leadership as their faculties undertook major changes in curriculum and governance, candidly sharing the frustrations, fears, and successes they met as their schools and their roles changed in the restructuring process.

In Chapter 7, a classroom teacher, a speech pathologist, and a university speech pathology professor share their experiences in developing a collaborative, push-in communication program at Central Elementary that eventually became a site for preparing novice speech pathologists in collaborative approaches. The authors describe their own experiences with "sharing children," the reactions of skeptical administrators and colleagues, and the opportunities this collaboration has created for children and university students.

Chapter 8 depicts the evolution of a major curriculum change at East Dale Elementary School. Gaston, Francis, Crescenzi, and Phillips share the story of envisioning a school that focuses on science, math, and technology; professional development; collaborative curriculum redesign; and the ongoing evolution of the school's vision and curriculum. Their story is a good example of the ongoing, recursive nature of restructuring. Their original goal was met some time ago, but the process of curriculum development continues as they see ways to improve their curriculum.

In Chapter 9, Field and Barksdale-Ladd detail the processes that reshaped Morgantown High School, a large high school with a stable, older faculty, and a tradition of academic excellence. Identifying five phases of change, the authors track the development of school-wide reforms that have transformed the school's curriculum, schedule, governance, climate, and relationships with the University and community.

In Chapter 10, Hoffman, McCrory, and Rosenbluth share stories from three schools to illustrate the mutual impact professional development school collaborations can have on schools and teacher education. Emphasizing ownership, the uniqueness of each site, and respect for each other's expertise, this chapter describes the gradual development of new collaborative partnerships to educate children and prospective teachers—partnerships that have created learning environments that seem to benefit all participants.

In some manner, each of the Benedum Collaborative's six restructuring schools is featured in these chapters—a small suburban primary school, a large comprehensive high school in a university community, an elementary school with a multicultural student population, and an elementary school, a junior high, and a high school in three different rural communities. Readers finishing Part II of the book should have a sense of how the PDS reform process might unfold in different schools, how relationships might evolve, and how participants can grow. Readers should also have a sense of the time, effort, patience, resources, and good humor the process requires. But most importantly, readers should have a sense of the opportunities that come with restructuring—the opportunities for lasting growth and change in the lives of public school children, university students, educators, and communities.

4

The Story of Two Changing Teachers

Sarah Steel, Rhonda Jenkins, and Diana Colebank

When we were asked to paint a word portrait of changing teachers in professional development schools (PDSs), we were excited about sharing the changes in roles and responsibilities of the teachers with whom we work closely in the Benedum Collaborative. The two PDS teachers featured in this chapter are just two of the many teachers in the Collaborative who have experienced professional growth through their efforts in school reform. We wanted to tell this story in a way that would inform the practice of others as well as authentically communicate all the elements of their change experience, including the emotional ones. Therefore, this chapter has been organized in a way that allows the reader to "enter into a conversation" with two teachers about their change through this school reform initiative.

Our conversations focused on issues in teacher change such as leadership roles in PDSs, collaborative and collegial relationships, opportunities for professional development, changes in teaching and learning occurring at schools, and their motivation to be a part of the current school reform movement. These conversations begin to answer questions about PDS teachers' experiences. Some of those questions include the following. In what areas of their professional lives had they experienced change? How pervasive were the changes? How substantive? And as the bottom line, how had their changes affected the lives of their students? The conversations with these two teachers proved to be descriptive, forthright, funny, touching, and ultimately informative. What they have to say about their lives in professional development schools contributes significantly to our growing body of knowledge about the changing roles and responsibilities of teachers in restructuring schools.

Context for Teacher Change: National Climate

To build a context for these portraits, it is necessary to look not only at the climate for teacher change in the national educational reform movement, but also at the teachers' own professional backgrounds and the work situations in which these teachers practice and learn.

Joseph Murphy of Vanderbilt University and the National Center for Educational Leadership succinctly summarized the two waves of educational reform of the 1980s in an article for the *Journal of Teacher Education*. Early in the '80s the first wave of school reform was a response to the outcry from the nation that the United States was lagging behind other industrialized nations economically. Reformers felt that schools were at fault for not adequately equipping students to be effective, capable members of society. To remedy this situation, reformers sought to "improve teacher quality through mandated, top-down initiatives, especially those of the state. . . . Early reform efforts that emphasized policy mechanisms such as prescriptions, tightly specified resource allocations, and performance measurements that focused on repairing components of the system and raising the quality of the work force by telling employees how to work. . . . These early reform initiatives focused on higher standards and harder work to right the course of education" (Murphy 1990, 51).

It wasn't long, however, before these reforms were found wanting. Many educators felt that reforms that aimed at merely tinkering with the existing educational structures and systems would not produce lasting, substantive change in education. Soon the second wave of school reform began. Now reformers called for "fundamental revisions in the organization and governance of schools. Educators in this group believed that continued repairs of the old system were not only unlikely to get us to our desired destination but might prove counterproductive. . . . Whereas reformers in the earlier era of reform called for change mandated from above, the second reform wave capitalized on the energy and creativity of individuals at the school level to effect change" (Murphy 1990, 51). Although this second wave of school reform, or what Cuban calls second order change (1988), calls for complete systemic change, it is the teachers in individual schools who will interpret and implement these changes. The role teachers play in restructuring schools has a significant impact on the success of the school reform effort. Like the Holmes Group, a consortium of U.S research universities committed to improving the quality of schooling, many experts in education are calling for the professionalism of teaching. To realize this "transformation of teaching from an occupation into a genuine profession" (Holmes Group 1986, ix), teaching professionals will be required to take on new roles and responsibilities. Many of these enlarged roles and responsibilities will take them "beyond their regular classroom assignments" (Smylie and Denny 1990, 241). These new roles can include "colleague, decision maker, leader and learner" (McCarthey and Peterson 1989, 1). Scholars studying restructuring schools emphasize the importance of teachers and their new roles. When Harvey and Crandall (1988) compiled a list of critical components of restructuring, a key component was to "rethink and alter the roles and responsibilities of educational personnel" (Harvey and Crandall 1988, 11). Moses and Withaker (1990) included redefining the role of teachers in their list of ten components of restructuring schools. And SERC's national forum, *Effective Restructuring: Putting the Pieces Together*, described five fundamental role changes for teachers in restructuring schools: "more involvement in the decision-making process, more collaborative working relationship with school principal, team teaching using an interdisciplinary approach, more opportunities for professional and personal development, become a facilitator of learning" (Feduk 1993). Changing teachers' roles and responsibilities to facilitate school reform is an abiding theme in educational literature and has been demonstrated repeatedly by teachers in professional development schools. These teachers are the linchpins of this second wave of school reform. As Michael Fullan comments, "Educational change depends on what teachers do and think—it's as simple and complex as that" (quoted in Rutherford 1985, 3). The portrait that follows of two teachers actively engaged in a school reform initiative illustrates this philosophy.

Context for Teacher Change: Teachers' Professional Backgrounds

Diana Colebank is an English teacher at Grafton High School in Taylor County, West Virginia. Diana graduated from a local teachers' college with a degree in history and English. At graduation, she had vague plans of teaching in college one day, but marriage and family commitments put these plans on the back burner. Three years later, Diana found herself in Taylor County and in need of a job. Even though she had no teaching degree, the local high school needed an English teacher, and Diana became temporarily certified via her high scores on the National Teachers' Exam. This began her life-long career at Grafton High School. Twenty years after getting her bachelors, Diana still had not found the opportunity to pursue a graduate degree. She felt intimidated by the large state university, the size of which, when compared with her graduating class in high school (twenty-nine students) or with the student population at the teachers' college (3000 students), was overwhelming.

Rhonda Jenkins, the Library Media Specialist at West Preston Junior High in Preston County, West Virginia, graduated from a local teachers' college with a degree in secondary education. For years she resisted working toward a masters degree as she felt higher education would not be able to fulfill her needs. However, after becoming involved in PDS work, she decided to pursue this degree. In 1993 she received her masters from WVU in secondary education with a specialization in Library Science. Rhonda had taught in several schools before she came to West Preston. Although she learned from each teaching situation, she always felt "stifled in environments that offered no opportunity to stretch or grow."

Both teachers teach in schools situated in rural West Virginia. Grafton High School is a consolidated county high school which serves about 700 9th–12th graders. GHS students come from families at the lower end of the socioeconomic scale. The statistics show that thirty-one percent of the student population take free or reduced lunch and that the dropout rate in 1988 was 25.9 percent. Traditionally, community members made their livings from coal mining and railroad work; however, these jobs are now disappearing. The population of Taylor County is decreasing, with the more affluent members leaving the state. As part of Grafton High's strategic planning, they created a vision statement that articulated what they would like their school to look like ten years from now. To reach their vision, the Grafton High School faculty agreed that they would focus on motivating all students to learn, with a special emphasis on their large population of students classified as "at-risk."

West Preston students have a very similar background to those at Grafton High. The majority of them come from farming or coal mining families. Eighty percent of the parents have not graduated from a four-year college. The lack of convenient public transportation and the distance of Masontown from a city have meant that access to outside resources has been severely limited. West Preston's vision statement included the ideas of progressive education where teachers taught an interdisciplinary curriculum that emphasized the community's rich mountain heritage and where students learned through democratic, "hands-on" instruction.

These teachers' backgrounds and work situations are not unique in West Virginia. These are not teachers from wealthy backgrounds who have worked in school districts with the material advantages that wealth can bring. However, these teachers are committed to the improvement of education in West Virginia. When we discussed their motivation for becoming actively involved in the work of a professional development school, they both spoke about that commitment. All schools applying to participate in the Benedum Collaborative as PDSs had to react to a set of Belief Statements about schooling. Rhonda said, "What motivated me to become involved in PDS were the Belief Statements. Statements such as 'All children can learn,' and 'All have the opportunity for success' struck a chord. That sounded like what I had always believed about learning and school." Rhonda was also motivated to become involved because she felt that she had something valuable to offer West Virginia University, specifically, the practitioner's perspective on schooling. Both Rhonda and Diana felt that being a part of a PDS was an opportunity to help students who were not motivated to learn. Rhonda noted, "We thought this was our chance to make a difference. We don't get very many chances." Diana agreed, saying that to her the definition of professional development school was opportunity.

Collaborative Working Relationships

Looking back on our lengthy conversations about their work in professional development schools, it became obvious that there were some pervasive themes in the dialogue. The following is comprised of outtakes from our conversations organized around the themes these teachers felt compelled to share. Since collaboration has been a hallmark of the Benedum Collaborative from its inception, it is not surprising that collaborative work relationships was one of the major themes of our conversations about their experiences in the Benedum Collaborative

How has your involvement in school restructuring and PDS affected relationships with your colleagues in education?

Diana: When our school got involved in restructuring, I was just one of the crowd, nothing special. I was the teacher who sat in the back of the faculty meeting and said very little. I got along with everybody on the staff. That has changed drastically! Now at faculty meetings I'm more likely to bring up issues and speak my mind, and once you begin to voice your position on important issues, you find that others may vehemently disagree. Conflicts arise and we have to learn to deal with that. However, I feel I've gained the respect of my faculty. Because they know how active I am in the Benedum Collaborative, they now consult me about issues that have resulted from our involvement as a PDS.

         My relationship with my principal has changed as well. We really act as partners and colleagues. He has come to depend on me more because he knows of my commitment to improving the education students are getting at GHS. He has been willing to try new things, work with us, and listen to our ideas. He respects us as professionals and he comes up with plenty of good ideas himself. It used to be that the principal's yearly evaluations made me very nervous. My stomach would be in knots and my knees turned to jelly. However, now I'm much more at ease with him. I really think that is a result of a PDS class I took where we were required to observe each other and discuss our teaching. My principal was my partner in this class and the repeated observations really helped put me at ease with him and see him as a true colleague, not just as my boss.

Rhonda: I've noticed a real change in my relationship with the county level administration. Last summer I took a class on restructuring that was being taught by the assistant superintendent of my county. Because he knew that I was actively involved in the Benedum Collaborative, he often called on me to share experiences with the class. All my thoughts were not received with enthusiasm, but the class members as well as the assistant superintendent always looked to me to be the voice of experience.

As a teacher in a restructuring school, I have had my share of conflicts with my principal. The faculty has begun to look to me to express faculty decisions at meetings. And it's true that I do think it's important to deal with issues openly, and I'll take the lead in doing that. Naturally this puts me in a position of conflict with administrators sometimes. For successful collaboration, it's vital that the administration be open to sharing decision making. I've felt that my faculty has been "allowed" to share in making decisions only in predetermined areas. We've had a taste of it, but we know there are limits. That makes for a very frustrating relationship with administration at times.

What is the nature of collegiality at your school now?

Diana: An example of dealing with colleagues in a new way for me is preparing and presenting staff development sessions for my staff. Before attending an Association for Supervision and Curriculum Development (ASCD) Conference dealing with topics such as "at-risk" students, a colleague and I were asked to share our experience with the staff when we returned. I had never done that before. I was always one of those people who sat in a conference and scribbled a few notes on a note pad. This time, however, I knew I had better listen carefully. My co-presenter and I spent a lot of time organizing the materials to be shared. All the work paid off because most of the people who attended said it was one of the best staff development sessions ever because it was really geared to their needs.

As part of the strategic planning to reach our vision, subcommittees were formed to address areas of need in the school. I've been actively involved in the subcommittee concerning "at-risk" students. This subcommittee has done a lot of research and worked hard to educate and sensitize our faculty concerning "at-risk" students.

How has your relationship with the University changed since you've been involved in PDS activities?

Rhonda: I had never been involved in designing university curriculum before! One of the goals of the Benedum Collaborative was to redesign the teacher education program at WVU. I had just finished my coursework in Library Science and was approached by a Library Science professor to work on a committee charged with creating the curriculum design in this discipline. I felt that I was an equal member of the group serving on this committee that was comprised of university professors, public school librarians, and county level administrators. My thoughts and experiences were incorporated into the final product. I think every teacher should have this experience because I came to realize what a complex and difficult task it is.

In the past, I thought WVU had no idea what the "real world" was like and that the classes offered weren't motivating or relevant. Thinking back on that now, I realized that my attitude and prejudices about the "ivory tower" were getting in the way of my learning. My attitude has completely changed since our collaboration through the Benedum Collaborative. Now that I have been in closer touch with WVU people I think they respond to our needs very well. In fact PDS teachers have asked for courses on specific topics, and they have been created to fit those needs. But I think it is crucial to my change in attitude that I have new and different kinds of interactions with WVU. No longer are they just standing in front of a classroom lecturing: they are partners on committees and in research. We are working together on the same problems with common goals.

Diana: Through my interactions with WVU I had the opportunity to attend a Southeastern Holmes Group meeting. At first I felt like a fish out of water at this meeting where professors and deans from member universities discuss issues in education. Then I realized they were discussing things my colleagues and I were experiencing. People from all over the nation were asking me questions about the Benedum Collaborative's reform efforts and for once West Virginia looked pretty good! That was a good feeling.

One interaction with WVU that paid off for me and my students was my collaboration with my student teacher. When I got involved in the Writing Project, I didn't know anything about computers except that I was scared to death of them. Now, at least, I can fool around with them and come out with a typed page. I was still leery about taking an entire class to the lab, however, since students can do some of the weirdest things with a computer and I was afraid I could never figure out how to help them. But because of my student teacher, I have now taken students to the computer lab. She was very familiar with IBM computers and because she was my partner, I felt brave enough to take twenty-eight students into the lab. This is a great example of how I learned from my student.

What opportunities for shared decision making are available at your school?

Rhonda: Although my faculty hasn't experienced a lot of shared decision making, my program has been greatly affected by one organizational decision made my faculty. Last year my principal told the faculty he was having difficulty placing some Special Education students for one of their class periods. One option was to place these students in the library for that class period. This would mean that the library media center would have to be closed at that time. Well, the faculty agreed that rather than lose that library time, they would absorb the extra students into their classes. This would allow the students and the teachers to have complete access to the library all day. I think that says a lot. It means that they appreciate having the library media center open and they see its importance to the school.

   Our Site Steering Committee that was formed to oversee the restructuring efforts made at our school never really was allowed to be a strong decision making group. We did come up with excellent ideas, and if the principal perceived them to be good, we got to go ahead with them. Otherwise they were not carried out. However, one idea that was supported by the majority of the faculty was to try to eliminate tracking at the school. As a faculty we studied the issue, made a plan, began implementation, and are now beginning to evaluate our success. It hasn't been all smooth sailing. Some of the faculty would prefer tracking, but they are going along with the majority for now.

Diana: A collaborative experience that really affected my work began with a class offered by our Regional Educational Service Agency (RESA). Some Grafton teachers and I took this class on the collaborative/ consultative approach. We really got excited about this approach that calls for Special Education teachers to team teach with the regular classroom teacher. As part of the class, my colleagues and I wrote a proposal to our principal about incorporating this technique into our curriculum. Even though using the collaborative/consultative approach meant rearranging our school's master schedule so that teachers could have joint planning time and rethinking how our resources would be utilized, our principal was convinced to give our idea a try. The collaboration between our learning disabilities teacher and me has had a profound effect on my teaching.

   It's interesting to note how closely Diana's and Rhonda's experiences are reflected in the literature on school reform. Judith Warren Little notes that successful schools are places where "teachers valued and participated in norms of collegiality and continuous improvement," and where "they pursued a greater range of professional interactions with fellow teachers or administrators, including talk about instruction, structured observation, and shared planning or preparation" (Little 1982, 325). Roland Barth (1991) places collegiality at the top of his list on ways to improve schools from within. He describes collegiality as the presence of four specific behaviors: talking about practice, observing each other teaching, working on curriculum, and teaching each other. Therefore, according to the literature, Diana and Rhonda are acting as true colleagues. However, the success of their schools will be determined by how pervasive and substantive the collaborative working relationships are. In schools where terms like shared decision making are only rhetoric, it's impossible to experience complete restructuring or success.

Professional Growth

Participation in professional development activities is critical to the school restructuring that is ongoing in professional development schools. Defining which activities qualify as professional development becomes quixotic in professional development schools. It's more than taking classes or attending conferences, though these activities are certainly a vital part of the learning taking place. It includes all the process, governance, and organizational skills teachers take on when pursuing work in their PDS sites. "Teacher knowledge includes knowledge of content and method, to be sure. But it also includes knowledge of policy systems, of professional organizations, and of a professional dialogue pertinent to teachers' work" (Lichtenstein, McLaughlin, Knudsen 1992). Rhonda and Diana emphasized the effect these professional development activities had on their professional as well as their personal growth.

How have you grown as a professional since your involvement in professional development schools?

Diana: Because our county is unable to send teachers to conferences or even pay substitutes for us when we're out of our classrooms, I was so excited about having the opportunity to participate in some national level conferences. As part of trying to reach our vision for Grafton High, our faculty explored options for learning how to help students who were "at-risk." As part of that effort some of my faculty went to the Association for Supervision and Curriculum Development (ASCD) conference in Orlando. I attended three excellent sessions. These people knew their stuff and I came home with tons of materials. I remember one session that really influenced how I teach now. The session was on mind, memory, and learning. For example, they presented evidence on how difficult it was for students to do two things at once such as taking notes and listening to lectures simultaneously. So now my class talks a while and then we stop and write a while. It's really a simple concept, but it's had a good effect on my teaching.

A different kind of professional development I pursued through the Benedum Collaborative was a visit to a restructuring school out of state. Fairdale High School in Kentucky had been restructuring for several years and were able to show us ways they had been creative in solving problems. It was unique because this faculty was able to talk to us from their own experiences. They even made predictions about things that might happen to us a few years down the line. By the way, those predictions were pretty much on target!

Some of the best professional development I experienced came from another teacher on my staff. As part of the collaborative/ consultative approach to teaching, our school's teacher of the learning disabled became my "partner in crime." We used to have these "classes from hell" composed only of LD students. At the same time I had LD students in my regular English classes, and I didn't know how to help them. I didn't know what to do with them because my traditional methods were not working, but I didn't know any other methods to try. Now the LD teacher and I team teach this class. What a difference this has made. She has been there to show me effective strategies so that these students can experience success in the regular classroom. For many teachers it might be difficult to have a colleague watching you work and then making suggestions on how you might do better.

I took a class arranged by WVU at the request of teachers in PDS sites. In this class called Observation and Discussion of Teaching, I remember reading an article about how teachers make about 1300 decisions a day. At that time I thought, "No wonder I don't know what to make for dinner!" I loved that class because it gave us a chance to examine what we think and do when we teach. You know a lot of times teachers just teach to "get through the day" without really reflecting on their goals and purposes in lessons. This class allowed me to make those important reflections.

Rhonda: There have been so many opportunities for professional development in this Collaborative. Recently I presented a research project done in collaboration with two university people at the West Virginia Educational Media Association. I had no idea going in what would be involved in a collaborative research project. It was a real challenge and I learned so much. The project dealt with the role of information access and utilization in PDS sites. In the project I got to work with all the Library Media Specialists in the six professional development schools. This research didn't just inform my university colleagues and me; it was the beginning of a series of professional development opportunities for the PDS Library Media Specialists. The research led them to want to learn more about exemplary Library Media Centers in the area and to visit some of these centers.

Although you might not think of it as a "professional development activity," participating in shared-decision-making groups has contributed greatly to my professional growth. Working with colleagues on the Site Steering Committee and the Cross-Site Steering Committee was a real learning experience. Becoming comfortable making presentations about our work in the Benedum Collaborative to Boards of Education and other groups also provided professional growth.

What personal growth have you experienced through this reform project?

Rhonda: I remember speaking at the Governor's Task Force on Education with my PDS colleagues as a major milestone in my personal growth through this collaborative. It was the first time I had participated at this level in education. Even though I was very nervous, the more I talked about the good things happening at my school the better I felt. It became very important to me to help them understand the wonderful possibilities inherent in working in professional development schools. But the most important part of that and other, similar experiences I've had through the project is that educators on the state, university, and even national level were showing me respect. Before this project, I didn't feel that anybody at the University was interested in what I had to say, but now I feel I have lots to contribute.

I read that burnout was not because of too much work but rather because of how teachers felt about the work. I know I'm doing much more work since I'm in a PDS but I feel energized. I feel I'm making a positive difference, and that's led to a whole new attitude about my work as a teacher. It used to be that when a student had problems at school, I was apt to blame that student or his background for the problems. Now I look to myself first. I look for options and, if I need to, I seek help so that that student has the chance to succeed. Instead of needing to blame something for problems, I try to come up with strategies to solve the problems that are blocking that student's ability to learn.

Diana: When I think of personal growth, there is this picture in my mind of
            Rhonda at the Southeastern Holmes Group meeting grabbing the
            microphone and saying, "I'll take that question." That was wonderful
            because it showed that we public school teachers felt confident about
            what we had to offer to the school reform movement. I know that my
            self-esteem as a professional, as a teacher, has gone way up. It's
            partly because I've learned so much, but it's more that I have a
            different perspective on what I know. I also feel that you get to a
            certain point in your professional life where you feel like you're
            doing the same thing over and over again. You just get bored with it.
            Then, with PDS, a whole new set of opportunities and challenges
            open up. You're doing different things, interacting with different
            people, sharing different experiences and your whole perspective on
            yourself and your profession changes.

                            Changes in Teaching and Learning

        Rosenholtz (1989) found in her study on teachers in the workplace, that
teachers were most interested in shared decision making around the themes of
curriculum and students. These were the areas that touched them the most.
Rhonda and Diana have both experienced great changes in curriculum and
instruction at their schools, and their students have enjoyed the results of these
changes. For Rhonda, it was the Foxfire approach to instruction that changed her
teaching most. She described it as a "religious" experience. This approach
incorporates hands-on instruction and a democratic style of learning. Students
are empowered to choose the learning strategies they find most relevant and
appropriate to their learning. In this student-centered teaching, Rhonda became
"more of an orchestrator or artist, giving up some authority and control to gain
student interest and involvement" (Lieberman 1992, 19). Diana's teaching life
changed substantially after her introduction to the collaborative/consultative
model of instruction. As she's already stated, this approach to instruction allows
students at all levels to interact in the same classroom, as well as allowing
teachers from the "regular" classroom to team teach with teachers trained in
special education techniques.

How has your instruction changed since you became involved in professional
development schools?

Diana: Through our involvement in the Benedum Collaborative, Grafton
            High was able to complete our computer lab. At WVU, I took a class
            called the Writing Project. I learned a lot about teaching the writing
            process here. I also learned about how computers can facilitate this

process. I feel like I finally know what to do in my classroom. After seventeen years of teaching I finally figured out how to do it!

Rhonda: Teaching library media skills in a school using the Foxfire approach to instruction and learning is wonderful. Instead of teaching individual skill units to students who can see no connection to that and what they need to know, I teach these information skills at the point of need. Students who have decided how they want to pursue learning certain objectives come to the library media center, and I can teach them what they need when they need it. Giving kids choices instead of deciding everything myself makes a world of difference in how they feel about what they are doing. Foxfire has also opened up opportunities to team teach with my faculty. Now we plan together how we can incorporate information skills into their Foxfire instruction. I find myself doing a lot of instruction on presentation skills. Since students are doing much more project-style learning in cooperative groups, I've begun teaching students and teachers production skills such as making transparencies and graphic plates. Once the kids see the relevance of what they are doing, it all becomes so much easier. I know I am a different teacher now.

What about assessment?

Rhonda: Well, with the Foxfire approach, pencil and paper tests are no longer good assessments of what they've learned. Instead, we're using journals, demonstrations, portfolios, and media products such as video tapes to enable us to evaluate the skills they're now learning.

Diana: I used to collect daily work from my students and record each assignment in my gradebook. At the end of the grading period, I would have about forty-nine grades to average! Now I have students keep a notebook of journal entries and their daily assignments, and it works so much better, for a couple of reasons. First of all, we check a lot of things together, so students get immediate feedback on how they're doing. All their material is in one place so that when test time comes, they can easily find what they need to study. It also helps them see the connection between their grades and these daily assignments. All of a sudden, dawn breaks and kids see "well, this is important, isn't it?" It's also acted as a great equalizer for the learning-disabled students in my class. Even if a child has a low reading level, he can finish daily work and keep it in his notebook. These notebooks also are a great tool to build in some reflection on work by students. They can look back over a semester of work and see how much they've changed and grown. It teaches students to be responsible for their work, to stay organized and, maybe most importantly, it has kept me sane! I can evaluate notebooks over a couple weekends every six weeks instead of being burdened by tons of papers each night.

Planning?

Rhonda: Planning for a class where students are choosing the learning activities is a challenge! In my classes taught through the Foxfire approach, I have to plan activities that students have chosen. Even though I'm often writing less in a plan book, extensive planning is involved. As a library media specialist, I know that I'd better have all the equipment and materials available for whatever activities these students plan. I've also noticed changes in my planning since our school has begun to eliminate tracking. I now make a real effort to plan for the diversity of students in my classes. Heterogeneous grouping is not what all teachers prefer, but I like it. I think it is more interesting for everybody, but it requires different kinds and levels of activities and more collaboration among the staff. I really think teaching this kind of group has forced me to be a better teacher.

Diana: Probably the biggest change in planning is that now I do it with my collaborative/consultative partner. Our schedules have been arranged so that we have a joint planning period. That was particularly critical the first year because my partner was teaching me strategies that would be effective for learning-disabled students.

How have the changes in teaching and learning at your school affected your students' lives?

Rhonda: There are so many examples, but I think I'll start by saying that our students are now so much more self-confident outside the school setting. I team taught a Foxfire social studies unit where the students organized a trip around West Virginia in order to learn about the state. To get this project off the ground, students were making contacts with adults over the phone and making travel arrangements. They were giving presentations to parent and community groups. They were using the university library to get information. All this experience out of the classroom dealing with adults in the "real world" has made a difference in their lives. I'm guessing that this is one reason, in the past, why our students dropped out of college after the first semester. It was too scary. If they needed help, they weren't assertive enough to ask for help. This is not going to be true for the students we're training now.

Diana: I really have two stories that illustrate changes in students' lives. As a faculty, our school began to search for ways to help those students who are classified "at-risk." A committee was created to attack this problem. One strategy suggested by the At-Risk Committee was the Buddy System. In this system, teachers are assigned one or two students to sort of look after during the school year. They become the teacher's buddy, and check in every day to chat about what's going on in their lives. Well, one of my buddies is such a unique kid. He's really smart, but you'd never know it from his grade average. He's got problems in his home with substance abuse, and you can see how hard his life is. I remember asking him to write about what it would be like to be snowbound, and he wrote this beautiful story from the perspective of a snowflake. I really think the Buddy System has sensitized our teachers to the very real problems these high school students are having. I hope that I'm helping my "buddies" to deal with all this stuff that gets in the way of success in school. The initial results from the Buddy System are good. We've seen real changes in grades from the students involved in this program.

The other change in students' lives that I've particularly noticed are changes in the lives of the LD students participating in the collaborative/consultative English classes. Before, the LD sections of English had the reputation of being a zoo. These students didn't have any reason to model good behavior. Now, they are in classes with cheerleaders and high achievers, students who do exhibit good behavior, and it's having an effect even beyond the classroom. It's great now to go to football games and dances and see some of these students who never attended these activities before. They are dating kids that before they never had the opportunity to meet. It's made a profound difference, not just in their classroom performance, but in their lives.

Barriers

Although great strides have been made in the professional development schools in restructuring and school reform, it hasn't been without cost. Barriers such as "time, money, unwillingness to change, state regulations, local school district goals/policies, and training" (Feduk 1993) have been cited as obstacles to successful restructuring. Diana and Rhonda discussed the obstacles they've faced in their reform efforts.

What are some obstacles you've faced in your school restructuring effort?

Rhonda: Whenever you try to change an organization drastically, there are going to be conflicts to resolve and obstacles to overcome. We've run into several in our work. Leadership at the county level has not always been supportive of our needs. I remember our assistant superintendent responding to a comment of mine about needing cooperation at the county level for our reform. He said that "there are some things you can do in your classroom and then there are some things that need to be left to the county." That kind of mindset is a barrier. Along those same lines, county administration has also asked us to limit our time out of the classroom. Even though this release time is paid for from the Benedum grant, the county doesn't see that long-range benefits might be worth that out-of-class time. It's not just the county, of course. I'm worried about being away from my class too often. It's been difficult weighing the trade-offs between missing class and future results coming from the work done out of the classroom.

Diana: A major barrier we've faced at Grafton High did not come from our county level. In fact, as long as it didn't involve money, of which they have very little, they have been with us all the way. Our obstacles came from our own faculty. Some faculty members have seen reforms come and go and thought that this restructuring effort was just another trend that would soon pass. They really didn't want to become involved. Other faculty members would participate as long as their own personal agenda was being addressed. However, if school-wide needs took precedence or if grant requirements had to be met, they were no longer interested in participation.

    I guess a real lesson we learned in our work is that group building is extremely important. We really could have used training in shared decision making. It sounds great when you're told that you will have the power to "reinvent" your school. The trouble is, making those decisions means you better be ready to deal with conflict and to build consensus. We've had some bruised feelings among our staff. Having been trained to work with children, and then doing that for years, you're not really prepared for working with adults. I would recommend that anyone undertaking school restructuring look into training for decision making.

    In addition to those named by Diana and Rhonda, school reform experts cite other barriers to restructuring and school change. Adam Urbansky, Vice-President of the American Federation of Teachers, commented on the need for *informed* shared decision making in restructuring efforts. In a videoconference on effective school restructuring, he stated that having more people involved in decision making did not necessarily make for better decisions, just ones that make more people happy. He argued that in order to make decisions that effected good results, educators must be trained to make informed decisions and be vigilant about evaluating and modifying these shared decisions once made (Feduk 1993).

Time has been cited as a barrier in school restructuring by many educators. In analyzing the role of time in collaborative school restructuring, Phillips and Wolfe (1993, 4) discussed "three dimensions to the variable of time in change projects: 1) time for the overall process of change to occur, including the institutionalization reforms; 2) time for the constituent parts or sub-processes of the reform project to be accomplished; and 3) time for individuals and groups to participate in the variety of tasks associated with a collaborative reform effort." Finding time to collaborate and restructure is crucial; however, "It is both unfair and unrealistic to expect teachers to somehow find the time for collaborative activities *and* continue to do everything they are expected to do already" (Scott and Smith 1987). External funding to provide released time for restructuring activities has been helpful to Rhonda's and Diana's professional development schools, but to institutionalize this change and make it last, these schools must begin to discover ways to reallocate resources at hand.

Leadership

When Barth (1988, 131) said, "Teachers harbor extraordinary leadership capabilities," he might have been talking about teachers such as Rhonda and Diana. Throughout our discussions on teacher change, Rhonda and Diana demonstrated their leadership capacity. If the conditions for effective school leadership include "demonstrating mastery of a knowledge base, a willingness to make decisions and to take responsibility for implementing them, and receptivity to new ideas and to learning from other teachers" (Rallis 1988, 646), then Rhonda and Diana can be called school leaders. Through their involvement in activities ongoing in their professional development schools, all the above conditions have been met. This theme of leadership is woven through all our discussions about their experiences in professional development schools. Just looking at the various roles these teachers are now taking on in their schools illustrates how teacher professionalism has become the "new paradigm for school management" (Smylie and Denny 1989).

What new roles are you playing since your school became a professional development school?

Diana: I'm doing so many new things since I became involved in PDS. In my own school, I participate on the Site Steering Committee. This committee is made up of the principal and faculty members who are committed to PDS work. I am the representative from this committee to the Cross-Site Steering Committee (CSSC). The CSSC has members from all PDS sites as well as from the University. Last year, I was elected co-chair of this committee that deals with issues that go across sites. I've written grant proposals for our school and even receive mail addressed to "grant writer." Other roles include graduate student, staff developer for my school and other schools in the area, and Holmes Group participant. That's pretty heady stuff for someone who four years ago was happy to just stay in her classroom and teach.

Rhonda: As I remember it, when I began representing my school at the CSSC, my role in my school changed overnight. All of a sudden faculty members began consulting me about issues related to PDS. Also, after a collaborative project done with a university partner in Library Media, the school began to see the role of the library media center and library media specialist differently. The faculty saw that the media center could serve as the information hub of the school as well as a center for building their interdisciplinary units. I started to become an equal team member in instruction. I wanted to capitalize on that, and so I began offering inservices to my faculty on library media as well as on PDS information. Another new role for me is team teaching a university class. I've been asked to present information to a Foxfire II class this spring. I've also participated in a Holmes Group meeting and presented research I conducted in collaboration with some university partners at a state conference. I guess you could say I've undergone a lot of change since I've become involved in this project.

Lessons Learned

As our discussions on school restructuring concluded, we realized that there were several "lessons learned" on Rhonda and Diana's journey to school restructuring that might benefit those beginning their own restructuring efforts.

What advice would you give to readers interested in beginning an extensive school restructuring project?

Diana   (1) Be prepared to work hard and invest a lot of time and energy in the process; (2) Get some training in conflict resolution and consensus building. You'll need it; (3) Don't get frustrated if things move more slowly and less smoothly than you would like. Change takes time and it isn't a comfortable process; (4) Focus and prioritize your efforts. Don't try to work on too many things at once. You won't accomplish enough on any of them to feel good about them, or you will burn out trying; (5) Keep records—they will be valuable to you and to others; (6) Celebrate your successes and learn from your mistakes.

Rhonda: If I were to offer advice to a school that was beginning restructuring efforts, the first suggestion would be to learn exactly how much restructuring the county or district administration will support. If administrators can offer genuine support for site-based management and shared decision making, then the possiblities can be exciting for the school community. However, if teachers enthusiastically begin restructuring efforts only to find that they are severely restricted in their input, then the teachers become frustrated. For administrators to "pretend" to empower teachers is worse than not to mention empowerment in the first place.

Once a district has made an honest commitment to restructuring, then the staff needs to be assisted with building group consensus. Staff development could be a college course or a workshop, but the important point to remember is that educators will need immediate assistance; they will need refresher courses or follow-up workshops once or twice a year for the entire faculty.

Most of all, individuals who agree to participate in restructuring need to be prepared to work hard. Working to achieve schoolwide goals should include the entire school faculty, with help from county administrators and university faculty. Much of the work to be done will be in addition to the demanding work of teaching. The work does not need to be burdensome if everyone contributes, but it can be very difficult if only a small percentage of the faculty is involved.

Conclusion

The idea that teachers act as the fulcrum of substantive change in education is not just a theory in the professional development schools involved in the Benedum Collaborative. There's congruency between what experts have determined to be the role of teachers in restructuring our schools and what's happening in some rural schools in West Virginia that have committed themselves to improving the education of their students. If we revisit what SERC listed as new roles for teachers involved in school reform: "more involvement in the decision-making process, more collaborative working relationship with school principal, team teaching using an interdisciplinary approach, more opportunities for professional and personal development, become a facilitator of learning" (Feduk 1993), we can see how far Rhonda, Diana, and many other teachers in the Benedum Collaborative have come in trying to move their schools toward a more effective way of educating their students.

What has been the most exciting thing about being involved with professional development schools?

Rhonda: If I have to choose one thing that has excited me about this exper- ience, I guess it's been the wonderful opportunities to grow. Once we became aware of the opportunities out there, started to take advantage of them and understand what restructuring schools was all about, the possibilities have been endless and very, very exciting. The fact that these innovative things are happening in regular school settings may make our work more challenging, but in the end working with different kinds of people and students to accomplish real goals is important and very exciting.

Diana: There are so many exciting things, it's hard to choose. One of the most exciting things about the whole project, as far as I'm concerned, is the development of mutual respect between some of my faculty and West Virginia University. I feel like I've learned so much from them, but also that my voice was heard and my practical experience was of value to them.

           I know it's been a learning experience. It's more than years of experience plus being willing to do the work. It's caring about what happens in your school. I know to some people it is just a job. It is just where they make money and when they walk out the door, that's it for them. They don't think any more about it. But for me it is another family. I care what happens here. I care about the people I work with and my students. And if I can do something to help make it better, then I will.

Journal Entries

As part of reflecting on our work in PDSs, Rhonda and Diana kept a daily journal. The following entries offer a glimpse into their busy, complex professional lives. The journals illustrate some of the hallmarks of school reform: collaboration, professional development, changes in leadership, and changes in teaching and learning. Perhaps better than anything else, these entries give a concrete picture of how teachers actively involved in school restructuring may spend their days. Besides teaching, these teachers spend a great deal of time outside the classroom meeting and collaborating with colleagues, grant writing, documenting and disseminating information to their faculty, the community, the local Board of Education, and their funding agency, as well as offering and pursuing professional development activities. As these kinds of activities go well beyond what is generally considered the "regular" duties of teachers, they illustrate the extraordinary commitment made by these two teachers in the Benedum Collaborative.

Rhonda: *Monday*: I have done my lesson plans and prepared materials for classes like all other teachers. During my planning time today, I need to assist two other teachers with their proposal to the Benedum Collaborative for funds to develop their hands-on units. We need to go over the proposal so that corrections can be made right away. Copies need to be distributed to the School Steering Committee before Thursday's meeting.

I read over my notes from last week's Cross-Site Steering Committee. I need to organize these notes so that I can get them typed and distributed to faculty members. I spent about fifteen minutes getting the notes ready to type.

Tuesday: Before school this morning, I began interviewing students about advantages that they have gained from our PDS activities. This information will be available in presentations to community groups and to the local Board of Education. The students are enthusiastic contributors. The interviews will take longer than I had thought. Without exception, the students feel more confident of their own abilities than they did before we became a PDS. Their oral communication skills have obviously improved. They seem to be enjoying school more. They are actually staying after school for academic activities, and not just for extracurricular activities.

In the afternoon I began collecting data from the faculty about the PDS activities in which they have been involved during the last month. This information will go into the monthly report that must be submitted to the Benedum Collaborative Staff. Although these reports tend to be cumbersome at times, they help to give a clear picture of what the school is really accomplishing.

Wednesday: I completed the interviews with students this morning.

Today the school principal, Dr. Mike Teets, and I met with the county Superintendent of Schools, Mr. Elmer Pritt, about Strategic Planning. Mr. Pritt offered his support in requesting a work day for the staff without students so that we could develop a school Vision and Themes. He enthusiastically agreed to add his recommendation to our request. We immediately began to make plans for convincing the Board of Education to agree to our plans. We will work on this individually and meet on Friday to compile our report.

After collecting the remainder of the data from the faculty concerning their PDS activities for the past month, I resumed working on the monthly report. I could not finish it at school, so I took it home to finish it.

At 7:00 P.M., I attended a meeting of the Masontown Home-maker's Club. They had asked a member of the faculty to explain what a Professional Development School is. They were interested in how our methods have changed. They wanted to know how our PDS activities were affecting students. They were very interested in knowing what kinds of support we are getting from WVU and from the Benedum Foundation. After their questions were answered, the group seemed very supportive. Some expressed interest in visiting and/or assisting with classroom activities. It was a very productive meeting.

Thursday: In the morning I finished typing a summary of last week's Cross-Site Steering Committee meeting. I made copies to dis-tribute to the School Steering Committee at today's meeting. I also made copies for the rest of the faculty.

I made copies of the monthly report for the principal's approval/input, for the school PDS file, and for the School Steering Committee. After Dr. Teets approved the report, I sent it to the Collaborative Staff.

I made copies of the proposals that are to be considered at today's meeting, and I distributed them to the committee members who are at the school.

After school we had a School Steering Committee meeting. We reviewed the proposals that had been submitted. Some changes needed to be made before the proposals were sent on to the Proposal Review Team. We decided to go ahead and approve the proposals, with the stipulation that the changes we recommended need to be addressed before they go on.

One of our major concerns at this meeting was to try to establish some time in our schedule for interdisciplinary planning. We discussed the matter for quite a while, and then we decided to use time after school. It did not seem possible to insert interdisciplinary planning time after the regular school day. Scheduling seems to be one of our toughest problems.

Members of the Steering Committee raised some questions today that I need to carry to the Cross-Site Steering Committee. They want to know whether our strategic plans are to be approved by anyone other than our own school community. They want to know how specific our plans need to be. We adjourned after two hours with more questions raised than we answered. This is not unusual.

I spent part of my evening preparing for a substitute for Friday, because I requested released time to work on a proposal.

Friday: First thing this morning I met with Mike Teets to coordinate our presentation to our local Board of Education. We are on the agenda for this Monday evening. It is important that we anticipate the kinds of questions that they will ask us. We will only get one chance to convince them that Strategic Planning is important enough to warrant a day without students. The Board will need to agree with us that the long-term benefits outweigh the short-term instructional time lost.

My main purpose in having a substitute today is to put together a proposal for the faculty to have our summer work funded. We will need the time to complete our Action Plans. Hopefully, we will also have time to do some interdisciplinary planning. It is important to meet the deadline for submitting this proposal, because all requests for funds for summer work must be submitted soon.

All members of the faculty know that I am in the computer room working on this proposal today, so during their planning time several of them will stop by to ask questions about proposals, committee meetings, or other matters related to the Benedum Collaborative. Sometimes this personal contact is important, even critical, to the success of our goals as a PDS; so I don't mind too much if I must complete the proposal after school or at home.

Almost every day I have something to do for The Benedum Collaborative. The paperwork is very time-consuming. There is always some communication from the funding agency or from WVU that must be shared with the school faculty. The work is demanding. But the rewards are great. When I see how excited students are about their schoolwork, then I know that it is worth the effort. When I see faculty members energized because of a new approach or a new technique that helps to make teaching fun for them again, then I know that I will continue to serve as their representative for as long as they want to be a PDS.

Diana: *Monday*: Today I'm not teaching at all. While a substitute covers my classes, paid for with Benedum funds, I'm in the computer lab (also paid for by a Benedum grant) writing a grant proposal for money to send teachers to ASCD conferences this summer. I am talking to travel agents about plane fare, preparing a budget, and writing a narrative which explains why we want to go to these particular conferences. By the end of the day the proposal will be ready to present to our site steering committee for approval before we send it on to the Proposal Review Team.

Tuesday: At the end of the school day, we have the site steering committee meeting where I present the proposal for discussion and approval. Greg, the principal, suggests that, although I have budgeted for four people to attend each of three conferences, I should tell the Proposal Review Team that we would like to have some flexibility— perhaps we will send three people to one conference and five to another. The proposal is approved and six copies are signed by the principal as our steering committee chair. He keeps the copies and sends them to the Benedum Collaborative office the next day.

Wednesdasy: No meetings today! I'm actually in the classroom all day. My Freshmen are learning about the writing process, thanks to Benedum support which allowed me to participate in the WVU Writing Project in the summer of 1990. Today we are clustering, a pre-writing technique that utilizes the right side of the brain. All of this new information about the brain is fascinating, and I have learned more about it and different learning styles through Benedum-sponsored classes and an ASCD conference. I tell my students a little bit about the different areas controlled by the left and right sides of the brain, and how you can tell which side is your dominant side. They are quite intrigued by the discussion, since they can apply it to themselves.

Thursday: Today began very early. We had an At-risk committee meeting this morning at 7:30 (classes start at 8:05). We have submitted a JTPA grant proposal for money to hire a much-needed counselor to work with our at-risk kids, but so far we have heard no response. Sam, our chairman, reports that our "Buddy System" students, who have been "adopted" by faculty members, have shown a marked improvement in their grades for first semester compared to last year. My two adopted students are doing better this year than they have since elementary school. It just shows how much difference a little kindness and interest can make in their lives. We just make it a point to talk to our kids on a friendly basis for at least a few minutes each day. If they are having a problem, we try to help with it or act as an advocate, so they feel that someone cares about them. I suspect more than a few kids will finish school due to this program.

We are also told that crisis team training is coming up in April. We will get six hours of training in how to help deal with kids who are in crisis because of family problems, death of a friend/family member, depression, etc. Last year we had a crisis when one of our students died as a result of a motorcycle accident. Some of his friends found out about his death when they came to school on Monday morning, and we were unprepared for the large numbers of grief-stricken students. That experience led to a proposal for training teachers to help deal with kids and their feelings in the event of another such crisis.

Later today my collaborative teacher, Janie, tells me we have an invitation to speak to people in a neighboring county about our collaborative consultation program. They were referred to us by Dr. Luise Savage, who is in charge of the collaborative consultation program at WVU. They want to know how our program is set up, what we do, and how well it works. I'm so glad we have kept data on our classes over the last three years. They have offered to pay us, so we have begun to see ourselves in a new role—the consultant!

Friday: This afternoon I go to the Proposal Review Team meeting at WVU. I'm on the committee because I am the PDS co-chair of the Cross-Site Steering Committee. Today we look at several proposals from the PDS schools. Most are for conference attendance or summer planning for new programs for the 1993-94 school year. Since I am the only proposal author present, I get asked enough questions about our proposal to make any murder suspect sweat! The proposal is finally approved with some excellent suggestions for modifications.

This evening I get a call from my principal, who is on his way home from a night class (he is working on his doctorate at WVU). He is calling on his car phone to see what happened with our proposal. I'm impressed; I've never been called on a car phone before. I tell him we are approved, and I tell him about the suggested modifications. He agrees that the modifications are sensible. He's happy. I'm happy. And soooo tired! It's been a long week.

Next week there are more meetings. On Thursday I will help chair the Cross-Site Steering Committee. On Monday I need to check with Van, my WVU co-chair, about the agenda. Normally I would have talked to him after the proposal review meeting, but he had to go teach a class. Besides the usual information items, subcommittee reports, and site reports, there may be some other interesting items to consider.

Also, next week our GHS steering committee will meet to hear about our grant proposal and the modifications. Then we can discuss further details about the conferences. We will also consider proposals from faculty members for Professional Development funds.

But that is *next* week. Meanwhile, it's the weekend, and I'm going to relax!

References

Barth, R. S. (1988). School: A community of leaders. In A. Lieberman, ed., *Building a professional culture in schools*. New York: Teachers College Press.

Barth, R. S. (1990). *Improving schools from within*. San Francisco: Jossey-Bass Publishers.

Cuban, L. (1988). *The managerial imperative and the practice of leadership in schools*. Albany: SUNY Press.

Feduk, M. (Producer) and Vance, G. (Director) (1993). *Effective school restructuring: Putting the pieces together: A national forum*. [Videotape]. Columbia, SC: The Satellite Educational Resources Consortium, Inc.

Harvey, G. and Crandall, D. P. (1988). *A beginning look at the what and how of restructuring*. The Regional Laboratory for Educational Improvement of the Northeast and the Islands for the Maine Dept. of Educational and Cultural Services' Restructuring Schools Project, Andover, Mass.

The Holmes Group (1986). *Tomorrow's teachers*. East Lansing, Mich.: Author.

Lichtenstein, G., McLaughlin, M. W., and Knudsen, J. (1992). Teacher empowerment and professional knowledge. In A. Lieberman, ed., *The changing contexts of teaching: Ninety-first yearbook of the national society for the study of education*, pp. 37–58. Chicago: The University of Chicago Press.

Lieberman, A., Ed. (1992). *The changing contexts of teaching: Ninety-first yearbook of the national society for the study of education*. Chicago: The University of Chicago Press.

Little, J. W. (1982, Fall). Norms of collegiality and experimentation: Workplace conditions of school success. *American Educational Research Journal* 19(3): 325–340.

McCarthey, S. J. and Peterson, P. L. (1989, March). *Teacher roles: Weaving new patterns in classroom practice and school organization*. Paper presented at the annual meeting of the American Educational Research Association, San Francisco.

Moses, M. C. and Withaker, K. S. (1990, Sept.). Ten components for restructuring schools. *The School Administrator*.

Murphy, J. (1990, Sept./Oct.). Helping teachers prepare to work in restructured schools. *Journal of Teacher Education* 41(4): 50–56.

Phillips, P. D. and Wolfe, J. M. (1993). *Collaborative school restructuring: The role of time*. Paper presented at the annual meeting of the American Educational Research Association, Atlanta.

Rallis, S. (1988, May). Room at the top: Conditions for effective school leadership. *Phi Delta Kappan* 69(9): 643–647.

Rosenholtz, S. J. (1989). *Teachers' workplace*, New York: Longman.

Rutherford, W. L. and Murphy, S. C. (1985). *Change in high schools: Roles and reactions of teachers*. Paper presented at the annual meeting of the American Educational Research Association, Chicago.

Scott, J. J. and Smith, S. C. (1987). *From isolation to collaboration: Improving the work environment of teaching*. (Synthesis Paper). Eugene, Ore.: ERIC Clearinghouse on Educational Management.

Smylie, M. A. and Denny, J. W. (1989, March). *Teacher leadership: Tensions and ambiguities in organizational perspective*. Paper presented at the annual meeting of the American Educational Research Association, San Francisco.

Smylie, M. A. and Denny, J. W. (1990, August). Teacher leadership: Tensions and ambiguities in organizational perspective. *Educational Administration Quarterly* 26(3): 235–259.

5

THE STORY OF A CHANGING ROLE: TEACHER RESEARCH IN ACTION

W. MICHAEL REED , DAVID J. AYERSMAN, AND NANCY E. HOFFMAN

Introduction

Although the notion of teacher-as-researcher, also known as action research, has been suggested as a professional development strategy for teachers since the 1940s (Myers 1985), there has been little evidence of significant implementation of the strategy until the 1980s. During the last ten years, the movement toward professionalizing teaching has heightened the need for action research as a strategy for teacher development (Myers). It has, likewise, addressed the ongoing failure to translate research findings into classroom practice (Cochran-Smith and Lytle 1990; Griffin 1983; Nixon 1987; Strickland 1988). In addition to professionalizing teaching and facilitating the process of informing teaching through research is the teachers' need to "reclaim" their classrooms via generating their own data and making instructional decisions based on their students' performance.

Teachers from various professional development schools collaborated with Human Resources and Education faculty at West Virginia University to conduct action research. This chapter shares that collaborative endeavor. Two of the PDS Belief Statements on which our work has been predicated specifically allude to conducting classroom-based research: "Teachers and administrators will share ideas and opportunities for professional development, including using and *contributing to* current research," and, "In a professional development school, the best of practice and the best of research [will] guide review and revision of curriculum and instruction."

It is one thing to state that teachers are to engage in research and allow research to guide their teaching and revision of teaching; it is another thing to do it. Historically, most research partnerships between practicing teachers and higher education faculty have focused on the higher education faculty's providing research assistance: setting up designs and analyzing and interpreting data (Feldman 1992). One reason has been that few teachers have had much, if any, training in conducting research.

To address the more difficult statement—that practicing teachers conduct research—a course was developed, tailored to address their needs so that they could conduct research in their own classrooms. We realize that the course—and what we are about to present in this chapter—does not reflect true collaboration between practicing teachers and higher education faculty standing side-by-side conducting research. We do believe that it begins to narrow the gap between the two groups, however. By our giving the teachers the tools to conduct research, they, when collaborating with higher education faculty, will be playing on "an even research field"; that is, there should be an equalization of roles (Carter and Doyle 1995). There will be less likelihood of delegating distinctively different roles to members of both groups, with higher education faculty less likely to always be the "research design," the "data analysis," and/or the "data inter-pretation" person.

Teacher-Researcher as a Means for Promoting Reform

Many researchers have recently suggested that one way to promote reform in our schools is to involve teachers in conducting research within their own classrooms (Casanova 1989; McCutcheon 1987; Sardo-Brown 1990). It has been found that teachers often improve their instruction (Johnson 1993; Kutz 1992), they become more reflective learners (Johnson), and they engage in professional growth (Johnson). In essence, teachers' practice often changes because of the action research they conduct (Fleischer 1994; Lehman 1991).

The implementation, however, has often proven to be problematic. Criticism of the quality of teacher research has led to desperate attempts to release teachers from the *burden* of research, rather than to develop teachers' ability to conduct research. The quality of the research by teachers has frequently been criticized. In an effort to reduce this criticism, there have been suggestions that the definition of teacher research be narrowed to naturalistic inquiry procedures in order to alleviate the necessity of establishing proficiency in statistical procedures (Goswami 1984). This, however, is not a viable solution. A broader definition of teacher research directly opposed to this suggestion is "any study conducted by teachers of their school system, school, class, groups of students, or one student, either collaboratively or individually" (Myers 1985, 5). To encompass more, rather than less, of the potential research designs and procedures available to teacher-researchers appears to be a more productive decision. Other critics of teacher research have suggested that the teacher be relegated to the position of assistant-researcher or teacher-partner (Graves 1981), which would lessen the research expertise required of the teacher. Although these suggestions may provide solutions to problems of quality in teacher research, they are not the most judicious.

Research conducted by practitioners allows teachers to investigate issues of immediate concern within their own classrooms and to incorporate the results into future teaching (Sardo-Brown 1992). "Developing a research tradition among classroom teachers is a way of changing institutional roles and shifting more of the responsibility for teaching expertise to teachers themselves" (Myers 1985, 2). Teachers are no longer sitting still while "experts" provide them advice and direction. Instead, by conducting research on why some lessons work and others do not, they are defining themselves as key members in the development of theory (Myers).

By conducting research, teachers contribute to the professionalization of teaching in general. "The teacher-researcher movement now underway among K–12 teachers is an important part of a professionalization project in which classroom teachers are establishing their special expertise in teaching and curriculum development" (Myers 1985, 1). Rather than allowing texts or administrators to direct the nature of their teaching, teacher-researchers are equipped to effectively reclaim their classrooms by presenting empirically supported arguments for their classroom decisions. If teachers are to create classroom communities in which students learn through active, collaborative inquiry, they themselves must have similar learning opportunities (Wells 1989).

One problem with encouraging teachers to conduct research is the absence of incentives provided by their institutions. While collegiate teachers receive promotions, commendations, awards, and tenure based on the research they conduct, teachers do not receive such extrinsic rewards for conducting research (Myers 1985). Perhaps the simplest solution to this dilemma is to focus on improving *intrinsic* rewards for teacher-researchers. One method of doing this is to develop public school/university collaborations that result in both the reward of collegiality and the reward of systematically analyzing one's teaching (Brookhart and Loadman 1992). To improve the quality of teacher research and encourage teachers to conduct research, collaboration should occur between universities and public schools so that teachers can learn research methods and designs.

Enhancing Higher Education-Public School "Partnerships" Via Action Research

Despite the fact that colleges of education have much in common with public schools, collaboration between the two groups has been quite rare. Action research has been a relatively frequent example of this limited collaboration.

One of the major benefits of this type of collaboration has been the reduction in lag time between research-knowledge generation and research-knowledge utilization (Cochran-Smith and Lytle 1990; Griffin 1983; Nixon 1987; Strickland 1988). Often, university-generated research findings are not disseminated to practicing teachers, and the implementation of what researchers have learned from their research seldom occurs. Likewise, university researchers often ignore the authenticity of classrooms in their more highly controlled treatments and, thus, may produce results that are not totally generalizable to specific contexts. Collaborative efforts by university and public school faculty may accelerate not only the process of research informing practice but also the process of practice informing research.

Although the volume of teacher-researcher studies is increasing, only a few of them, by comparison, feature higher education and public school faculty. For example, Oja (1984) explained a project in New Hampshire in which teams of university and middle school faculty investigated the relationship among teachers' developmental stages, the process of collaborative research, and individual teachers' change. In another study (Lind 1984), higher education participation in action research involved student teachers who had been trained to conduct action research as part of their preservice training and, while student teaching, investigated topics. As they conducted their studies, they relied on practicing teachers as knowledge-experts and assisted their fellow student teachers in working through problems. Huling's (1982) study focused on the efforts of six research teams comprised of university researchers, public school teachers, and staff developers. Membership on a team was determined by the nature of the research topic. Huling found that by conducting research the teachers' attitudes toward research improved dramatically.

In their book, Bissex and Bullock (1987) present numerous studies conducted by public school teachers and graduate students. Collectively, the studies support the notion that the sense of professionalism of both groups of educators increased as a result of working together. Through collaborative efforts they acquired a better understanding of research, how it might be used to inform practice, how it could allow them to regain control over what occurred in their classrooms, and how it affected them as learners. Many of their findings reflect those in the collections of teacher-researcher studies presented by Goswami and Stillman (1987), by Shanahan (1994), and by Eisenhart and Borko (1993). Often the benefits teachers receive from engaging in such efforts parallel those that university faculty typically experience: the teacher (a) becomes more knowledgeable about the instructional situation, (b) can better defend his or her approach to teaching, and (c) can better influence higher-level decision making (Kennedy 1985).

Smulyan (1983), Stansell and Patterson (1987), Lytle and Cochran-Smith (1990), Carter and Doyle (1995), and Elliot (1983) have stated that a precaution that should be heeded in collaborative efforts is that such efforts need to "equalize" roles. Given the different research backgrounds of higher education and public school faculty—that is, university professors are likely to have more extensive research skills—it is easy for university-based collaborators to be given research design responsibilities and for public school teachers to administer the treatment. Ideally, such responsibilities should overlap so that the research is successful and both collaborative partners learn from one another.

Summary

We have limited our review of related research to teacher research that views action research as a means of reforming teacher education and a vehicle for enhancing the collaborative efforts between public school and university faculty. Although teacher research comes in various forms, has implications for a wide range of teaching and learning arenas, and has the potential for forcing us to rethink what and how we teach, we focused on the notions of reform and collaboration because of the purpose of the teacher-as-researcher course. The year-long course provided the teachers with instruction on the skills they needed in order to conduct their research, established a network of fellow teacher-researchers, helped them approach the implementation of their research in a systematic fashion, and showcased their efforts for other teacher-researchers.

The Teacher-Researcher Course

The ten teachers who enrolled in the *Teacher as Researcher* course represented four of the six original professional development schools (PDSs) participating in the West Virginia University Benedum-sponsored educational reform effort. One of the reasons the schools were chosen to be PDS sites was the teachers' willingness to engage in a variety of risk-taking activities, one of which was to conduct classroom-based research. The course was designed to prepare them to conduct such research.

Central to the course's intent was establishing a research mindset, at times conceptually destroying the teachers' previous attitudes toward research. In fact, a considerable amount of time was spent directly and indirectly challenging their prior beliefs about research. Even though they were not opposed to research—their taking the course attested to that—they did not feel unconditionally positive about research or were not completely confident they would succeed at it. An early exercise they engaged in was taking a few moments to write down the process or the steps they typically employed when planning and teaching units. Consistently, their responses reflected the following steps: (a) they obtained a sense of where their students were in relation to the content—usually through pretesting or knowing what the previous year's curriculum was; (b) they developed the curriculum based on ability—that is, that they knew low-ability students were often taught the same content but were taught differently than high-ability students; (c) they recalled what had worked with previous and similar students; (d) they taught the unit; (e) they determined how well their students had learned the content; and (f) they modified the unit for the next group of students who would receive the instruction.

Once these steps were formulated, we then attached research terms to them. Finding out where their students were in relation to the content was labeled *Pretest. Ability Level* was labeled *Blocking Variable* with the understanding that even if students of varying abilities received the same instruction they would be expected to perform differently. More important was the awareness that the teachers preferred to develop different curricula for the varying abilities. This awareness then allowed us to label students as *Sample* and to decide that ability level would be a characteristic of the sample. We then pointed out that a fairly automatic blocking variable was gender. Performance by boys might differ from performance by girls. Their instruction was then labeled *Treatment.* A few teachers stated that they often made decisions as they taught and wondered if that violated the term, treatment. Our position was that any change was acceptable as long as they had a sound reason for it. By including the change in their final report, their results would be considered within the context of their design. Testing their students at the end of the instruction was labeled *Posttesting.* Changes they would make in the curriculum when they next taught it were labeled *Future Research*—or more importantly an excellent example of *Research Informing Practice.* We offered the point that, although any well-designed and well-conducted study answers the research questions, it also poses new questions.

The purpose of the exercise was simple—we wanted to make the teachers aware that they conduct research when they make decisions about instruction and teaching, and that they simply have not viewed their teaching as research. Although they began to see research—and especially what they were doing as they taught—differently, some were still skeptical. Their concern was based on the distinction between applied and pure research. We then posed a scenario of a highly controlled, lab-situated study and asked them whether or not they would have any problems with applying the results to their classrooms. They began to understand that, while their research was not pure research, it perhaps had more relevance to their particular classroom context. Highly controlled studies ignored what they faced most of the time: the dynamic nature of their students, beings hardly willing to be highly controlled. We then explained that, although their research designs would be "muddy," they had a greater chance of impacting their teaching because the real-life, authentic dynamics of their classrooms had been part of the treatment.

In addition to helping the teacher-researchers see that they conducted research all of the time, it was important that we help them demythologize research by pointing out that research did not need to be difficult. We attempted to help them understand that their research questions or topics were important. Some of the teachers were university faculty spouses and believed that classroom-based topics simply were not as important as the pure research conducted by their university spouses working in laboratories.

The goals driving much of the curriculum were: (a) helping the teachers acquire the skills to conduct research; (b) facilitating topic selection; (c) locating resources; (d) making the teachers more critical consumers of existing research; and (e) assisting in the construction of a design that fit their usual teaching as well as accommodating the time-related demands of their teaching. At the end of the instruction, two concerns remained: (a) providing continuity, and (b) constructing a support network.

The *Teacher as Researcher* course extended from Fall 1991 through Fall 1992. The teachers met once a week during the months of September and October. During this period they received instruction on general research design principles and examined both qualitative and quantitative research methodologies. Two texts were used in this course to help them acquire both quantitative and qualitative research skills.

Studies representing both quantitative and qualitative methodologies were read, discussed, and, through classroom exercises, experienced. For example, they responded to Daly and Miller's (1975) Writing Apprehension Test. We then discussed how the instrument scores could be used as either an independent variable or a dependent measure. The scores could be used as an independent or blocking variable to group an existing sample into low, medium, and high apprehension groups and then determine other types of writing-related changes using other measures. For example, one approach might be to have students write essays at the beginning of a unit and then at the end and determine whether one apprehension group produced better writing than another. The Writing Apprehension Test scores could also be used as a dependent measure in a pretest/posttest design by determining whether the students' writing apprehension changed due to the treatment—or to the instruction. We added a qualitative component to the writing apprehension example by explaining how the teachers could then interview some of the low apprehension students as well as some of the medium apprehension and high apprehension students. Another qualitative analysis was to conduct a text analysis of the essays they produced. Although the teachers were informed of the combined quantitative/qualitative approach, we explained that either one by itself was certainly sufficient—that, in fact, the research questions dictated the analysis they would employ.

Guest teacher-researchers from the West Virginia University Writing Project presented their studies during this part of the course. These teacher-researchers were selected for two reasons: (a) to provide models of action research, and (b) to help demythologize research (we felt that hearing practicing teachers present their research would be more valuable to the prospective teacher-researchers than hearing higher education faculty present their research).

November was set aside for the teachers to formulate a research plan and gather the materials they would need. Although the class did not meet formally during the month, we were available for them to meet with us during the hours the class had met during the previous two months. They could also set up appointments at other times.

The class met during the first week in December so that teachers could present their research plans and explain problems they were facing, as well as react to each other's plans. Having to articulate their plans proved to be invaluable, in part because they began to solve some of their own problems. They also surprised themselves by talking like researchers. We met once again in early January to articulate their refined research plans and to assure that the teachers had all the materials they needed.

Spring semester was spent conducting studies. Monthly meetings were held to touch base, discuss problems, and collaborate in problem solving. At a late spring meeting the teacher researchers explained their preliminary findings. We also discussed formats for the final written reports, which were written during the summer. The papers were submitted in early fall for a preliminary reaction. Also, meetings were held to prepare for their teacher-researcher conference presentations. About fifty teachers attended the half-day conference in early October. The teacher-researchers then spent the next month and a half finalizing their reports so that they could be included in a book showcasing their research.

The Teachers' Research

The ten teachers designed studies on nine topics: (a) opinions about a school's program; (b) learning styles of West Virginia Foxfire teachers; (c) the relationship between school policy and student attendance; (d) teachers' use of a library media center; (e) the effects of a Foxfire-based approach on CTBS scores; (f) students' and parents' attitudes toward tracking; (g) the employment patterns of high school students; (h) the effect of practical activities on students' attitudes toward physics; and (i) why certain students fail art.

Measuring Opinions about Schools: One Survey for Students, Staff, and Parents

This study by Etta Zasloff, a guidance counselor at East Dale Elementary School in Fairmont, centered on students', school staff members', and parents' attitudes toward the school's various programs and activities. Her findings were quite extensive, with the majority of the school's programs receiving grades between "good" and "excellent." She cleverly decided to look at various facets and programs of the school and the percentage of people responding "no feeling or don't know." Zasloff assumed that a person's lack of opinion or knowledge was based on that persons not being apprised of the program and that a logical next step for the school would be to better inform people of the programs. The programs that were most familiar were the media-library program, the music program, and the computer and technology program. The following areas were the best known to the respondents: teachers and methods used when teaching, grading and report cards, a safe and welcome feeling at the school, and the cleanliness and attractiveness of the school.

An Examination of Learning Styles among West Virginia Foxfire Teachers

This study by Joyce Lang and Clorinda Ammons, teachers at Suncrest Primary School in Morgantown, focused on the learning styles, as measured by the Kolb Learning Style Inventory, of teachers participating in the MountainFire project, a statewide affiliate of Foxfire. The findings on eighty-three of the 114 MountainFire teachers were, likewise, quite extensive. One set of results showed that the teachers who shared the characteristics of perceiving with feelings and intuitions far outnumbered those who preferred to use their intellects when meeting new situations. Lang and Ammons explained that this learning style fits well with the experiential, hands-on learning that the Foxfire approach emphasizes. They complemented their Kolb-related findings with McCarthy's Hemispheric Mode Indicator.

The Relationship Between School Policy and Student Attendance

This study by Fern Thorn, an English teacher at Grafton High School, was based on three data sources: (a) faculty and student input on the attendance policy; (b) policies from area schools; and (c) information provided by the attendance officer. Of the 647 students responding, sixty-one said that they attended school because it was the law; twenty-three said they attended because their parents made them; 156 said they attended because they wanted to learn; ninety-nine said they attended because they wanted to be with their friends; and 308 said they attended for all of the reasons previously stated. Thorn's study also presented a set of proposals for the school's attendance policy based on both student and teacher input.

The Effect of Practical Application Activities on the Attitude of High School Physics Students

Keith Ross, a physics teacher at Grafton High School, wanted to find out whether practical physics activities would influence his students' attitude toward physics. The activities were integral to the instruction across forty sessions. Ross set up a pre-instruction/post-instruction design and compared their early attitudes with their later attitudes. Some of his findings included (a) a seventeen percent increase in students' seeing a connection between what they studied in physics and their everyday life; (b) a twenty-five percent increase in their seeing a connection between what they studied in physics and their intended career choice; and (c) a thirty-four percent increase in their opinion that physics was useful for their life.

The Employment Patterns of Students at Morgantown High School

This study by Edie Jett, a marketing teacher at Morgantown High School, involved 1,053 students. Jett found that 74 percent of the student-respondents lived in a two-parent household and 59 percent were from households earning $30,000 or more per year. A little more than 33 percent of the respondents were employed. About 32 percent of the employed students worked in fast-food restaurants, and 23 percent worked in retail/wholesale sales. Sophomores worked fewer hours than juniors, who worked fewer hours than seniors. Jett also included gender comparisons in regard to pay. Interesting—and alarming—is that 21 percent of the females reported earning less than minimum wage, although only 7.3 percent of the males did. Almost 30 percent of the males earned more than minimum wage, whereas only 12.1 percent of the females did.

Failing in Art: Who Fails, Why Do They Fail, and How To Help Them Change

Beverly McClung, an art teacher at West Preston Junior High School in Arthurdale, focused her research on why nine boys failed art the previous year. The nine boys responded to an interest survey, the Peirs and Harris self-esteem test, and an attitude survey. They were also interviewed. Most of the boys did not feel good about school although they felt school was important. Even though the majority of them stated that their families supported them in school, only half of them received help on homework at home and only one had his homework checked at home. Fewer than half of the students stated that they were sometimes talked to by teachers while the remainder stated that they were never talked to. McClung felt that a lack of attention was the major reason these nine students were not doing well. In fact, she suggested that receiving attention via being interviewed may have been the reason several of the boys began doing better in the art class they were repeating.

Impacting Students' Education Through Teachers' Use of the Library Media Center

This study by Judy Kelly, the director of the library media center at East Dale Elementary School in Fairmont, addressed the following issues: (a) by circumventing any logistical problems teachers had in accessing media materials, they would then be more likely to use the media center; and (b) through seeing their teachers use library materials, students would more likely use the materials. Kelly first kept track of teachers' use of the media center and found a variety of patterns, which included (a) that teachers who taught more than one class used the library more than those who taught only one class, and

(b) that those who had a planned, written curriculum tended to use the library more than those who did not. Kelly then interviewed ten teachers on how she might help them integrate media-center-related use in their curricula.

A Study of Preston County, Valley District's Attitude Toward Tracking

This study by Rhonda Jennings, a mathematics and social studies teacher at West Preston Junior High School in Arthurdale, was based on the question, What is the County's attitude toward tracking? All eighth graders and parents of the eighth graders enrolled in Jennings's classes responded to a survey on these attitudes. Tracking was based on band membership—that is, if a student was enrolled in band, he or she essentially went through an instructional day with other band students. Both students and parents were relatively comfortable with the band-based tracking system, even those who were in groups often labeled less intelligent. Jennings's conclusion, in part, was that the system was perceived to cause few problems and, therefore, did not merit changing.

An Evaluation of an Innovative Teaching Method: The Effects of the Foxfire Teaching Approach on the Comprehensive Test of Basic Skills (CBTS) Scores

Linda Campbell, a teacher at Wiles Hill School in Morgantown, was interested in determining whether a sharp rise in a certain group of students' CTBS scores was due to their having been exposed to a Foxfire-based curriculum. Campbell's curiosity was tapped when the CTBS scores for the 1990–1991 third grade class rose more sharply than the scores of the third grade classes she had taught in 1988–1989 and 1989–1990. The 1990–1991 class was the first to receive a Foxfire-based curriculum. Further evidence came in the form of particularly impressive improvement in the sections of the CTBS that paralleled the Foxfire curriculum in her classrooms: (a) language mechanics, (b) social studies, (c) reading comprehension, (d) language expression, and (e) reading vocabulary. Pupils' knowledge in areas related to subject matter not taught with a Foxfire approach—math, science, and reference skills—had very little growth.

Summary

The ten teachers designed research plans that helped them better understand and/or make decisions about their teaching (Ross, Campbell, Jett, and McClung); about their non-teaching roles (Zasloff and Kelly); about school-related issues (Jennings and Thorn); and about teacher characteristics (Lang and Ammons). Collectively, they employed both quantitative and qualitative methodologies; they administered widely used as well as self-made instruments. Most valuable perhaps was that each study addressed a topic the teacher-researcher was interested in pursuing.

Teachers' Attitudes Toward Action Research

We also collected data on the ten teachers and explained our findings to them. We felt that employing them as research participants would capture the spirit of the course: systematically analyzing our own teaching—as they were with their teaching. We also felt that this might make research more meaningful to them; they could understand the results of our study within the framework of what they were doing and had learned. We used three sources of data: (a) the Stages of Concern instrument (Hall, Rutherford, and George 1977); (b) field notes, response logs, and taped discussions during the class meetings (September through January); and (c) structured interviews of four of the ten teachers (after conducting the research).

Stages of Concern

Background. The Stages of Concern data deal with the changes in the ten teachers' attitudes toward teacher-as-researcher as a result of taking the course and conducting their studies; that is, we collected data at the beginning of the course (September), the end of the course (January), and after they had completed the studies and had written the research reports (August).

The 35-item, Likert (0 to 7) Stages of Concern instrument (Hall, George, and Rutherford 1977) measures different types of concerns toward an innovation—in the case of this study, teacher as researcher. The seven types of concerns are Awareness, Information, Personal, Management, Consequence, Collaboration, and Refocusing. The first four concerns are self-oriented, whereas the final three deal with external matters. The instrument has been proved to be valid and reliable.

The first stage of concern is Awareness; a sample statement is *I am not concerned about teacher-research.* The second is Informational; a sample statement is *I would like to know more about action research.* The third is Personal; a sample statement is *I am concerned about how becoming a teacher-researcher will affect me.* The fourth is Management; a sample statement is *I seem to be spending all of my time getting materials ready as a teacher-researcher.* The fifth is Consequence; a sample statement is *I am concerned about how action research will affect my students.* The sixth is Collaboration; a sample statement is *I am concerned about relating what I am doing as a teacher-researcher to what other instructors are doing.* The final stage of concern is Refocusing; a sample statement is *I know now of several approaches for conducting action research.*

Findings. The teachers' Awareness concerns did not significantly change as a result of the ten-week course; however, they decreased significantly from the period between the end of the course and the end of the action research:

$F(2,18) = 10.99$, p = .0008. The Scheffe F-ratios were (a) from Pre-Treatment to Post-Treatment (.89); (b) from Pre-Treatment to Post-Action Research (10.5); and (c) from Post-Treatment to Post-Action Research (4.98). See Table 5.1.

TABLE 5.1

Means and Standard Deviations (in parentheses) for the Seven Stages of Concern at the Pre-Treatment, Post-Treatment, and Post-Action Research Points

	Pre-Treatment	Post-Treatment	Post-Action-Research	F	p
Awareness	69.3 (32.43)	59.4 (29.97)	37.5^1 (23.28)	10.99	.0008
Information	92.0^2 (10.92)	56.9^2 (15.04)	41.5^2 (15.64)	48.58	.0001
Personal	87.3^2 (7.97)	52.5^2 (14.34)	40.8^2 (14.31)	60.338	.0001
Management	84.0 (19.01)	67.0 (12.78)	42.2^1 (18.08)	11.31	.0007
Consequence	42.0 (22.23)	48.8 (30.79)	76.6^3 (17.47)	20.97	.0001
Collaborative	62.0 (22.16)	58.8 (26.02)	91.2^3 (5.57)	18.1	.0001
Refocusing	83.8 (8.79)	78.0 (14.63)	93.9^3 (4.04)	9.07	.002

1 = significant decrease at the Post-Action-Research Point
2 = significant decrease from Pre-Treatment to Post-Treatment to Post-Action-Research Points
3 = significant increase at the Post-Action-Research Point

The teachers' Informational concerns decreased significantly between the pre-treatment and the end of the course and further decreased due to conducting the action research: $F(2,18) = 48.58$, $p = .0001$. The Scheffe F-ratios were (a) from Pre-Treatment to Post-Treatment (22.34); (b) from Pre-Treatment to Post-Action Research (46.24); and (c) from Post-Treatment to Post-Action Research (4.3). See Table 5.1.

The teachers' Personal concerns decreased significantly between the pre-treatment and the end of the course and further decreased due to conducting the action research: $F(2,18) = 60.338$, $p = .0001$. The Scheffe F-ratios were (a) from

Pre-Treatment to Post-Treatment (31.25); (b) from Pre-Treatment to Post-Action Research (55.8); and (c) from Post-Treatment to Post-Action Research (3.53). See Table 5.1.

The teachers' Management concerns did not significantly change as a result of the ten-week course; however, they decreased significantly from the period between the end of the course and the end of the action research: $F(2,18)$ = 11.31, p = .0007. The Scheffe F-ratios were (a) from Pre-Treatment to Post-Treatment (1.85); (b) from Pre-Treatment to Post-Action Research (11.81); and (c) from Post-Treatment to Post-Action Research (3.94). See Table 5.1.

The teachers' Consequence concerns did not significantly change as a result of the ten-week course; however, they increased significantly from the period between the end of the course and the end of the action research: $F(2,18)$ = 20.97, p = .0001. The Scheffe F-ratios were (a) from Pre-Treatment to Post-Treatment (.72); (b) from Pre-Treatment to Post-Action Research (18.68); and (c) from Post-Treatment to Post-Action Research (12.06). See Table 5.1.

The teachers' Collaborative concerns did not significantly change as a result of the ten-week course; however, they increased significantly from the period between the end of the course and the end of the action research: $F(2,18)$ = 18.1, p = .0001. The Scheffe F-ratios were (a) from Pre-Treatment to Post-Treatment (.15); (b) from Pre-Treatment to Post-Action Research (12.1); and (c) from Post-Treatment to Post-Action Research (14.9). See Table 5.1.

The teachers' Refocusing concerns did not significantly change as a result of the ten-week course; however, they increased significantly from the period between the end of the course and the end of the action research: $F(2,18) = 9.07$, p = .002. The Scheffe F-ratios were (a) from Pre-Treatment to Post-Treatment (1.18); (b) from Pre-Treatment to Post-Action Research (3.57); and (c) from Post-Treatment to Post-Action Research (8.86). See Table 5.1.

Discussion. Over the time the teachers participated in the course and conducted their research, significant changes occurred in each type of innovation concern. Instruction significantly affected only two concerns, significantly reducing Informational and Personal concerns. Completion of action research caused a second significant reduction in Informational and Personal concerns. Instruction neither significantly decreased Awareness or Management concerns nor significantly increased Consequence, Collaboration, or Refocusing concerns. Completion of action research did significantly affect these five concerns: Awareness, Management, Consequence, Collaboration, and Refocusing.

While these findings suggest that a course alone can accommodate Informational and Personal concerns, it is interesting to note that actually planning, conducting, and reporting action research further reduced teachers' Informational and Personal concerns. A course that gives information about conducting research and encourages teachers to personalize that information by applying it to research scenarios of interest to them was certainly a positive experience, but the opportunity to conduct action research and fully apply what they had learned seemed to make research information more real and more accessible. It also increased their personal store of information, since the completion of a specific action research project entailed gathering more information and developing more expertise on specific research techniques.

Significant changes in Awareness, Management, Consequence, Collaboration, and Refocusing concerns occurred only after teachers conducted action research. Their ongoing concerns about managing the research tasks decreased; they discovered that they could find the time to conduct and write-up their research. Their surety about the consequences of their conducting research also changed at this point. They began to see benefits for their students, themselves, and their school that they had not seen initially. Collaboration concerns also increased. They were now much more comfortable talking to other teachers about their research, they were sure that other teachers wanted to hear about their research, and they thought it was important to talk about research with their peers. They also began to refocus and see when action research was appropriate and how it could help improve teaching.

Summary. The findings indicate that the instruction on teacher as researcher, although it provided the essential foundational information for subsequent action research, fell short of the impact we had hoped. Even though the ten-week instruction decreased such self-based concerns as Information and Personal, indicating that the teacher-researchers had received not only sufficient general information on teacher-researcher but also personally specific information, the instruction did not affect their self-based Awareness and Management concerns or any of the externally based concerns—Consequence, Collaboration, and Refocusing. However, as a result of the teacher-researchers' conducting their research, not only did their self-based concerns decrease even more but also the external concerns increased. These findings indicate that, in order for the later, external concerns to be affected, teachers must conduct research. Through this experientially based action of inquiry, the teachers obtained a better sense of how to manage the acquisition of knowledge related to action research, as well as how to conduct the research. Likewise, via the research experience, they became more comfortable with the idea of collaborating with other teachers—not only in terms of being co-investigators but also in terms of serving as research resource people for their colleagues. A shift in the Refocusing concern reflected their becoming critical "consumers" and users of action research; such a shift indicates that they began to distinguish researchable ideas from unresearchable ideas, as well as usable findings from unusable findings. It is clear that to have a real impact, action research must be conducted—not just considered.

Emergent Attitudes During the Course

Journal entries, field notes, and audiotapes of the class sessions and other meetings served as the data sources. Based on a text analysis of our data, five themes emerged: time, confidence, perceptions of others, camaraderie, and professional growth.

Time. Concerns about time were a major and constant theme. Early in the experience, time concerns were related to finding time to do the course readings: "You've got to be joking. All this for next time?" As the teachers learned more about action research, the time concern shifted from time for reading class assignments to time to find and read research literature in the library. "By the time I find 'appropriate, relevant literature' to read, I'm asleep! I work all day! I need more time!!" "I want time to read all the fascinating things I see that aren't even exactly on my topic." "She suggested I also read Ladd's research. Where's the time to do that?" Then came concerns about time to design instruments and conduct and write up the study. "Feeling the pressure of time, I have spent my minimal waking hours and some sleeping moments contemplating the survey instrument." "I'm absolutely fascinated by process described. Want to do this instead of survey. How unrealistic to expect to have the time. There must be a way to record audios and transcribe them technologically." "This [writing] is so hard when you don't have time to sit down and think. This is a summer job for a teacher, not something to do during the [school] year." "I'm never going to finish this. Other teachers keep coming in to ask me how it's going and then I can't interview the kid!" "I mean, you can't do it at home every night because the dishes have to be done and the lessons planned and this isn't what I get paid to do. I want to, it's important, but I need real time, school time."

As they moved through the process, the teachers simply accepted that there would never be enough time, and doing the research became something to "fit in somewhere." They seemed to think only about finding time to do what they perceived to be the next step, rather than trying to plan time for the whole process. "If I think about all the work, I'll lose it." All of them expressed frustration over the lack of time, noting that they could not possibly do action research all the time and do "the job I get paid for."

Confidence. Teachers' confidence clearly increased as they moved through the process. One teacher expressed the evolution of confidence as well as anyone could. After the first class, she said, "This is overwhelming. How can I do this? Maybe I should drop." Three months later, she arrived at the point most of the group seemed to see as their ending stance: "It's still overwhelming, but it's manageable. Not every day but sometimes." Between these two points, however, a lot of things affected teachers' confidence in their ability to do action research. Successfully completing action research obviously built confidence, but the ups and downs the teachers experienced seemed to be strongly associated with two particular experiences.

An important factor in teacher confidence seemed to be language. The teachers spoke of a "language barrier," describing much of what was written about research as unnecessarily "jargony," "unclear," or "too complex." Their comments about the accessibility of research language began with inquiries like, "What is epistemology?" and "Why would someone use a word like phenomenology?" (In fact, nine of the ten teachers frequently had specific and negative reactions to specific terms. Phenomenology, hermeneutic, and epistemological were some of the terms most often cited as irritants.) As the teachers read more for class and began to read the literature on their topics, they made comments like these. "Is the author trying to make me feel stupid? Because he's doing it. I feel really stupid." "I wasn't validated by this reading. I was confused!" One participant became very upset about the "language" of research, saying "I about went crazy. No wonder teachers think they can't [do research] or is it we just refuse to waste our time writing paragraph after paragraph of drivel. Is redundant phrasing required?"

On the other hand, the participants were delighted with the presentations made by practicing teachers who had completed action research in the past. They found these reports to be "inspiring," "exciting," and evidence that "Teachers can ask their own questions in their own language and it's OK." No matter how much they read about teachers doing research, the chance to read research written by other teachers and talk with the teacher-researchers was very important to them. Their confidence seemed to be greatly affected by that experience, and they often referred to that experience as a confidence builder and a motivator. As one said, "She did it and that means I can do it, too."

Perceptions of others. The participants in this experience came from four schools and had a variety of interests, but they had a common concern about doing action research: How will others perceive me and my research? They were unsure how other teachers would react to them as researchers, they were unsure how their principals would react, and they were unsure about the effect on students.

Choosing the research topic brought out these concerns. No teacher lacked ideas to research, but all but one of them expressed concern about others' perceptions of their research topic. "What if I find something my principal sees as negative?" "If the data include negative things about the school or about another teacher, what do I do?" "Do teachers dare to investigate or research things they are really passionately interested in?" "A problem I see arising [is that] from an administrative point of view these efforts are going to appear mutinous. Should we not tread lightly on the first topic or two and then go in for the more controversial issues?" "If we [teachers] all do individual research, how will the education system maintain its uniformity? Do you really think politicians will let teachers do what they think is effective in their classrooms? No!" (Note the relationship between these comments and Dempsey's discussion of professionalism in Chapter 1.) These concerns were evident in class discussions, in many informal conversations, and in journals. Every participant expressed some concern with others' perceptions, and five indicated that their choice of topic was influenced by what they perceived to be "safe" in their school and acceptable to their principal.

The responses from other teachers and students were an initial concern which faded rapidly, at least partly because the participants chose topics that were "safe." The participants reported that their colleagues and their students were very supportive and very interested in their research. Most reported that students and teachers asked a lot of questions about what they were doing and were very helpful.

Camaraderie. The participants in this study were encouraged to express their feelings, raise questions, and interact freely with one another. Reports on their progress and their concerns were part of every meeting, and group problem solving was encouraged. Their progress as teacher-researchers was clearly related to these interactions. After some initial discomfort, they found class discussions about research topics and procedures to be an important part of their growth and an important support. It was common for a class discussion to include a comment like, "Oh. I'm glad you have that question, because I . . ." and for journals to mention a specific comment or question that had been helpful to them. Several participants noted the value of sharing their thoughts with other novice researchers, and the conduct of the participants made it clear that they valued each other's ideas. They rarely missed a meeting, and despite all their concerns about time, they were often early in arriving and late in leaving class. All but two of the participants had entered the class with another teacher from their school, which meant that eight of them had a natural "research buddy" at their school. As one teacher said, "I need to know I'm not suffering alone. It helps to talk with her. If she can solve her problems, so can I."

Professional knowledge. Every teacher wrote and spoke about the growth they had experienced through this process. This was first evident in the identification of possible research topics. No one lacked topics to research. As one put it, "At first I had no ideas, then I had a topic a week, then a topic a day. Now I keep a book to write all my topics in, for later." Another teacher was very excited about sharing action research with other teachers. "They don't know what they're missing. This is how you get control of your teaching. This is how you get to make decisions that are right for you and your kids. Every place is different." "This is real. Regular research is irrelevant to regular classrooms. This is a way to validate what works in my real room." "Research is learning."

"I feel excited about this. I have learned that research is not just looking up material. [It is] not dull because the researcher can choose the topics to be researched. The fact that I can apply it to my classroom means everything to me because, if I can't use it, I don't want to spend my precious time on it." "Teacher researchers have the ability to ask questions that have never been asked before. This is important stuff." "All teachers should have to know about this. Why don't we know this?" "My school is ripe for learning from teacher research. [I'm] ready to work on something substantial." When asked what they had learned, teachers spoke of research skills gained, jargon acquired, and sleep lost, but most of their comments related to personal growth in professional knowledge and confidence. "I really do research all the time when I make decisions about materials and assignments and plans. Now I know I can communicate that in a professional way and make a contribution to others. At first I was afraid if I spent twenty minutes less on grading papers, I wasn't doing my job. Now I know that the time I spend on this makes me a better teacher. I look at my teaching as problems to be solved."

Summary. The issue of time was usually expressed in the context of finding the time to acquire the skills and knowledge to design and conduct the research while also teaching. They referred to the amount of time needed to read the materials assigned to them as they prepared for each class meeting, the time needed to read the research related to their topics, and the time needed to design instruments as well as to conduct and write up the research. While they complained about not having enough time, they resigned themselves to the necessity of all the work so that they could acquire the skills and knowledge to conduct their research.

The teachers' gain in confidence can best be described in the going-from-the-unknown-to-the-known framework. Their initial lack of confidence was based on their preconceived notions of research—that research had to be mostly statistical and that it had to be immensely important to the research world at large (or was finding out why their students did not learn important to anyone other than themselves?). Until they conducted the studies, their confidence was not at its pinnacle. They did feel that two other factors helped them gain confidence: (1) overcoming the language barrier (that is, getting used to the research and theoretical terms included in both the class-assigned and topic-specific readings), and (2) having teacher-researchers present their studies during the class meetings.

Initially, they were concerned about how their fellow teachers would perceive them as they conducted research. Their concern centered mostly on the possibility of finding results that teachers and principals might not like. One way they accommodated this concern was to choose fairly safe topics when topics extended outside their own classrooms. Given the "safe" nature of the topics, they found teachers, administrators, and students to be very supportive of and interested in their research.

Given their initial lack of confidence and concerns about how fellow teachers would perceive them, the camaraderie that formed helped them work through some of their problems and concerns. Class meetings were spent, in addition to acquiring new skills and knowledge, helping them solve problems they were having or raising concerns. That they often arrived early and left late and that there were virtually no absences attest to the importance of the camaraderie.

A final theme was professional growth. The teachers began the class not being able to identify any researchable topics. That changed to having one a week and then one a day. Many ended up keeping notebooks to list all the topics they might want to research. They also began to view research as being addictive. Many of their comments centered on the notions that: (1) other teachers did not know what they were missing; (2) conducting research allowed them to gain control of their teaching; and (3) they became better at making the right decisions for themselves and their students. They also sensed a degree of autonomy and empowerment because they could choose their own topics. They felt that their research was important because they could use it to confirm their teaching or to change their teaching. The following comment best sums up their professional growth: "I really do research all the time when I make decisions about materials and assignments and plans. Now I know I can communicate that in a professional way and make a contribution to others. . . . I know that the time I spend on this makes me a better teacher. I look at my teaching as problems to be solved."

Teacher Reflections After Conducting the Action Research

Our method for collecting these data was structured interviews with four of the ten teachers enrolled in the course. The overarching question guiding the interviews was: "How have studying research methods and research design and conducting research influenced teacher perceptions of themselves and their profession?" The four teachers were selected because they represented different sub-groups: one is a high school teacher (Edie Jett), two are elementary teachers and co-investigated their topic (Clorinda Ammons and Joyce Lang), and one is a guidance counselor (Etta Zasloff). Edie Jett teaches high school marketing and has ten years of teaching experience; Etta Zasloff is an elementary guidance counselor with twenty-three years of school experience; Clorinda has taught for sixteen years at the primary level and now teaches a third grade class; and Joyce Lang has more than thirty years of teaching experience and now teaches a third grade class also.

Numerous trends emerged from the four interviews. Almost without exception, they stated the following. They wanted to take the course so that they could acquire the skills needed to conduct research. Via the course, they felt that someone at West Virginia University would be identified who could be their research contact person. Somewhat leery of research before the course, they became less intimidated by it in part because they had a network of other teachers taking the course. They also realized that research was not restricted to statistical analyses. Although they all expressed desires to conduct further research, time was a critical issue to them. The course and conducting research heightened all four teachers' sense of professionalism.

Scenario One—Edie. Edie has taught marketing at the high school level for about ten years. She has her bachelor's plus fifteen graduate credit hours although she, in fact, has sixty-seven graduate hours and is currently working on her master's in Adult Technical Education. Edie used survey data to examine the employment patterns of 1,083 students in her high school. She chose to take the *Teacher as Researcher* course so that she could use it as a vehicle for conducting research on a topic in which she was already interested. She also felt that she needed a "mentor" or someone she could go to for help in the area of research and that this course could provide that.

When asked about positive aspects of the course, Edie especially liked "the networking with people" and "seeing what everyone else was doing." She felt that "not being so alone" and "having people" were important aspects of the course. She went on to say, "I don't feel good about getting someone to help, but in that class they were right there. I was able to work with others." As a result of a grant she submitted, Edie was able to obtain computer software that has helped her to analyze the questionnaire data she gathered as part of the research requirement of the course. She feels that using this software "removes the statistical burden" of conducting research. Despite this, Edie claims to have "learned a little bit about this chi square thing" as a result of the course.

Perhaps the most important positive aspect of Edie's taking this course has been the change in her perception toward research. Prior to taking the course, her feelings centered on negative emotions and aspects of research, which she found intimidating. In describing her feelings prior to the course, Edie stated "I don't think mathematically," and that statistics are "not something that I want to do." She frankly admits that "I didn't really know what I was doing" with action research prior to the course. She felt "scared" and said she had "anxiety" about the statistical "burden" involved with research. These responses can be compared with her feelings about research after the course, which were much more positive. She readily admits that she "is excited to do it again," and that one way of describing her feelings "would be empowerment." Edie stated that "it really helps your self-esteem," research now "has real meaning," and she "is tickled to death that [she] did it." In discussing her own study, she mentions "I think the validity of my data is wonderful. I think it is really on target, and it compares to the national levels very well. It is so neat that this employer update has come out of this. We are also sending it to the Board of Education, and my students are aware of it." Another positive aspect has been the recognition Edie has received for her study. She was nominated for an award given by a regional television station for her efforts in establishing partnerships between area businesses and her students. Now that she has finished her study, she "is anxious to get it in the faculty lounge so everyone can see it."

At one point, when she was feeling overwhelmed by her study, Edie mentioned to the instructor that perhaps she had "bitten off more than she could chew." Her instructor quickly responded, "No, you'll just be chewing longer" which helped her to realize that, despite the size of her study, she could do it.

Edie's future research plans are to conduct her survey again to obtain more recent data. "I need new data. I am current now but soon I will be telling them old stuff." Since the course, she has completed another survey with the board of directors and has maintained the employer update she established. She uses it to inform the employers about the data from her first study about high school students who work.

"I guess I am doing [research], I am doing it all the time" was one realization Edie admitted. One benefit of the course has been that Edie now feels she "can think through how to collect the data and do something about it." She is currently "looking for research questions" and feels she "can do more." When asked about her plans for future research, Edie emphatically stated, "I would like, I would *love* to do more if I had the time."

Scenario Two—Etta. Etta has taught kindergarten and primary grades for fifteen years. She is currently a guidance counselor and has been for the last eight years. She has a master's degree in elementary education guidance and counseling, plus thirty graduate credit hours, and is taking classes as a result of incentives offered by the Benedum Collaborative for PDSs. She also "got really interested in research from a grant-writing course" she had taken.

Etta took the *Teacher as Researcher* course as a way to develop some expertise in research. She suggested that the primary reason she was interested in research was because "grants need a research component," and also because she "was just interested." She expressed a desire to "contribute to the literature," because so little of what teachers do is actually recognized or publicized. She feels that many wonderful things occur daily at her school but stated, "it is almost like reciting a beautiful poem in the wind and nobody ever writes it down." She sees research as a means of transcribing these activities into a useful method of sharing with others.

Etta described her perception of research prior to the course as "something someone assigned you to do," and said that she was "not that much into it." One concern she had prior to the course was "how to do a project that is valid that someone could learn something from." She describes the course as doing "a really good job of that." Following the course, her perspective was, "Now I see it as the same as evaluation. All learning is basically research." Her initial, more narrow "perspective was broadened to include so much more."

When asked to describe aspects of the course that were especially helpful, Etta recognized the "collaboration with others," and mentioned that "it was interesting to see what others came up with." She stated that "the collaboration helped" and that research "is not something to do in isolation." She also mentioned that "I like to collaborate with the ideas, but the real work I like to do alone." Other positive aspects of the course were that "I learned to really focus. Research can get too big." The enthusiasm of her comments was evident. She recalled that "we usually got so involved we stayed late, tossing out ideas and all of us collaborating to help that person to develop the design." She mentioned the guest lecturers as beneficial, but really stressed that doing the research herself was crucial.

Obstacles to conducting research were seen by Etta to be the "lack of equipment" and her inexperience with computers; as she mentioned "I am still struggling with the computer part." Time constraints were also mentioned as an obstacle: "So much time, I just don't have that kind of time." "[There] are only so many hours in one day" indicated this as well. She admitted that "all of my research was done at home," and that there is "just no time."

Etta feels that teachers who conduct research are "fantastic" and that "they are growing." She feels that the course has "helped me to be more confident" and that "it improved my professional development."

An integral part of the course has been the change in Etta's perspective. She now states, "I understand what to do, how to do it, I am comfortable doing it." She recognizes the need to remain current: "I need to get some more data" and ways of facilitating the data analysis procedure. "I would like to, if I can, get it automated." Most important is the change in perception described by Etta as "It's how I view the world now."

Etta is currently working collaboratively as part of other research efforts. She feels that she "will continue to do research" and is actively recording memoirs of her living relatives in hopes of someday transcribing them for other members of her family. She hopes "to take better case notes now in hopes of future research." "I have realized [the importance of] all the things that come across my desk."

Scenario Three—Clorinda. Clorinda has been teaching for sixteen years at the primary level. She has completed a master's in reading and has an additional forty-five graduate credit hours. She now teaches the third grade. She chose to take the *Teacher as Researcher* course because she had been "hearing a lot about it and didn't want to miss anything." She adds that "mostly we were curious about what this teacher researcher stuff is." She had also been exposed to learning styles with a colleague. They had predicted certain outcomes for Foxfire teachers. They wanted to "follow through and see if our predictions were correct."

Prior to taking the course, she felt that "research was something out there but [I was] not too much interested in [it]," and that it was "heavy number stuff," which was intimidating. Clorinda admitted that "a lot of us didn't know what it was," but that this course was "designed to meet our needs." She admits, "I knew at the beginning that I wouldn't turn into a researcher, but I wanted to know more about it."

Following the course, she realized that research "didn't have to be such heavy number stuff. We deal with it all the time." Clorinda gives the course credit for helping her to "develop new respect for research" and because it "showed us that teachers *could* do research." She stated that "we could all choose our own topic" and felt that this was a positive aspect of the course. Her perspective on research has changed. She now realizes that she "never thought about what we do in class as research, but if we follow through it is." In fact, Clorinda describes the course as providing "validation that a lot of what we do is research but not a document with a lot of numbers in it." She now feels that she "values [research] more" and that as a teacher she has changed. "I will never be the teacher I was, I thought I was pretty good but I have begun to see how much better I can be" demonstrates this new self-image.

Positive aspects of the course involve collaboration with her peers and beginning to see the importance of research. She placed particular emphasis on the importance of "being able to share these interests with other teachers," "learning from each other," and the "inside view of what everyone was struggling with by sharing in discussions."

Her biggest obstacle to conducting research involved time constraints. She made repeated references to the lack of time for research in her schedule. "The course showed me it was possible to do research but difficult because of time"; "[it] takes me away from my classroom work"; "[I am] still not convinced I would do a lot of research because of the time commitments"; "if I have to choose how to spend my time, I choose to spend it on things I do with my students"; and "although it could be expanded into research, I just don't have time for it" are only some of her twenty-two references to a problem with "time" in her sixty-minute interview. She explained that her time was typically spent "training preservice teachers, training and development with other teachers, and acting as a teacher-leader," a responsibility imposed by being on committees and acting in other leadership capacities within her school. Other obstacles were that the "design part at the front end and the analysis at the end would be where I would need help." She has realized a new complexity to research, in that answering some questions only leads to other questions. She admits that she "can't just look at the numbers. [I] have to realize that there is more complexity." "Mixing qualitative and quantitative allows you to find out more."

Clorinda admits that she may not conduct future research simply because of the time factor. She also feels "I wouldn't do it if I had to do it by myself. I would want collaboration with the university or someone to work with me." She has not completely ruled out the possibility of future research, however. She states that "I would have to be very motivated to continue to conduct research. I am not going to go out looking for it. It may be something to evolve from another need, and I would have someone work with me." She has developed an appreciation for those who conduct research and has offered to support them in any way she can. She sees it as "a responsibility of her profession to share" the demands of teaching and conducting research.

Scenario Four—Joyce. Joyce has taught for more than thirty years and is now teaching third grade. She has her master's plus forty-five graduate credit hours. She worked collaboratively with Clorinda on the learning styles and Foxfire teacher study. She also took the course as a means of learning research so that she could conduct the study with learning styles. She claims she needed the course because she had already collected the learning style data and had "no clue as to what to do with it." She describes the *Teacher as Researcher* course as the "perfect opportunity for us to figure this out."

Prior to conducting her own study, she felt that research was something she "wasn't capable of doing." She explained that "teachers aren't trained for conducting research." Her view of research led her to believe that "I am not that kind of person." She expressed some anxiety about computers and statistics: "if I have to learn to use a computer I'm outta here." Even before the class she felt "I knew I had much richer data than those in the lab [or traditional research facilities]. I had the perspective."

Obstacles that Joyce encountered when conducting her own research were time and ignorance. "We assumed everyone would know how to fill out these forms. WRONG! We mailed them to some people hard to reach, and they filled them out incorrectly. Because of this our data may not be accurate." She anticipated that her sample would have been bigger and that it would be a straightforward process of answering the initial research questions, but "the more we looked at the data the more questions we had. We had to decide which questions to answer." "We discovered a lot of questions that we didn't think of. We expected it to be straightforward." She thinks that "the problem with people not doing [research] is that they are already overworked and underpaid."

For Joyce, some positive aspects of the course included the collaboration she experienced and the relationships she established for future direction. The "collaboration was important. I feel comfortable that I can go back for guidance, but a lot of people can't. Others are farther away." Joyce feels fortunate that her school is geographically so close to the University. She enjoyed "the interaction that went on in the class. We were all fumbling at the same time." In her case, she sees research as something "to keep the adrenaline going" after thirty years of teaching. "I think it's challenging. I like the challenge of looking at something in a new light. I think you look at kids differently. You really see a whole new perspective." In her study, Joyce was investigating an issue that had concerned her for some time. She said "I was intrigued that I was wrong. I expected certain outcomes, and it didn't come out that way." Joyce stated that the instructor made her see things differently. "I really could do it, [the instructor] helped me to see that," and "he was fulfilling a need that I had," were comments that exemplified her feelings about the instructor's influential role in the course.

Following the course she felt that "professionally we do grow. In isolation sometimes you just don't have a clue." Joyce now realizes that research does not have to be "rows and rows of numbers"; and since she "is not that kind of person," she is excited that research "doesn't have to be sophisticated [or quantitative]." She didn't know about qualitative research prior to the course. She now perceives it to be quite useful in helping to answer some of her research questions. She felt that the "guest speakers" and the "collaboration" were aspects of the course that were especially helpful in conducting her own research. She admits that she now has "more questions than I did before."

Joyce expressed a desire to continue to conduct research: "I am sure I will." But she admitted that, based on her previous experience, her next study "probably won't be the same." Even now she feels that "I need some of that guidance" that she received during the course. She isn't looking to publish her findings but wants to "continue to collect data and look at things differently." She wants to focus more on her own students as subjects of research so that she can "be a better teacher." Joyce feels that all teachers should "do [research] at least once," and that "I would like to see more teachers do it. It isn't for everyone, but more should do it, more of us out there that could do it if they only gave it a try." She also expressed a desire for the collaboration to be "ongoing" between the public schools and the University. (Joyce and Clorinda continue to collaborate on research in their classrooms. They are currently working with a WVU faculty member to study the impact of fine arts integration.)

Summary. The stories told by these four participants focus on two issues: (1) the *Teacher as Researcher* course, and (2) teachers conducting research themselves. It is not possible to separate the two issues or to combine the four stories without losing the richness of the individual experiences. Admittedly, there are many commonalities across the four interviews, but each story is also unique. Conversely, attempting to synthesize these stories is beneficial in that it can provide useful information for the course design and new insight into action research as well as into each of the individuals.

The collaborative aspect of the course appears to have been a key aspect for all four participants. Each enjoyed the networking and sharing of ideas among their peers. Many cited this as the most helpful aspect of the course. The encouragement provided by others seemed to be crucial in motivating these teachers to conduct their own research. Without other, more extrinsic types of reinforcement, this is readily understood. Recognition was mentioned as one reward for action research.

The role of the instructor was also critical in maintaining motivation and encouragement among the teachers. All comments regarding the instructor were favorable, and he was often mentioned as having played a very influential role in each of their experiences. He supported them when it was needed the most. The angst that most of the teachers felt toward statistics was overcome by using computer software, hiring others to perform this task, and introducing them to qualitative methods.

It is apparent that the single biggest obstacle to conducting action research is time. Every teacher mentioned it, and most of them expanded on it more than once. Generally, they see teaching as their primary concern, and they feel that research detracts from their time to plan for teaching. In an effort to solve the time problem, the teachers suggested having specialists, graduate students, or some other person serve as a research "person." Unfortunately, these suggestions violate the notion of action research to some extent. Those who did feel confident enough to continue conducting research admitted that they would need some type of assistance. None of them appeared ready to begin by herself. There were some specific aspects of the research process which made the teachers uncomfortable. For some it was the computer, but for most it was the statistics. Others mentioned the area of forming the research design, and some mentioned the analysis of the data. Although some problems were encountered during data collection, this appears to be the only area where everyone felt comfortable. Ongoing collaboration with the University and maintaining the relationship with the instructor were suggestions for alleviating these concerns.

There were several comments referring to a change in perspective following the course. The respondents appeared to have generated more questions from having taken the course, rather than simply having answered preliminary questions and received satisfaction. Taking the course and conducting their own research appeared to have opened their eyes to many new questions and ways of thinking. There was a collective realization that much of what they do every day is research. Research is no longer the intimidating mystery it previously was. They see the utility of it now. In fact, Clorinda mentioned that she now sees research as a "professional responsibility." They see it as a way of making themselves better teachers, even though they considered themselves good teachers when the course started. Following the course, many of them desired to continue to conduct research, but only with collaboration, guidance, further assistance, and time.

Confidence also emerged as a continuing attitude. They felt that they had overcome negative attitudes and anxiety toward research and were relieved to find out that research did not have to be only statistics. They all stated they were glad that they took the course and conducted their research. They were very pleased that they found out it was something they could do. One teacher even began to employ some of what she had learned to investigate a topic related to her family lineage. All four made the statement, "I feel more confident [about conducting research]."

Many of their professional growth statements were similar to those given during the class meetings: (1) conducting their own research empowered them; (2) it increased their self-esteem; (3) research made them better teachers because the topics were personally meaningful; and (4) research was a part of their teaching and professional lives. Some new dimensions were that they (1) found that their topics were useful to others, (2) felt they needed to continue to remain current in terms of the research, and (3) gained a new respect for research.

Two new, dominant attitudinal themes emerged as a result of the interviews: (1) publishing, or informing others; and (2) the course. They were interested and excited about sharing the results with other teachers. They felt that they could contribute to the literature of classroom-based research and saw that as a necessity because so little, according to them, of what teachers do is recognized or publicized. They felt that the course had made them focus on one idea or topic. Some of them already had some data. Through the systematic nature of the course, they learned how to separate what they needed to concentrate on from other ideas or unrelated information. The course also met their specific needs, as it was designed to do.

Two other, less dominant attitudinal themes, although just as critical as the others, were (1) support, and (2) conducting research. At this point, they were concerned about support not only from fellow teacher-researchers but also from the instructors of the course if they were to conduct research again. They all felt that conducting the research was critical—to employ what they had learned, rather than just having learned the information.

Lessons Learned

Probably the most important lesson learned was not to underestimate the amount of time needed to prepare teachers to do their research and for them to conduct it and prepare the research report. Originally, we felt we could cover the research information in six to eight three-hour sessions. As the teachers attended the sessions, they would automatically translate such information into what they were already doing in their classes, they would have instruments handy to administer, and they would be quick to analyze their data and interpret their results—all in the course of one semester, yes from September to December.

Perhaps we were not that foolishly optimistic, but we were not that far from expecting just that. Time was a critical issue . . . time in terms of teachers' needing the time to process what they were being taught and time in terms of their conducting their research. Because we were interested in the long-term effects of this inquiry-based experience, we decided to pay close attention to their attitudes. The purpose of the course was not just to have nine studies at the end of it, but rather to help the teachers form positive attitudes about research. In the long run, we wanted them to continue to conduct other studies, to instill in their fellow teachers a desire to research their classes, and to develop some addictive attachment to the process of research informing practice and practice informing research. Holding them to a brief timeline would have probably ruined all of that—and we probably would not have had the nine studies either.

Although we are often forced to adhere to semester-structures and three-credit-hour-structures, teacher-researcher courses require a certain flexibility. This should not be much of a surprise to higher education faculty. After all, we did not acquire all the skills necessary to conduct our dissertations, formulate and design our studies, conduct our studies, and write them up *in one semester*. And most likely we were not facing up to 150 students each day at the same time. Not understanding this difference may be as monumentally offensive to teachers as higher education faculty pontificating to teachers on how they should teach their classes. This particular lesson learned also needs to be considered when developing prospective teachers into prospective teacher-researchers.

A second lesson learned was the importance of having successful teacher-researchers explain their studies. Not only are they more likely to present classroom-based research, but also they are proof to the other teachers that teachers can conduct research. It is one thing for a university professor to discuss conducting research with teachers; it is much more convincing to teachers when another teacher claims it can be done and then explains how he or she succeeded at it.

A final lesson learned was continuity. As the interviewed teachers stated, they would like to conduct more studies but believe they need the continued support of the instructor. Unfortunately, university resources are often such that even that one person cannot continue to set aside the same amount of time he or she did when teaching the course. And one person as sole support is simply not sufficient if other teachers would like to conduct studies. An answer is to rethink university faculty's teaching assignments to formally include more continuous work with teachers. Perhaps an extension to this answer is to dedicate some of a college's resources to developing centers for teacher research.

These three lessons come quickly to mind in the context of our ten teachers. Others may be reflected in Cochran-Smith and Lytle's words:

To encourage teacher research, we must first address incentives for teachers, the creation and maintenance of supportive networks, the reform of rigid organizational patterns in schools, and the hierarchical power relationships that characterize most of schooling. Likewise, to resolve the problematic relationship between academic research and teacher research it will be necessary to confront controversial issues of voice, power, ownership, status, and role in the broad educational community. (1990, p. 10)

References

Bissex, G. L. and Bullock, R. H. (1987). *Seeing for ourselves: Case-study research by teachers of writing*. Portsmouth, N.H.: Heinemann Educational Books, Inc.

Brookhart, S. and Loadman, W. (1992). School-university collaboration and perceived professional rewards. *Journal of Research in Education 2*(1): 68–76.

Carter, K. and Doyle, W. (1995). Teacher-researcher relationships in the study of teaching and teacher education. *Peabody Journal of Education 70*(2): 162–174.

Casanova, V. (1989). Research and practice—We can integrate them. *N.E.A. Today 7*(6): 44–49.

Cochran-Smith, M. and Lytle, S. L. (1990). Research on teaching and teacher research: The issues that divide. *Educational Researcher 19*(2): 2–11.

Daly, J. and Miller, M. D. (1975). The empirical development of an instrument to measure writing apprehension. *Research in the Teaching of English 9*: 242–249.

Eisenhart, M. and Borko, H. (1993). *Designing classroom research: Themes, issues, and struggles*. Needham Heights, Mass.: Allyn and Bacon.

Elliot, J. (1983). *Paradigms of educational research and theories of schooling*. Presented at the Sociology of Education Conference, Birmingham, England.

Feldman, A. (1992). *Models of erquitable collaboration between university researchers and school teachers*. Paper presented at the annual meeting of the American Educational Research Association, San Francisco. (ERIC Reproduction Services Document No. 349 293)

Fleischer, C. (1994). Researching teacher-research: A practitioner's retrospective. *English Education 26*(2): 86–124.

Goswami, D. (1984). Teachers as researchers. In R. Graves, ed., *Rhetoric and composition*. Montclair, N.J.: Boynton/Cook.

Goswami, D. and Stillman, P. R. (1987). *Reclaiming the classroom: Teacher research as an agency for change.* Upper Montclair, N.J.: Boynton/Cook Publishers, Inc.

Graves, D. H. (1981). Where have all the teachers gone? *Language Arts 58*: 492–496.

Griffin, G. A. (1983). *Interactive research and development on schooling: Antecedents, purposes, and significance for school improvement.* Austin, Tex.: Research and Development Center for Teacher Education.

Hall, G. E., George, A. A., and Rutherford, W. L. (1977). *Measuring the stages of concern about an innovation: A manual for use of the stages of concern questionaire.* Austin, Tex.: Research and Development Center for Teacher Education.

Huling, L. L. (1982). *The effects on teachers of participation in an interactive research and development project.* Austin, Tex.: Research and Development Center for Teacher Education.

Johnson, R. (1993). Where can teacher research lead? One teacher's daydream. *Educational Leadership 51*(2): 66–68.

Kennedy, C. (1985). *Teacher as researcher and evaluator: One suggested solution to some recurrent problems in ELT and ESP.* Presented at the National ESP Conference, Vitoria, Brazil.

Kutz, E. (1992). Teacher research: Myths and realities. *Language Arts 69*(3): 193–197

Lehman, B. (1991). Practicing what we preach: A personal perspective on "knowing and doing" in university teacher education classes. *Action in Teacher Education 13*(1): 22–27.

Lind, K. K. (1984). *Action Research: Helping student teachers understand and solve classroom problems.* Presented at the annual meeting of the Association of Teacher Education, New Orleans.

Lytle, S. L. and Cochran-Smith, M. (1990). Learning from teacher research: A working typology. *Teachers College Record 92*(1): 83–103.

McCutcheon, G. (1987). Teachers' experience doing action research. *Peabody Journal of Education 64*(2): 116–127.

Myers, M. (1985). *The teacher-researcher: How to study writing in the classroom.* San Francisco: Bay Area Writing Project.

Nixon, J. (1987). The teacher as researcher: Contradiction and continuities. *Peabody Journal of Education 64*(2): 20–32.

Oja, S. N. (1984). *Developmental stage characteristics of teachers participating in a collaborative action research project.* Presented at the annual meeting of the American Educational Research Association, New Orleans.

Sardo-Brown, D. (1990). Middle level teachers' perceptions of action research. *Middle School Journal 22*(3): 30–32.

Sardo-Brown, D. (1992). Elementary teachers' perceptions of action research. *Action in Teacher Education 14*(2): 55–59.

Shanahan, T. (1994). *Teachers thinking, teachers knowing,: Reflections on literacy and language education.* Urbana, Ill.: National Council of Teachers of English.

Smuylan, L. (1983). *Action research on change in schools: A collaborative project.* Presented at the annual meeting of the American Educational Research Association, Montreal.

Stansell, J. C. and Patterson, L. (1987). *Beyond teacher research: The teacher as theory builder.* Presented at the annual meeting of the National Reading Conference, Clearwater..

Strickland, D. S. (1988). The teacher as researcher: Toward an extended professional. *Language Arts 65*(8): 754–764.

Wells, G. (1989). Foreword. In G. S. Pinnell and M. S. Matlin, eds., *Teachers and research: Language learning in the classroom.* Newark, Del.: International Reading Association.

6

THE STORY OF TWO PRINCIPALS: CONSTRUCTING LEADERSHIP, BALANCING TENSIONS, AND CREATING RELATIONSHIPS

VAN DEMPSEY WITH THOMAS HART AND SUSANNE LYNCH

Introduction

Rich conversation during the now-extending decade of school reform has focused on the lives of teacher and context of teaching, with our understanding of the complexities and ambiguity of the professional worlds of teaching building constantly. While our work with the Professional Development School concept in West Virginia has drawn heavily from that understanding to come to grips with how schools might be restructured and current practices reconsidered from teachers' perspectives, we have paid less attention to what the world of principals has been like during the reform efforts, and what principals' lives might be like in PDSs in the future. This has not been by intention. Principals have been crucial in the reform efforts in each of the PDS sites and have played major roles in the design, direction, and strategies of the cross-site activities.

While teacher empowerment and expanded teacher decision making have been in our focus now for quite some time, our attention is starting to include more directly the roles, values, beliefs, uncertainties, and ambiguities created for principals of PDSs. This chapter is a portrait of two PDS principals: Tom Hart of Morgantown High School and Sue Lynch of Suncrest Primary. It describes how working in Professional Development Schools has changed their identities, roles, values, and beliefs as principals, and how their schools and the teachers with whom they work reflect that. These portraits will, hopefully, give a sense of the "leadership mindscapes"(Sergiovanni 1992a, 1992b) that have been constructed by and with these two principals while they have taken part in the reform efforts in their schools. These portraits include attempts to capture how those mindscapes are reflected in the teachers with whom they work, acknowledging that such mindscapes are "socially constructed" (Berger and Luckman

1967) realities within the school communities. These portraits are a representation of the beliefs and values, perceptions and feelings of Sue and Tom as they reflected on their experiences as PDS principals over the course of two interviews apiece. They include, as well, commentaries, developed through focus group interviews, from teachers in the two schools who have worked closely with the two principals over the last few years in the development of the PDS idea. These portraits also are an attempt to describe the "collaborative play" (Smylie and Brownlee-Conyers 1992, 153) that has been constructed at Morgantown High and Suncrest Primary.

Sue Lynch is the principal of Suncrest Primary School, a kindergarten through third grade elementary school in the Monongalia County school district. It is located in a residential area about one mile from the University. The faculty of the school is a senior faculty, with one teacher having worked in the school since the early 1960s. Upon becoming a Professional Development School, the faculty made a commitment to developing the "4MAT" instructional strategy as the central focus of their reform.

Morgantown High School is one of two high schools in the city, and is located in South Park, one of the oldest residential areas in Morgantown. Morgantown High School enrolls more than 1200 students and has a faculty of more than eighty. Since its opening in 1927, the school has had a reputation of academic excellence, with multiple National Merit Scholarship semifinalists year in and year out. Morgantown High School chose to focus on the enhancement of scientific and technological learning and instruction as the key to their reform agenda, and has invested a great deal of energy in curriculum integration and a new "block" schedule (using ninety-minute teaching blocks rather than fifty-minute blocks of time).

It is notable that both of these schools were known as "good" schools in the district when they were selected as Professional Development Schools, and did not suffer from reputations that might have made them the focus of reform to avert educational crises. Both Suncrest and Morgantown High have for some time been seen by the Morgantown community as having solid educational programs.

Leadership as Balance: Tom Hart

Tom Hart's professional experience began more than three decades prior to the PDS work at Morgantown High School with the reform initiatives that marked the aftermath of the Sputnik crisis and the resultant proliferation of funding for educational programs in science and math. In the mid-1960s Tom participated in a series of National Science Foundation (NSF) institutes for the teaching of chemistry and physics. After graduating from college in 1963, he attended an institute on the Chemical Bond Approach (CBA) to teaching

Chemistry, sponsored by NSF. After teaching for one year, and then conducting research comparing CBA approaches to other teaching strategies, Tom worked on weekends in staff development sessions in West Virginia to introduce teachers to the then "modern approach" to teaching chemistry. He broadened his perspectives to include physics teaching and working with computers.

In interviews, Tom alluded to the rapidity of the changes in science learning and science teaching that went on in the mid-1960s, changes that took him away from approaches focusing on the transmission of science knowledge to teaching strategies more attuned to developing understandings of theoretical foundations and discovery learning. As he recalls:

> The course that I had was teaching about what chemistry was, and when we made these changes we were actually going in and doing chemistry and doing laboratory reports the way a chemist might do them in the laboratory. So there was quite a difference in philosophy and a change in what was going on from one to the other.

Tom came to Morgantown High School as a substitute teacher in 1967. After completing a degree in administration, he became assistant principal of the school in 1971, a position he held until 1989, when he became the principal. In his interview, Tom devoted a great deal of reflective conversation to those years spent as assistant principal, connecting his own experience to the histories of past administrators of the school. Tom was only the third person since World War II to serve as principal, with his immediate predecessor having held the position for more than twenty-five years. Tom describes a leadership style that during that quarter of a century was authoritarian:

> What the principal said, the principal got done. The principal was the boss, and everyone knew that, recognized that and accepted that. Now that does not mean that the principal flaunted his power or anything like that. But everyone knew that there was very little, if any at that time, questioning of what was going to be done.

But during his time as assistant principal, Tom observed changes in his predecessor that foretold the PDS ideal that was to come to Morgantown High School. Many of the security, risk, and trust issues that would mark the school as a PDS came to affect Tom's predecessor and Tom himself. Tom describes a conversation he had with his former principal:

> I know as the years went on and [he] would come to me and would say, "I'm losing control. I don't feel like I'm in control any more." It was a terrible feeling for someone who had been trained under a principal who

had absolute control, to someone who started into that mold and then all at once he felt things were eroding away from him and that was a bad thing to happen. He didn't feel that he could take a hold of things and get things done the way he wanted to get them done, and that was true.

He adds:

I know that during the times that I was in this office for eighteen years we made progress, and we changed and we moved as the times sort of dictated. But it was the principal's vision of what ought to be done and very little real—and I said very little—not meaning none. But there was very little real input from the faculty.

Tom credited the departure of the principal at least in part to this transition:

I honestly think that one of the reasons that [he] retired at the time that he did was because he just got frustrated with the fact that things were changing and he was losing the control that he felt was necessary to run a good school.

Tom's transition into the principal's role and Morgantown High School's into the PDS idea were concurrent events in the life of the school. Both occurred in 1989, a period that Tom describes as a "good time as for as change in administration is concerned." Tom felt early in his tenure as principal that leadership required the building of consensus around the issues the faculty addressed and the activities it pursued.

You know, we have shifted from a place where the principal was really almost a dictator with little input from teachers. Really, very little. When the final decision was made the principal made that decision. Now that does not mean to say that every decision is a consensus type of decision. There are certain decisions that the principal does make, I mean more or less unilaterally. However, most of the decisions that we make at this school that are of major consequence such as direction the school is going, such as curriculum change, Those kinds of decisions are made basically from a consensus point of view.

Being the point person for that transition has not presented Tom with a particularly easy or simple task, a matter complicated by the fact that the Morgantown High School faculty is one with a great deal of experience, represented by tenure. Change for Tom and the school has required more than just desire on the part of the principal, state mandates to set up teacher decision-making structures such as a faculty senate, or changes in the personality of the principal's office. Tom works against the legacy of a faculty accustomed to another leadership model and not well versed in collaborative decision making, empowered teachers, and consensus.

> As you are probably aware, the State of West Virginia decided that all at once we would change by making a law and put in faculty senates and there was going to be all this collaboration, all these kinds of things, and they said boom, you are there, you do it. Well, we have made a lot of progress along that way, but our teachers need to understand how to work in that mode, too. Because many of the teachers have been here for many, many years. The average tenure is fifteen to sixteen years. So they worked under a principal that the principal said these are the ways we are going to do things. This is what we do. This is how we do it basically. And then all at once they are told you've got input. Well, some people I think, think that input means that you have the control to say what's going to happen and then you have to start to learn how to work together and how to put ideas together and share ideas and, in a professional way, sit down and discuss differences and look at things. And we really didn't have the chance or opportunity to do much of that in the past.

Tom feels he and the faculty are able to reach the best decisions they can through consensus, not necessarily because any particular plan is the "best," but because it is a plan that best represents the "hybrid" of multiple ideas, thinking, and investments. Although the process of building consensus sacrifices short term efficiency in decision making, long term resistance to an unowned plan would likely cause failure. As Tom has learned, "If you allow [the teachers] to come up with the same solution [that he might have forced], then they are going to feel a part of it and they are willing to accept that."

Yet Tom has also learned in his role as a PDS principal that searching for and even reaching consensus does not come without risks and threats to individual feelings of security, including that of himself and the faculty.

> I know it's very difficult for me to make those changes that I may want them to make. And even if you want to make changes, it is difficult to do. It's, it's a real threat sometimes. There is a lot of security in what you presently are doing and if we go from a traditional seven period day next year to one in which you may have a two hour block of time and those classes are meeting maybe three days a week as opposed to fifty minutes a day for five days a week, then those teachers are going to have to change what they are doing.

This sense of insecurity that comes with the necessity for change is not removed by consensus decision-making strategies, but it is shared. Tom does not feel that he can eliminate insecurity in his faculty while the school experiences the kinds of transitions it has as a PDS, but he does feel that top-down requirements and mandates guarantee a high degree of insecurity among those acted by the change. To help reduce the insecurity and the anxieties associated with it, he has tried to work under the premise that "Everyone has got to move along together." He acknowledges a tendency to get too far out in front of the faculty, or to use his power as principal to say, "We are going to do this; this is the way we are going to do it." He feels that to avoid some of the problems associated with the distance that can develop between himself and the teachers, "You move along together." In that, he feels there is a greater sense of security. Over time, as the faculty at Morgantown High have participated in the change process on a number of fronts in both individual and group situations, Tom feels that the anxiety has been reduced, and the level of insecurity about being a PDS has abated as the process has been experienced more often by more of the faculty.

During the school's transition from an authoritarian leadership style to one based in faculty participation and consensus, Tom has had to learn about his own tendencies and his own insecurities. He has learned that he has to be "more sensitive to what their feelings are," and that he has to be sensitive to his own tendency to "jump in and move things right along" when he believes strongly in what he wants to do but has not yet sold it to his faculty.

> You've got to realize that you may have spent a lot of time preparing yourself for this change and just all at once it is thrown on someone else and they may not be ready for it. And I think I have become more sensitive and have tried to put myself in their positions and mentally put myself in that position to see what it is that would be difficult for them.

Tom recognizes that there are aspects of his evolving leadership style that have been frustrating, both for himself and for the Morgantown High School faculty. There have been times when the rush to get a plan in place has taken precedence over the faculty's participation in the development and implementation of the plan. He also understands that he has acted in the past on the assumption that a sense of vision that he held was shared by the teachers more than it actually was. He therefore was less attentive to communicating his perspectives and ideas than he might have been had he not taken their understandings for granted.

> If you could take your vision and immediately plant that in someone else's head, and in their thoughts, then you could move quickly. But that communication, of trying to communicate that direction that you're going is very difficult. And you can sit down and talk about it, but it takes a

while for it to actually take root and start to grow. And I think that initially I was maybe a little too ambitious as far as what I expect to be able to happen right away.

Sharing the vision with his faculty does not complete the communication necessary for leadership as Tom sees it. The shared vision has to also carry shared investment, and as Tom thought about it:

I think there does have to be a certain amount of enthusiasm for something, but you've got to be very careful that you're able to instill that enthusiasm or that vision in others before they can catch on to it. You don't want to run away and leave them. And I think that there were times that I was a little too impatient with people for not understanding what I was envisioning.

Tom has also learned that much of the anxiety that his predecessor felt when he began to lose control over the school is a normal part of the transition in leadership for a PDS principal. "Sometimes I feel that way, also, because I create a situation in which I encourage teachers to be involved." That loss of control creates its own set of problems for leadership, because as Tom has turned more of the decision making over to the faculty, "You just never know what's going to happen." As the "what" unfolds and things begin to happen for the school through the process, Tom, though in less control, is no less a principal and no less a participant in the process of change. He sees his role in the context of change as assisting the teachers, once they have set upon a course, with the negotiation of barriers and obstacles, and helping them understand when insurmountable barriers have been reached.

And you've got to be careful too, at the very beginning to let people know. Yeah, we want to move in this direction, but at the same time there may be some barriers. So when we run into those barriers, let's look at how we can work together to get around those things.

This growing understanding and awareness of and sensitivity to problems in the change process for a PDS creates communication on a new level probably not enjoyed by Tom's predecessors, and certainly critical to the transitions going on in Morgantown High School. The connections developing between Tom and the teachers foster better understanding about each others' roles in the school and in the process of decision making. Tom recognizes that the faculty has become more aware of the problems that he has to deal with as a principal, and feels a heightened degree of sensitivity and understanding toward him on their part.

> In the past they just weren't aware of what went on in this office. They just know that they wanted to do this and it wasn't done. And that's very discouraging. But now, they want to do something, if it can't be done at least they know the reasons why.

> And so I think it's a matter of working together, understanding where each person is coming from. Where the teacher is coming from. Where the administrator is coming from. And trying to work together such that you can put your thoughts together and be able to work through a situation as opposed to not seeing the reasons for something happening.

This enhanced communication, with the advantage of multiple voices and multiple perspectives brought to bear on problem solving and the development of ideas for the school, provides a way around the barriers that might otherwise be impassable for the faculty and Tom.

> So I get ideas from them as to how things can work when from an administrative point of view I would say, ah, I don't know if we can do that. But when we sit down and start looking at it, we finds ways that yes, maybe we can work this out. We can't fit it in the same mold that we did before, but we'll change the mold.

And he adds on this same point:

> But I think once we are able to look at it from their point of view and my point of view there's always middle ground that we can work in. And that's important. In the past it wasn't that type of communication that I feel it should have been. And that's one of the things that I try to do.

Some of Morgantown High's faculty feel that Tom has a vision of what the school might become, and that he articulates that vision to teachers for their consideration. Tom's vision centers on the issue of students being able to anticipate change, which requires that his teachers be able to understand and anticipate change. This entails change in not only what students are taught, but the instructional techniques and practices through which they are taught.

> And I also think that change is not improving, necessarily improving upon what we are presently doing. I think that change many times has to be a radical departure from what we have been doing. And doing things just completely differently.

Tom has also gained some measure of success in articulating that vision to the teachers, developing understanding among the faculty for his own ideas for the school and what they might mean. As one of the teachers puts it:

> Let me suggest that he sees education as more than transmission of information. And so therefore he sees teachers' roles as being very different in the classroom.

A colleague followed:

> Part of his concept is that we not only change, or alter some of the styles in which we teach, and the delivery and gathering. Not just gathering of information, but the process of using that information after it has been gathered sometimes in alternative methods in what we traditionally use.

One place where Tom sees that kind of change going on at Morgantown High School is in the transition from a traditional fifty minute per subject schedule to a ninety minute per subject schedule on alternating days. The transition took several years for the faculty to develop, moving from a series of preliminary discussions as part of the school's decision to become a PDS to implementation of the strategy in the 1993–1994 school year. The new schedule was a result not only of changes in the allocation of time for instructional delivery, but of reconsideration of what objects could be integrated or linked together in the new configuration. Tom sees this change as "something radically different from anything else were ever done," and as representative of the kind of risk taking in which he thinks the school's faculty should engage.

The scheduling change represents a restructuring activity for Morgantown High that has prompted pointed thinking and talking about school change and what it means to be a PDS. Tom's ability to envision what the school might be had become clearer to the faculty members, prompting discussion of Tom:

> First of all, I think . . . he has some very definite ideas. I mean he definitely knows what he wants to do and I think he listens very well.

Another teacher says of his leadership style in relation to the schedule change:

> Tom generally in my dealing when I go one on one and ask for this he takes it all into consideration. He is a darn good listener and he will research and take a look and ask other people.

But Tom's experience with the schedule change has brought to the fore many of the tensions that come with being a principal in a PDS that is moving to new decision making structures and strategies. Being the principal at Morgantown High School demands that Tom strike a balance between wanting to share decision making with the faculty, and having to play many of the more traditional principal's roles. As many of the details in the implementation of the new schedule ran into rough spots, and disgruntled constituents began to voice their complaints, Tom became the focus of much of the questioning and criticism—even though the decision to go to the new schedule had been a faculty decision. And the implementation problems raised questions of a general nature, not just specific to the activity at hand. As one of the faculty members suggests:

> So I think there's no question that Tom has a vision. I think many people sometimes question whether we have the skills to get to that vision or not. But I think you know he certainly does have a point where he wants us to be. But then when you have things go wrong like we have over the last several weeks you start to have the doubters as to whether we can ever get there.

In such a situation, Tom seems to be expected to have one foot in the world of the traditional principal and one in the more inclusive, empowering realm of a principal who practices shared decision making. In times of trouble, teachers have sometimes expected Tom, perhaps unconsciously, to be more of the traditional leader. As one teacher voices the frustration:

> But there are decisions on often little things that slip by. Maybe it was raised here about this scheduling change and all of that there were not some deadlines placed, that we have this in place before we move on. And I think that is one of the reasons for some of our discontent right now, that there were not those clear guidelines and people who look to the leadership for some of those guidelines.

One teacher is more direct about longing for some of the vestiges of more traditional leadership:

> There are so many choices to make and so many ways you could go that I think that some people would like a little traditional leadership to go along.

The teachers who discussed Tom's role as leader recognized that he was caught between leadership styles, and that even though the school was moving toward more participatory decision-making structures, he was still the person upon whose desk many criticisms and ultimate responsibilities would rest. "The buck stops here," one teacher said of Tom's role. "The bottom line is he is responsible."

Some of the teachers recognized that Tom is also caught in organizational tension outside the school: While he may support new decision-making structures within the school that might mean autonomy and responsibility spread across the faculty, Tom is still principal in a school district that has certain expectations of its principals. A teacher described the tension as he sees it play out in Tom's work:

Now [the district administrators] talk about how they support the PDS and they support this and that, but then they want Tom to have all these piddley little reports on their desk at exactly the right time and so on. I think he is trying to be a new leader. But again the pressure—it gets back to what I said in the beginning. The pressure from above and below and faculty members who aren't necessarily wanting that new leadership.

According to the faculty, by supporting their decision making and teacher empowerment, Tom cannot escape the "catch-22" of having to respect the flexibility and autonomy the faculty need, while being under the gun when things don't go so well. "He's going to be darned if he does, and darn if he doesn't," as one of the teachers summarizes the tension.

In the end, Tom's was quite naturally the most articulate voice describing the tensions and frustrations that have come with being the principal of a PDS like Morgantown High School. Frustrations arise for Tom over the preponderance of problems that develop as the school works through the kinds of changes the faculty desires. Problems seem to Tom to be a natural part of the process, but the frustration comes in the tendency to sometimes fixate on the problems rather than the possibilities. This does not mean that there aren't times when attempts to change meet failure, but without the focus on the positive, solutions or alternatives might seem more limited than they actually are. Tom is also frustrated sometimes by the lengthy time that the change process seems to take. That time is a result, according to Tom, of the amount of thinking, planning, and questioning that goes on among the faculty as options and ideas are considered. Another instance of Tom's frustration with being a spokesperson for the change process and the ideas that might come out of it occurs when, having garnered the support to bring the changes about, he sees his supporters retreat when the ideas become reality. As Tom put it:

People will initially say let's make changes. That's good. But when it really hits you in the face that we really are going to do it, then people start backing down from that, and say well, maybe we shouldn't do this.

But it is frustrating for me to, for our faculty. For the faculty to say to me on a number of occasions over the last two years let's make changes in our schedule. And then finally I say yes, let's go for it. Here are some possibilities. Let's go with it. And then all at once people are saying, well, I don't even know what you're talking about. Why are we doing this? And I have to remind them we're doing this because you said that it was important for us to do.

During his tenure as the principal with the PDS concept at Morgantown High School, Tom has learned some things about himself and adapted, at least to some degree, to the new kind of leadership required of him. He has come to understand the difficulty of changing the way professionals operate in a school attuned to reforming its practices. He has had to change just as he has advocated change for those around him. As he describes his own participation:

I think maybe part of the reason that we didn't make changes a little sooner is I maybe didn't feel that comfortable with change myself, and needed that incubation period for things to start changing. I feel much more comfortable with the changes that we're doing. Whereas before I would think, my gosh, am I turning down what's been successful for the last seventy years.

Second, the kinds of change issues with which the school is dealing present problems that have not been experienced before by most of the faculty. "The problems that you face are new problems that you've never seen before, therefore trying to come up with solutions to new problems can be even more difficult." Tom, in coming to grips with this challenge, reflects

It's easy as a principal to say these are the directions that we are going to go. What types of things we are going to do, and have everyone just jump on the bandwagon and you go with it. But when you encourage people to seek alternative ways of looking at something, the principal's way is not the right—is not the way. What evolves is something the entire group comes together with. And me learning to deal with that and learning to understand that when I say something, I know that there are going to be a number of voices saying something differently. And you've got to have some confidence in yourself and realize that they are expounding a certain point of view. I have a certain point of view. Neither one of those points of view are necessarily the right thing. But maybe a combination of those things could be more right than any one individual view.

Sue Lynch: Sharing, Connection, and Communication as Leadership

Sue is the principal of Suncrest Primary, where she has served as principal or half-time principal since 1979. Sue first came into contact with Suncrest as a half-time principal while also working with North, another elementary school in the district. She eventually left that school, then began splitting time between Suncrest and Wiles Hills. In the 1993–1994 school year she became a full-time principal at Suncrest.

Sue's background in different schools placed her in roles where the skills at collaboration and teamwork that have marked her work at Suncrest began to develop. Her earliest thoughts on being a teacher and principal were not particularly positive:

My mother was an elementary school teacher. And the one thing I had always said that I would not do is be an elementary school teacher. "Oh look, see Dick run and jump and play ball. Oh see Spot, see Fluff." All that was all over my house and everything I ever owned would be at school at some time because mother would borrow it. And she taught in a country school so I had her for my teacher for four years. So it was grades one through six in one room in this country school. So I never wanted to go into elementary education.

Although initially Sue sought a career in secondary teaching. she ended up in elementary teaching. beginning in a nursery school and then moving to an elementary school in the Monongalia School District after completing her bachelor's degree. She completed her master's degree, an intern principal's program, and then moved into administration in an elementary school. In her first position, she was a "teaching principal." She worked with grades four, five, and six in a two-room school building. After one year, became the "supervising principal" at another elementary school, where she completed her certification to become a principal. After three years, that school was closed, and Sue moved on to North Elementary in 1979. At North, Sue was the principal of Curriculum and Instruction, and worked with another administrator in a situation she called "dual principals." She describes her work at North this way:

I really could see a lot of possibilities in that position at that time because I dealt totally with programs, teachers, parents, students. I handled all of that and had the time to meet with curriculum planning, cooperative teacher work. . . . And we had a group of nine people in each of the subject areas so we could talk for one through six in reading. We could talk about one through six in math. We could meet in subgroups in that big school and it really worked well.

A few years after her arrival at North, Sue's co-principal retired, Suncrest Primary was added to her responsibilities at North, and an assistant principal was hired. With the addition of Suncrest, Sue's student population responsibilities combined 700 at North and 210 at Suncrest by the mid-1980s. In a subsequent redistricting and reorganization at the district level in 1990, Sue left North, retained Suncrest, and added Wiles Hill, an elementary school similar in size to Suncrest. Sue cites a change in her responsibilities at North as the impetus for her move into the Suncrest-Wiles Hill arrangement:

> As head principal up there, it was how do you get the money to pay the xerox bill. And how do you raise, take care of this. And a lot of it was just business then, book work and paper work. And I didn't want to do that. That's not what I liked best. I liked working with teachers, staff development, those kinds of things. So I shifted here to Suncrest.

Several things are clear about Sue's leadership at Suncrest. She is a facilitator and a supporter of the work that the teachers do, and much of what she describes as her own leadership style concerns what she sees in the teachers' work and experiences. Much of what Sue says she enjoys about her work as principal relates to how she sees the faculty change.

> What I like about this job—especially working with teachers there—are new things. Things are different. The challenges come in all the time. But I can see people grow, too. And kind of learn together. And I think that's what built this part of our program, the PDS part, that I enjoy the most. Because I've been able to see my teachers, especially during this particular phase, really develop.

With the PDS concept at Suncrest, she enjoys the opportunity to share decision-making responsibilities, and to broaden participation in the responsibilities of running the school. While at Suncrest Sue has been able "to get people to buy in" to decision making, so that she hasn't had to be the sole arbiter.

One benefit of leadership at Suncrest, as she has experienced it, is that her teachers participate freely, and do good grassroots work in the development of plans and ideas, even if consensus is sometimes hard to reach. Sue credits the free participation in part to the degree to which teachers at Suncrest are willing to share with her and with each other. She thinks this sharing contributes to her own ability to share decision-making opportunities with the faculty, and is at the heart of the teachers' abilities to make choices about their own professional lives as well. The shared decision making works for Sue because she fears that more mandated change in the school would not lead to change at all, and would probably weaken whatever leadership status she might have When the Suncrest faculty decided to participate in 4MAT training as part of their professional development strategy, the faculty worked out the plan for their own development and training, a process that Sue feels has worked well for the group, certainly better than if she had devised the plan and then tried to deliver on her own as principal.

> They agreed that *everybody would be trained*. If I had come in here that spring and said OK folks, we're going to take thirteen hours at the University, or we're gonna take twelve hours at the University and then you're gonna take about another nine hours some place else over the next two to three years they would have told me where to go. You know, get another job. We don't need this here.

Sue has seen herself move into the role of a facilitator of professional development for the Suncrest faculty. Her interactions with the faculty have begun to center on helping the teachers create their own opportunities for professional growth and changes in the way the school works with the students, 4Mat being the centerpiece change. She sees her role as having gone beyond, or become different from, instructional leader, because that does not capture the full scope of her work with the teachers.

> So it's, it's a whole different perspective. I am a facilitator. I try very hard to understand and follow what their interests are with which they're working. I am not expert in any particular point.

In the process of becoming a principal-as-facilitator, Sue has learned that she has to "let go" of much of the traditional principal's identity. One key trait to let go of, and even dispel in some cases, was her power over the faculty, or at least the perception that she had power. Her own perception of the power exchange was in the form of "Here, help yourself," recognizing that with new forms of power for the faculty came new forms of responsibility. Sue feels that that transition has not been a particularly easy one, particularly where the acceptance of power to make decisions was not as quickly met with the assumption of responsibility for the use of power in the decision-making process at Suncrest: "It isn't a one-way thing."

In many cases, the new decision-making arrangements at Suncrest have worked well. Teachers do not go "through" Sue with as much of their professional interactions outside the school as they might have in the past. Teachers are now taking care of much of the scheduling of their own professional activities, either outside the school or with other teachers inside the school, that traditionally would have been worked out with the principal or at least contingent upon her approval, including teacher interactions with each other, with teaches at other schools, with the University, and with the school district central office.

Much of the school's capacity to operate under these kinds of relationships and understandings depends, according to Sue, on the constant communication that goes on at Suncrest. Sue includes supporting the interactions that go into that communicative strategy as part of her role as facilitator. The level of trust and support that is a part of this interaction moves leadership into the group and increasingly out of the hands of the principal. In that sense, the teachers have taken on the responsibility that comes with empowerment, albeit shared with Sue.

> They are a very go-getter group. They set their goals and they really push to get there. They've done far more than I think I could have ever guided them.

In a practical sense, that has meant giving some of the routine principal's traditional job to the faculty, as well as developing among the faculty an understanding of what those routine jobs are about. One example was Sue's attempt to give the faculty control over budgetary decisions, and then tying that to cross-grade level work and decision making:

> I wanted to see us move from a kindergarten, a first grade, a second grade, a third grade to a K–3 program with ties between the grades. A perfect example of that is it's very expensive in consumable materials to outfit your kindergarten and first grade. Third grade is not as expensive. So in the past appropriations of funds would be a little heavier in kindergarten and first grade. Well then the third grade teacher says, well, if the kindergarten teacher gets four hundred dollars to spend and I only get two hundred dollars. I realize there's two different groups of kids. But I only got two hundred dollars. They don't really see why. But if you can get people to walk in someone else's shoes for a while and see the consumable materials, the hands-on kinds of materials that you need so that they can understand what the others person's needs are, you're gonna get a better picture. And you're gonna get a tie. So we've tied together financially.

This process has also facilitated teachers moving in and out of each others rooms more freely and created more contact between colleagues within the school. Teachers spend time covering for each other across grade levels, which brings teachers in contact with different levels of learning. Teachers are also able, under such conditions, to free up time to spend working collaboratively or to pursue opportunities such as staff development within the school site and with other sites. As Sue said, "So now we're not only sharing monies, we're sharing planning and we can do a school wide activity." Sue also gives more of her time helping teachers who need to be outside their own classrooms or working in a colleague's classroom. Sue benefits by working more closely with the day-to-day activities in the classrooms and by supporting teachers in endeavors outside the school.

This degree of interaction and role sharing is made possible in part by the amount of time that the teachers at Suncrest and Sue invest in meeting as a group for planning. The group meets every Tuesday morning as a staff and once a month as a "faculty senate." The group meets at least four times every month, and some months as many as six times. This means communication is a principal's responsibility and increasingly a faculty responsibility, and it provides Sue with an abundance of opportunities to "touch all these people." Sue also feels that her constant interaction with the faculty reduces the number and the scope of problems that might develop in the school. The groups interact regularly enough that "nothing is there so long that it gets to be a big, big problem." As she describes the sharing and the group leadership that is developing, "They're making choices and learning and sharing. I'm not having to provide that."

The faculty's decision to go to 4MAT as the key curricular and instructional change for the school not only has changed the school in an instructional sense, it has represented much of what the school is symbolically and what Sue is as a leader. Sue highlights the adoption of the 4MAT strategy as a major turning point in her own professional development and a turning point for the school.

> Careerwise, for me the turning point in my personal staff development, you know, professional growth, came in the commitment to work with the teachers on the 4MAT program.

> That's the start. I think that started it. Kind of like retreading. You know what I mean. Just really relearning a lot of things.

The 4MAT program is a learning styles strategy where teachers attempt to accommodate instruction to four learning styles quadrants that tap into different learning characteristics. The strategies incorporate left and right brain activities in each of four learning styles. The four quadrants (grossly simplified) are: 1) those who want to know "why"; 2) those who want to know "what"; 3) those who want to know "how"; and 4) those who want to know "what if." Not only do the teachers and Sue try to recognize how instruction and learning might be better accomplished through a recognition of the different styles in their students, they attempt to be sensitive to each others' differences as professionals in their day-to-day interactions. Sue feels that this attention to different needs and tendencies has helped the faculty members learn about each other, and in her mind "that's one of the strongest things that has happened" in Suncrest as a PDS.

> And I think that it has helped all of us at my school as adults working with parent volunteers, working with outside agencies working with just

anybody. You kind of get an idea of how to . . . help them visualize
something that is not particularly their favorite way to work. So I think
we've really come a long way with that.

The increased interaction, the enhanced communication and the interpersonal understandings that have developed at Suncrest have become hallmarks
of increasing team leadership, with Sue as a facilitator of the team. Sue uses the
metaphor of the hand to describe the professional culture of the school, and the
palm of the hand as her place in the school. "We work like a hand, you know.
The thumb doesn't work without the rest. The little finger can't do much without
the rest." And she continues in describing her role as the principal by saying:

> I think I must be the palm. I have to hold them all together. Sometimes it's
> just a part. I think part of my job is to keep us connected and keep people
> caring and support them. You know, much like the palm supports the
> fingers.

And Sue sees those aspects of her role as principal-as-facilitator reflected back
to her from her faculty. She respects the ways that the faculty works together,
how they work out differences as a group. The faculty sets the direction and
decides how they want to get there, while Sue provides the support from her
end. Sue has learned that as her faculty takes over more and more of the
responsibility for the school, they need her more, not less (reflected in the fact
that in the 1993–1994 school year she became a full-time principal for
Suncrest).

Sue has come to gain strength as a leader from the degree of responsibility
that the faculty has assumed, and from the support that has come with the
enhanced communication, interaction, and sharing.

> I have a lot of trust in them. They've learned that. They know that I trust
> them and trust their judgment, and respect their expertise. And that I am a
> willing learner right along with them.

Sue has come to appreciate her own leadership abilities and style by
witnessing the degree of trust that the teachers have developed for each other,
and the respect they are gaining for each others' opinions and advice: "I think
they've really grown in their positions."

Sue's impression of what her leadership style is and its meaning are born
out in faculty impressions of her as a principal. Not only do the teachers feel the
empowered status that Sue has tried to generate, they feel the support that she
gives them in the process of creating new decision-making structures. As one of
the teachers at Suncrest said, "One of the things that I find almost contradicts

itself is that she allows us to be leaders in a lot of ways but yet we find we're needing her more and more." Another describes what Sue's leadership has instilled as "ownership":

> You know, we kind of go to her and say, you bow, what about this and by her giving us the freedom we then have that ownership. And then of course the leadership follows after that. But I think ownership became, or came before leadership. I think that has helped us a lot to grow as much as Sue has talked about, is because we feel a Commitment to that.

The faculty also recognizes Sue's role in pulling together the ideas for the group, and being the support in the center. They have felt supported by Sue's ability to fill in for them in ways that limits on their time do not allow. One such role that Sue plays for them is providing the coordination for a group of teachers who are involved in many different instructional and professional development activities at once. Sue helps to build the connections among different people who have developed different roles, and her support helps the teachers accommodate to the new demands on their energies and schedules. Sue also helps the teachers build the confidence to accept the responsibility that comes with being empowered and being decision makers for the school.

The teachers also see Sue as providing a conduit with the school district central office gaining support externally for the ideas and strategies that the teachers value while protecting the faculty in situations where central office support may not be immediate. One of the teachers comments on this role for Sue:

> Sue knows the system better than we do as classroom teachers. I mean we know what affects us directly. And we're learning more as we emerge as leaders and kind of spread out into other things. But we need that expertise that she brings.

Sue added that she did see part of her work as "keeping them in the county." In many cases the faculty wanted to change in ways that might have come in conflict with ideas or regulations external to the school. Sue took on the task of buffering the external constituents. "And then that kind of just puts our plan in both the PDS sector as well as presenting it to the county, or to the on-site team or whoever happens to come to review us."

Finally, Sue has learned a few things about herself as a principal in a PDS. She has found that she has had to learn to be a risk taker, having not been one to take a risk without prompting. As she says:

> I'm much more comfortable in doing things and watching and then maybe experiencing it later. So I had really tried to do that. I've tried to be a risk

taker. With my faculty you have to do that because they have all kinds of wonderful ideas. So I'll, we'll, let's go with it.

And Sue, in the end, describes the rewards of being a PDS principal at Suncrest in terms of what she sees in the teachers with whom she works:

I really enjoy being a part of this. It is a lot of work, but you know it's very rewarding. It's almost as rewarding to see a teacher grow as it is when the teacher says how thrilled she is to see the student grow. When I see them take on and accomplish tasks that really have made them use the talents that they have with other teachers and with other adults, or even with the parent groups. You know, presenting to a parent group. I can see how far they've grown in working and that strengthens me. It really is wonderful to have had the opportunity.

Contextual Leadership Lessons

Much can be gained from the stories of people who have experienced the PDS process from perspectives such as those of Tom Hart and Sue Lynch. Although their experiences and the points we can gain from them are probably not generalizable to all Professional Development Schools in all contexts, they may provide some insights for others who are sharing or about to share experiences that connect to Tom's and Sue's. Murphy and Beck capture the essence of their struggles and opportunities well:

Principals must find their authority in their personal, interpersonal, and professional competencies, not in formal positions; they must cultivate collegiality, cooperation, and shared commitments among all with whom they work. (1994, 15)

These same characteristics are cited by Rosenblum and her colleagues (Rosenblum et al. 1994) as the basis for good leadership, and for supporting the quality of life of teachers in the change process as well. Their works include a focus on vision and values, empowering others, modelling risk taking, a focus on people, and a commitment to educational quality. The experiences of Sue and Tom reflect these qualities as well.

Tom is in transition, trying to achieve balance in many different ways at Morgantown High School. Tom and the faculty are sorting out the proper balance between their shared desire for Tom to be an envisioner and speaker for the change process, and his need to be a listener and facilitator of the changes that result. This creates the combined responsibility of assuming a new leadership style that calls for participatory decision making, consensus building, facilitation, and support, while at the same time retaining the traditional position of ultimate responsibility at the top of the organizational hierarchy. In that sense, he is a point person for a school that is grappling with the transition from an "organization" to a "community" (Sergiovanni 1992), a transition that at times disempowers him greatly as a leader at points where he is expected to exercise power. His struggle is to exercise power at a point where the transformation process seeks to empower others, while adhering to socially negotiated terms with his faculty. Tom and Morgantown High School are living through the experience of changing from a bureaucratic organization with professional tendencies to a professional community with bureaucratic tendencies.

In his role as principal of a PDS, Tom must deal with security, risk, and fear issues that result from the process of becoming a different kind of school. While those concerns are not his alone—the faculty participate in their construction—he does take on alone the responsibility of confronting them. And in the process of dealing with those concerns and the tensions they produce, Tom's position as principal sometimes puts him at the fulcrum of several balancing acts. First of all, Tom is looking for a balance in the requirements placed upon him to be both a bureaucratic leads and a facilitator of faculty leadership. Second, and connected to the first, Tom has to balance the legacy of a faculty tempered by more authoritarian principals in a school with a history of top-down leadership. He therefore must not only struggle with his own tendency to be more authoritarian, he must struggle with a seasoned faculty that knows that there is a certain "security" in more top-down leadership strategies. There are also times—such as during the period of the schedule change—when that historically accepted, more authoritarian leadership style gives the impression that there are easy solutions to problems. Third, Tom is balancing between his own tendency to provide a vision for the school based on his own ideas of what should be, and his recognition and respect for the faculty's responsibility and power to develop a vision for the school. Teacher empowerment does not necessarily negate Tom's desire or responsibility to participate, but it does create for an uncertain if not ambiguous leadership and participation context that must be sorted out (or at least made more comfortable). Finally, and generated out of the first three, Tom has to live with the sometimes uncomfortable and frustrating role of supporting participatory decision making while knowing that he will still be the "decision maker of last resort" in some cases.

Sue has been able to draw on her past experiences in a more positive way than Tom. Her leadership experiences have been for the most part in situations where she was a co-principal or a teaching principal. She has also experienced situations where the teachers with whom she worked took on responsibilities of leadership because they shared Sue with another school. This has provided Sue with leadership contexts that by nature and necessity have been communicative and oriented toward establishing connections across roles. Sue has also been able to rely on the strength of those relationships to nurture teamwork, group decision making, and group leadership. She has not only put a great deal of effort into the construction of professional connections and communication at Suncrest, she has been a willing participant and supporter of them. The closeness of the group of professionals in the school has nurtured and been nurtured by a sense of trust and respect by Sue for the teachers, and Sue tends to assess her own identity as a leader by the qualities she sees in the teachers. She has been able, through her leadership, to help the teachers construct a sense of "ownership," while concurrently becoming a leader in the eyes of those who claim the ownership. In that sense, both leadership and ownership are constructions that Sue and the faculty share.

There are also leadership themes that are part of the experiences of both Sue Lynch and Tom Hart, and that have come to define leadership for each of them. As in the change process for teachers, principals do not become new kinds of leaders through prescription. The process of examining new possibilities and coming to terms with appropriate leadership styles is highly contextual. As Hallinger and Hausman (1994) argue:

> Although the importance of the principal to the success of school restructuring is often asserted, there is no consensus among practitioners, researchers, or policy makers as to the appropriate role of the principal in a restructured school. (173)

Both Sue and Tom would probably make that claim as well. As principals, they effect change within the context of history, their own histories and their schools'. Suncrest has a history of sharing a principal, which has probably fostered some degree of independence on the part of the teachers, and a set of expectations about the teacher-principal relationship. At Morgantown High, on the other hand, the history of a much more direct form of leadership, compounded by a senior faculty with a great deal of time under that leadership style, has created a group of teachers who are much less likely to have experienced a high degree of school-wide decision-making authority. This historical context should not be taken lightly. The social and historical context of change, particularly in a role as visible as "leader," can provide key insights as to where particular sensitivities might be found in a school considering restructuring issues and questions. And as Bowers (1984) argues, one way to gain ownership over the construction of a culture is to examine its history, thus making more evident the meanings and beliefs by which those in the culture operate.

Sue and Tom have also experienced the tensions that come with being the leader of a school that is looking for new ways of looking at schooling, while participating in a broader organizational structure (central office) that may not be moving as quickly toward new ideas, if it is moving at all. They therefore work at a point of tension between the desire for change and the bureaucratic tendency to preserve the status quo. They suffer from the simultaneous demands of top-down and bottom-up decision-making and leadership strategies. They are being asked to provide the bridge between the pressures of organizational models of school from above and the needs of school as community from below (Sergiovanni 1992). Cuban, synthesizing a collection of research on the nature of the principalship, summarizes the tension as this:

> What becomes apparent from these studies and an awareness of the post's origins is a DNA of principaling. Positioned between their superiors who want orders followed and the teachers who do the actual work in the classrooms, principals are driven by imperatives of which they have little control. Their responsibility to act far exceeds their authority to command; their loyalties are dual: to their school and to headquarters; the professional and political expectations for what should occur in the school conflict; they are maintainers of stability and agents of change. In short, embedded within the principalship is genetic material, to extend the metaphor, that shapes to a large degree (but not totally) what principals do. (Cuban 1988, 61).

Cuban's analysis can also be extended to the tension that Tom feels within his school to still carry some of the characteristics of a bureaucratic leader, particularly when risk taking seems to be a bit riskier. Both Sue and Tom live in the administrative buffer zone between school and the broader educational community. Sue and Tom are coming to grips with this responsibility, and possibly transforming it. Murphy and Hallinger (1992, 80–81) discuss the redefinition of roles that such a position and the roles therein present for principals, and highlight its "ambiguity," "uncertainty," "complexity," and "turbulence." They add to that commentary on the general role of principaling the "schizophrenia" that comes with higher organizational level calls for simultaneously decentralizing and centralizing authority in schools.

The look "up" into the organization of a school from the perspective of Sue and Tom does not give the same light on the change process that looking "into" the school community does. Looking into that community, they see characteristics they share with teachers, albeit colored by the historically different nature of the roles of teachers and principals. Cuban argues that teachers and principals share three binding elements: 1) both work in bureaucratic organizations; 2) both tend to be (at least for much of their experiences) solo practitioners; and 3) both seek professional autonomy (1988, 180–182). One more characteristic that both teachers and principals would seem to share in Morgantown High School and Suncrest Primary is that as much as they can they are attempting to resist 1), and 2) change outright 3). As the connections, communication, and relationships in the schools have become mere constructive, they have developed as leaders together, and have developed autonomy mutually, a phenomenon Cuban describes this way:

> Decisions blend facts, values, beliefs, perceptions and experiences. Those decisions and the actions taken in their wake become the marginal autonomy available to teachers and administrators, which is a necessary (but not sufficient) condition for leadership. (Cuban 1988, 190)

Smylie and Brownlee-Conyers (1992) argue that the successful negotiations of the tensions involved in role redefinitions by principals and teachers create the time necessary for school improvement. They argue that this negotiation and redefinition are born out of several characteristics of professional life in schools for teachers and principals, including "ambiguity and uncertainties" about their inter-role relationships, the "interests and prerogatives" of players in the new relationships, "expectations for teacher leadership," "interpersonal obligations," "strategic interaction" to construct relationships, and "key events" in the development of new relationships (162–169).

This set of issues and concerns is not far from Sergiovanni's emphasis on the characteristics that come to define a school as a community, and mesh well with the kinds of issues Sue and Tom have raised as principals of Professional Development Schools. Sergiovanni (1992) argues that:

> Communities are defined by their centers. Centers are repositories of values, sentiments, and beliefs that provide the needed cement for uniting people in a common cause. Centers govern the school values and provide norms that guide behavior and give meaning to school community life. (41)

He further points out that as schools come to be seen as communities in this sense, and a sense of the collective identity becomes more established, "a principal can afford to give much less attention to the traditional management functions" (42). Murphy and Hallinger (1992, 82) argue that at such a point principals become "transformational leaders," move from centralization of decisions to participatory structures, enhance and support the decision-making opportunities for teachers, and rely more greatly on interpersonal relationships and communication with teachers as a mark of leadership.

In such a community, Sergiovanni argues, the "motivational rules" are transformed. "What is rewarded gets done," and "What we believe in, think to be good, and feel obligated to do gets done" (Sergiovanni 1992, 44). This aptly describes the work that Tom Hart and Sue Lynch pursue in their efforts as principals of Professional Development Schools. They are both coming to define who they are as leaders through their relationships with the teachers with whom they work, and teachers are beginning to reflect back to them the kinds of participation and teacher leadership they are seeking to establish. Both are still wrestling with having feet in both the "old school" and the "new school" of leadership, and each in his and her own way is dealing with unique and common concerns and questions. But they are both becoming new kinds of leaders for new kinds of schools.

References

Berger, P. L. and Luckman, T. (1967). *The social construction of reality: A treatise in the sociology of knowledge.* Garden City, N.Y.: Doubleday Anchor.

Bowers, C. A. (1984). *The promise of theory: Education and the politics of cultural change.* New York: Longman.

Cuban, L. (1988). *The managerial imperative and the practice of leadership in schools.* Albany,: State University of New York Press.

Hallinger, P. (1992). The evolving role of American principals: From managerial to instructional to transformational leaders. *Journal of Educational Administration* 30(3): 35–48.

Hallinger, P. and Hausman, C. (1994). From Attila the Hun to Mary had a little lamb: Principal role and ambiguity in restructured schools. In Murphy, J. and Louis, K.S., eds., *Reshaping the Principalship: Insights from transformational reform effects*, pp. 154–176. Thousand Oaks, Cal.: Corwin Press.

Murphy, J. and Beck, L. (1994). Reconstructing the principalship: Challenges and Possibilities. In Murphy, J. and Louis, K.S., eds., *Reshaping the principalship: Insights from transformational reform effects*, pp. 3–19. Thousand Oaks, Cal.: Corwin Press.

Murphy, J. and Hallinger, P. (1992). The principalship in an era of transformation. *Journal of Educational Administration*, 30(3): 77–88.

Rosenblum, S., Louis, K.S., and Rossmiller, R. (1994). School leadership and teacher quality of work life. In Murphy, J. and Louis, K.S., eds., *Reshaping the principalship: Insights from transformational reform effects*, pp. 99–122. Thousand Oaks, Cal.: Corwin Press.

Smylie, M.A. and Brownlee-Conyers. (1992). Teacher leaders and their principals: Exploring the development of new working relationships. *Educational Administration Quarterly* 28(2): 150–184.

Sergiovanni, T.J. (1992a). *Moral leadership: Getting to the heart of school improvement.* San Francisco: Jossey Bass.

Sergiovanni, T.J. (1992b). Why we should seek substitutes for leadership. *Educational Leadership* 49(5): 41–45.

7

The Story of Changing Practice:
Classroom-Based Collaboration as a Model
for a Communications Program

Jennifer Borsch, Ruth Oaks, and Cheryl Prichard

This chapter describes one aspect of the reform work going on at Central Elementary, a collaboration between the school and WVU's speech pathology preparation program. (See Chapter 3 for more background information on the school.) This collaboration is not rooted in the redesign of teacher preparation like the efforts described in Chapter 10 or in a school-wide initiative like the reforms described in Chapter 8. This collaboration has not restructured the school like the efforts described in Chapter 9. This collaboration began with one teacher and one speech pathologist who were both unhappy with the impact their work was having on children. After the teacher describes the origin and evolution of the collaboration, the authors briefly review the literature on classroom collaboration and speech pathology programs. The chapter then analyzes the impact of the program on participants and closes with a personal assessment by the teacher. Lists of resources and readings are provided in appendices.

A Classroom Teacher's Perspective: In the Beginning

In the beginning, there was a need. Although I was an experienced teacher, I still was unable to meet all the needs of my class of twenty-two third graders. Included in my class were two hearing impaired boys who were main-streamed into my classroom for the first two periods every day for math and handwriting. We somehow managed to communicate, although no one in my class, including me, knew sign language. The boys always arrived late, did what they had to do and left, with little interaction with the other children in the class or with me. When we were reciting our times tables, their presence became more of a challenge. The day I remember especially well began with their BURSTING into the room, DUMPING their books onto their desks, and

CLOMPING back to me in the back of the room. One of them fastened the auditory trainer around my neck, while the other one climbed onto my lap, perusing my grade book. As each child finished the times table recitation, the hearing impaired boy would announce to the rest of the class the grade I had just recorded. Neither of them said their times tables—after all, they were deaf. That day at lunch, I talked to our speech-language pathologist, Jennifer. I was quite upset that the hearing impaired children were not following our third grade classroom rules. Our conversation continued on the phone that night. We agreed that the two boys could learn their times tables and could sit in their seats and listen to the others.

Together, Jennifer and I developed some strategies. I was determined to try them and hoped they would work. I spent the next week working with the two boys and the class. I encouraged the boys to follow our classroom rules, which an interpreter signed to them. They were very willing to try to abide by them. I also found that in a situation where the boys' only task was to listen, it was certainly much more satisfying if the microphone to the auditory trainers was held by the speaker. The boys' behavior improved. I was proud to report to Jennifer at lunch a week later that things were certainly going better in the third grade math class. The boys were listening and were even reciting their times tables, even though one boy was saying, "Pip time nine is pipty pour." Jennifer let me know in no uncertain terms that he could say those words and should be required to do so.

Jennifer realized that there was no carryover of the speech skills she worked so diligently on in her pull-out therapy sessions; she had been feeling successful! Jennifer and I talked and came to the conclusion that somehow we together could see that the boys learned the skills and practiced them in their mainstreamed classroom. The most logical solution was for Jennifer to come into my classroom, not as an observer but as a partner to work on the communication skills for all the children in the third grade room, not just these two targeted boys.

So we met and we planned. We talked on the phone at night, before school and after school, on our joint lunch hours, and worked out our plans to teach together. What fun we had! We both were a little intimidated about teaching in front of each other, but that quickly ended after we realized we were exchanging far more encouragement than criticism.

When we first began, our principal did not favor the collaborative project. I was told that my class would have to give up the thirty-minute afternoon recess to make up for the time Jennifer "wasted" in my room. When I tried to explain that my work with Jennifer blended beautifully with my language arts program, I was again admonished to make up the time. This less than enlightened view did not deter us at all. The class loved what we were doing, and they never seemed to object to missing recess for a day.

Our mutual desire to continue and indeed expand the collaborative communications program prompted us to write a proposal requesting that the Benedum Collaborative support our program. Support to continue the program was forthcoming, and Jennifer became our Communication Consultant. She came to our school one day a week and worked with the classroom teachers in kindergarten through sixth grade, teaching communication skills to all the children in the school.

As our core communications program became established, it soon became evident that we needed to tap additional resources, as well as to begin to promote our program as a training site for students and other educators. Cheryl Prichard, a speech-language pathologist and an assistant professor in the Department of Speech Pathology and Audiology at West Virginia University (WVU), agreed to become a new collaborative partner.

Our team, now consisting of a classroom teacher, a speech-language consultant, and a university faculty member, began to design and implement a preservice training program to allow graduate students in speech pathology to experience the collaborative model first hand. (A more detailed discussion of the preservice training site will follow.) We wanted to involve preservice pathologists because working with children in a public school therapeutic setting presents so many challenges for speech-language pathologists. These challenges include scheduling difficulties (trying to accommodate classroom activities, teachers' schedules, school schedules, and the speech-language pathologist's schedule), allowing time for planning and paperwork, finding an adequate or appropriate place to work, accessing available funding for supplies and materials, obtaining parent support for home follow-through, and assuring carryover of learned skills from the treatment setting to other contexts. The communication class program at Central has successfully resolved the lack of skill carryover from the therapy room to the classroom. We wanted to share this model with prospective speech pathologists.

Does the Literature Reflect Real Life?

What we have done at Central is often advocated in the literature on speech pathology. The recent professional literature and the presentation circuit are replete with discussions of why classroom collaboration is a viable model for speech pathology, how it should be done, and suggestions for who should assume the responsibility (Achilles, Yates, and Freese 1991; Christensen and Luckett 1990; Cooper 1991; Ellis, Schlaudecker, and Regimbal, 1995; Magnotta 1991; Moore-Brown 1991; Russel and Kaderavek 1993; Secord 1990). Publishers are rushing to bring forth materials for classroom communication activities in various subject areas. Unfortunately, the literature is also replete with research that documents the reluctance of speech-language pathologists and classroom teachers to implement the classroom collaboration model.

Prerequisites for Collaboration

The literature on this sort of collaboration reflects the same issues evident in Chapter 2. For successful collaboration to occur, the collaborators must focus on the child and be prepared to work together to reach their mutual goal. A genuine respect between partners is essential. Collaboration is facilitated when there is a belief that educators who bring together diverse areas of expertise are more likely to have a positive impact on children.

What makes the Central collaborative partnership so successful, so comfortable? The success of any new program is due to the willingness of the participants to take risks. The teacher's reflections emphasize this:

> I used to be very afraid of change. I felt I was a good enough teacher. I knew my children learned from me. They always succeeded in the fourth grade, and frequently I saw some of their names on the Honor Roll at the local high school. I received no hate mail from the parents, and the children spoke to me if they saw me at the mall. I must be doing OK. Our PDS work encouraged me to change, not by anything that was provided me or told me, but because one of the basic goals of the project is "risk-taking." Their philosophy emphasizes that there are no mistakes just "little tries." I began to say to myself, "Well, if I can't make a mistake, why not try a few new things?" The steps I have taken have been small and rather few in number, but I see in myself a whole new teacher with an entirely new attitude when I look in my locker mirror today.

Several factors have been identified in the literature as necessary for developing a collaboration project to improve communication skills. The most important factors for the program at the Central included: (1) establishing rapport, (2) identifying target students, (3) establishing goals, and (4) performing/conducting lessons through a variety of modes. Our rapport grew as we planned to address a mutual goal. We have used a number of modes of collaboration in the collaboration project at Central. These are listed in Table 7.1.

Central Elementary School as a Preservice Training Site for SPA Students

Are speech pathology students prepared to function in a classroom collaboration program?

Although professionals in the field are implementing collaborative programs and are urging others to do the same, and publishers are rushing to capitalize on the market for classroom-based materials, there is little evidence that preservice preparation programs for speech-language pathologists and

TABLE 7.1

Different Modes of Collaboration at Central

---

1. The teacher and speech-language pathologist team teach mutually identified lessons during whole language activities.
2. The speech-language pathologist teaches a specific lesson in the regular classroom to all students related to a topic as requested by the teacher (the lesson may be curriculum related or based on some other classroom need).
3. The speech-language pathologist teaches disability awareness to all students in the school (especially related to the health curriculum).
4. The speech-language pathologist teaches a lesson to the regular class emphasizing specific communication skills (listening, speaking, or thinking).
5. The classroom teacher teaches a lesson or adapts a planned lesson to supplement the communication skills being taught by the speech-language pathologist.
6. The speech-language pathologist or classroom teacher teaches a lesson to the regular class based on a particular student's IEP goals.
7. The speech-language pathologist develops learning stations for the classroom (to be supervised by the teacher).
8. The speech-language pathologist observes and monitors target students while the teacher is conducting a regular lesson or one that has been mutually planned.
9. The classroom teacher observes and monitors target students while the speech-language pathologist is conducting a regular lesson or one that has been mutually planned.
10. The teacher and speech-language pathologist jointly select an area to be targeted for the class.

---

teachers are teaching students how to begin the process of collaboration. The majority of training institutions are providing limited, if any, instruction in the classroom collaboration model. A study by Prichard and Borsch (1991) revealed that the majority of speech-language pathologists working in West Virginia reported that the classroom collaboration model was not a model for which they felt they had been adequately trained. In fact, most of the speech-language pathologists reported that they had learned about this model of service delivery through their own reading, attending professional development workshops, exchanging information with colleagues, or simply by plunging in and doing it.

How did our preservice classroom collaboration program begin?

As one part of a grant-funded effort to prepare speech clinicians for service in rural areas, the "Rural Project" graduate students enrolled in the Department of Speech Pathology and Audiology at West Virginia University take specialized course work to help meet the challenges of working in a remote or rural setting. A portion of a course focused on alternative service delivery models (alternatives to the traditional "pull-out" model). This seemed to be an ideal place to provide some beginning instruction in the collaborative model. Initial efforts centered on reading journal articles, viewing videotapes, and guest lectures by a speech pathologist (Jennifer Borsch) and a classroom teacher (Ruth Oaks) who had been working collaboratively. While this seemed a reasonable beginning, it was not enough. One day, one of the students raised her hand and somewhat timidly said, "I think this is probably a good idea and it seems that all these people who are doing the collaborative programming are convinced that it works, but I just can't picture how you actually do it." As teachers, we believe the Chinese proverb "Tell me, I'll forget. Show me, I may remember. Involve me, and I'll understand." This seemed to be a perfect opportunity to involve the students, that is, to actually let them try some classroom collaboration activities. Since Ruth and Jennifer are believers in the collaborative model and are ardent in their belief that the program that works for them will work for others, they were willing to accept some student participants. Thus, a group of graduate students were able to begin their training in classroom collaboration at Central. The program began with four students, and eventually eleven graduate students were able to participate. Jennifer, as Central's communication consultant, and Cheryl, as the university clinical practicum supervisor, served as the on-site supervisors for the graduate students.

How did the program operate?

The collaborative classroom placement option was eventually required of students supported by the rural grant. Each student supported by the grant spent one morning each week at Central for one semester. The practicum experience was divided into three phases: observation of the supervisor presenting lessons, teaming with the speech-language pathologist clinical supervisor to present classroom lessons, and direct classroom programming delivered under clinical supervision. During each semester, four or five students and two supervisors comprised the Communications Team. Two or three students were assigned to each supervisor. Supervisors and student clinicians consulted with classroom teachers and other specialists, such as the reading specialist, the teacher of the hearing impaired, and the building-level administrator.

As part of the observation phase, student clinicians observed the classroom teachers in their respective rooms during routine activities. The students were instructed to observe the teachers' styles of interaction with the children; the daily schedule of classes; the means of discipline employed in the classrooms; materials that were utilized; and the overall "personality" of each class. In a second phase of observation, the student clinicians observed their supervisor in the classroom directing communication activities for two or three sessions in each classroom. Initially, student clinicians were instructed to simply "watch" the session to determine how the students were responding to the activities and to the supervisor. No observation sheets were required for the initial communication activity. The student clinicians met with their supervisor to discuss the sessions, ask questions, and review the procedures used. Additional observations of the supervisor directing communication activities were also required. In these subsequent observations, the students were instructed to complete formal observation sheets and were asked to target students who seemed to be having difficulty. Again, followup meetings were held to discuss the sessions that were observed. Upon completion of the observations, the students participated in a team teaching exercise with the supervisor. This exercise varied from classroom to classroom. In some classes, they helped to model appropriate responses for selected activities; and, in other classes, they worked with a small group within the class. In each of these instances, the supervisor was responsible for determining goals and activities and for gathering materials or determining the prepared materials to be utilized in the class. Students participated in this team teaching mode for two or three sessions. Following the team teaching experience, the supervisor determined the goals and activities and suggested materials and resources for approximately two additional sessions. For the remaining weeks of the semester, the supervisor served in an advisory/consultative role and discussed each session with the student clinicians, but typically did not participate in the session. For the team teaching sessions and the student-clinician directed sessions, the supervisor provided verbal and/or written feedback to the student clinicians regarding their performance.

Weekly planning meetings were held to provide supervisor feedback, review the student evaluations of the communications activities, discuss problems, and brainstorm future goals and activities. As the semester progressed, the students assumed more of a leadership role in these conferences, and the supervisor served more as a consultant.

How did the student clinicians respond to this new practicum experience?

The initial responses from the students varied. Some expressed feelings of curiosity, excitement, anxiety and skepticism. All of our students were enrolled full-time in the graduate program, two had worked as clinicians in school settings prior to returning to graduate school, some of them had completed traditional placements in the schools, some had hospital placements, and all of them had experience in the Department's outpatient clinic. None had participated in a collaborative program like this one.

The concerns expressed initially by the student clinicians centered on maintaining control of a large number of children in the classroom, finding enough activities to keep the class involved for a half-hour session, and working in the classroom with the teacher present. As the semester progressed, the students expressed less and less anxiety. Near the end of the second semester, one student related the following: "At the beginning of the semester, I was just sick each Thursday night [because she visited Central on Friday mornings], knowing I was going to have to stand up in front of the class and direct the lesson. As the semester went on, I began to look forward to it. The kids really looked forward to us coming and it was fun."

As a group, we had numerous discussions about the issue of "therapy" being fun. With respect to therapy, the student clinicians seemed to hold the idea that if it does not taste bad, it cannot be good for you. Our students were in the habit of having to devise games and locate reinforcers to get clients to respond. Being faced with a room full of eager students who actually wanted to communicate was a new experience. Throughout the semester, the student clinicians remarked about students in the classes who had been hesitant to talk at the beginning of the semester but by the end of the semester were actually volunteering to be called on.

As a part of a final evaluation for the semester, the supervisors met with the student clinicians and solicited comments and suggestions for improving the program. Each of the students expressed the idea that this program should be continued and indeed expanded. The students suggested that this experience should be made available for all students who will work in the schools. They indicated that, while working in the classroom was initially a bit intimidating, it was a positive experience and one that was a real "confidence booster." At the end of the semester, one student stated, "I'm sure I'll try this now. I don't think as a new clinician I would have been comfortable doing this if I hadn't had the opportunity to try it as a student." Students who have completed their graduate education and are now working in school settings continue to call and request materials that they used in the Central program or call and tell us about some new materials they have found or developed. Many of the students completed semester-long externship placements in school settings after completing their collaboration placement and encouraged their externship supervisors to permit them to do some classroom-based programming as part of their practicum experience. They have indeed taken their experiences with them and seem to feel confident enough to share them.

How did the faculty and students at Central respond to the collaborative program?

There have been many changes at Central as a result of our collaborative communications project. Some have been immediate and obvious; many have been subtle. We have experienced changes among our teachers and our students. Central is a school that serves many international children. Recently, we had fifty-four children from twelve countries other than the United States. Since our school has only 120 children, we have a large group of children for whom English is a Second Language (ESL).

Because of our population of international and hearing impaired children, we decided to teach sign language to all the children and teachers in the school. What fun we had with that! Talk about carryover . . . try signing the week's new spelling words with the classroom teacher perfecting her signing ability right along with the children. It has done wonders to bridge the gap between the children with hearing impairments and the other children. The children with hearing impairments love to teach the rest of us new signs or help us perfect our signing. Sign language is a language in which they all can communicate. One of our third-grade girls from Nigeria loved to sign and worked continually to perfect her signing. She told us that in her country only the very rich people knew sign language. She dreamed of stepping off the plane when her family returned home that summer and signing her greetings to the people of her country. "They will all think I am a very rich lady."

The children have grown in other areas as well. Their oral communication skills and confidence in public speaking have improved greatly. When we have all-school assemblies, we now have no trouble getting any elementary child to lead the Pledge or introduce guests. At a recent "Terrific Kids" assembly, where fourteen children were honored, a fifth grade child did the introductions while a second grader led the Pledge of Allegiance. Our teachers agree that this confidence can be directly attributed to the Communications Program, which emphasizes effective speaking skills in every classroom.

As a result of having the SPA graduate students work with them to emphasize certain aspects of subjects we are teaching, the Central students get increased opportunities to use skills they learn in the regular classes. Our students have responded very positively to the idea of having WVU students working with them. They respond favorably to others giving ideas. Having young, educated people come in and tune in to what we are doing is something innovative and educational to our students. Competition has decreased among our children and sharing and encouragement have increased, due to the involvement of the WVU SPA graduate students.

Once the teachers at Central began opening their doors to let others work with their children, they found they liked it. They enjoy collaborating with the SPA students and their supervisors because it adds a new dimension to their teaching. By working together to decide on the needs of the children, then jointly agreeing upon the activities to help meet those needs, they achieve a collaborative effort that is satisfying to all.

The various teachers at Central all seem to interact differently with the SPA people. Some teachers have their lesson plans ready well in advance of the date they are due so they can share them with the SPA students, who take the plans and build their lessons around them. For example, when the SPA students realized that the third grade was beginning a month-long unit on a book entitled *The Mouse and the Motorcycle*, each of the three graduate students who worked in that classroom checked out a copy of the book and read it. Their activities for the month tied in with the book. Other teachers share long-term goals and encourage the development of parallel lessons taught by our SPA collaborative partners on subjects ranging from dinosaurs to Native Americans to Hanukkah. Still other teachers have not felt as comfortable sharing lesson plans with the SPA students and expecting their lessons to mesh with what is going on in the classroom. In those cases, the SPA students have observed in the classroom and reviewed the children's performance on a variety of tasks with the teacher, to identify and develop appropriate activities.

Changes in the area of self-esteem are evident. Central's focus on enhancing self-esteem leads logically to a number of activities that emphasize communication. With the new confidence our children have in their speaking skills, we have witnessed improved self-esteem. Children are initiating conversations with teachers, volunteering for speaking parts in school assemblies, and encouraging other students to participate. These are indeed positive steps.

A second area of change now in evidence is that teachers are allowing and sometimes inviting others into their classrooms to work with them. They have seen how successful this collaboration can be and how good they feel when someone is sharing their load with them. The teachers are now more open to letting people from other departments of the University come in and work with them, are going into each other's classrooms to work collaboratively, and are more comfortable with the push-in Chapter I model.

Resources and Materials

We found that many of the materials and ideas that we were using in the classroom were being adapted and modified for use in the clinic with individual clients (see Appendix A for a list of resources). As one student explained, "If things are practical and reasonable, it just stands to reason that the clients are going to profit more from doing those things."

So, were there any problems?

Of course there were problems. Many of the problems are the same as those reported by other clinicians and teachers who are attempting to incorporate this type of service delivery into their own schedules. The major concern of the graduate clinicians, the Central faculty, and the supervisors was lack of time available for ongoing consultation among the group of teachers, graduate students, and supervisors.

During the program at Central some teachers remained in their rooms and actively participated in the activities and some left their classrooms when the SPA group entered. In some cases, "consulting" with the teacher meant catching her on a break between classes in the hall or leaving notes or telephone messages. The student clinicians reported that they found this somewhat frustrating but could not see an alternative, given the severe time constraints of being in the school only one morning each week. The student clinicians also reported that the thirty-minute sessions we had scheduled were not really long enough to complete some of the planned activities.

At this point in the development of our collaborative program we have identified positive outcomes for all of the participants. For the Central students and teachers, the positive outcomes include: (1) kids initiating conversations with adults other than their own teachers; (2) kids volunteering to emcee at school assemblies; (3) kids demonstrating more effective speaking skills; (4) kids' improved self-esteem; (5) kids loving it; (6) teachers letting others in their classrooms; and (7) improved communication in general. For WVU Speech Pathology and Audiology students and faculty, the positive outcomes include: (1) hands-on experiences in collaborative classrooms; (2) exposure to curricula at various levels (K–6); (3) opportunities for positive interaction with teachers; (4) experience in the classroom—while others are just reading about it; (5) it is fun; and (6) students and supervisors love it.

Final Reflections . . . from the Classroom Teacher

It's Monday morning and I'm not depressed! I ask myself why, and for a long time, I can't explain it. I have taught school for twenty years and in three states. Weekends have always meant laughter, dialogue, camaraderie, and fun. That used to end on Monday mornings, when that other part of my life called "school" began. Monday morning used to be rough. But now school is starting to be more like my weekends. I start every Monday with my collaborative partners—students and clinicians from the WVU Department of Speech Pathology and Audiology. They enter my once closed (and it would have been locked, if it had been permitted) classroom. They skillfully work with my third graders, helping them master communication skills. The signs they have taught my students for "slow down," "speak louder," and "keep eye contact" are being used throughout the lesson, not by the SPA students, but by the children themselves. There is no havoc in my room . . . I thought there would be with four non-teacher adults (three graduate clinicians and a supervisor) leading the lesson. What I am experiencing is a group of professionals who have combined their expertise with mine to provide the best possible program for my children. What we are doing is fun! We laugh, we talk, we learn . . . before we bring the collaborative lesson to the children as well as while we are doing it. My Mondays are really becoming like my weekends!!!

References

Achilles, J., Yates, R. R., and Freese, J. M. (1991). Perspectives from the field: Collaborative consultation in the speech and language program of the Dallas independent school district. *Language, Speech, and Hearing Services in Schools* 22: 154–155.

Christensen, S. S. and Luckett, C. H. (1990). Getting into the classroom and making it work! *Language, Speech, and Hearing Services in Schools* 21: 110–113.

Cooper, C. S. (1991). Using collaborative/consultative service delivery models for fluency intervention and carryover. *Language, Speech, and Hearing Services in Schools* 22: 152–152.

Ellis, L., Schlaudecker, C., and Regimbal, C. (1995). Effectiveness of a collaborative consultation approach to basic concept instruction with kindergarten children. *Language, Speech, and Hearing Services in Schools* 26(1): 69–74.

Magnotta, O. H. (1991). Looking beyond tradition. *Language, Speech, and Hearing Services in Schools* 22(3): 150–151.

Moore-Brown, B. (1991). Moving in the direction of change: Thoughts for administrators and speech-language pathologists. *Language, Speech, and Hearing Services in Schools* 22(3): 148–149.

Prichard, C. L. and Borsch, J. (1991). *Alternative service delivery options in rural public schools*. Paper presented at the annual convention of the American Speech-Language-Hearing Association, Atlanta, Ga.

Russell, S. and Kaderavek, J., (1993). Alternative models for collaboration. *Language, Speech, and Hearing Services in Schools* 24(2): 76–78.

Secord, W. A. (1990). *Best practices in school speech-language pathology*. TX: The Psychological Corporation.

Appendix A: Selected Resources for Collaborative Programs

The following list of materials may assist classroom teachers and SLPs who are interested in beginning a classroom-based collaborative program. While no attempt has been made to provide an exhaustive list, there is sufficient variety to begin to develop a program.

Ameel, K., Paganucci, P., and Rohovsky, K. (1992). *Language links: Whole-language activities based on children's literature*. Tucson: Communication Skill Builders.

Auslin, M. S. (1978). *Pro-ed idiom series raining cats and dogs*. Austin, Tex: Pro-Ed.

Auslin, M. S. (1990). *Dormac idiomseries—out of this world*. San Diego: Dormac Inc.

Bilgo, A. and Kleinhans, S. (1992). *Sounds like fun reproducible articulation stories and games*. Tucson: Communication Skill Builders.

Borsch, J. and Oaks, R. (1992). *Collaboration companion*. East Moline, Ill: Lingui-Systems, Inc.

Burden, C. P. (1991). *Literature gems.* Allen, Tex: DLM.

Children's Language Institute (1990). *Developing preschool language programs: A guide for the slp.* Tucson: Communication Skill Builders.

The Early Education Team The Capper Foundation (1990). *Project kidlink: Bringing together disabled and nondisabled preschoolers.* Tucson: Communication Skill Builders.

Hasse, E. and Hansen, L. (1991). *Collaborate! celebrate! The curriculum-based cooperative language learning in the classroom social studies & science 6th grade.*

Heerman-Jones, C. and Kalat, A. (1991). *Collaborate! celebrate! The curriculum-based cooperative language learning in the classroom social studies & science 3rd grade.*

Hurst, C. A. (1990). *Once upon a time an encyclopedia for successfully using literature with young children.* Allen, Tex.: DLM.

Jeffries, P. and Schroeder, S. (1991). *Collaborate! celebrate! The curriculum-based cooperative language learning in the classroom social studies & science 4th grade.*

Lantz, K. and Parker, K., (1991). *Collaborate! celebrate! The curriculum-based cooperative language learning in the classroom social studies & science 5th grade.*

Lockhart,B. (1987). *Read to me, Talk to me—Language activities based on children's favorite literature.* Tucson: Communication Skill Builders.

Paris, J. and Tracy, S. (1983). *Myths.* San Diego: Dormac Inc.

Paris, J. and Tracy, S. (1989). *More myths.* San Diego: Dormac Inc.

Paris, J. and Tracy, S. (1984). *More fables.* San Diego: Dormac Inc.

Plourd, L. (1990). *Learning language dramatically: Acting out stories in the classroom.* Tucson: Communication Skill Builders.

Plourd, L. (1990). *Classroom listening and speaking (CLAS) by Themes.* Tucson: Communication Skill Builders.

Plourd, L. (1989). *CLAS preschool.* Tucson: Communication Skill Builders.

Plourd, L. (1989). *More CLAS K–2.* Tucson: Communication Skill Builders.

Plourd, L. (1989). *CLAS 3–4.* Tucson: Communication Skill Builders.

Riley, A. M. (1987). *After school communication activity book.* Tucson.: Communication Skill Builders.

Pritchard, E. and Stamos, M. (1991). *Collaborate! celebrate! The curriculum-based cooperative language learning in the classroom language arts for 3rd grade.*

Simon, C., ed. (1991). *Communication skills and classroom success assessment and therapy methodologies for language and learning disabled students.* Eau Claire, Wisc.: Thinking Publications.

Smith, M. S. and Hanson, K. (1991). *Collaborate! celebrate! The curriculum-based cooperative language learning in the classroom language arts for 4th grade.*

Staff of The Communication and Learning Center (1987). *125 ways to be a better student.* East Moline, Ill.: LinguiSystems.

Stitt, S. (1985). *Learning center activities for speech therapy.* Tucson: Communication Skill Builders.

Strommer, A. (1993). *Listening lessons for the classroom curriculum.* Oceanside,Cal.: Academic Communication Associates.

Wilson. C., Lanza, J., and Evans, J. (1992). *The IEP companion: Communication goals for therapy in and out of the classroom.* East Moline, Ill.: LinguiSystems, Inc.

Woude, J. and Italiano, N. (1991). *Collaborate! celebrate! The curriculum-based cooperative language learning in the classroom.*

Other Readings

ASHA (1991). A model for collaborative service delivery for students with language learning disorders in the public schools. *ASHA, 33* (suppl. 5): 44–50.

Borsch, J. (1989). *Improving communication skills in the classroom.* Presentation at the West Virginia Speech-Language-Hearing Convention, Wheeling, W.V.

Dodge, E. P. (1992). Social skills training using a collaborative service delivery model. *Language, Speech, and Hearing Serices in Schools 23*: 30–135.

Elksnin, L. and Capilouto, G. (1994). Speech-language pathologists' perceptions of integrated service delivery in school settings. *Language, Speech, and Hearing Services in Schools 25*(4): 258–267.

Friend, M. and Cook, L. (1992). *Interactions: Collaborative skills for school professionals.* White Plains: Longman Publishing Group.

Fujiki, M. and Brinton, B. (1984). Supplementing language therapy: Working with the classroom teacher. *Language, Speech, and Hearing Services in Schools 15*: 98–109.

Holzhauser-Peters, L. and Husemann, D. A. (1988). Alternative service delivery models for more efficient and effective treatment programs. *The Clinical Connection (Fall)*: 16–19.

Holzhauser-Peters, L. and Husemann, D. A. (1989). Alternative service delivery models: Practical implementation. *The Clinical Connection (Summer)*: 18-21.

Idol, L., Paolucci-Whitcomb, P., and Nevin, A. (1986). *Collaborative consultation.* Austin, Tex.: PRO-ED.

Nelson, N. W. (1989). Curriculum-based language assessment and intervention. Language, Speech, and Hearing Services in Schools 20: 170–184.

Norris, J. A. and Hoffman, P. R. (1990). Language intervention within naturalistic environments. *Language, Speech, and Hearing Services in Schools 21*: 72–84.

Norris, J. A. (1989). Providing language remediation in the classroom: An integrated language-to-reading intervention method. *Language, Speech, and Hearing Services in Schools 20*: 205–218.

Pery, T. L. (1990). Cooperative learning = effective therapy. *Language, Speech, and Hearing Services in Schools 21*: 120.

Pickering, M. (1981). Consulting with the classroom teacher to promote language acquisition. *Topics in Learning and Language Disabilities 2*: 59–67.

Saricks, M. C. (1989). School services and communication disorders. *ASHA (June-July)*: 79-80.

Simon, C. (1987). Out of the broom closet and into the classroom: The emerging SLP. *Journal of Childhood Communication Disorders 11*: 41–66.

Simon, C. S. (1990). *Into the classroom. The slp in the collaborative role.* Tucson: Communication Skill Builders.

Staab, C. F. (1983). Language functions elicited by meaningful activities: A new dimension in language programs. *Language, Speech, and Hearing Services in Schools 14*: 164–170.

West, J. F., Idol, L., and Cannon, G. (1989). *Collaboration in the schools.* Austin, Tex.: PRO-ED.

Westby, E. C. (1990). The role of the speech-language pathologist in whole language. *Language, Speech, and Hearing Services in Schools 21*: 228–237.

8

STORY OF A CHANGING PROGRAM: WEST VIRGINIA'S FIRST SCIENCE, MATH, AND TECHNOLOGY CENTER

MARY ANN GASTON, RAYMOND FRANCIS, JANET CRESCENZI, AND PERRY PHILLIPS

> Eastdale students are clearly aware of the changes in curriculum and teaching brought about through the SMT Center. Commenting on these changes, students said: "The technology is different." "We're like the computer school." "You could call this the school of the future." "We have the Internet." "We have a line even to the White House!"
>
> —(Student interview data gathered in 1995)

Introduction

Since becoming a Professional Development School (PDS), we at East Dale Elementary have completely transformed our approach to curriculum and instruction in science, math, and technology. Our change agenda is based on an evaluation of student needs, societal changes, and emerging directions in science, math, and technology education. We have benefitted from strong administrative leadership, a skilled and committed faculty, and the opportunities for teacher-directed staff development that have been part of our participation in the Benedum Collaborative. The result is an ongoing professional development program for teachers and a state-of-the-art science, math, and technology center where students at all grade levels participate in integrated, hands-on experiences that emphasize critical thinking and problem-solving skills.

In 1989, when East Dale applied to become a PDS, we began to envision our future. Later, as a PDS we had a unique opportunity to do long-range strategic planning. Our vision for the future included "establishing a K–6 program which integrates mathematics, science, and technology to best prepare students for the changing world they will be facing." Because we had no space available in our school for an SMT Center and the innovative new program it would house, we had to raise money to construct an addition to our building. This prompted our faculty and administration to develop an action plan, which included raising money through dinners and a "buy a brick" program. We also sought funds through the local school system and various competitive grant programs. This was a very complex and expensive endeavor, but the entire school community pooled its talents, resources, and energies to accomplish our goal.

West Virginia's First Science, Math, and Technology Center

In 1990, our dream came true; and, through a variety of funding sources, we established our state's first elementary Science, Math, and Technology (SMT) Center at East Dale. The laboratory classroom and adjoining conference room and office were built from local community fund raisers ($100,000), with donated services from the Marion County Board of Education. Furnishings were purchased with moneys awarded through the Benedum Collaborative ($48,000). A competitive Dwight D. Eisenhower Mathematics and Science Award (DEMSA) grant of $410,000, awarded over a three-year period, provided SMT staffing, teacher training, and equipment, and released time to develop hands-on integrated activities to support the new curriculum design.

The SMT Center has been a collaborative effort from the beginning. With the assistance of WVU, the Benedum Collaborative, and Marion County Schools, we have become active agents of curriculum reform. Five key ideas have been interwoven throughout our reform effort: collaborative planning, staff development, site-based curriculum development, implementation, and evaluation. Although we will discuss these ideas separately in the next sections of the chapter, it is important to note that integration of these ideas characterized all aspects of our reform effort.

The planning for building our SMT Center, developing our curriculum, and designing our staff development reflected our PDS commitment to shared decision making. As a PDS, we had an infrastructure already in place to establish a collaborative relationship with West Virginia University (WVU) faculty. Representatives from West Virginia University and East Dale School visited model programs in elementary science, math, and technology. Following these visits, the team members collaborated to incorporate outstanding elements of each model into an exemplary design appropriate for our rural, Appalachian students.

Since we wanted our state-of-the-art learning environment to be guided by a teacher-driven model of curriculum development, we established curriculum teams which began meeting during the first year of the project. This team approach was chosen because it seemed likely to promote teacher ownership and changes in actual classroom practice, which would translate into increases in student performance. The first task for curriculum teams was to develop an SMT Center philosophy from which all SMT Center activities would evolve.

In a process facilitated by the SMT Center Director, curriculum teams explored a variety of research sources, including reports from Project 2061, the National Center for Improving Science, the National Council of Teachers of Mathematics, the National Science Teachers Association, the National Science Resource Center of the Smithsonian Institution, the California State Department of Education, the Texas State Department of Education, the California Restructuring Science Program, and the West Virginia Education Goals (draft). The teams then developed our SMT Center philosophy, which emphasizes: (1) providing opportunities for students to build practical knowledge through personal experience and exploration; (2) maintaining a psychologically safe, student-centered atmosphere; and (3) developing conceptual understanding through integration of science, math, and technology. To assist us in implementing this philosophy at East Dale, we established four SMT Center goals: (1) to provide teacher training that enhances teachers' ability to provide hands-on instruction in science, mathematics, technology, and related disciplines; (2) to develop a hands-on curriculum that will integrate science, mathematics, and technology with other disciplines; (3) to provide for the integration of our media center with the SMT Center for the purpose of research and project development; and (4) to increase community and parental involvement in the education of children.

In addition to the SMT Center philosophy and goals, we constructed a series of belief statements to guide development and implementation of the curriculum. The belief statements committed us to: (1) student learning experiences that develop connections between curriculum and students' own life experience; (2) a classroom atmosphere that supports experimentation and exploration; (3) promoting in-depth knowledge of a few concepts to best prepare students for more advanced study; (4) designing developmentally appropriate, hands-on activities that help students develop connections between concepts; and (5) using the interrelated nature of science, mathematics, and technology to generate powerful learning experiences that enhance conceptual organization and integration of content. As decisions needed to be made about curriculum or staff development, reference to these belief statements ensured that our decisions were congruent with our ultimate goals.

Staff Development

Scientific literacy for all Americans can be realized only if students have teachers who are fully qualified to teach science. Therefore, staff development was a vital component of our reform. After designing the curriculum and developing the objectives for the SMT Center, we chose four nationally recognized programs as the centerpieces of our staff development program:

Project AIMS; Box-It/Bag-It Math (K–2) and Math in the Mind's Eye (3–6); the marine science project, For Sea; and Lego Early Childhood, Technic and Lego Technology Programs.

Project AIMS (Activities that Integrate Mathematics and Science) is a one-week-long intensive workshop that provides teachers with hands-on experience in the integration of science and mathematics. The AIMS program has several specific attributes: (1) it creates more time for science by integrating science with mathematics and other disciplines; (2) science-mathematics relationships are shown in the three-dimensional real world through use of concrete materials, symbolism, graphic representation and interpretation, and the scientific method; (3) a balance of science processes, content, and questioning are integrated via hands-on experience; and (4) positive student attitudes toward science are created.

Our new curriculum is based on the belief that young children learn best when they are actively involved in hands-on experiences with a variety of materials; therefore, students who can tell, draw, or act out a story problem to explain their solution are closer to understanding than those who complete numerous worksheets. In Box-It/Bag-It Math (K–2) and Math in the Mind's Eye (3–6), teachers learned ways to help students at varying developmental levels think about mathematics "visually." These approaches enable teachers to help students develop and retain a variety of mathematical skills and increase their problem-solving abilities in developmentally appropriate ways.

Because East Dale is located approximately seven hours from the nearest ocean, most of our students had not been exposed to any form of marine science and consistently scored low on the oceanography section of the state-mandated Comprehensive Test of Basic Skills (CTBS). Therefore, we chose a National Diffusion Network marine science project that has been validated nationally, "For Sea," to provide students with information concerning the world of water. Our staff development program included an overview of the philosophy of the program, text implementation procedures, and hands-on experiences that familiarized the teachers with relevant materials.

Technology has been a fundamental force in the development of human culture. In fact, the shaping of tools marked the beginning of civilization, and technology has enabled us to change our world and "reach farther with our hands, voices, and senses" (Project 2061, 1989). If students are to be prepared for the technology of the coming century, the literature suggests that they must be allowed to create and build realistic working models based on problem-solving situations. However, few technology curricula exist that are appropriate in a K–6 environment. The Lego Technology Program, a one-week-long program, provided our teachers with hands-on experiences in the integration of technology into the physical sciences (K–6). Teachers learned how to present problem situations and allow students to explore, investigate, simulate, and invent solutions using technology.

The staff development programs have clearly affected what happens in our classrooms. As one Eastdale teacher reflected on the changes she had made in recent years she said,

> In every teacher's life there is something that has transformed them professionally. For me, it has been technology. Through the use of multimedia, my classes have become more exciting and, I must add, more appropriate for the children. The possibilities are endless in showing animated representations of action verbs, exploring communications across generations, or accessing art collections throughout the world. Technology has brought the world to my fingertips.

As our reform work has continued, we have tried to share what we are learning with other schools. In 1993, we sponsored a professional development conference, Visions, to share our ideas with other educators. We have also shared our work in science, math, and technology education through a series of workshops and camps for educators and children and family activities for the school community.

Curriculum Development

East Dale Elementary faculty supported by the SMT staff (coordinator, teacher/aide, and secretary) designed an integrated curriculum that may serve as a model for the other rural schools undertaking the reform of science, mathematics, and technology educational delivery. Working in teams across grades and disciplines, East Dale teachers and SMT staff designed a tentative SMT curriculum framework around conceptual organizers and content organizers. Our initial conceptual organizers are presented in Table 8.1.

We then established a tentative, spiralling sequence of developmentally appropriate themes and topics for students to interact with at each grade level. This sequence is depicted in Table 8.2. We did not want to depend on "one shot" learning experiences, so we chose to introduce, revisit, and expand on concepts over the elementary years. For example, developmentally appropriate concepts like organization are heavily emphasized in the early grades, while more complex concepts like change are emphasized in the middle grades. Although the concept of systems, which is emphasized earlier, is not a focus in the upper grades it continues to be used as a conceptual organizer.

Since curriculum development, staff development, and pilot testing were going on simultaneously, our initial curriculum framework was regularly adjusted as we learned. After several years of learning, we now depict our spiral SMT curriculum structure, which is given in Tables 8.3 and 8.4.

TABLE 8.1

Initial Conceptual Organizers

Organization:	organize and classify the world around us
Systems:	movement of matter, energy, information, and ideas through an identified pathway
Cause and Effect:	exploring causes and explanations for predictable events
Scale:	relative and absolute quantities
Models:	developing functional representations of real life events and objects
Structure and Function:	exploring the relationship between physical characteristics of objects and organisms, and their function
Diversity and Variation:	exploring discontinuous and continuous properties as well as the differences which exist within an organized system
Change:	exploring and applying ideas concerning the types and kinds of changes which occur in the natural world

TABLE 8.2

Use of Conceptual Organizers by Grade Level

Conceptual Organizer	Grade K	1	2	3	4	5	6
Organization	•	•	•				
Systems		•	•	•			
Cause & Effect			•	•	•		
Scale			•	•	•		
Models			•	•	•		
Structure & Function			•	•	•		
Diversity and Variation					•	•	•
Change					•	•	•

TABLE 8.3

Spiral SMT Curriculum Structure—Conceptual Organizers

ORGANIZATION (O):	
Organization:	organize and classify the world around us
Systems:	movement of matter, energy, information, and ideas through an identified pathway
Structure & Function:	exploring the relationship between physical characteristics of objects and organisms, and their function
INTERACTION (I):	
Cause & Effect:	exploring causes and explanations for predictable events
Diversity & Variation:	exploring discontinuous and continuous properties as well as the differences that exist within an organized system
Change:	exploring and applying ideas concerning the types and kinds of changes that occur in the natural world
REPRESENTATION (R):	
Scale:	relative and absolute quantities
Models:	developing functional representations of real life events and objects

We have translated this conceptual and content organization into developmentally appropriate themes and topics for students to explore at each grade level (K–6) and established specific learning outcomes that are the foundation for teacher-created integrated science, math, and technology activities. More than 400 activities were developed and field-tested in the lab setting over the first two years of our work. We have revised these activities to reflect the feedback teachers and students have provided after field testing the lessons and compiled the activities in three teacher resource books: *Down and Under* for grades K, 1, and 2; *Out and About* for grades 3 and 4; and *Above and Beyond* for grades 5 and 6.

Evaluation

We believe that successful reform in elementary science, mathematics and technology programs are possible only within the context of an ongoing and effective evaluation system. The East Dale SMT Center evaluation plan has involved the following activities:

TABLE 8.4

Spiral SMT Curriculum Structure—Content Organizers

SCIENCE (S):	
Living World:	studying plants, animals, and ecology
Physical World:	exploring matter and energy
World of Earth and Space:	examining earth, space, and weather
MATHEMATICS (M):	
Number Sense:	determining quantity as well as recognizing patterns and meaning of numerals
Number Operations:	utilizing binary operations including addition, subtraction, multiplication, and division
Spatial Sense & Geometry:	describing and working with spatial relationships and geometric models
Measurement:	recognizing and using standard units of measure in determining distance, weight, time, and money
TECHNOLOGY(T):	
Communication:	considering electronic and non-electric forms and systems of communication
Manufacturing:	relating to production of consumer goods
Transportation:	identifying the methods of moving items from one place to another
Construction:	working with various types of building structures

National Science Teacher Association Guidelines for self-assessment: The East Dale administration, faculty, and parents have completed a comprehensive examination of the science and mathematics program before and after the implementation of the SMT Center.

The Concerns-Based Adoption Model (C-BAM): Teachers' understanding and perceptions were tracked throughout the process using C-BAM instruments.

Implementation Logs: Teachers recorded their lab experiences (i.e., overall appropriateness of materials, developmental appropriateness, availability of time to complete activities, etc.) immediately after each lab session.

Comprehensive Test of Basic Skills (CTBS): Third and sixth grade science and math scores for the 1990-1991 school year through the current school year were used to evaluate overall student performance.

Validation team of external educators: employed to determine the degree to which the SMT Center has accomplished the goals and objectives established by East Dale Elementary School and The Benedum Collaborative.

To date, the evaluation procedures we have employed have shown extremely favorable results. CTBS scores for third and sixth grade students have increased significantly in both math and science. C-BAM surveys indicate that our teachers have progressed from being uninformed and concerned about the SMT Center to becoming informed and comfortable with the changes. The teacher implementation logs are a formative evaluation strategy that has been extremely helpful in ongoing refinement of our SMT activities. An analysis of student interview data collected in 1995 reveals that "the most visible reform initiative at East Dale, both in terms of being physically apparent and embedded in students' descriptions of their opportunities to learn, is the Science, Math, and Technology Lab." Student comments emphasized the importance of "hands-on" learning in science and math. When asked how they learn best, students responded, through "using manipulatives", "with manipulatives you can see where the problem is and correct it. Like we do in science. There are lots of hands-on materials there." "I like hands-on because you can see for yourself how it does. When teachers show you stuff on the board, you don't really understand it, but when you do it, you can see for yourself how it does." Our children are getting what we wanted them to have—meaningful learning experiences in science, math, and technology.

Implementation

Our original plans for the new SMT program are now fully implemented and, funded by a variety of competitive grants awarded to the SMT staff, we have established numerous additional programs for teachers and students across West Virginia. Some of these initiatives are described here.

An Evening Under the Stars

An Evening Under the Stars was a collaborative effort between East Dale's SMT Lab and Morgantown High School's Astronomy Club. (Morgantown High is one of our "sister PDSs" in the Benedum Collaborative.) By working together, we were able to offer more than 500 stargazers of all ages an opportunity to participate in an evening astronomy program that involved both learning stations outside the SMT Lab and numerous activities inside the lab. Adults and students alike were mesmerized by Greek mythology explaining early civilization's interpretation of astronomy. Participants discussed changes in space flight over the years, then moved outside the lab to launch rockets into space. Students and parents explored a student-constructed mock planetarium providing a representation of the Spring Sky constellations. The evening concluded with multiple observation points outside the lab exploring the solar system beyond. This program helped to expand the learning environment beyond the classroom walls, enabling students, their families, and other community members to explore the planets and constellations surrounding our planet Earth. Because astronomy has stirred our natural curiosity in science over the ages, and space travel has captured the imagination of many in contemporary times, this was a natural opportunity to foster intergenerational math and science learning.

Soar To the Future

Women are playing an increasingly important role in professions focused on science, math, and technology and we recognize the need to target and enhance our girls' future career choices. We designed Soar to the Future to encourage and support fifth and sixth grade girls' interest and experiences in science, math, and technology. The students had the opportunity to work on a variety of science, math, and technology lab experiments over the three-hour event. The activity-based learning plan involved students in building a kaleidoscope, designing a curve stitching pattern, creating a tabletop model of the constellations, and exploring the technology of a circus pulley representation. The girls were assisted throughout the evening by female students from local colleges who are majoring in science, math, or technology.

Math in a Bag

Children learn math by doing, but many parents do not understand that, feeling that they do not have the training or background necessary to help their children "do math"or thinking that math must always be done with paper and pencil. If our children are to go beyond simple computation to higher-level math skills, they need to have many and varied math experiences. Parents can help provide these experiences if they are given the resources and strategies to do so. By sponsoring Math In a Bag, we provided teachers, parents, and children in grades K–6 with training, literature, manipulatives, and activities that make math understandable and fun. Now parents can help their children develop math skills and interest in math by doing "hands-on" projects with them at home. Together they can see how math relates to the real world. Because the children will read a quality literature book that goes with each activity and will be writing about their experiences, the activities also link reading, writing, math, and fun.

Throughout the project, we encouraged parents and students to share their thoughts, feelings, and needs concerning the "Math in a Bag" ideas that they use.

The Rivers Program

Rivers have been a major factor in West Virginia's history and will continue to be important in the future. We wanted our students to explore this important aspect of their state, so we chose to work with the Rivers Curriculum, created by Southern Illinois University. The program helps us to prepare West Virginia students for an environmentally and scientifically sound future through a variety of engaging learning activities that teach chemistry, biology, earth sciences, geography, and language using a hands-on format and focusing on local rivers. The program also involves our teachers in collecting river data and sharing this information with local, state, and federal scientific agencies through a telecommunication system known as SOILED NET.

The Rivers Curriculum is designed around five content units—chemistry, biology, earth science, geography, and language arts—to be used by the teachers during a one-month period. Each unit is organized around field trips to a river and followup classroom experiments. East Dale Elementary, in collaboration with Southern Illinois University, West Virginia University (WVU), and Fairmont State College, provided the training necessary to implement this curriculum to both practicing teachers and preservice teachers.

In addition to these four programs, we have added to our SMT program a variety of professional development sessions that acquaint teachers with many different approaches to teaching science, math, and technology. We want to be part of the significant shift in attitudes toward science, math, and technology that is occurring in our nation, and are continuously striving to stay abreast of the latest advances and to share these ideas with our students, teachers, and community.

Our experiences in planning, implementing, and evaluating the SMT Center have led to a broader review of our school. This review in turn has led us to reexamine and revise our strategic plan. Our current strategic plan (which is included in our PDS biography in Chapter 3) focuses on three broad areas: education, collaboration, and motivation. We have chosen to address some of our content concerns by developing a curriculum based on the Core Knowledge program. We have also reshaped our schedule to allow longer blocks of time which facilitate the use of instructional technology and collaborative learning. Our curriculum has moved toward a whole language approach, implementing thematic units, and integrating the fine arts. We have begun a number of programs to support and motivate our children. In short, our work in creating the SMT Center was not the end of our curriculum change—it was an important starting point for many curricular changes which continue at East Dale.

Summary

As young children embark on a life-long journey of learning, they naturally want to discover and explore all aspects of life. An effective elementary science, math, and technology program can build on these natural tendencies, offering learning experiences that stimulate curiosity, foster investigative skills, encourage critical and creative thinking skills, and build conceptual understandings. At East Dale Elementary, we set out to create just such a program for our children and our faculty. We felt that this goal required an entirely new approach to education in science, mathematics, and technology and we refused to let any of the traditional barriers to school change prevent us from developing this new program. Through the collaborative efforts of WVU, the Benedum Collaborative, the community, and the East Dale faculty, our new Science, Math, and Technology Center—coupled with the continually evolving curriculum we have designed for it—provides the necessary experiences for all children to be scientifically literate, active participants in their journey of life-long learning. One Eastdale teacher described the changes this way,

> Being a Professional Development School has provided many opportunities for me to grow professionally. I have become a more secure teacher of science because of the training I had in hand-on, student oriented teaching strategies. This training led to the development of a curriculum that is child centered rather than content centered. I think we now look at the needs of the children in the area of science. This new curriculum provides opportunities for children to explore science on a personal basis. This had led us to involve students in more group exploration than in the past. Also, the types of assessments used have changed dramatically. We now use more performance assessments using experiments, assessments that are more real-life centered.

Life at Eastdale has changed for children and for teachers. It will continue to change because every time we improve something, it helps us see more possibilities.

Note

East Dale Elementary's Science, Math, and Technology Center is a collaborative venture involving everyone in our school. Because East Dale's teachers are so important to this project, we consider them the "co-authors" of this chapter.

References

AAAS (1989). *Project 2061: Science for all Americans.* New York: Oxford Press.

The Benedum Collaborative (1991). *Characteristics of the novice teacher and characteristics of an effective teacher education program.* Morgantown, W.V.: Author.

East Dale Elementary School (1992). *Gold medal schools design.* Fairmont, W.V.: Author.

9

The Story of a Changing School

Teresa T. Field and Mary Alice Barksdale-Ladd

School restructuring is a developmental process that involves changes in rules, roles, and relationships (Schlecty 1990). Successful restructuring efforts require that teachers identify their own goals, design methods for reaching their goals, and move toward achieving selected goals at their own rates.

In order to develop understandings of the processes involved in school restructuring and the components of school restructuring processes that encourage or inhibit successful changes, it is important that we study schools engaged in these processes. Morgantown High School (MHS) has been involved in a restructuring process over the past four years. The school was identified as a Benedum Collaborative professional development school in January 1990. The Benedum Collaborative provided human and monetary resources for teacher release time and pilot projects, and also provided connections and new perspectives from University collaborators. In this chapter, we describe the restructuring processes in which Morgantown High School (MHS) has been engaged. We will summarize the results of documentary evidence, interviews, and participant observations gathered over a period of three years (Field 1992). First, a context will be provided for the changes in the school. Then, phases of activity will be described as the school community progressed through the restructuring process. Finally, we will discuss changes in the people who make up the school community, the processes they used to make decisions and communicate with one another, and programmatic changes that have resulted.

A Place to Begin

Examinations of change require observation at different points in time. Thus, before we investigate current change processes at Morgantown High School, we must look at the school prior to 1989. Looking at the past gives us a context for understanding change processes, and the knowledge of traditional norms and structures in schools provide foundational understandings of change.

Morgantown High School is situated in a neighborhood of tree-lined streets and turn-of-the-century houses that has recently been named a National Historical District. Organized in a horseshoe-shaped pattern with a recently renovated football stadium in the center, the school campus includes the main classroom building, the auditorium, and the gymnasium/cafeteria/and a renovated related arts building. The architecture of these nearly seventy-year-old red brick structures blends nicely into the residential area. As evidenced from both the 1927 Morgantown High School Dedication Program as well as current documents and publications, the school has long been viewed as being on the cutting edge of technological, academic, athletic, and vocational programs.

"Tradition," "stability," and "academic excellence" were words used in a variety of contexts by many groups describing MHS. In the past, the school was rated one of the ten best high schools in America, and MHS usually has the greatest number of National Merit winners and finalists in the state. MHS students have gone on to attend the nation's most prestigious universities and have received appointments to U.S. military academies.

Using a departmentalized system to organize content areas of instruction, MHS offers a broad, varied curriculum that exceeds the requirements of the state department of education. Students who wish to continue their studies in a discipline beyond MHS's offerings or who wish to take courses not taught at the school can opt for University release periods. This allows these students to enroll in courses at West Virginia University (WVU) during regular school hours.

The attendance area of the school reaches from the most rural sections of the county to neighborhoods near the University, creating diversity in the student population. The school population of tenth through twelfth graders is approximately 1300, with 95 percent White, 2 percent Black, 1 percent Asian, 1 percent Hispanic, and 1 percent American Indian. This population is fairly stable, with 92 percent of the student body spending three years in the school. Most of the students are college bound; 60 percent plan to attend a four-year college. An additional 14 percent of the students plan to continue their education in some other way. Almost one-third of the students hold part-time jobs while attending high school.

The MHS faculty is also non-transient and well educated. More than half of the teachers have been at MHS for more than twelve years. Three of the approximately ninety faculty members hold doctorates, with more than sixty holding at least one master's degree. The faculty is active in local, state, national, and international professional organizations. Several of the teachers have received county, state, or national awards for teaching excellence in their content disciplines.

The MHS administration, which has been extremely stable, utilized a traditional top-down decision-making approach prior to 1989. The current principal is only the third person to serve in that role since before World War II.

He had served as assistant principal at the school for eighteen years prior to his selection as principal in 1989. The traditional management style of former principals apparently went unquestioned by the school faculty and the community at large. A veteran teacher made this observation: "When I started here 3,000 years ago under [a previous principal], nobody ever made any decision in the whole county when he was here but him. There was never, ever, any input from anybody. That was how I was initiated into teaching."

The stated philosophy of Morgantown High School as noted in yearly reports provided to the Board of Education has focused upon providing each student with a variety of experiences that develop the ability to function productively in an ever-changing world. The school's three-part mission, found in the current faculty handbook, is to: (1) provide all students with knowledge, development of skills, and enhancement, understanding, insight, and aesthetic appreciation; (2) encourage positive social and emotional growth; and (3) ensure that each graduate exhibits mastery of the subject matter.

The Impetus for Change

The MHS faculty began to discuss their involvement in restructuring after several MHS faculty and administration members were asked to serve on the Benedum Collaborative Professional Development Schools Team. Four MHS faculty members worked with this group, helping to create the Benedum Collaborative Professional Developmental School Belief Statements, which guide professional development school (PDS) activity. Having identified the Belief Statements, the group went on to design the application process, used by schools in applying to become a professional development school (PDS), and specified selection criteria that would be used in screening the applications and selecting PDS sites.

The faculty members who had been members of the PDS teams recommended to the MHS faculty that the school complete the application process, and they led this effort at the school. MHS completed the application process in January 1990 and was selected as one of six Benedum Collaborative PDSs in February.

Why did MHS want to become involved? Through the discussions and reflection involved in the completion of the application packet, the faculty identified some issues that were important to them. First, the faculty noted that, because the strong academic programs of the high school focused primarily on the college-bound student, there was a need for the development of programs designed to meet the specific needs of the average and at-risk learner. The faculty was somewhat surprised when their data-collection effort for the application packet revealed that a majority of their students were from rural areas, a revelation for the MHS faculty. Thus, it was determined that the faculty needed to reconsider current school programs and activities in light of the population that was actually being served. It was felt that curricular and organizational changes were needed in order for MHS to become more effective in these areas. By becoming involved in the restructuring effort, the faculty benefitted from the University community's assistance, which allowed them to initiate and implement changes. Also, the Monongalia County school system and the Superintendent of Schools created an atmosphere that supported risk taking and provided leadership opportunities for teachers and administrators.

First Steps in Restructuring

In the Fall of 1989, the faculty began to read, think about, and discuss school reform and restructuring. For the next five years, the entire school community would struggle with developing and understanding a school vision and then working to make it a reality. A review of data from across these five years reveals distinct phases of activity in this restructuring project. Five phases of activity can be identified: (1) Phase One—Finding the Courage to Dream; (2) Phase Two—Looking Beyond Tomorrow into the Twenty-first Century; (3) Phase Three—Moving From Paper to Practice; (4) Phase Four—A Time for Action; and (5) Phase Five—Major Changes. We will describe each phase of activity and the associated changes in people, processes, and programs at the school.

Phase 1—Finding the Courage to Dream

Phase 1 began with the development of a school-wide understanding of the PDS process. This understanding was a part of the preparation for, and actual completion of, the application to become a PDS. The teachers and administrators had difficulty dreaming about the possibilities and opportunities presented to them by a PDS. Most of the teachers were unfamiliar with recommendations from organizations such as the Holmes Group, which identifies the need for closer ties between public schools and universities.

The development of a common understanding of educational restructuring and organizational change resulted from interactions that led to completion of the school's application to become a PDS site. Learning and practicing group process skills were the first steps in communicating options and soliciting input into the design process needed to complete the application. Using nominal group process techniques, common readings, and instructional and testimonial videos to spark discussion, the faculty developed a common understanding of what a PDS might look like.

The level of knowledge and understanding of these processes on the part of the four faculty members who served on the Benedum PDS Team, and the fact that one of the teachers had visited a PDS site (connected with another university), provided the MHS faculty with advantages that some other schools did not have. The processes that had been used by the Benedum PDS team for developing documents and guidelines became models for interactions at MHS. Thus, the MHS faculty was successful in creating and sustaining the kinds of interactions that allowed for the production of an impressive set of documents for the PDS application. Describing this part of the PDS process, one teacher said, "I think a PDS has to evolve. I'm not certain that we know what it's going to look like and that's the really nice thing about it. It evolves through the needs and goals of the faculty, the students, and the administration."

The professional discussions that were organized around the application process were, for many faculty members, the first opportunities that had been offered for them to informally share their thoughts on teaching and learning with their colleagues. With ninety faculty members scattered through three large buildings, years could go by in which teachers had no need and no opportunities to discuss education and teaching with many of the other teachers. But that changed. A need was created and supported by discussion groups, steering committees, and shared decision making. Decisions were being made at the school, and many people hoped to become a part of those decisions. Phase 1 ended with Morgantown High School's collaborative completion of the application on January 5, 1990.

Lessons learned in Phase 1. School history and tradition played an important role in the earliest phases of change. Because MHS was perceived by the faculty and the community at large as a traditional college preparatory school of innovative teachers and programs, many faculty members found it difficult to identify curricular weaknesses, information deficits, and needs to change from a traditional top-down model of management to a more open, collaborative model. Also, the traditional relationship between WVU and MHS faculty affected initial interactions of the two groups. The faculty was skeptical of the University's "hidden agenda" for change. For example, some teachers felt that public school teachers would "not really be heard" in the discussions of school reform, but would be asked to do most of the changing and work. Additionally, there had been a negative interaction between the Monongalia County school district and the University more than fifteen years prior to The Benedum Collaborative. Despite the long period of time that had passed, the memory of this event had not been forgotten and it colored initial attempts at collaboration. Many teachers mentioned it in their interviews. It was clear that at the end of Phase 1 there was a need for MHS and WVU to continue working to develop common understandings and a basis for trust, if a successful collaborative relationship was to be established.

Phase Two—Looking Beyond Tomorrow into the Twenty-first Century

Phase 2 began in February 1990, with the selection of MHS as a PDS site. The School was selected from a pool of fourteen applicants as one of six

Benedum Collaborative PDSs representing a four-county area of north-central West Virginia. The creation of PDS committee structures, the piloting of shared decision-making processes, and the elicitation of faculty involvement in curricular and pedagogical changes were major focuses within this phase.

There were many opportunities for the exploration of new decision-making processes. The creation of a Site Steering Committee was one of these opportunities. This committee served as the policy-making and governing body for PDS activities in the school. The Site Steering Committee was made up of teachers, administrators, University faculty, business partners, and parents. One of the first activities engaged in by the Site Steering Committee was the creation of a process for sharing information with the school community and for writing grants to receive funding for larger projects.

Each site was provided with $2,000 in start-up funding and released time for teachers to plan and discuss the PDS concept. During Phase 2, it was fully recognized by the Site Steering Committee that new challenges such as site-based management, collaboration, and shared decision making should be attempted in an environment in which participants felt comfortable in taking risks. Participants needed to be able to experiment and evolve with the process. It was also recognized that such an environment and the skills for participating in such an environment could not be developed overnight. Inherent in this atmosphere was promotion of the idea that failure at these new initiatives was not possible. "Little tries" had to be accepted and rewarded. It was also recognized that the administration in a restructuring school must engage in learning new processes of leadership and decision making and that the administration should also be supported in these efforts. The Site Steering Committee worked hard to build a supportive environment for shared decision making, risk taking, and change. During Phase 2, it was clear that the faculty noticed differences in the school. As one teacher noted: "I think one of the things that anyone can see, if they are around here for a while, they can see a lot of decisions being made from the bottom up, from the faculty, instead of everything coming from the principal. We put a lot of input into the decisions made here. And that's not always been the case."

Once selected as a PDS site, MHS overcame several obstacles in order to create a cohesive unit. One component of this action was the development of improved communication patterns and norms. New communication processes were created to get faculty members interacting among themselves, with the administration, and with the school community.

From the Benedum Collaborative Staff, the MHS Site Steering Committee learned that in order to guide and sustain restructuring, it was essential that MHS collectively develop a vision for the school. A school vision represents the dreams and hopes of the school community for what the students will be like when they leave the school system. A well-articulated vision was perceived as one of the keys to a successful restructuring effort. The processes used to develop the vision, to create a sense of ownership in the vision, and to make plans to carry out the vision were important components of Phase 2 at MHS.

As the Site Steering Committee organized and took initial steps toward the creation of a school-wide vision, they built upon the tradition of excellence already in existence at the site. But with tradition can come aversion to change. Breaking up a top-down management model and instituting a shared decision-making process was difficult. Acquiring proficiency in this new skill required instruction and authentic practice; the skills needed to be used in solving real-life problems.

It was during this phase of activity that MHS used a strategic planning process presented to them by Dr. Neil Bucklew, then-President of WVU. The outcomes of this process were a school vision and five strategic planning themes. The school's vision was to "become a school for the 21st century." The five themes identified by the faculty were: (1) restructuring, (2) critical thinking, (3) professional enhancement, (4) student success, and (5) technological enhancement. These themes became the focus of staff development and school improvement activities. The identification of the themes and the development of rationales for each were the culminating activity of this phase of work (see Table 9.1).

The identification of five specific theme areas led to the opportunity for individuals, departments, and interdisciplinary groups to meet for the purpose of discussing the five themes and designing methods of addressing each theme. The establishment of the five themes helped the faculty in that they began to see what their participation in a PDS meant. One teacher explained: "Part of the problem was in how vague things were. Until I saw the themes, I really didn't understand." The identification of the themes also helped to focus interest on areas of concern for many educators throughout the school.

Teachers began to seek collaborators from the University and from the community to assist in the discussion and design of activities related to the theme areas. Two teachers who had had little involvement prior to the identification of the five themes made the following comments: "I think I understood what the vision of a school for the twenty-first century was, but when we got the themes, we were able to see how they related to what we were doing in our classrooms and that made a lot of sense"; and, "I think we became more aware of what we need to do [to reach our goal], what can be done, and we're now trying to move in that direction."

Lessons learned in Phase 2. Effective communication was essential to the change process. The need to improve communication at MHS was identified frequently during Phase 2. Ineffective and inconsistent communication patterns were identified. These communication patterns involved the presentation of information to individuals about the Benedum Collaborative, Site Steering Committee activities, and school-wide initiatives and opportunities. Unfortunately,

TABLE 9.1

Morgantown High School's Strategic Planning Themes

Restructuring

We realize that changes in management, scheduling, and curriculum are needed. Teachers' roles are changing; there is a need for opportunities for greater involvement in the decision-making process. Curriculum redesign, curriculum integration, and schedule revision may be needed to insure that all our students are successfully prepared for the 21st century.

Critical Thinking

We will emphasize the integration of information with higher levels of learning, rather than focusing primarily on the accumulation and transfer of knowledge.

Professional Enhancement

In the school of the 21st century, where real learning will occur, all teachers will be part of the community of learners. The personal academic growth of our faculty will require both continued content area updating and training in new instructional techniques including the best of modern technology and educational research. Attention to content and technique will also be central to our role in the training of future teachers.

Student Success

Our student body is diverse in background and ability. We will have high expectations for all students. Our students need to be motivated to succeed, to participate, and to identify positively with Morgantown High School. By working with every student and making each one feel a part of the school community, we will foster enthusiasm for our school and promote student success.

Technology Enhancement

In order to prepare our students for the 21st century, we will implement technology effectively in our classrooms.

suggested solutions to these problems were not addressed by steering committee members at this time.

Leadership sources and forces changed as needed to support work toward the MHS goals. Four changes in leadership were identified in Phase 2. First, there was the initial identification of leaders for the PDS process at MHS. While some of the PDS leaders had traditionally been school leaders, others had not, so we saw a change in the leadership constituency at the school. Second, the teachers who had taken on leadership responsibilities as members of the Site Steering Committee worked through a process of negotiating what their roles would be in leading change activities at MHS. Third, there was the changing role of administrative leadership at MHS, the leadership of both the principal and the county administration. As the teachers negotiated what their new leadership roles would be, administrators also negotiated their new leadership roles. Fourth, for some teachers, a change in the level of personal and professional empowerment was noted. As teachers took on leadership roles in PDS activities, they began to feel that they were more empowered as teachers.

Learning about and living through change was a frustrating experience. During Phase 2, we found that the types and degrees of frustration identified by participants decreased as their involvement and understanding of restructuring activities increased. Originally identified as barriers, then as obstacles, and finally as stresses or frustrations, the importance of change issues was closely related to faculty perceptions of their effects on school activities. Specifically identified concerns in Phase 2 were: (1) understanding the change process, (2) time, (3) resources, (4) changes in scheduling, (5) living with ambiguity, and (6) faculty involvement in project activities.

Phase Three—Moving from Paper to Practice

Phase 3 involved the early stages of translation of the school's vision and themes into changes at the school. These changes were to include new and expanded leadership opportunities for educators and the creation of new organizational patterns within the school. The faculty and school community moved from "the what," or the mere identification of themes, to "the how" of accomplishing these goals.

This phase was a very active one for an expanded group of teachers, and new leadership opportunities were created for many. Key events of this period included visits to other restructuring sites and the staging of a professional development opportunity known as the "September Snow Day." Benedum PDS grants that had been funded in the previous phase were underway during this period, and the successes of these projects interested others in developing proposals to be funded.

Teachers at MHS began to identify the need to look outside the school to consultants, to other sites engaged in restructuring processes, and to informational groups and organizations. The idea that information should be sought from a variety of sources outside the school was new for MHS faculty and administrators. Other sources were identified within the site, as faculty members began to collaborate and share with each other.

It became clear that there was a need for further development of the site-based management system. In order for site-based management to work effectively at MHS, the Site Steering Committee then took steps to improve communication processes within the school. The purpose of improving communication was to articulate the vision and create an atmosphere where faculty members could feel ownership in the process. Newsletters, presentations, and bulletin boards were created to ensure that the faculty was kept up to date on opportunities and responsibilities associated with restructuring.

There were numerous discussions about the need for a room in which to meet and plan and where a professional library would be housed. Also, there was a need to find a place for the IBM PC provided to each PDS site by the Benedum Collaborative. The Site Steering Committee found a janitor's closet that was large enough to hold a conference table and a computer workstation. Then work began on designing and creating a Professional Development Center (PDC) for MHS. The improvements to this space were partially funded by a portion of the $2000 in "start up funds" provided to each site by the Benedum Collaborative. The decision about this expenditure provided the group an opportunity to practice shared decision-making processes in a situation that led to a very tangible change in the school.

The PDS became a gathering place for teachers to talk about professional issues, to hold meetings with student teachers, or to spend planning time. While a "Teacher's Lounge" existed, it became a place where "people just go to vent." The PDC became a location for professional discussions and debates. In the School Bulletin, the original teacher's lounge was soon referred to as the "Xerox Room," as few teachers frequented it for any purpose other than to make copies.

The Site Steering Committee also worked to increase faculty involvement in project activities. The goal was to involve as many people as possible and to expand the ownership of the project to the faculty at large. This was difficult to accomplish, and some felt that they failed at this mission. The move from restructuring ideas to restructuring realities was more difficult, and required more effort than the members of the Site Steering Committee had anticipated. We noted that, as a result, there was some distrust and disillusionment about the project.

Efforts were made to create better connections with WVU that would result in professional development activities. Graduate school courses were offered at the site. Additionally, WVU teaching methods professors presented staff development programs to teachers who worked with WVU students in their classes. The goal here was to create greater congruence between WVU's teacher education program and student teacher supervision. A related activity involved placing a WVU doctoral student at MHS as a site supervisor for student teaching and other field experiences. These expanded opportunities, and the fact that they were initiated by the faculty at the site, created a sense of ownership among faculty members who were involved.

"Frustrations" and "barriers" were identified by many participants during Phase 3. Tasks that at first appeared simple became quite complex when they were approached collaboratively, when they were attempted for the first time, or both. Although these complexities were noted as concerns, it did not appear that they kept faculty members from attempting new activities. The fact that money was available to support these endeavors drew many teachers to participate, despite their concerns. But even with increased participation and teacher learning, there were faculty members who chose not to become involved in restructuring activities at MHS.

During this phase of activity, the initial Benedum Collaborative grant ran out, and a continuation grant was renegotiated. There was a lag in access to funding; and, when the continuation grant was funded, there were changes in the processes used to support site activities. The site continued with planning and discussion but was stalled on several major projects during the period in which funding was not available. This lull in activity allowed for reflection on the project to date; some participants were satisfied with the progress the school had made toward the school vision, while others were disappointed at the slow rate at which change was occurring at the school. When access to funding was restored, some faculty members believed that momentum had died and changes in project criteria might have created a gap that could not be bridged. Confusion was found in descriptions of the restructuring process at that time. For example, one teacher said: "When one person said 'restructuring' I didn't know what to think. When you say 'restructuring,' it doesn't mean the same to everybody. Yet, we used to get together and talk about it—but all think we meant the same thing. We now need to get together and talk about it so we can come up with a common understanding of what it means."

The Site Steering Committee recognized that after almost two years since the inception of the project, there were faculty members who still did not understand the PDS concept or wish to actively participate in restructuring activities. In order to provide information and instructional opportunities, and as a "celebration" of the five themes, a professional development conference was planned.

The professional development conference envisioned by MHS faculty members was a day-long conference modelled after professional conferences in education; calls for papers were distributed within the school and University communities, keynote speakers were enlisted, and decorations, handouts, and other materials were assembled. In order to make it possible for all of the faculty members to attend the conference, some special arrangements were needed. At the request of MHS faculty members, the county administration approved the cancellation of classes at MHS on the day of the conference—as if it were a "snow day." Hence, the conference was named the "September Snow Day." More than 200 people from the school, the county, the University, and other PDS sites participated. The September Snow Day event had a great impact on the faculty and the work that came after. Two representative quotes from teachers explain: "[The Snow Day] provided a forum for the entire school community to discuss and learn and grow. The Superintendent, the janitors and secretaries, students, parents, and University people, plus colleagues from other schools, were able to participate." "It allowed us to show each other the kinds of things we're doing in our classes and what we have learned in the past year as a

PDS. It also gave us the opportunity to learn from other schools and experts on technology, learning styles, the Foxfire approach, and other things we have an interest in." The knowledge gained and the common understandings developed poised the MHS faculty on the verge of action.

Lessons learned in Phase 3. Collaboration, while a time-consuming process, creates an environment that supports school change. Our discussion of collaboration refers to the collaboration between MHS and WVU; the collaborative relationships developed among teachers within MHS; and collaboration between the administration, the faculty, and the school community. During Phase 3, participation in restructuring activities strengthened past and current collaborations and created the opportunity and need to develop new and innovative relationships. The collaborators began to develop understandings of what it means to collaborate, and they took steps that built a foundation for future work together.

Creating an atmosphere of trust and risk taking allows for growth, development, and creative problem solving. The data revealed that sharing, providing support for innovations and "little tries," and developing an open dialogue helped create an atmosphere where teachers were able to experiment, stretch, learn, and grow. Effective communication and commonly held expectations were identified as fostering the development of trust. Pilot projects, brainstorming sessions, and authentic situations that required professional and/or personal trust had to be attempted in order for those involved to believe that a safe and trusting atmosphere actually existed. The history of past interactions, the willingness to take responsibility for actions, and time were necessary to support the development of this environment.

People participated in change activities for a variety of reasons. The reasons identified for participation and involvement in restructuring activities varied, with no predictable pattern. A common reason identified was a "need" to take a role in the Project. When people thought they could be a help to the school, their students, or their department, or if they thought they could "better" themselves either personally or professionally, they became involved. Others did not initiate participation, but served in various capacities because they were asked or felt they had some responsibility to the group, even if this was not a major focus of their own work.

Many saw the opportunity to participate as a professional obligation to improve the school for their students and for the University field experience students who trained there. An administrator noted: "They're not in it for the financial rewards, but for the excitement of being involved in something really exciting!" A teacher stated: "If there are going to be changes made, say, in my schedule or curriculum, I'd like to get my two cents in and share my ideas with others." Others viewed the project as a way to fund pet projects that would improve programs and practice at MHS: "Well, my personal feeling is that the way you get people involved is by getting them to work on short-term projects. The number of people who are going to want to work on long-term projects is limited, but, if a short-term project is meaningful and interesting, the number that are likely to participate is much higher."

Participation in change activities fosters personal and professional growth. "All in a professional development school are learners" was taken to heart by the PDS participants at MHS. The participants had learned a great deal. They demonstrated professional growth as they discussed what they had learned about change, restructuring, and improving instructional practices. There was personal growth as they learned about themselves—what motivated them and how they learned. The faculty and school community showed that they had learned about each other, as well. Teachers learned more about their colleagues and about their administration. These changes resulted in a better understanding of the process of change and the context of the site. As one teacher said during a meeting: "The P.D. in PDS stands for professional development!" Another observed: "I think what PDS means to me is that the faculty is motivated to find ways to develop themselves professionally, not only individually, but as a group, a department, an interest group, or whatever the case may be."

Several MHS teachers noted that their professional growth had been enhanced because they had taken advantage of special PDS courses taught at school sites. These courses included: (1) Discussion and Observation of Teaching, (2) Teacher as Researcher, and (3) Critical Thinking Skills. In addition to the classes, a professional library, videos, and the support of Benedum Grant funds to send faculty members to conferences had been very important to some teachers: "I don't have lots of time to go to graduate school or to take classes; my summers are kind of dictated. So this is a way of staying abreast of the current issues and changes in education. Even the discussions at meetings are beneficial to this."

Phase Four:—A Time for Action

Phase 4's title, "A Time for Action," was taken from a comment made by a faculty member during an interview: "This is the time for action. We must move toward attaining the goals and activities associated with the five themes. If we don't do something now, we'll never succeed."

Activities during this phase were aimed toward getting the faculty moving. The next step required dedication to the visions and themes and meant that forces had to be mobilized to design and initiate plans for making the school's vision a reality. Faculty input into planning and faculty commitment to accomplishing these goals were identified by participants as a needed focus of the Site Steering Committee and the faculty. As one teacher reflected: "I don't think we see apparent changes because we're still at the point where we're talking about philosophical changes. So there are not things that you can put your finger on. And some of us need to see something happen."

The first actions taken by the school during this phase of activity were necessitated by a change in criteria in the new grant agreement. Long-range strategic planning was required of all PDS sites. The first step in this strategic planning process was to train school-level facilitators to monitor and direct an open process of discussion and planning in each site. Ten MHS teachers were trained as facilitators, and the site is currently using previously identified themes in the creation of action plans to guide future school improvement activities.

Phase 4 activity focused on the theme of restructuring. The Site Steering Committee noted that, if radical changes were to come about, then major organizational restructuring must occur. MHS had identified a number of goals that they felt would support their themes and allow them to reach their vision. These goals included: (1) flexible scheduling, (2) curricular changes, which included interdisciplinary teaming, (3) heterogeneous grouping, (4) alternative assessment, and (5) the creation of a Teacher Education Center to provide support for the clinical supervision of student teachers and other field experience students. The Site Steering Committee recognized that achieving these goals would require (1) expertise that was not locally available, and (2) a coordination of efforts, which had not been attempted in the past. In response to this dilemma, the steering committee endorsed a plan to work with several consultants from Kentucky who had worked in a restructuring high school for almost five years. These university faculty members and public school teachers and administrators assisted MHS in developing a sequenced and integrated plan.

There remained a need at the school to explore the implications of restructuring from the view of those who were currently involved in the process. To this end, the faculty organized a "Restructuring Institute" that brought MHS faculty members together with University and public school personnel from Louisville. In addition to sharing their experiences, strategic planning themes were discussed and decisions made regarding next steps for the school. This "end of the year" activity included provisions for monetary support for summer work by faculty members involved in planning and implementing change.

During Phase 4, the MHS faculty recognized the need to involve students in an activity that would support their adjustment during high school. Collaboratively, the teachers and students designed a "Teen Forum." The Teen Forum was a conference that put the entire student body in contact with experts in such areas as drugs and alcohol, stress, family problems, peer pressure, and dating. Just as the September Snow Day allowed teachers to learn more about innovations that would affect their lives, the Teen Forum afforded students at MHS the opportunity to make choices and learn more about issues important in their lives.

The beginning of the 1992–93 school year brought "September Snow Day 2." The second Snow Day experience focused less on outside experts and more on internal experts: teachers shared successful restructuring activities they had piloted over the previous year and discussion groups met regarding specific restructuring plans, especially alternative forms of scheduling.

The September Snow Day activities, the Restructuring Institute, and the Teen Forum provided the school community with a voice in the direction and planning for change at MHS. As one teacher commented: "Knowing teachers planned and carried out such a special activity really makes you feel good about yourself and what we can accomplish when we work together."

Lessons learned in Phase 4. The development of new structures and programs can happen. It just takes patience, flexibility, and time. The focus of Morgantown High School's vision is to become a school for the twenty-first century. This entails creating new programs and the structures to support and make them a success. But change takes time, as does the development of new structures and programs. There are several pilot programs affecting change currently underway, as well as radical changes in scheduling, instructional techniques, and the use of technology in teaching.

Phase Five—Major Changes

The time after the Snow Days and Restructuring Institute was primarily focused on adopting a new schedule. However, before the faculty was willing to make a major change, they had many questions and concerns that needed to be addressed. Which model was most appropriate for MHS students and faculty? To find answers, teams of MHS teachers, with support from the Benedum Collaborative, researched the literature and visited several schools in neighboring states before sharing the various possibilities with their MHS colleagues. Deliberations and discussions of the pros and cons of the various options took place in MHS throughout the school year. However, shortly before student scheduling in the Spring of 1993, the principal sought and received a consensus of faculty support for a four-period block schedule with ninety-minute classes that would meet every other day. This decision was a major one for this mature, traditional faculty—they would be the first school in the state to implement block scheduling. The very fact that this faculty was undertaking this radical move was a real testimonial to the impact that the previous few years as a PDS had had on the faculty. They were now willing and reasonably accustomed to being risk-takers and innovators.

The faculty quickly recognized that, if the new ninety-minute classes were to be successful, the teachers would have to use more innovative teaching methods. Ninety-minute lectures would not only be unacceptable, but they would also most likely be fatal! To address this need, about half of the MHS faculty participated in an all-day summer workshop taught by a University faculty member who shared her expertise in collaborative teaching strategies.

This workshop was followed up with a similar one, but a mini version, at the beginning of the school year. It provided the vital information for those who had been unable to attend the summer workshop and was a refresher course for those who had attended.

The new schedule was implemented at the beginning of the 1992–93 school year, and everyone waited for the problems and complaints to begin. Much to everyone's surprise, especially the administrators', faculty and students alike adjusted more readily than anyone could ever have predicted. The data collected two months after school started revealed that only two of the almost ninety teachers were dissatisfied, and even those two did not favor returning to the old schedule. The teachers agreed that the new schedule was far less stressful than the previous seven-period day. Because they shared their Independent Research class with at least one other teacher, they had gained some additional planning time.

The students who were surveyed also expressed a high level of satisfaction with the new schedule. They enjoyed not having to prepare for all of their classes every night, and many of them found having a study period beneficial because they could not only do some of their homework but also had time to go to the library and guidance office or schedule and complete makeup work.

During that first year, the major complaints did not focus on what took place during the instructional periods but rather on what occurred during the Independent Research Period. The teachers were especially displeased with the inconsistent discipline and lack of structure and policies, believing that the IR period needed to be more uniform. A committee of teachers and administrators developed guidelines for the next year's IR classes; the result was a much more positive experience the following year.

Because of the options and flexibility that the new schedule provided, teachers were able to start thinking about curricular modifications and teaming options. Special education teachers adopted the inclusion model and began teaming with regular education classroom teachers. At first, both groups of teachers had reservations about the new approach and were understandably doing some "turf protecting," but they were so successful that the program has been fully accepted by both groups.

Additional teaming was undertaken in 1992–93 by several English, social studies, art, and music teachers, who piloted a "Linking the Humanities" course for honors level tenth and eleventh graders. Because of their success, additional honors level sections were added, and a comparable course will be piloted for de-tracked remedial and on-grade level students for the 1995–96 school year. Without the new schedule and the options it provided, it is highly unlikely these curricular changes would have been attempted or would have been so widely accepted.

In December 1994, the county superintendent announced that MHS would be adding the ninth grade in the Fall of 1997 and that $8 million had been made available through SBA funding to begin the renovations and additions that MHS would need to accommodate these additional students. So the faculty is once again deeply involved in the examination and reexamination of scheduling, curricular, and philosophical issues. However, because of the faculty's restructuring experiences over the past five years in a PDS, the fact that the next couple of years will be filled with disruptions, distractions, and hard work is not only being accepted but is also being anticipated as a challenge and a unique opportunity for reform.

Lessons learned in Phase 5. The implementation of new structures and programs can happen, but it takes leadership and dedicated faculty members who are willing to devote the time required to design and implement change. The new schedule was a major change at MHS, not only in the actual time schedule, but because it provided tangible evidence to a traditional faculty that something new could be an improvement and that they could identify and do whatever was necessary to adapt and make a major change successfully. The faculty recognized that they had to do "their homework" before they could make an informed decision. By studying the issues and options, they felt reasonably comfortable and willing to make the change. They were fortunate in having a leader who recognized the importance of having the faculty arrive at this decision through consensus and not by win/lose voting, so that it became something all were reasonably committed to.

The old adage, "success breeds success," is very true in this instance. Because of the success of the new schedule, the faculty is willing to pursue the challenges of redesigning the curriculum and addressing other innovations, with special emphasis and concern for the new ninth graders who will added in 1997. So the restructuring goes on and on and on.

Discussion

Through the PDS application process, open discussions, professional reading, and reflection, many of the teachers discovered that while many things had changed in the world in the previous sixty years, few changes had occurred at MHS and much had gone unnoticed. The faculty found they were not meeting the needs of a large segment of the student population, in particular those who were at risk of not being successful at MHS. Traditionally, MHS had been recognized for academic excellence, National Merit winners, and Ivy League-bound graduates. These traditions had been supported by little turnover in leadership throughout the history of the school and, until recently, a relatively stable student population. During the application process, the faculty discovered that the student body had changed in recent years, but that the programming at the school had not changed to meet the needs of these individuals.

The MHS tradition held a great deal of power at the school and in the community and may have prevented the early involvement of some faculty members. Many are now looking at building on past successes and creating new traditions that will support a continuous review and development of programs to meet the changing needs of the students, the community, and society.

Identified as a leader in academic standards, this school was not accustomed to playing catch-up. By and large, the faculty has been willing to do everything in its power to become a model of a restructuring high school. Thus, while tradition may have played a role in a slow start for MHS as a PDS site, it may also play a role in maintaining a commitment to being "on top" as a PDS site. One teacher said her goal was to, "within a few years, have buses full of teachers heading from Louisville to Morgantown to see how it is done," just as MHS teachers visited Fairdale High School in Louisville to see a model of a restructuring high school. That goal has been realized.

With restructuring comes the need for new or improved processes to facilitate new interactions, leadership opportunities, and the creation of new structures. Teachers and administrators become learners. They must learn about the change process, their student population, current trends in education, collaboration, and systematic, long-range planning. As Fullan and Parks (1981) noted, change is a process, not an event. The teachers involved in this project are finding out that the process is tiring and time-consuming, and it requires that they rethink their daily interactions.

In order to disseminate information, plan for change, and document the processes being developed, communication has been a key component in this change initiative. Communication has been difficult for the Morgantown High School faculty. The issue of communications was already a concern prior to becoming involved with the Benedum Collaborative. The size of the faculty, the size and configuration of the physical plant, and the lack of need to communicate or collaborate as fostered by the previous administrators created an environment where communication problems could, and did, build. Instead of communicating with colleagues, people came to work, shut their doors, taught their courses, and went home. This is no longer the case.

While learning about teaming, shared decision making, and site-based management, a need was created to discuss topics within departments, with the Site Steering Committee, or with those in a content area of interest. When the need was created, there were no effective processes in place for fulfilling this need. This initially caused great frustration among the faculty. While individual interactions within existing organizational structures began to improve, there were still many concerns and complaints about the communication of information from the Site Steering Committee to the rest of the faculty. And while ways to combat these problems were discussed at Steering Committee meetings, the followup on these solutions initially proved to be ineffective in meeting the needs of faculty.

Additionally, the Steering Committee was identified by several of those interviewed as being "elitist," since two of the most active members had doctoral degrees. This intimidated some people, while others stated that the Site Steering Committee was a "closed group" or a "secret society" that was making decisions for the rest of the school. Although Site Steering Committee meetings were open to the public, they were not attended by the public of MHS. This concern has dissipated as other faculty have joined the committee and involvement has broadened but communication remains an ongoing area of concern at the school. It is evident in current efforts to prepare for adding a ninth grade at MHS that the school has learned a great deal about how to foster involvement and communication within the faculty and with the larger school community.

Although the Site Steering Committee has been criticized regarding their communication processes, it is important to point out that this group was most effective in "steering" the faculty toward successful restructuring. They remained focused on the task of identification of goals and movement toward reaching those goals. While keeping this focus, the Site Steering Committee continuously identified problems in current processes and sought collaborative solutions to these problems.

Many PDS participants were surprised at the complexity of making changes and the chain of reactions that followed when a single aspect of the organization changed. The fact that they were participating in a project that was breaking new ground did not reassure the majority of those involved. Time to communicate and participate was a secondary issue for the teachers. Many teachers became creative at finding time to collaborate. Released time, stipends, the use of county staff development time, and other options created from department to department were identified by faculty members as allowing them to write grants, research topics, attend conferences, and design programs. The faculty have learned that change is a very complex and time-consuming activity.

Change is also an energy-consuming activity. Those who have taken leadership responsibilities in the project alternate from "tiredness" to "total exhaustion" to "exuberance" as new programs are initiated. One Site Steering Committee member commented: "If we don't get some help, we'll be worn out and exhausted, and fade into the distance." The original leaders have sought to expand the faculty's understanding of and involvement in leadership activities and are seeing some new leaders emerge as the current restructuring emphasis evolves.

Dealing with ambiguity, constant modification of process, procedures, and products, and the need to develop common understandings about ever-changing processes is very difficulty for many faculty members. Statements such as, "just tell us what to do or how to do it and we'll be happy to help" and "not another change, I just completed it this way!" have been common at MHS throughout the PDS process. March (1984) noted the importance of recognizing the multiple realities of teachers and the need to consider all of those realities in plans for change. While it may be important to recognize and include the multiple realities of teachers in plans for changes, it is probably more important to recognize that no realities are fixed. The recognition and inclusion of multiple realities of all the participants in a PDS will be a continuing struggle as new processes and understandings are continually being created. Pioneers must learn to accept that they may often go down the wrong path. The destination is still in view; a new direction must to be taken to reach it.

An additional issue has been the level of coordination and integration needed for lasting change to occur. Many of the faculty have begun to recognize that change can no longer be viewed as an avenue to short-term, isolated activities, but rather as a long-term plan to improve the quality of education for the students at MHS. Sizer (1991) points to the interdependent nature of change in schools; change any one component and the others will be affected as well. This revelation has been made and continues to be made at different times, during different phases, for different people engaged in the PDS process at MHS.

The type of organizational change that involves the creation of a well-articulated, collective school vision and a long-range strategic plan for reaching this vision is foreign to most public school teachers. Through the strategic planning process, the identification of themes and development of action plans that are all research-based and grounded in sound practice, the faculty has been able to see how the many small pieces of the curriculum, schedule, and organization interact and react to even the smallest changes. Also at issue was the congruence of curricular and assessment issues. Faculty realized that, when planning separately or in small groups without a common vision or purpose, situations could be created that were detrimental to a clearly sequenced and integrated program that meets the needs of the whole student.

Change did not occur as quickly or as dramatically as the participants had thought, hoped, or planned. MHS has taken steps to achieve their goals and develop programs around their identified themes. Teachers, students, parents, and University personnel have worked to drastically alter the daily class schedule and plan curricular changes that will create a more appropriate learning environment for all students. These changes grew out of many hours of discussion and program development, courses, seminars, and pilot projects. These changes have been very successful.

Still, many of the initial changes that resulted from the school's involvement in restructuring were not tangible "things" that could be "shown" to the community. Faculty members in PDSs could not say, "See, we have totally overhauled our teaching practices," or, "Our student test scores have increased by ten percent as a result of these activities." Early changes were in some cases tacit or attitudinal. Other changes were philosophical or, in some cases, personal.

These changes were described by teachers with statements such as, "I'm now more sensitive to those kids," or, "I am more aware of my own philosophy about teaching."

This too changed with the 1993–94 school year, when the restructured MHS schedule and course structure were implemented. Courses now meet in ninety-minute blocks of time on alternating days, thus allowing for more frequent use of hands-on activities and the utilization of a variety of other innovative instructional strategies. Several exciting new programs have been developed in conjunction with the new schedule: a team-taught humanities course, an expansion of a mastery learning integrated math program, and redesigned science programs.

The days of coming in and shutting the classroom door have ended at Morgantown High School. The faculty has moved reforms from paper to practice, using their best thoughts and professional judgment, current research, University and business partnerships, parents, and students to create a changing school for the twenty-first century.

References

Field, T. T. (1991). *Establishing professional development schools.* Paper presented at the annual meeting of the Association of Teacher Educators. New Orleans.

Fullan, M. (1991). *The new meaning of educational change.* New York: Teachers College Press.

Huberman, M. (1983). *Understanding change in education: An introduction.* Paris: UNESCO.

March, G. I. (1988). *The empowerment of teachers.* New York: Teachers College Press.

Schlecty, P. (1990). *Schools for the 21st century.* San Francisco: Jossey-Bass.

Sizer, T.R. (1991). No pain, no gain. *Educational Leadership 49*(10): 32–34.

10

THE STORY OF CHANGING SCHOOL-UNIVERSITY RELATIONSHIPS

NANCY E. HOFFMAN, GWEN SOCOL ROSENBLUTH, AND KAYE MCCRORY

Introduction

The process of changing school-University relationships began several years ago, when we initiated the Benedum Collaborative with its commitment to restructuring both public schools and teacher education at WVU. For many years, the University, like other teacher preparation programs, had cooperated with local schools to provide prospective teachers with field experience and student teaching placements. The schools and the University had enjoyed a reasonably pleasant, but distant relationship. Students were assigned to various schools for their practice, with prospective elementary education teachers spending considerably more time in field experiences than prospective secondary teachers. Supervision was done by University faculty or graduate assistants; as the literature depicts (Guyton and McIntyre 1990; Kennedy 1992), it was infrequent and lacked both thematic focus and continuity. Although field experiences and student teaching were seen as important by all participants, especially teacher education students, there were concerns about the impact of these experiences on both the schools and the teacher education program as teacher education enrollments increased. University faculty felt that student teaching was too much an apprenticeship that did not support the use of theory or the implementation of best practice. Public school faculty expressed frustration with the brevity of student teaching assignments and the teacher's role in evaluation and placement. Teacher education students were concerned about the amount of field experience they had and about varying expectations from schools and the University. All participants felt they had too little control! In short, it was a traditional teacher preparation program.

As the Benedum Collaborative began, student teaching and field experiences, which had long been the major point of contact between the schools and the teacher preparation program, were a natural starting point for discussion and collaboration. After all, each party had a real stake in field experiences, and supplied different experiences and complementary expertise. Examination of field experiences was a good starting point and has proven to be a productive focus for restructuring both teacher education and schools. Our pilot work has taken two basic forms: Teacher Education Centers (TEC) and demonstration sites. These pilot efforts have produced some valuable outcomes: caring relationships among students, children, and teachers (Duquette 1994; Noddings 1987); opportunities for reflection on and uncertainty about the technical and ethical aspects of teaching (Clarke 1995); and an appreciation for the backstage complexities of teaching that is rare in beginning teachers (Rust 1994).

This chapter will describe the nature and evolution of these new forms of school and University interaction and the impact of these changes on practicing and prospective teachers. First, these collaborations will be described as they have evolved into Teacher Education Centers at two sites: Suncrest Primary and Morgantown High School (MHS). Then we will discuss the development of demonstration sites at Central Elementary and MHS. We will close with a discussion of the impact of these connections on practicing and prospective teachers.

Teacher Education Centers

Suncrest Primary School

The Teacher Education Center (TEC) concept originated at Suncrest Primary in 1990. Suncrest Primary is a small school serving a residential area about a mile from the University. The school draws from an area that includes families from all socioeconomic levels, and has a history of strong parental involvement. When this project began, the principal was responsible for two schools. (She is now responsible only for Suncrest.) The school has eight teachers: two teachers for each of the first three grades, a Head Start teacher, and a kindergarten teacher. The faculty consists of women, mostly over forty, who have taught at the school for a number of years. The school served as a WVU student teaching site although the teachers did not accept early practica students. When Suncrest applied to be a PDS, their application indicated they had two major goals: (1) teaching in ways that were more responsive to students' learning styles, and (2) improving preservice teacher education. They felt an obligation to contribute to the teacher education program and had some ideas about how it could be improved.

In the Spring of 1990, shortly after Suncrest was named a PDS, the teachers invited the University's director of field experiences to come and talk with them and parent representatives about the student teaching program. The faculty expressed frustration with the brevity of student teaching assignments and with the inconsistent quality of University supervision. They felt that they could do more to prepare a student teacher if that student were assigned to the school for a longer time and supervision were more frequent.

As we discussed our experiences, we listed our common concerns. Opportunities for preservice teachers to develop professionally were limited by the length of placements. Because there was not enough time for students to learn the context and refine their own work, they did not get a sense of how children developed over time. They saw only fragments of curriculum and were not at the school long enough to become members of the school community. Even in a school that involved many parents, there was really no way for students to experience any significant work with parents. The teachers felt that just as students began to "really get into it," they had to leave for another placement and start over, from the same point they had begun at their previous site. As one teacher said, "Sometimes I see a problem and I know I can't solve it in the time I'll have with them, so I just don't say anything. What good does it do to upset the student, and maybe the supervisor, over something I can't change?" The teachers were frustrated by the feeling that student teachers were "like ships that pass in the night" and felt there was little incentive to mentor a novice who was with them for such a brief period.

We also realized that the current system did not encourage students to learn from one another. There was no small, familiar peer group to help them and no ongoing association among students at different points in the program. The system, which was intended to allow students to see a diversity of children and receive a variety of feedback, did not seem to be achieving its goals. Students were not demonstrating that they actually comprehended the diversity they encountered in going to different schools; they seemed more attuned to personal survival than to children. The system also limited contact with more experienced students and discouraged teachers from giving students meaningful feedback and involving them in the school community. As we considered these problems, we realized that there was a lot of diversity within Suncrest Primary. Families from all socioeconomic levels were represented, and the classroom teachers had very different personalities and used a wide variety of approaches in their teaching. We began to think that we could better achieve our goals by having students spend more time in one school than by having them go to five different schools for "diverse experiences."

State certification requirements precluded student teachers' staying in the building longer than eight weeks, so we began to explore other ways to extend Suncrest's contact with prospective teachers. The Suncrest faculty had not accepted early field experience students for a number of years, feeling that the University expectations for these students were too disruptive to their program. After vigorously discussing the value of some field assignments, we decided that

222 Hoffman, Rosenbluth, and McCrory

it might be possible to establish a program in which a small group of students completed all their field experiences (except the middle school level student teaching placement) at Suncrest. That meant that each student would complete the four semesters of field experience required in the program at Suncrest: a semester of early childhood field experience, a semester of literacy field experience, a semester of methods "block" field experience, and the eight weeks of early childhood student teaching. Students would leave Suncrest to do their middle school placement in the second half of student teaching. Suncrest teachers would have nearly two full years with a teacher education student. We finally decided to set up cohorts of three students, which meant that there would be twelve WVU students in the school every semester but only three of them would be new, and only three of them would leave.

We continued to explore the question of supervision, which was more difficult to answer. The teachers wanted the same supervisor every semester, and it was a logical request. Why put students in a building for an extended period of time so they learn more about children, curriculum, and teaching and then send someone as a supervisor who does not know the context? We needed the supervisor to be familiar with the school's program, students, and teachers, effective in helping students improve their work, and, obviously, present in the school much more than was common. We tried to match these expectations with the current structure of University teaching loads, and found no match. This led us to consider other options, and it became obvious that the logical person to play the role we were describing was someone on the Suncrest faculty. The faculty knew one another, they knew their students and their program, they were always there, they would know the University students, and many of them were strong, experienced cooperating teachers. After examining the role we wanted a supervisor to play, we concluded that if one of the teachers could be free every morning, she could meet all the needs we had defined. We decided we wanted to create a new role: site supervisor.

We had involved parent representatives throughout our discussions; but, as this program began to take shape, parents became more important than we had ever imagined they would be. They had, understandably, expressed some concern about the number of strangers introduced to their children's lives because of University field experience placements. They thought having a small group of students work at the school for two academic years would be a better arrangement for the children, and we agreed. As we began to talk about the possibility of releasing a primary teacher from her classroom for half a day, the parent perspective was again very helpful. Working with the parent representatives, we were able to garner parental support for the program, which they saw as reducing the number of "passing strangers" in the school, improving the supervision of student work with their children, and creating more opportunities for flexibility and individualization. They also expressed a commitment to helping prepare teachers who would be sensitive to children's needs and interested in working cooperatively with parents. As we proposed our ideas to the county school system and the University, it was very helpful to have parents with us saying this program would be beneficial for their children. That was the first question asked in both places! In fact, when the formal proposal to establish the TEC at Suncrest was introduced, approved, and funded in the summer of 1990, it was originally presented by a parent.

Working within the county school system's hiring structure, we posted a job description and conducted interviews for the site supervisor position. A first grade teacher at Suncrest who was an experienced cooperating teacher was selected as the site supervisor. The principal and the first grade teacher then interviewed candidates and selected another teacher for the critical role of first grade co-teacher. This teacher would teach the first grade class when the site supervisor was supervising University students. The two teachers have now co-taught successfully for five years.

In the Fall of 1990, the TEC "opened" for business. The Suncrest site supervisor and University's director of field experiences selected three students in each field experience and assigned them to the TEC, deliberately choosing students who were vocal, had strong academic records, and seemed to work well with others. Starting any new program is a challenge, and we wanted a strong start-up group! In the first year of the TEC's operation, the site supervisor took a course in clinical supervision and completed an independent study that focused on developing the TEC program. These experiences helped in more fully developing the TEC program, deciding what staff development needed to be done and when, working out strategies for making placements, and encouraging peer mentoring among the teacher education students. The site supervisor also began attending meetings at WVU as part of the faculty for the "block" and other field experiences. Her voice as a classroom teacher has been valuable in helping faculty to redesign or develop alternatives for a number of field assignments.

Although Suncrest TEC students have the same course expectations and field assignments that other WVU students have, their experiences are much better coordinated than other students' experiences. First, the students must apply and be selected for the program. Interested students complete an essay on the benefits they expect the program will provide them and they will provide the school if they are selected. The essays are screened and likely candidates are interviewed by the site supervisor and field experience director. The three students selected begin their first semester at Suncrest with introductions and orientation: learning what and where the facilities are, having names and photos posted as TEC students, meeting the teachers and the more experienced TEC students, interviewing some of the itinerant professionals who serve the school, becoming familiar with the school's service area, and starting a portfolio, a requirement for TEC students. Because the first semester field experience takes place in Head Start or kindergarten classes, which are held in an annex building, these orientations are an especially important part of the first semester. The orientations are conducted by the site supervisor, who also confers with students and teachers on their field experience assignments.

In the second semester, TEC students complete a literacy field experience in a grade one, two, or three classroom. In this setting, they are introduced to team planning and are expected to explore school and county library resources as part of their assignments. Their work is observed by the site supervisor, who works closely with the students and teachers to monitor their growth. At this time the students also begin to familiarize themselves with the teaching by employing learning styles and integrated units, which are both important parts of the school's program. This semester also provides opportunities for some first looks at site-based management, child study teams, and parent involvement.

In the third semester, TEC students return to Suncrest for "block," a much more extensive field experience. Placements for "block" and student teaching are planned to address the needs and interests students have demonstrated. In this semester, they begin to attend school governance meetings, receive considerable training in learning styles instruction, and tour the neighborhood. Professional development seminars are conducted by the site supervisor and other faculty members as needs and interests are recognized. By this time students seem to have identified teachers whose styles or practices particularly interest them, and they often arrange to spend extra time with those teachers. These students begin to make a more significant contribution to the school.

Before the student teaching semester starts, TEC students begin research for the integrated unit planned to accommodate a variety of learning styles that will be collaboratively developed in student teaching. This unit is a major curriculum development effort and an important culminating experience. During their eight weeks of student teaching at Suncrest, TEC student teachers also attend a Board of Education meeting, work with parents, mentor less experienced TEC students, participate in all-school meetings, spend a day with the principal, and complete their portfolios.

In the Spring of 1992, another program for preservice teachers was begun at Suncrest at the request of a parent group and influenced by a tutoring program developed earlier at MHS. This weekly after-school tutoring program for children who require extra attention and support is known as FLIP (Fun Learning in Progress). The program is coordinated by a Suncrest teacher who provides orientation and initial training, oversees the tutoring sessions, and conducts reflective seminars. Prospective teachers, typically freshmen and sophomores, have an opportunity to earn one elective credit by tutoring a child, using plans prepared by the child's teacher. This experience helps them clarify their career goals while also helping children.

Morgantown High School

Morgantown High School (MHS) has long been noted for outstanding academic programs, which have produced an exceptional number of National Merit Scholars. The school's academic programs include a long-standing arrangement allowing MHS students to begin early study at WVU. Despite this cooperative arrangement and the school's proximity to the University, there was little interaction between the faculty at MHS and the WVU teacher education program. Many MHS faculty felt that University faculty did not respect the public school teachers' expertise and sought to work with them only to advance their own research agendas. University faculty seemed to read the "MHS attitude" accurately and found the school a difficult place to work on the rare occasions they were allowed access. There was a perception at the University that the school would only accept the most outstanding student teachers and then did not give them a very good experience. Student teacher placements in academic areas were rare. As late as the 1988–89 school year, this large school accepted only nine student teachers and three pre-student teaching field experience students. Student teachers did not feel accepted and often indicated they found MHS a difficult place to work. One MHS teacher described the faculty's attitude toward preservice teacher education as "mixed and basically unenthusiastic."

As part of the application process to become a PDS, MHS had to describe how the school would collaborate with WVU in the preparation of preservice teachers. Responding to the question required the faculty to formulate a role for themselves in preservice teacher education. Since the Benedum Collaborative focused on both PDS and the redesign of teacher education, the MHS faculty began to see some possibilities for work in improving preservice teacher education. Many MHS faculty chose to serve on PDS development and teacher education redesign teams, experiences that increased the contact between MHS and WVU faculty and tore down some of the barriers, imaginary and otherwise, that had built up over the decades. Working on these teams, MHS faculty felt their expertise was valued, and a new openness to work with preservice teacher education began to emerge. These new relationships and this new openness meant that, when the call came asking for student teaching and pre-student teaching placements, the response was a little more positive. The school accepted a few more pre-student teachers in the 1990–91 school year.

In the Spring of 1991, several experiences came together that led the MHS faculty to consider a new way of working with preservice teachers. First, the development of a school vision and action plans made the teachers realize that they had pupils who needed one-on-one academic tutoring that they could not provide because of class size. Second, their work with pre-student teachers made them realize that the preservice teachers would benefit from more and earlier field experiences. Meanwhile, at the suggestion of the principal, a third experience was initiated. The University director of field experiences held two meetings at the school to discuss the future of field experiences at MHS. In these meetings, which were attended by a significant portion of the school's faculty, the teachers expressed some openness to more work with teacher education students and vented frustrations with some earlier experiences. (Hearing someone from the University say that their concerns were legitimate seemed to be an important part of these meetings.) A number of teachers who had not been willing to accept a student teacher now indicated they would be willing to "try it." These three factors led the teachers to ask the University director to help identify a way to use University students as tutors.

In a series of meetings that extended into the summer, we designed a pilot tutoring program that would give teacher education students an opportunity to engage in earlier field experiences and MHS pupils an opportunity to receive one-on-one assistance directed by their teachers. The teachers would identify the students who would be involved, and they would also develop the plan and materials they believed were needed. They would then share these with the tutor. After the lesson had been taught, the teacher would seek feedback on the student's progress and any problems and/or concerns the University student might have experienced. The situation was ideal for collaboration because the project met a real need in both organizations, and all participants could make real and different contributions to the discussions. The result of these discussions was a pilot program known as the Academic Assistance Program (AAP), which has now been operating successfully for four years. AAP has spawned two other site-based tutoring programs, and our experiences with the program helped us decide to make a year of tutoring the first field experience in the redesigned teacher education program. Our success with this program certainly contributed to the expanded MHS-WVU collaboration.

In the Fall of 1991, WVU faculty, responding to a request from MHS teachers, provided a half-day professional development session on the teacher education program. To give the MHS faculty a fuller understanding of the teacher education curriculum, both the core pedagogy courses and the discipline's content and pedagogy requirements were discussed. Once again, WVU and public school faculty came together in a way that met a need for both groups. This kind of information sharing and communication encouraged MHS teachers to work with more WVU students in a more informed way.

As MHS teachers expanded their work with WVU students, they became concerned about integrating the teacher education students more fully into the school. They needed "more time" with the teacher education students, and they wanted to use the time that they had more efficiently. The University director began experimenting with a way to address the problem in 1991, when a group of students completed both pre-student teaching (Spring 1991) and student teaching (Fall 1991) at MHS under the direction of a generalist University supervisor. The supervisor was a doctoral student who had done some supervision at the school in previous semesters in his content area, science, and had taught the general methods course taken during the pre-student teaching field experience. The cooperating teachers and teacher education students were enthusiastic. Even though the experiences at MHS were of no longer duration than those in the past, the teachers felt the teacher education students performed considerably better than previous student teachers who had been assigned to the school only for their student teaching. The teachers were also impressed by the seminars held on their site each week, noting that the student teachers gained insight and support from these meetings and learned a great deal from one another. The student teachers were equally positive about the experience (Francis 1992). Both groups enthusiastically recommended similar experiences for future student teachers. The support for a generalist supervisor was a new idea at MHS. In the past, it had been assumed that content knowledge was required of a University supervisor. Because having a site supervisor who was an expert in every content area was not possible, this shift in thinking was an important change.

In the Spring and Summer of 1992, plans were made to initiate site-based supervision and cohort groups at MHS. An English teacher at the school was selected as site supervisor, and a TEC was established at Morgantown High. Unlike the elementary education program, the WVU secondary education program required only one semester of field experience prior to student teaching; therefore, cohort groups at MHS spent only two semesters at the school. In the first semester, selected students (like the Suncrest TEC, admission is limited, and interested students must apply) spent six to eight half-days at MHS for their pre-student teaching field experience. In the second semester, they completed their first student teaching placement at MHS. This placement was initially an eight-week placement. In 1993–94 it became a fifteen-week placement, and in 1994–95 we settled on a thirteen-week placement. To satisfy certain certification requirements, students did their second student teaching placement, which has varied from eight to one to three weeks, at a middle school. TEC placements are arranged by the site supervisor in consultation with the principal and field experience director.

The site supervisor, who teaches English in the morning and supervises TEC students in the afternoon, has developed a sequence of orientation and professional development activities for TEC students assigned to the school. Prestudent teachers become familiar with the school and its mission, the faculty, and the resources available as part of their orientation during pre-student teaching. They also work closely with one teacher in this experience, planning and implementing classroom instruction. At the end of the pre-student teaching, student teaching placements are finalized, and TEC students begin to prepare for their student teaching assignments.

During student teaching, the scheduling of professional development has varied, but, based on feedback from TEC students and teachers, a schedule that features intensive staff development in the first two weeks of the placement and weekly seminars thereafter has evolved. Student teaching seminars build on the information gained in prestudent teaching. During the first two weeks of the placement, student teachers meet with a number of MHS faculty and staff. They meet with the principal, who discusses the school and its philosophies and answers questions based on their concerns. They meet with the assistant principal for a thorough grounding in the school's discipline and attendance policies. They meet with the coordinator of the Student Assistance Program, who informs them of the programs available, warning signs, and the referral process, which they are encouraged to use. The librarians meet with the student teachers to share the vast resources available in all content areas, to explain the policies and procedures for using the resources and facilities, and to demonstrate the available technology used for research. Student teachers meet on at least two occasions with the head of the special education department, who shares information on IEP's, student needs, teaching strategies, and the school's collaborative-consultative program. Student teachers also meet with MHS's technology coordinator who provides several workshops that introduce the student teachers to the instructional technology available at MHS. Student teachers consult with the technology coordinator and their cooperating teachers to select technology appropriate for their content area and ways to successfully implement it in their instruction. If additional training is needed, arrangements are made to provide it at MHS. The site supervisor provides training in using writing as a mode of learning, and a University faculty member provides a workshop on promoting critical thinking. All TEC students receive monthly calendars of MHS's extracurricular events which they are encouraged to attend. They also attend Faculty Senate and/or faculty meetings, participate in professional development offered while they are assigned at MHS, and contribute to curriculum redesign at the school, which in the Fall of 1993 moved to a new schedule of ninety-minute periods, meeting every other day. Since communication is a constant concern in a large school such as MHS, and teachers have limited time to meet, the site supervisor sends weekly memos to cooperating teachers and TEC students to keep everyone informed and focused.

MHS has changed from a school that in the 1989–90 year grudgingly accepted eight pre-student teachers and nine student teachers to a school that hosts all sorts of students and makes them feel welcome. Since the 1992–93 academic year, MHS has annually hosted about a dozen AAP tutors, about twenty pre-student teachers, about twenty student teachers, about 100 educational psychology student observers, and between fifteen and twenty science methods students. Even more exciting than the growth in numbers has been the growth in faculty interest and enthusiasm. MHS teachers like having student teachers, and the student teachers feel welcome. Student teachers consistently report that they are treated as faculty members and supported by the whole school. Even teachers who do not work with student teachers in their own classrooms help the TEC students by providing technology training, sharing resources and materials, or simply being a willing sounding board for their ideas and/or concerns. If a student teacher is upset, the site supervisor is sure to hear about it from a number of teachers, all of whom will have offered assistance or support. Having a supervisor at MHS to coordinate activities and assist cooperating teachers and TEC students is certainly one reason for the change in attitude. The responsibility MHS has assumed for teacher preparation also allows the faculty to take great pride in the graduates of their TEC. When a former TEC student is offered a job, it is good news for the entire MHS faculty, because they have played an important part in the preparation of that student.

Just as introducing and implementing site supervisors and a modified field experience at Suncrest Primary and Morgantown High School have had a significant impact on the WVU teacher education program, so have demonstration sites.

Demonstration Sites

Morgantown High School

MHS was our first example of a demonstration site, a program in which a number of WVU students spend a limited period of time in a public school to observe and, in some cases, participate in a model program. Demonstration sites allow a large number of students to see real teachers use the practices they are learning about in their University classes. The first program began in the fall semester of 1991, when approximately twenty WVU Science Methods (C&I 144) students became actively involved in preparing and presenting lessons to students at MHS. In August, three MHS science teachers contacted a WVU professor and asked if she would be interested in placing her science methods students in a practicum situation. She was eager to do so, and together the public school teachers and University professor devised a curriculum outline that included the responsibilities of the students and the mentors, general requirements for the high school placements, learning goals for the students, and evaluation methods to be used by the MHS mentor teachers. The students were placed with one of the three MHS teachers. They began to visit the high school in late September and observed several classes and labs, including astronomy, biology, and chemistry. The WVU students maintained ongoing contact with the mentor teacher throughout the semester. Eventually, the students were assigned lessons to prepare. They were required to write plans for a predetermined lesson, have these reviewed by the mentor, prepare the necessary materials for the lesson, and eventually teach the lesson to students. The format for the lesson plans was presented in their WVU Science Methods class. The University professor sent evaluation forms to the mentor teachers, and students were scored on several aspects of their performance. A percentage grade was given for the presentation of the lesson. In addition, suggestions for improvement of the lesson were added. Students prepared a second lesson that was a lab activity. The same format was followed. These lessons were inquiry activities. Students were to practice the methods they had studied in class and had observed at MHS. In addition to classroom activities, most of the University students accompanied MHS students on a field trip to the Carnegie Science Center, acting as chaperones and observing the students outside their classroom environment. Many said that this experience was extremely valuable.

Several of the WVU students volunteered to tutor MHS students who were having difficulties in science. They made appointments to work with the students after school or during the class period, under the guidance of the mentor teacher. Some of these students were working with the MHS Academic Assistance Program, but a few simply volunteered, to gain experience.

Three of the University students who were in this methods class were eventually placed in their pre-student teaching and student teaching experiences at MHS. They emphasized how valuable their previous experience at MHS had been and how easy the transition to student teaching was, compared to their classmates who had not had the same series of placements. Two more of the students also did substitute teaching at MHS and often referred to the value of having a teaching placement at MHS during their Science Methods course. Because of the success of this demonstration site, other schools have been added to the list of placement sites, to lighten the MHS mentor teachers' load.

Central Elementary School

A second demonstration site, focused on elementary literacy instruction, has evolved at Central Elementary, a PDS located in downtown Morgantown. A number of the students in this K–6 school are transient because the school's service area includes downtown apartments and WVU's graduate family housing. The school population typically includes children from between ten and twenty different countries, many of whom do not speak English. When the school became a PDS, its vision included an emphasis on whole language and literacy. A number of efforts at Central were directed at promoting language development and literacy, including a push-in speech and language program, an award winning push-in Chapter I program that used a whole language approach, and the "Students as Authors" project created and developed by students and teachers to publish and market books written by children for children.

A WVU literacy faculty member studying collaboration and empowerment in all PDS sites became concerned about the amount of WVU faculty involvement in the sites. She decided to try to foster more collaboration between University faculty and public school teachers. Since she had previously talked with the Chapter I teacher at Central and knew that she was interested in collaborating with the University, she contacted her. After some discussion, they decided to form a group with a literacy orientation. Reluctant to call it anything as formal or "University" as a study or research group, they settled on the name, Literacy Discussion Group (LDG). They also decided that, if the group were to be truly collaborative, there would be no agenda. Rather, the group members would decide what they would do. Setting a meeting time after school on Wednesdays, they invited all teachers in elementary PDSs and a number of WVU literacy faculty and graduate students to attend a first meeting in January 1993 at Central. (However, the invitation letter indicated that, if teachers from other schools chose to be involved, the group would rotate meeting sites so that no one group would have to do all the travelling.) At the first meeting, the attendance was light—there were the two organizers, two of the faculty member's doctoral students, another WVU literacy faculty member, and a third grade teacher from Central who was not particularly interested in discussing literacy but assumed that the LDG was a "Benedum sponsored" activity and, therefore, deserved her support. As the six people present began to talk about what they might do, one of the WVU faculty members expressed some concerns about the literacy methods course she was teaching. Her students were having difficulty understanding some of the material she was presenting because they had no context for it; they had never seen it done. Because the field experience did not start for another month, the group began to talk about ways to give the students an authentic context, and settled on the idea of having all ninety of the under-graduate students in literacy methods visit Central and observe a typical morning in the third grade class. The LDG planned this experience, and on the appointed Wednesday, the third grade class met on the stage in the all-purpose room and the WVU students observed for three hours. The husband of one of the WVU instructors volunteered to videotape the morning session, which began with math. After math, the Chapter I teacher came in to involve the children in whole language activities. Then the third grade teacher did her basal reading lesson.

On Friday, after reviewing the tape, the Central teachers went into the literacy class. They gave a short presentation, using sections of the video to illustrate their discussion of what they were doing and why. The literacy students raised questions, and the group discussed what they had seen. The activity went well and was a success for the LDG; in retrospect, however, it may be that the activity served another purpose in the development of the LDG, because the tape revealed two things about the third grade class that no one had noticed on Wednesday. First, the election portion of the Chapter I teacher's activity had been completely and silently controlled by one child. Second, the WVU students felt that the third grade teacher favored the ESL students. Open discussion of these issues was difficult, but that shared experience seemed to bond the LDG into a cohesive group.

Having finished their first project, the LDG began talking about new options. One of the graduate students, an experienced teacher, raised a question about why her junior high reading students had invariably disliked reading. Was it just the nature of junior high students or was it something that they had learned in school? The group began to talk about whole language as a strategy that responded to students' interests and might keep them interested in reading. Since the third grade teacher had previously indicated she was a "dyed in the wool" basal teacher, the group was quite surprised when she indicated that she might try some whole language "for a while" with the LDG's help. (What she did not tell the group for several months was that, when she had watched the videotape, she had noticed that the children were much more actively involved in whole language instruction than in basal instruction.) It was agreed that the third grade teacher would conduct an experiment during the last twelve weeks of school. First she would teach a six-week basal unit, and then she would teach a six-week whole language unit that the group would design. Before any of that instruction began, the LDG planned to gather some data using the basal pre and post tests and reading attitude surveys. As a group, the LDG selected books, designed activities, and planned a classroom schedule for the whole language unit. At the completion of the sequence, there was evidence that the children did just as well on the basal tests during the whole language unit when they received no instruction on the basal material as they had during the basal unit. The attitude surveys and observations of the class indicated major changes in the children's attitudes and in their roles in the classroom.

In the Fall of 1993, the LDG's membership expanded to include a few more WVU faculty and a few more Central teachers. The group began to consider its next project. Initially, discussions centered on the teachers' new groups and problems they were facing, with less focus on literacy than in the previous year. The group did some work on portfolios, because that was a concern for some members. At the end of October, a new LDG project suddenly "popped out" while the Chapter I teacher interacted with WVU literacy methods students who had been placed with her. One day, she asked their WVU instructor why she did not address the writing process in the methods course. Since the instructor had devoted a month of her course to that topic and her students had used the process to publish a book of their own work, she was quite shocked to hear that the same students did not know how to use the writing process with children. This discussion led the LDG to discuss how this could happen and to conclude that it might be helpful for literacy methods students to immediately practice what they had learned in the field experience, by directly relating class theory to personal practice. The group began talking about ways to redesign the literacy methods course. As the discussions progressed, the WVU instructor debated how much change she was comfortable with. As they planned, it was realized that the logical place to teach the course was at the school and, after some soul searching, the WVU instructor decided to try it. With support from a group of Central teachers and the school's principal, the Central faculty agreed that the course could be taught in their library for two of its three weekly meetings, and four teachers agreed to provide field experience sites for the literacy students on Mondays and Wednesdays.

Based on observations of students' field performance, the LDG developed a revised syllabus, adding several elements and changing some assignments. During the 1994 spring semester, one section of literacy methods was taught at Central two days a week. Because that winter's weather had closed both the local schools and the University more times than ever before, the syllabus was revised and re-revised to accommodate the weather as well as the interests and expertise of two Central teachers, who were not part of the LDG but wanted to be involved in this particular project, and the needs of the students in the class. A number of the sessions were taught by members of the Central faculty while the WVU instructor taught their Central children. After the instructional portion of the class, University students implemented what they had learned with their assigned small group of first-, third-, fifth-, or sixth grade students under their University instructor's supervision. It is interesting to note that while the Central teachers were involved in the course, they were not very much involved in the field portion of the course, often spending that time away from their classrooms. The LDG recognized that the role of the teachers in the field component and the weak relationship between the students and the cooperating teachers would need to be addressed if the experience were to be repeated. They reviewed and revised the course before repeating it in the fall.

Over the next two semesters, Central faculty's participation in the literacy methods course gradually increased to include all the teachers in the school. Each semester, input is sought from Central faculty, Central students, WVU faculty, and WVU students. This feedback is used to make further modifications in the course. The course now involves instructors from WVU, Central, and some other schools, each contributing in their particular area of expertise. This demonstration site has not only enriched the experiences of teacher education students, it has forged new, collaborative relationships among veteran teachers, WVU faculty, University students, and children.

Impact of Changing Relationships

Preservice Teachers

Our teacher education students recognize that their experiences as part of the changing relationship between the PDSs and the University are worthwhile.

Most of the experiences that have grown out of our collaboration are not required in the current teacher education program, although many of them are an integral part of the redesigned program which began in 1995. Our students compete for admission to these pilot programs, knowing that they take more commitment, more energy, and, in the end, more time than the traditional program. Why do they prefer these programs? Is it just because they are new? Is it because the students whose parents are teachers advise them, at least according to some students, to "get into one of those [pilot programs]. That's how teacher education ought to be done?" After dozens of interviews with students who have participated in these programs, we have gleaned some ideas about why these programs are considered so beneficial to teacher education students.

TEC students have a sense of belonging in their assigned schools. They are "Suncrest students" or "MHS students," and they can tell you their school's vision, they know where everything is, and they are known. They feel a part of the school, and that makes an important difference to them. As one student said, "It's not like some teacher just said, 'Yeah, OK, I guess I can take a student teacher.' The school really wants us there, and they want us to succeed. They're proud of the stuff they're doing, and they're always showing us things. . . . We're [TEC students] all part of the staff. It's great." Students also value the time spent with practicing teachers. As one said, "I think like a teacher now and it's because when you get to know teachers and spend a lot of time with them, you think differently. . . . I hear some of the others [student teachers] talk about school and I know they're missing the important issues . . . things I learned a long time ago."

TEC students also have a sense that they belong to the TEC student group as part of their particular cohort and as part of the larger group of more and less experienced TEC students. At Suncrest, it is typical to see older TEC members sharing ideas and information with "the young ones." In exit interviews, Suncrest TEC students frequently mention their gratitude for the support and help received from more experienced students and their pleasure in being able to assist less experienced students. "When I hear them saying, 'That's hard,' or 'Bobby really has an attitude,' and I can help them, it makes me realize how much I've learned." No TEC student feels that progress through the teacher education program is painless, but there is a sense of the "shared ordeal" that Howey and Zimpher (1989) found was part of effective teacher education programs. As one MHS TEC student said, "When I have a kid who's giving me fits, the others know who he is, and they give me ideas and then I'll know some of their kids. We're all in this together."

TEC students think the site supervisor makes an essential difference in the program. "She's always there and she helps me figure out what to do when I have a problem." "My friends at other schools don't see their supervisors that much. I see mine all the time." "Since she knows everybody here she could help me figure out what was going on." "My teacher and I really get along and she's doing things now that she saw me do. . . . I like that. If my supervisor didn't know us both so well, I don't think we would have been matched up." The supervisor's availability, familiarity with the school and faculty, and credibility as a "real teacher" are valued by TEC students. "I couldn't figure out why my third period class was so rude to me. I asked Dr. Hoffman for ideas and she gave me three or four but she didn't know the kids. Dr. Rosenbluth knew the kids so she could help me more. I ended up doing something Dr. Hoffman suggested; but, because my supervisor knew the kids, I didn't have to guess which was the best thing to do." In exit interviews or conversations, every TEC student recognizes the importance of the site supervisor being "the right kind of person." When pressed to identify what makes a person "right" for the job, they talk about a positive approach, openness and approachability, communication skills, flexibility (but not elasticity), expertise as a teacher, liking people, and political skills. Many students have indicated that the site supervisor "makes or breaks" the program, and we agree with them.

Another advantage students see is the continuity of feedback they receive and the high expectations which are held for them. "I wasn't very organized that semester so Mrs. McCrory put me with Mrs. Dyer the next semester and, boy, did I get organized! She's incredible. Now I know how to organize and I do it. I have to." "When I needed to try a different way of handling some things, my supervisor sent me to see what some other teachers do and then we talked about it with my teacher and decided what I should do. . . . They were really working to help me and I didn't want to disappoint them so I did what they asked. . . . It was hard, but it worked." Students also comment on the growth they see in their own work over time and on the fact that a lack of growth cannot be hidden. "She's always there to check on you, not like Big Brother or anything, but she's there and you know it. It made me work harder." "I have some friends who aren't serious about teaching. They don't understand why I do all this. I tell them it's a good thing they aren't at my school. It's NOT a good place to be if you just want to goof around."

Perhaps the words that best illustrate the difference a TEC program can make for preservice teachers came from one of the MHS participants. "On the first day of my friend's student teaching, she couldn't find a parking place, so she was late. Then her teacher was absent, and the principal didn't even remember she was coming. She didn't know anybody and nobody talked to her. She was really upset. I told her it would get better, but I don't think it has. I'm working on plans and units and the computer, going to the kids' games. She's still worrying about things like where to get an overhead. It seems like a waste of time. I mean she's not even thinking about important things. She just wants it to be over so she can have her own class. Her teacher is nice to her and everything, but it's a waste."

TEC students are learning to teach in places where they form caring, connected relationships with children, experienced teachers, and peers— relationships that Dempsey, in Chapter 1, suggests may be at the heart of the teaching profession. These connections and relationships help TEC students understand that teaching is not simply an intellectual endeavor, it is a moral endeavor that affects children's lives. That understanding makes them more committed to learning to teach well.

Practicing Teachers

If the preservice teachers think the changes that have developed in TECs are good, the practicing teachers think they are terrific These teachers are working with more preservice teachers more often and investing more energy in that work. There is a new sense of ownership and pride in the work teachers do with teacher education students. Comments such as, "The University doesn't care what we think," or, "That's theory, forget about it because it doesn't work," are rarely heard. The teachers talk about "our students," "our tutors," and "our TEC." When a TEC student gets a teaching job, it's good news for everyone at the school. That is their student! Why is this working? What does it change for teachers? We have talked about this with a number of teachers to try to determine what this change means for them. We think it means several things: a sense of ownership and commitment, an opportunity to mentor, an impetus for change, increased professional communication, more control over their time, and benefits for their pupils.

The belief that teachers are first and foremost responsible for their own pupils had long discouraged MHS teachers from allowing a "beginner" to teach their pupils and "slow them down." How do you go from that view of the world to a belief that having WVU students in the school is a good idea? Very slowly! First, you review all the history: who had a terrible student, what the University supervisor did not do, what was the worst content error of all time, who was the worst cooperating teacher ever. Air it all until all the history and all the ghost stories have been told. Then, you begin to talk about the concerns, and sooner or later something "pops out"—something small that can be done successfully and built on. You keep talking and something else appears; that is how relationships are built, through purposeful, positive, personal contact. As trust and under-standing build, collaborative work becomes possible. As collaborative work actually gets done, a sense of ownership and control develops and the project is "ours." Individuals know that they have a stake in the effort and have some control over what happens. Involving teachers in the evolutionary planning of joint projects lets them know they can have a real impact on outcomes.

When teachers are committed to working with preservice teachers, they need time to make an impact. Having the TEC students "around long enough" seems to be a universal reinforcer. If teachers are committed to making a difference and the schedule makes that unlikely, commitment will die. The scheduling changes that have been part of the development of the TECs are critical, because they allow the students and the teachers to work together long enough for real mentoring to take place. An important source of motivation for experienced teachers is their belief that they have wisdom to share. It is one reason the TEC teachers spend time with TEC students, much more time than ever before. Another reason why TEC teachers devote time to working with TEC students is the return they see for their pupils in extra help, new ideas, and better beginning teachers. Teachers feel that they have found ways to better prepare prospective teachers without sacrificing their pupils' learning.

Teachers acknowledge that one of the benefits of having TEC students, site supervisors, and evolutionary planning is more opportunities for professional communication. Evolutionary planning promotes discussion of professional issues among colleagues who have not talked about such issues in the past. TEC students can be a crutch in these conversations. A veteran teacher who may not be comfortable admitting "I don't know anything about that" can easily arrange for the TEC student to ask about that "new stuff." Site supervisors whose work takes them into many classrooms are a source of professional communication and a source of referrals. They may know who else is interested in an idea or whose student teacher has faced a similar problem. TEC students bring an endless stream of questions and ideas to be discussed and developed.

Working with TEC students can have some unexpected benefits. Everyone expects the novice to learn from the experienced teacher, but it can work in reverse also. At the TECs, students are rarely told that a strategy learned at the University is "ivory tower." Instead the teachers work with the TEC students to effectively implement the strategy, even though they may not like it or use it. This seems to foster change. When a TEC teacher assists a novice in implementing an unfamiliar strategy, the teacher has a safe, convenient opportunity to evaluate the new strategy, see how it works, and vicariously rehearse it. There is, of course, nothing to prevent any cooperating teacher from using the same process, but it seems to happen much more often in the TECs. We believe that this is because TEC students try a greater variety of strategies, since they are focused on instruction (rather than survival) and are given support for risk taking. The students implement strategies that are clearly related to the school's mission, and teachers in TECs typically spend more time working with their protégés.

We have seen this vicarious learning occur in a number of places. For instance, the Suncrest teachers now incorporate the learning cycle in their science teaching and literature units in their literacy instruction. These strategies were part of the undergraduate methods courses before the TEC developed but they did not become part of Suncrest's curriculum until recently. As the TEC students worked with their teachers to implement these strategies, the teachers saw that the strategies fit the school's goals, became comfortable with them, and integrated them into Suncrest's program. At MHS, student teachers are required to integrate instructional technology into their teaching. We have seen that requirement, which the teachers support, lead to an increase in teachers' use of technology. For example, a teacher who has never used any kind of technology (including an overhead projector), despite participating in professional development, recently began using some complex interactive technology independently. The TEC student in that classroom had integrated it, and the teacher had learned with him.

Another, more subtle change has also occurred. MHS TEC students meet regularly for seminars. The site supervisor documents the content of the seminars in memos, and TEC students often discuss the experiences of other students with their cooperating teachers. One topic of discussion this year was developing a belief statement or philosophy of education, something that one of the cooperating teachers has always worked on with his TEC students. Another cooperating teacher has expressed an interest in learning more about the area, because it seems helpful to the TEC students and she is committed to helping them.

The development of Central Elementary as a demonstration site also seems to be related to some changes in teaching practice. Involvement in the LDG and the literacy methods course seems to have promoted a greater openness to change for some Central teachers. There is not a lot of discussion about "maybe I'll change." Instead, changes in literacy practices appear to come suddenly, usually with the assistance of a colleague or the LDG. Occasionally, teachers reveal later that they had been considering the change for some time and one of the demonstration site experiences provided the impetus.

Even though the demonstration site at Central is quite different from the TECs, there are some important similarities in the development and impact of these efforts. All the new relationships have grown from joint planning in situations where both parties had a stake in the situation and there were extended interactions between WVU and public school faculty that built trust and under-standing. In short, these relationships reflect careful attention to the literature on collaboration presented by Shive in Chapter 2 of this book. In each of these situations someone has taken a leadership role in facilitating the process of change, tending to documentation, and seeking input from a variety of stake-holders. These new relationships have fostered reflection, experimentation, and collaboration which enrich the experience of prospective teachers, experienced teachers, and children. It is difficult to believe that we were once distant and distrustful partners in teacher education. These new relationships create a caring, connected context in which novice and experienced teachers collaboarate to construct and apply professional knowledge in ways that have a positive impact on the lives of children. We do not always agree and we are never going to be "finished" with this collaborative change effort, but we are very pleased with the changes these new relationships have made in our preparation of teachers and our own professional development.

Reference

Clarke, A. (1995). Professional development in practicum settings: Reflective practice under scrutiny. *Teaching and Teacher Education 11*(3): 243–261.

Duquette, C. (1994). The role of the cooperating teacher in a school-based teacher education program: Benefits and concerns. *Teaching and Teacher Education 10*(3): 345–353.

Guyton, E. and McIntyre, D. J. (1990). Student teaching and school experiences. In W. R. Houston, ed., *The handbook of research on teacher education*. New York: Macmillan.

Howey, K. and Zimpher, N. (1989). *Profiles of preservice teacher education: Inquiry into the nature of programs*. Albany: SUNY Press.

Kennedy, M. (1992). Establishing professional schools for teachers. In M. Levine, ed., *Professional practice schools: Linking teacher education and school reform*. New York: Teachers College Press.

Noddings, N. (1987). An ethic of caring. In Joseph Devitis, ed., *Women, culture and morality*, pp. 333–372. New York: Peter Lang.

Rust, F. (1994). The first year of teaching: It's not what they expected. *Teaching and Teacher Education 10*(2): 205–217.

PART III

THE OUTCOMES OF RESTRUCTURING: PROBLEMS AND POSSIBILITIES

OVERVIEW OF PART III

In 1993, Fullan noted the dearth of data on the impact of restructuring in general and professional development schools in particular, emphasizing the importance of such information for professional development schools because of the relative vagueness and ambiguity of the PDS concept. Evaluating the outcomes of restructuring is extraordinarily complex: the concepts are sometimes vague; the desired outcomes are sometimes intangible and rarely documented by standardized tests; and the relationships between various aspects of restructuring are unproven. Webb-Dempsey reminds us in Chapter 12 that many evaluations of reform have examined adult outcomes and the most important test of restructuring's value is its impact on students. Fullan (1993) has described another aspect of restructuring through PDS, the university side of the PDS partnership, as "understudied, and underdeveloped" (127). What does restructuring mean for students, for teachers, and for universities, particularly colleges of education? In Chapter 13, Hawthorne explores the potential impact of restructuring using the professional development school approach on colleges of education.

In Chapter 11, Saab, Steel, and Shive examine teachers' notions about the outcomes of professional development school reforms. The authors examine the literature on outcomes, which is minimal, and share teachers' anecdotal evidence of positive changes. Finally, the authors share two examples of synergistic collaboration that integrate professional development, teacher empowerment, curriculum development, and student outcomes assessment. These compelling examples are evidence of the powerful impact restructuring can have on all participants. The chapter will help readers envision collaborative endeavors that meet the needs of all participants and document the kinds of restructuring outcomes teachers "know" are occurring.

In Chapter 12, Webb-Dempsey analyzes the problems and possibilities in designing assessments of PDS work. She shares the process of designing an assessment that is driven by the values and goals of individual restructuring efforts, addresses both individual and cross-site goals, and provides a variety of data on student, teacher, school, and university outcomes. The process, which readers could adapt for other contexts, has several purposes: (1) to document teachers' involvement in PDS; (2) to document the impact of PDS on public school students; (3) to document the impact of PDS on preservice teachers; (4) to develop an ongoing system for assessing changes related to site-based and cross-site initiatives; and (5) to build PDS faculties' capacity to do assessment.

In Chapter 13, Hawthorne addresses the thorny issue of change within colleges of education involved in PDS reform. He begins by examining the literature to define the impact professional development school reform work should have in higher education. He then addresses the question of what the changes might look and feel like in the life of a college of education, offering the reader a set of guiding questions to consider in assessing the impact of professional development school reform in higher education. Finally, he explores the impact of the Benedum Collaborative reform efforts on the College of Human Resources and Education at West Virginia University. Readers will find that Hawthorne addresses an area Fullan (1993) describes as receiving "little attention in the literature" (126) in great depth and with great passion.

The final section of the book addresses a critical question for all those engaged in or considering restructuring, a question that is the heart of all our efforts and all our stories. "Have we authored our work in such a way that lives have changed for the better, most importantly, the lives of children who are crowded in school and classroom corridors, and together with their teachers, are hard at the work of creating their own very important educational stories?" (Carter 1993, 11)

11

TEACHERS' PERSPECTIVES ON SCHOOL CHANGE: LESSONS FROM THE CLASSROOM

JOY FAINI SAAB, SARAH STEEL, AND JERRALD SHIVE

Introduction

In a professional development school humanities class, where students learn concepts related to English and the Social Studies, the teacher is sitting in a student's desk in the back of the room while two eleventh graders show a model they built of Huckleberry Finn's raft and discuss the symbolism of the raft in Twain's classic of American literature. Another student reads his essay written in the language of Huck about events that might occur after the novel's end.

While teachers and students alike recognize that this class is markedly different from what they've experienced in the past, how much of the change can be credited to PDS? How soon might participants in reform initiatives expect to see changes like these in the classroom? What effects does restructuring have on teachers? What effects do innovations like an integrated course that incorporates alternative assessment have on the students? And what effects do changes in organization, professional practice, and educational process have on the life of school? Teachers in Benedum Collaborative professional development schools are implementing and examining reforms that will lead to some of these answers. They are providing lessons from the classroom for all participants in reform initiatives. Unlike Chapter 12, which addresses the design and assessment of the entire Benedum Collaborative, a *major* undertaking, this chapter focuses on smaller, individual pieces of the restructuring story. In this chapter we will examine some of the literature on the outcomes of restructuring, share what teachers have to say about their experiences in professional development schools, and fully describe two examples of smaller "reinvented" assessments that made evaluation of particular reform efforts a collaborative activity between public school and university partners.

The questions raised earlier about the multiple impacts of restructuring are important ones. With the current wave of reform, educators have made a conscious decision to concentrate their efforts not only on student outcomes but also on the structures that support learner-centered schools. In fact maintaining a balance "between process and content," i.e., between working on "teacher learning and collaborative decision-making [and] the implementation of specific projects aimed at improving learning for all students" is named as a "lesson in restructuring schools" (Lieberman 1991, 23). Lieberman states that, if one of these is given precedence over the other: "In the first case, the team's work is likely to be considered meaningless and the experiment in shared decision making judged a failure. In the second case, the project, though perhaps well conceived, is likely to fail" (1991, 23–24). Perhaps the reason so many earlier reform efforts produced only short-term change is that they limited their focus— addressing improving students' learning but not addressing the processes and structures that allowed that improvement to occur and persist. Darling-Hammond (1992) suggests that this wave of school reform will be no more successful than those of the past if the changes are not "deeply rooted in the professional structure of our schools, in the policy structure of the schools, or in the political structure of this country" (21).

It is the belief of educators working in the Benedum Collaborative's PDSs that attention must be paid "up front" to the restructuring of education; that without a strong commitment to examining the rules, roles, and relationships of all stakeholders in education no long-lasting change will result. In fact, one of the three main goals of the Benedum Collaborative was "to establish collaborative processes, strategies, and structures that will make the changes last." (Benedum Collaborative proposal, 1989, 12). We based our activities in the early phases of the Benedum Collaborative on the belief that "the nature of the professional community that exists [in a school] appears more critical than any other factor to the character of teaching and learning for teachers and for their students" (McLaughlin 1992, 20). Without a focus on structure and professional development, there is a danger that the current wave of reform will last no longer than the earlier attempts at systemic change did. Over the past eight years, Benedum Collaborative participants working in and with PDSs have invested a great deal of time and energy on that focus of restructuring.

Evidence from Other Reform Initiatives

Across the nation, those involved in educational changes are struggling with ways to assess the impact of PDSs on the participants in reform efforts. Kyle (1993) reports that across all educational levels, schools that had been involved in the reform initiative in the Louisville area outperformed comparison schools on a wide variety of achievement measures.

Lee and Smith (1992) conducted a study to determine the effects of school restructuring on the achievement and engagement of middle-grade students. After examining a variety of measures, the researchers reported that, "Although the magnitude of effects is generally modest, the elements of restructuring investigated here are positively and significantly associated with the academic achievement and engagement with schooling of American 8th graders" (Lee and Smith 1992, 29).

A professional development school faculty working in collaboration with the University of Wisconsin-Milwaukee demonstrated a change in their approach to reading instruction that was influenced by the philosophies connected to the school's reform efforts. This PDS faculty went from "an ineffective basic skills approach to reading, in a school context focused on student deficits, to an approach to literacy that emphasizes experimentation, growth, and risk-taking as part of school culture. . . . As teachers observed students' successes, they also began to feel successful, which resulted in more teacher efforts to create conditions for more student success. Success was a generative force" (Jett-Simpson 1992, 20).

Studies like those cited above contribute to the growing knowledge base on the impact of current reform initiatives such as professional development schools and school restructuring. However, we are still very much in the beginning stages of gathering information on the significance of these movements for each stakeholder in the process. Educators involved in school reform have found that the issue of time has played a key role in gathering student outcome data. To date, most of the research and writing on professional development schools focuses on key issues related to restructuring, collaboration among the various stakeholders in education, and the educational change process. Often, particular innovative programs ongoing in PDSs are showcased. However, documentation on how all of these factors combine and synergize to impact children's learning in PDSs is rare. For example, when describing the efforts being made at Lark Creek Middle School, a PDS participating in the Puget Sound Professional Development Center's educational reform initiative begun in 1987–1988, Grossman comments, "As yet, there are few data on whether or not students are learning better under the new approach to curriculum and instruction" (Grossman 1994, 66).

Perhaps this dearth of information on PDS impact on students and other participants in the projects shouldn't be too surprising. There is evidence that in a more traditional paradigm, where high assessment standards are imposed externally, teachers may feel pressured to meet those standards even at the expense of what might be best for students (Darling-Hammond 1992). If building a collaborative partnership for school reform is something to which educators in both public schools and universities do not attend, then the results will either be meaningless or not forthcoming at all. Therefore, it's not surprising that in systemic reform, like that undertaken by the Benedum Collaborative and its PDSs, a great deal of time has been taken to nurture the collaborative reform initiatives.

Conversations with Teachers

While some data has been gathered in relation to programs that are a part of PDSs' reform efforts, project participants are only now beginning to ask themselves the bigger question about the overall effect of PDSs on schooling. A comment made by one teacher in a primary PDS captured what many PDS teachers in the Benedum Collaborative feel. She said, "I know that the investment we have made in professional development and restructuring has paid off for my students. I'm just not sure I can tell you how I know that." It's important that we begin to explore ways we can gauge the impact learning in a PDS has on students, because "Student data are certainly critical to judging the quality of educational reform" (Whitford 1994, 96).

In conversations with Benedum Collaborative participants, teachers talk about the impacts of the reform efforts on themselves and their students as members of professional development schools. The following sections, determined by these conversations, describe what these teachers feel are the major categories for reform in their classrooms. Background information on each Benedum Collaborative PDS, which will provide a context for the following sections, is included in Chapter 3 of this volume.

The Restructuring of Time

The restructuring of time has been evident in a few of the Benedum Collaborative schools as they focus on effective curriculum and instruction. One of the PDS high schools incorporated the restructuring of time as a main directive throughout its Benedum Collaborative reform work. Through innovative professional development arrangements (see Chapter 9), this faculty worked in collaboration with WVU and external consultants to build understandings about what restructuring might mean to their particular site. Out of three years of study and work, this high school made the decision to completely restructure their master schedule.

Restructuring the master schedule of a large high school is an incredibly complex undertaking. During school year 1993–1994, the school community committed itself to operating under an innovative alternating 4 by 4 schedule. This eight-period schedule is somewhat like a university schedule in that it consists of two sets of four ninety-minute periods that alternate daily. The large blocks of times provided in the ninety-minute periods have opened the door for the implementation of a variety of new teaching strategies.

As the school began working with the new, restructured schedule, several faculty members thought it would be useful to reflect on and document its impact on the lives of the school community. Benedum Collaborative participants from WVU collaborated with the PDS's site steering committee to develop and implement a formative assessment of the restructured schedule. To begin the process of assessing the schedule, a Design Team was formed. The roles of the Design Team included: designing a process for the assessment study, making recommendations on the construction of research instruments, naming parent and student participants for the study, and monitoring all stages of the assessment. The Design Team's work was reported to the PDS's site steering committee and was open to input from this group.

Components of the study included: a faculty questionnaire about the restructured schedule, brief teacher interviews, anecdotal information that expanded on responses, focus group interviews with students, and brief telephone interviews with a random sample of parents. Analysis of the data is ongoing although the initial responses seem to be very positive. The main purpose of this assessment is to provide the MHS faculty with information that will help them gauge the impact of the schedule reorganization and plan for the future.

This lengthy and complex collaborative design process acts as an illustration for that balance between process and content that Lieberman (1991) mentions as a lesson in school restructuring. After devoting literally years to the process of restructuring time in the PDS high school, faculty members are now ready and able to examine the impact this restructuring may have on participants.

In the survey completed by teachers, several impacts of the schedule were mentioned. Several teachers noted that the new schedule that alternates the periods allows for flexible use of time by the students. Now they have two days in which to use outside resources to complete assignments. Some teachers added that this alternating also makes the school day "less monotonous," as each day is not exactly like the one before it. One math teacher described what he saw as an advantage to the ninety-minute periods. He noticed that his children operating below grade level were finding more success on a schedule that allowed them to be introduced to a concept, practice it, and master it in one sitting. For once, these students were experiencing closure on learning a concept. Teachers also noted that the longer periods of time facilitated the incorporation of innovative strategies into their instruction. One teacher commented, "I am more comfortable with spending the time necessary for cooperative learning."

This restructuring of time in the school day has also provided some unique challenges for the school community. Most teachers noted that the period of flexible time students have every other day is not being used to its best potential. (They have now restructured that time.) Some teachers miss having daily contact with students. Absences can pose problems since students who miss one day are actually missing two days of instruction. Also, with the new instructional strategies that involve hands-on activities and cooperative learning, making up work is difficult. However, in general, most teachers indicate that the advantages outweigh the disadvantages.

Another example of the restructuring of time at the high school involves the redesign of the math curriculum. The new math curriculum integrates the traditionally separate disciplines of geometry and algebra. The redesign also includes the mastery approach where students can move at their own pace through the material. Because some students require more time to master concepts, schedule changes were made that allowed students to continue their work in the summer if necessary. One teacher whose child attends the school described how restructuring the math curriculum affected his child. His child, who is identified as Learning Disabled/Gifted, was able to master all the units of the math class due to his being able to finish the class in the summer. It was this innovative restructuring of time that helped account for his success. The teacher/parent commented, "I don't know what I would have done sending [my child] through traditional math and science classes."

Participants in PDSs have also developed a commitment to the preparation of highly qualified novice teachers. This has become a goal to which classroom teachers are dedicated. One teacher expresses it this way:

> [T]he other commitment we have is that we think that we are doing a pretty good job [and] we want to help groom the next generation of teachers and give them good experiences to draw on when they are in the classroom

Another teacher notes that there were few student teachers in his school prior to the beginning of the Benedum Collaborative. Most of the animosities between higher education and the schools that limited school participation in clinical experiences have now been lessened. Some teachers became involved specifically to try to improve public school and higher education relationships.

At two sites, half-time site coordinators are paid with project funds. One teacher states that "our teacher ed. center . . . helps us . . . so we feel like we are sharing what we have learned with the next generation of teachers." The on-site coordinator also helps to introduce student teachers to the school and curriculum. At one of the sites she "gets the principal and the librarian to come in and the student assistance program people to come in and they all get knowledge of this."

Teachers recognize that student teachers and clinical experience students do create some interruptions in the program and the classrooms. However, as one teacher says: "we think that is outweighed by the richness in the experience. It gives them another adult role model."

Another teacher suggests that regular classroom teachers learn from the student teachers.

> I have seen several examples of where . . . the student teachers are gone
> [and] the teachers are trying to do some of the same things that they have
> seen modeled by student teachers . . . that to me is really the positive thing
> about all of this because it helps *you*. It is not just them, it is us. And I try
> to impress upon them, 'you are here to help teach us some new tricks and
> some new ways of teaching and doing things.'

This same teacher perceives that student teachers influence the learning of
students both directly and indirectly over time as new ideas are introduced.

> That clearly translates to the kids in the classroom, because if we have
> somebody who wouldn't touch a computer and the student teacher hauls a
> computer with the CD ROM in there . . . it doesn't change them overnight
> and it is . . . tough . . . but it does result in different things going on in the
> classroom.

In addition to clinical experiences associated with particular classes, as
well as student teaching, students from the University contribute to school
reform in other ways. They voluntarily contribute time to extracurricular
activities, for example. At one high school, University students participate in a
student assistance program that provides tutoring to high school students in
different subject areas.

Because the College of Human Resources and Education at WVU has
developed a new novice teacher preparation program, the PDS relationship is
particularly critical. The new program is heavily clinically based and school/
university collaboration is key to the success of the program. Including a professional internship, each student will spend six consecutive semesters in a professional development school. The preservice teacher will also design and conduct an
applied research project and school and university faculty will work closely
together on research projects. Every course in the new program has a practicum
attached to it, and novice teachers are constantly reminded of the close connections between theory and practice and the necessity for teachers to be inquirers.

Assistance with At-Risk Students

Concern for at-risk students is a common theme in the strategic plans
developed by professional development schools. Academic success, positive
attitudes toward school, and self-esteem are emphasized in a number of PDSs'
goals. Examples of such newly created at-risk programs for West Virginia professional development schools are described below.

The Buddy System. At one high school the Buddy System was an idea that
grew out of the work of the At-risk Committee at the school. The Committee

reviewed the research on teaching at-risk students as well as selected approaches to helping at-risk students in the classroom. They selected the Buddy System as an approach that might help students in their school.

Teachers compiled a list of students they judged to be at-risk. Each faculty member in the school then "adopted" at least one of the students. Each day the faculty member talked with the student to see if he or she had any problems. Other teachers were contacted regularly to check on the student's progress. As a result, the dropout rate decreased from more than twenty percent to roughly ten percent. A teacher commented on her perception of this Buddy System.

> I think there were a lot of kids who felt a difference in the life in the school because somebody was interested in them. Somebody was actually talking to them like a person everyday. I know from just working with the kids that I worked with that there were some who were ready to quit school and turned around and decided to stay. And that is what we were trying to do.

The teacher also noted that there was a marked difference in the grades of the students who were identified to participate in the Buddy System. Failing grades, in particular, declined.

Missing Links. At an elementary school the faculty set up a mentoring program for at-risk students called Missing Links. Former students of the elementary school who are now in the ninth grade came back to tutor fourth, fifth, and sixth graders in their old elementary school. Evidence of the program's success includes comments by parents who say that Missing Links is making a real difference in their child's life.

Teen Forum. Another example of how the At-risk focus was addressed occurred when students from one high school attended a regional and state teen institute consisting of a three-day health-related conference. When the students returned, they established a Teen Forum, for which help from school organizations and private business was organized. Workshops were presented by medical professionals, police officers, professional counselors, and social workers. Topics included suicide, eating disorders, sexual assault, alcoholism, and drug use. Participants included members of other professional development schools, as well as business partners in education.

External funding of counselor. One high school has a half-time counselor funded by the Job Training and Partnership Act. The counselor focuses on dropout prevention but he also works with classes on parenting, adult roles and functions, and conflict resolution. He has held group discussions in English, Home Economics, Journalism, and Media Productions classes. Other topics for discussion included teen suicide, teen pregnancies, and drug and alcohol abuse. Other PDSs are currently discussing how the resources of government and private agencies can be brought to bear in a coordinated way on the problems that affect children and adolescents, including their performance at school.

Collaboration with Chapter I. An elementary school was nominated for the Chapter 1 National Recognition Program. The school committed itself to build their knowledge base about teaching and learning related to students at-risk, to use instructional models that reflect current reading practices, to develop a strong collegial relationship between the Chapter 1 and the regular classroom teacher, to actively involve parents in student learning, and to seek other funding to support student needs. In this innovative program, the school publishes and markets books created by student authors from K–6. The children's books provide reading material for each grade as well as increased funding to support the reading program. In 1996, this reading program was chosen as an award-winning model of excellence by the International Reading Association.

Curriculum Change

The teachers in these professional development schools have been involved in a wide variety of curriculum changes. It seems that since becoming a PDS, the faculty at these schools report increased collaborative, integrative, and innovative curriculum changes. Some examples are described below.

Elementary Science/Mathematics/Technology Lab. One elementary school had as its goal to build a Science/Mathematics/ Technology Lab for elementary students. The faculty designed this lab, obtained funding through grants, and built the lab as their first project after becoming a PDS. A teacher describes the effects this lab has had on students:

With the SMT (Science/Mathematics/Technology) lab, which is the first thing we had Benedum's help with, the students . . . benefitted. I brought test scores. They've gone up consistently in science and math since we built that and also the interest inventories you do with the CTBS have really gone up, especially with the girls. The girls were not that interested—maybe 40 percent of thcm [befure] and now 75 percent of them in science and math. That's exciting! The counselor for the eighth graders was saying she couldn't believe the difference in our students that feed in there about how they are interested in science and math so I thought that was good. And . . . we won the World Championship of the Odyssey of the Mind. A lot of it when we traced it back had to do with the fact that the science/math lab-critical thinking skills that we tried to work into that and that is a big part of that Odyssey of the Mind.

Science/Mathematics Lab. Another school also increased the technology in their existing science/math lab by adding CD ROM capabilities to their equipment. This expansion also was a result of a grant writing project designed by the teachers with support from faculty from WVU. One teacher describes the technological results:

> The critical thinking that we do there (science/math lab) mostly blends in science and math but we also do the brainstorming in there like we did with Odyssey of the Mind. . . . We have the CD ROM set in there. . . . Our children are rural and with Internet we are hooked up all over the nation and it just gives them more of a global feeling.

In addition to the increased use of technology, many of the PDS teachers describe the integration of student-centered methodologies in their classroom. One school wrote grants for some of the teachers to attend seminars on the 4-MAT system and the Foxfire approach to teaching. These teachers, in turn, conducted faculty development workshops to share their new ideas with their colleagues. One of the third grade teachers describes the curriculum changes that occurred:

> One of the things, because of the focus that we have on learning styles, one of the things that is most different about our school now is that we present things in many different ways to the children. We make a point to use a variety of instructional strategies so that children have many opportunities to succeed. . . . We have to give them many opportunities to succeed and also to stretch and what we do often is we feel like we haven't thrown out the baby with the bath water, we have kept . . . a lot of what was good before. We still use textbooks, but we enhance that a lot and the textbook is not the Bible any longer it is just a resource and we use a lot of other activities that are not textbook-oriented. . . . You know five years ago I would not have ever tried some of the things that I do in my classroom and would not have encouraged my children to try either . . . so I think that has been an important change also. And it is because of the training, and in our case . . . it's been training . . . in the 4MAT system and . . . training with the Foxfire techniques which lead to that too.

Chemistry in the Community. Another curriculum change that highlights the collaborative nature of the instructional planning that has occurred in many of the PDSs, is a new course about Chemistry in the Community. This course was developed by teachers in an effort to connect students to science content in a more meaningful manner. As one high school teacher describes it:

One day a teacher came . . . to my room and said . . . we have this scenario and it is how you do chemistry. It is a divorce from the theoretical . . . the final outcome is where there is a stream running through town and the fish were dying and the question really had to do with oxygen content . . . and the problems with that. . . . That course is very clearly having an impact on our curriculum and what is happening is . . . people from around the state and other places across the nation are looking at what they are doing in that class.

Integrated Arts Curriculum. One primary school started with a focus on learning styles in their original strategic plan. As they studied the research on learning styles, the focused on the work of Bernice McCarthy and the 4MAT system for instructional design. As these teachers attempted to integrate a variety of teaching methods to meet their students' needs, they were increasingly drawn to the integration of the arts to allow for more exciting and effective divergent teaching and learning. Recently, the third grade teachers collaborated with the PDS faculty liaison to create an Impressionist Unit to teach critical observation and thinking skills. This unit was very well received by the children, parents, and community members as they interacted with classroom activities. By 1996, all teachers at this primary school were consistently creating collaborative curriculum plans that integrate the arts across all curriculum areas.

Teacher and Student Empowerment

The teachers from professional development schools in West Virginia consistently describe feeling increased empowerment in their roles as educators since becoming part of a PDS. Often this increased sense of ownership results in increased risk taking as well. Teachers describe involving their students in decisions in which they had not previously participated.

An elementary teacher describes empowerment as being a result of training received through PDS-sponsored classes. She notes a shift in the way she views her role in the classroom, which has affected the students in a dramatic way, explaining it in this manner: "I have had training in awareness, because I know about building a democratic classroom and giving students choices."

Elementary student-organized store. The teachers describe changing the manner in which curriculum decisions are made. Students in professional development schools are increasingly becoming involved in instructional design decisions. One teacher describes a project in her school in which students play an integral role:

The children have a lot of input. The biggest thing I can think of in my classroom is a school store. The kids do all the ordering and they decide what we are going to sell. They decide how much it is going to cost and they are completely in charge. There are teams that we hire in the morning and in the afternoon and it is completely in their hands. They make all the decisions. They are there 8:00-9:00(A.M.). Two girls that are advanced placed . . . are very young . . . all the way up to one ten-year-old, and they are making all the decisions with just a little bit of guidance from me but mostly they check in with me once in a while or they say something is running out and they . . . decide on the prices and they keep the shelves stocked. Benedum didn't fund the school store. It was the risk taking. I knew about risk taking. I knew that was a big risk . . . kids to run a store . . . [and] we were able to pay our bills.

Student interest inventory. Teachers describe focusing more on student needs during decision making, since becoming a PDS. Students are at the center of attention now, as teachers redesign a plan for curriculum and instruction for their schools. As one high school teacher describes it:

When we got together for our dream session, our strategic planning, it was student driven . . . what they needed. We have the counselor in with each group, we have four groups and we had her rotating around with each. These are our students' interests. We did an interest inventory.

Increased pride and respect. Teachers also speak of an increased pride and respect among students and teachers within the professional development schools. Students are described as acting as mirrors that reflect increased empowerment and pride back to the teachers. As one elementary teacher reports:

I asked (a couple of sixth graders), "What changes do you notice since Benedum, what good things have come out?" They said . . . "You get to go to conferences like to New York and Texas. When all the teachers come back they are real excited."

Student-centered methodologies. Teachers describe shifting toward student-centered methodologies as one result of becoming empowered in their teaching situations. These PDS teachers tend to pass their feelings of empowerment onto their students by involving them in the decision making in the classroom. Teachers who have taken Foxfire classes also describe a similar phenomenon. In Foxfire classes teachers study student-centered instructional processes based on the democratic educational principles of John Dewey. Many Foxfire teachers report adopting student-centered methodologies after reexamining their role in the educational process (Deay and Saab 1994).

Increased Reflection and Inquiry

The teachers from these professional development schools said that they are more involved in reflection and strategic planning since their schools have become PDSs. Increasingly, this planning seems to focus on the needs of the students. As one teacher says:

> One of the other things we have noticed and actually worked very hard on is raising our CTBS scores [standardized achievement tests], because they were pretty abysmal the last couple of years. I think two years ago we had the fine distinction of having the lowest basic skills scores in the state . . . when we focused on CTBS . . . and had the time to sit down and work on it (which we never had before because they never gave us the time to really sit down and do that) then we knew where to go with it. We know what to do.

This teacher went on to describe how her faculty worked collaboratively to determine what the students needed to increase their achievement:

> This was school-wide . . . we perceived a need and we said we have to do something and so we did—math people, science people, etc. . . . but it's ongoing . . . . you can't just say OK we fixed it, because every year you have a new bunch of kids and you have to look at it . . . And those scores are really *way up* . . . in everything this year!

Teachers also describe being involved in careful examination of student-centered methodologies. The increased time allowed for reflection often resulted in cooperative planning around student-centered activities. As one third grade teacher said:

> I think our whole (strategic) plan came from our interest in learning styles because before we had an opportunity to apply to PDS, we were noticing and becoming aware—what the teaching manual says to do just isn't working for all kids. Here is this child and there are some children in my room that I have this gut feeling are smarter than what they are appearing to be. This child has got something and how do we reach it? That grew from that experience and some of the observations we were making in our classrooms—so our whole plan was built on trying to find out more about learning styles. Not only finding out about it but how can this impact our teaching. How can this theory, this research, impact our teaching? The research by itself just didn't do it for us. We still didn't know how do we translate that into changing our teaching process or practices so that this

child can get the benefit from this research. I think that is what we learned
how to do.

The same teacher discussed how her faculty has begun to look at the need
for different types of assessment as a result of their redesign of curriculum and
instruction and their increased reflection about their teaching:

I'm pleased with the kinds of assessment that we are doing now within the
project. . . . Our teaching is so different, our assessment has to be different
and then we are still dealing with a report card with A, B, C, which
doesn't cut it. . . . What is an A or what is a B? What does that tell you?
We are really struggling with that now and we are trying using art as an
assessment tool sometimes. We are trying to cross that line of subject
matter in our curriculum. When you start doing whole language and
integration with little kids, . . . I think that at least through our experiences
with the professional development schools we have become aware that we
have been allowed and had the opportunity to go to some workshops and
things, but still when it comes time to put to practice in my classroom it is
still hard and we are hoping to come up with a new type of report card.

Many of the teachers from PDS schools describe the benefits of increased
time for reflection and inquiry. Often substitutes were hired so that teachers
could have release time to be involved in collaborative planning efforts with
their colleagues. Throughout our conversations, teachers expressed their
appreciation for the chance to meet during the regular work day or during
summer workshops to engage in strategic planning in a professional manner.
This is a deeply valued aspect of becoming a professional development school.

Professional Development

Meaningful professional development has long been recognized as a
partner of school reform and improvement. Increasingly in PDSs, teachers are
involved in the establishment of professional development directions for their
sites. Teacher perceptions of the effects of professional development on their
schools range from direct to indirect impact and include outcomes related to
both content and pedagogy. Professional development within schools in the
Benedum Collaborative included work at West Virginia University, professional
conferences, and in collaboration with other schools and universities.

Interviews with sixth graders who had just graduated from one of the K–5
PDSs were particularly revealing. A student noted that one teacher at the school
had been named "Teacher of the Year" because "they sent you to those
conferences and that looks good on a person's resume." The excitement was
clearly contagious and students were aware of it. Exemplifying that feeling was

a student who commented to a teacher, "I am proud because you are proud. I can tell since we have been in the Benedum Collaborative you are more proud of our school." That teacher says that she is sure that is true:

> We feel more confident now as teachers and we have taken on the leadership role . . . and they sense that. You don't think that they know what it is but then they have a sense of the change that is going on.

Teachers in the Benedum PDSs are increasingly asked to provide professional development sessions to their colleagues. The Microscale Collaborative at one high school, for example, resulted in the design of microscale lab activities that were also presented at state and national science teachers association meetings. Teachers from PDSs have made conference and workshop presentations on learning styles, whole language, integrated arts instruction, portfolio assessment, integrated curriculum science and math instruction, and the meaning of being a professional development school. Some of these presentations have been made at national meetings of the American Association of Higher Education, the National Science Teachers Association, the American Association of Colleges for Teacher Education, the American Educational Research Association, and the National Council of Teachers of Mathematics.

Teachers also collaborate with university faculty to gather information on topics related to curriculum in their schools. In one instance, they are reviewing research on Core Knowledge, the focus of curriculum in one elementary school. The PDSs have also begun building a video library on various topics that interest PDS participants. Videos include *Breaking the Mold: Education Policy for a High Performance Future*, a teleconference focusing on Tech Prep, youth apprenticeship, school reform, presentations by Ann Lieberman, and school-to-work transition. Two high school PDSs are exploring these issues. The National Center for Research in Vocational Education (NCRVE) teleconference on Alternative Assessment, which focuses on performance assessments, student projects, and portfolio assessments is part of the library. *Exploring Internet*, which deals with information technology, and *School Reform: From Vision to Reality with Technology* are being used by an elementary PDS site and WVU technology education students.

Collaborative staff members share information about professional development opportunities at each Cross-Site Steering Committee meeting. The CSSC also formed a special committee to deal with professional development. That committee formed an elementary and a secondary professional development network for the purpose of sharing professional development activities. The elementary network has arranged for a series of presentations by the participating PDSs on learning styles, whole language, and the Student Authors Program. Each of these is a central focus of the curriculum at one of the elementary sites. The networks also serve as a means of drawing in faculty to participate in the activities of their own PDSs. The network facilitates information exchanges about practical ideas that are working successfully in classrooms.

Funding for professional development can be accessed four ways: through a competitive Site-based Collaborative fund, through each site's Professional Development Fund, through a $1000 discretionary fund allocated to each school, and through collaborative grant writing to seek external funding. One such grant allowed teachers and students from selected West Virginia PDS sites to participate in an exchange program with Russia.

Any PDS site may submit a proposal to the Site-Based Collaborative fund proposal review team. In order to be considered for approval the proposals must be closely tied to the school's strategic themes and action plans, they must have potential for the broadest possible impact at the school and they must have potential for lasting change.

The Professional Development Fund makes funds available to faculty based on their own proposals to their own site's steering committee. The amount in each fund is determined by the number of faculty at the PDS site. Thus each site is responsible for managing its own funds and determining the relevance of each proposed project to the site's strategic themes and plans.

One elementary school developed a proposal for professional development that facilitated classroom teachers and WVU student teachers working together to create interdisciplinary units to teach students with different learning styles. Student teachers, teachers, and the school principal worked together to create the necessary planning time to create the units. They also presented the results of their work to other PDS faculty and parents.

Faculty from Benedum PDSs visited two high schools in South Carolina (a Coalition of Essential Schools site and a high school that operates on a block schedule format) to learn about the issues that arise in adopting a new schedule. The implementation of a new parent forum was also an outcome of this professional development activity. The forum informed parents on various aspects of the PDS work at the high school. Faculty from that same high school also traveled to Louisville, Kentucky, to visit another PDS. As a result of that trip, teachers in social studies, for example, came back with new ideas about doing group work and teaching integrated social studies.

An elementary and a secondary PDS collaborated to provide *A Night Under the Stars* for the entire elementary school community. More than two hundred students and parents involved themselves in hands-on astronomy activities. The high school students acted as guides and assisted with the telescopes and other equipment. The same elementary school also offered an after-school workshop called *Soar to the Future* that engaged fifth and sixth grade girls in hands-on math and science activities. Another series of workshops on Family Math helped parents learn ways to teach their children math concepts using ordinary materials found in their homes.

Because of this school's math and science activities, it has received a grant from the Appalachian Regional Educational Laboratory to expand the *Night Under the Stars*. The school has been identified by the Annenberg Foundation as one of the top 300 math/science programs in the nation. They also received a $10,000 grant from the Eisenhower Math/Science Consortium for a Rivers Program in collaboration with Southern Illinois University. A total of thirty-eight West Virginia teachers will be prepared in teaching science, geography, and language arts using the rivers theme. Three of the thirty-eight participants will be preservice teachers from West Virginia University. The Benedum Collaborative also assisted in the financing of connecting the school to Internet, which will permit students to communicate with other students in the state and nation.

These examples of professional development activities demonstrate a more meaningful trend in inservice teacher education. As Ann Lieberman (1995) states, "The conventional view of staff development as a transferable package of knowledge to be distributed to teachers in bite-sized pieces needs radical rethinking. It implies a limited conception of teacher learning that is out of step with current research and practice. . . .To make reform plans operational, teachers must be able to discuss, think about, try out, and hone new practices" (591, 592, 593).

The teachers' stories suggest that good things are happening and there are bits of data to support that feeling, but the stories we have shared thus far are not examples of "reinvented" assessments in which the evaluation of particular reform efforts becomes a collaborative activity between public school and university partners. What happens when all the elements and players in professional development schools come together in "reinvented" assessment? We want to share two examples that bring together curriculum development, teacher professionalism, collaboration, professional development, and assessment in ways that benefit all participants. These stories of restructuring, through a Literacy Discussion Group in one case and collaborative curriculum redesign in the other, are examples of the ideal.

The Literacy Discussion Group

A good example of a restructuring initiative that has produced rewards for all participants is the Benedum Collaborative's Literacy Discussion Group (LDG), based at Central Elementary. The LDG was begun collaboratively by a WVU assistant professor in Reading and a Chapter 1 Reading teacher at Central. The membership consisted of teachers from PDSs (predominantly Central), university professors, and graduate students. The LDG's meetings had agendas that were intentionally left open so that teachers would feel free to bring any issue connected to literacy to the group for discussion.

Early on, a focus for the group became whole language. One teacher, who had been an active member of the group but had never felt comfortable with the whole language approach to language instruction, agreed to "give up" the basal reading text and teach through a whole language approach for six weeks. She would only agree to this if the LDG would agree not only to support her throughout this risk-taking endeavor but also to support her decision to return to the basal text at the end of the six weeks if she chose. The LDG willingly agreed. The whole language unit was collaboratively designed by the LDG in order to give the PDS teacher the support she required. As part of the planning process, the group set up a study that would measure student attitudes toward and skills in reading after being instructed with the basal for six weeks and again after being instructed with whole language techniques for six weeks.

The assessment of the student data was also collaboratively done by the LDG. The results of the study proved quite persuasive to the PDS teacher as well as to the LDG. While there was no significant difference in reading skills achievement when whole language strategies were used, "this research indicate[s] that a holistic approach to the teaching of reading increases the students' interest level in reading, both as an academic endeavor and as a pleasurable pastime" (Isenhart et al. 1993, 6). The results of the study conducted by the LDG were collaboratively presented at a national reading conference. The PDS teacher has never returned to her basal text as the sole resource for her language instruction. The LDG is an example of the "reinvented" assessment that can make evaluation of particular reform efforts a collaborative activity between public school and university partners in school reform.

Developing an Integrated Curriculum: Beyond Cut and Paste

Increasingly, participants in curriculum reform efforts at professional development schools realize that they are spending their time in new and different ways. University faculty liaisons and public school teachers find themselves collaborating to create innovative instructional plans. Often their efforts are planned, implemented, and researched through a team approach. A recent example of this type of collaboration is a project entitled *Beyond Cut & Paste: A University-Public School Collaboration to Integrate the Arts in the Elementary Classroom*. During the 1994–95 academic year, a university faculty member designated as a liaison collaborated with two third grade teachers at a PDS to plan, implement, and research a project that focused on the integration of the arts in the teaching of other content areas. This project was a result of the years of professional development work the liaison had done with the school.

The professional development and service that the liaison provided to this PDS began in 1990 as they were developing their strategic plans for professional growth. During this planning phase the liaison and the PDS faculty developed a strong collaborative relationship. The development of the strategic plan led to the invitation to the liaison to provide instruction in the current instructional methods the teachers were trying to reform. This instruction was provided in the following classes: Learning Style Research, Models of Teaching, Creative Arts in the Classroom, Foxfire, Creative Mathematics Instruction, and Developmentally Appropriate Instruction.

As the teachers, student teachers, and liaison collaborated, they began to develop plans for instructional changes in the classrooms. First, they designed a series of research-based units that integrated the arts in the 4MAT unit plans to teach a variety of content areas. Once these unit plans were created, the team collaboratively developed the research plan for studying the implementation of these units during the 1994–95 academic year.

The liaison from West Virginia University visited the school every week during the implementation of these units. Data collection methods included classroom observations, videotapes, photos, collections of student projects, student journals, parent surveys, student surveys, written responses from parents, unit plans, lesson plans, teacher journals, and notes on weekly collaborative reflective sessions.

Student and community responses to this curriculum reform were very positive. Examples of their comments follow.

Sample Third Grade Responses to the Integrated Arts Units

Ahmad: "My favorite thing in third grade is the Watery World poems. I like it because you get to make your own poems. You can color and draw your own pictures."

David: "I like the puppets unit because I like making puppets because you can use old junk and make neat puppets and can help people recycling, and a cleaner planet, and (have a) very neat new toy too."

Michael: "I learned more about poetry than I wanted to."

Brendan: "It was fun when we did puppets for our book reports, because it let us use our imaginations."

Lauren: "I like the poetry because we did a lot of art and we learned about different animals."

Christy: "I liked the Watery World stuff because I did a lot of art work and learning."

Calli: "I like third grade because we get to do fun stuff and art work to learn a lot of stuff."

Student Survey Data for Integrated Arts Unit

On a scale of 1-5, the students responded to the following questions:

[1=not at all, 2=not much, 3=neutral, 4=somewhat, 5=very much]

Did you like this poetry unit?

Rating:	5	4	3	2	1
Number of Students:	16	3	1		

Did you like to write poetry before this?

Rating:	5	4	3	2	1
Number of Students:	4	2	7		5

Do you like to write poetry now?

Rating:	5	4	3	2	1
Number of Students:	14	2	2		

Sample Parent Responses to the Integrated Arts Units

Parent 1:   "I am very impressed with the students, the quality of work, and the presentation. I hope you'll continue the arts program. The integration of the arts with the standard classroom programs can only give our kids an edge on their peers. Susan has thoroughly enjoyed the projects and learned above and beyond reading and math. I am also excited about the children's opportunities to present orally to small groups, adding to their growth and self-esteem. I also value the opportunity to visit the classroom."

Parent 2:   "Mixing art and music with creative writing and reading is such a good idea. I'm sure the kids enjoy it. Poetry sounds boring to most, but I bet the kids didn't see it that way."

Parent 3:   "I appreciate both the time and effort that went into making this unit a fun and creative way of learning and teaching. I am glad that the parents were invited to come and see the presentation so that our children had the opportunity to show off both their hard work as students and your hard work as teachers! Very well done by all, I would give the entire effort an A+!"

Parent 4:   "I felt this was a very creative and stimulating learning experience for the kids. The presentation part was very important, also—it certainly had to help them develop confidence in public speaking. This is education of the highest quality—the kids discover that they have abilities they don't know they have."

Parent 5:   "The 'Watery World Poetry' presentation performed by the third grade students was excellent. An early effort to develop an appreciation for poetry and writing is essential if our youth is expected to expand in such arts. I only hope Jason's future teachers recognize the

Parent 6:
importance of these kinds of programs and encourage the seeds you've planted to grow. Please keep it up!"

"I have never seen children as enthusiastic as yesterday, when they were full of experiences from the practice session. Finally, I am very grateful that my daughter has the opportunity to experience education of such high caliber in a public school! One would expect this sort of a lesson in an extremely and progressive private school. It's great that all children have an opportunity to benefit from it. Thank you!"

This work ultimately culminated in the peer-reviewed acceptance for presentation of this authentic research at the annual meeting of the American Educational Research Association. This project has also been submitted for publication in professional journals. This collaborative restructuring initiative exemplifies the meaningful connection of higher education's teaching, research, and service expectations with the needs of teachers and students in a professional development school.

Conclusion

Professional development schoolteachers tell stories of significant changes in planning, curriculum, and instruction that have impacted the lives of their classrooms and their school communities. These teachers believe that these positive changes have been a direct result of becoming a PDS school. Much of the growth that has occurred seems to be related to the professional development and empowerment of the teachers. Their professional growth spills over to encourage the active involvement of the students in PDS communities. Ann Lieberman (1992) describes the power of these connections in her introduction to *The Changing Context of Teaching: Ninety-first Yearbook of the National Society for the Study of Education.*:

A growing body of research into new practices is helping us to understand that schools must develop collaborative, inquiring workplace environments for teachers at the same time that they are being developed for students. Many teachers involved in restructuring schools recognize the connection between their own development and the development of the students they teach; between their increased role in decision making and providing more choices for their students. Perhaps this obvious, yet elusive idea, provides the conceptual framework for the current reform movement.

Wilson, Peterson, Ball, and Cohen (1996), in their longitudinal tri-state research on educational reform, point out the effects of changes on reform participants,

The new policies demand many changes: in standards, curriculum, assessments, and instruction. But underlying them are changes more fundamental still: different views of knowledge and different ideas about the nature, purpose, and scope of school subjects. The reform instruments represent new conceptions of learning and a serious commitment to serve a diverse student population well. They also entail new images of good teaching (469).

Teachers involved in the Benedum Collaborative demonstrate their understanding of the process of school reform as they share stories of the instructional, assessment, and professional changes they are making in their classrooms and in their lives. After eight years of involvement in the Benedum Collaborative, the teachers regard professional development school reform as a positive force having a powerful impact on the lives of the participants. As the collaboration between WVU and the professional development schools matures, we are becoming more adept at using our complementary skills and abilities and effectively integrating the demands on higher education faculty and teacher education students with the needs of K–12 children and teachers. These stories of restructuring through a Literacy Discussion Group in one case and collaborative curriculum redesign in the other are examples of the ideal. They are models that reflect the interdependence of reform and professional development as described by Sykes (1996,466): "a professional community can serve as a source of insight and wisdom about problems of practice."

References

The College of Human Resources and Education, West Virginia University (1988). *Partners for progress: A collaborative project for educational improvement in West Virginia. A proposal to the Benedum Foundation.* Morgantown, W.V.: Author.

Darling-Hammond, L. (1992). Building learner-centered schools: Developing professional capacity, policy, and political consensus. In J. Banks et. al., *Building learning centered schools: Three perspectives.* New York: Teachers College, Columbia University.

Deay, A. and Saab, J. (1994). Teachers' perspectives of student-centered learning communities. *Journal of Research in Rural Education 10*(2): 108–115.

Field, T. (1991). *Toward a shared vision of education reform: Establishing professional development schools.* Paper presented at the annual meeting of the American Association of Colleges for Teacher Education, Atlanta.

Grossman, Pamela L. (1994). In pursuit of a dual agenda: Creating a middle level professional development school. In L. Darling-Hammond, ed., *Professional Development Schools: Schools for Developing a Profession*, pp. 50–73. New York: Teachers College Press, Columbia University.

Isenhart, J., Rudden, J., Johnson, R., Oaks, R., Nedeff, A., Barksdale-Ladd, M. (1993). *Comparing basal and whole language instruction in one third grade classroom.* Unpublished manuscript.

Jett-Simpson, M., et al. (1992). *Portrait of an urban professional development school.* Paper presented at the Annual Meeting of the American Educational Research Association, San Francisco.

Kyle, R. (1993). *Transforming Our Schools: Lessons from the Jefferson County Public Schools/Gheens Professional Development Academy*, 1983–1991. Louisville, Kentucky.

Lee, V. and Smith, J. (1992). *Effects of school restructuring on the achievement and engagement of middle-grade students.* Madison: University of Wisconsin, Center on Organization and Restructuring of Schools.

Lieberman, A. (1992). Introduction: The changing context of education. In A. Lieberman, ed., *The changing context of teaching: Ninety-first yearbook of the National Society for the Study of Education*, pp. 1–10. Chicago: The University of Chicago Press.

Lieberman, A. (1995). Practices that support teacher development: Transforming conceptions of professional learning. *Phi Delta Kappan 76*(8): 591–596.

McLaughlin, M. (1992). *What matters most in teachers' workplace context?* pp. 92–139. Stanford: Center for Research on the Context of Secondary Teaching, Stanford University.

Sykes, G. (1996). Reform *of* and *as* professional development. *Phi Delta Kappan 77*(7): 465–467.

Whitford, B. (1994). Permission, persistence, and resistance: Linking high school restructuring with teacher education reform. In L. Darling-Hammond, ed., *Professional Development Schools: Schools for Developing a Profession*, pp. 74–97. New York: Teachers College Press, Columbia University.

Wilson, S., Peterson, P., Ball, D., and Cohen, D. (1996). Learning by all. *Phi Delta Kappan 77*(7): 468–476.

12

RECONSIDERING ASSESSMENT TO BE REFLECTIVE OF SCHOOL REFORM

JACI WEBB-DEMPSEY

Introduction

Nearly five years into the Benedum Collaborative Professional Development Schools initiative, a comprehensive longitudinal assessment was launched. The initial phase of the assessment focused on the experiences of teachers in the five original professional development schools (PDSs) and was intended to document and describe the impact of efforts to develop a professional culture of teaching while engaging in the process of school reform. While the documentation of the changes in the conditions of work for teachers and the impact of those changes for teachers was a necessary first step in the assessment of the PDS initiative, the restructuring and reculturing undertaken in the name of the Benedum Collaborative was not only intended to make the participating schools places where teachers renew their professional practices on an ongoing basis, but also better places for the preparation of new teachers and, ultimately, for children to learn. Thus, in any attempt to comprehensively capture the results of this initiative there are three immediate populations for whom the simultaneous restructuring undertaken by the public schools and the University should be expected to have an impact: participating teachers, students in the teacher education program at West Virginia University, and public school students. The second phase of the assessment has sustained the focus on the experiences of teachers, but has broadened in scope to include the impact of the initiative for preservice teachers and the students in the PDSs. By attempting to establish a connection between changes in the "rules, roles, and relationships" for teacher culture and changes in the experiences of students, this work moves a step beyond traditional evaluation research on restructuring efforts.

One set of challenges presented by this assessment is unique to the nature of the Benedum Collaborative initiative: the history of relationships and research efforts in the schools and the University and the magnitude of attempting to adequately describe the impact of PDS across thirteen schools. Another set of challenges represents issues that confront any attempt to assess the impact of such change efforts. The way these challenges are dealt with in the assessment of PDS can either undermine the integrity of such initiatives because guiding beliefs about the nature of PDS are compromised or can support the effort by reflecting the underlying attitudes, beliefs, and values concerning what PDS can and should be about. This chapter focuses on three issues: 1) the challenges to traditional forms of assessment inherent in the complex restructuring and reculturing that creates professional development schools and makes teacher professionalism explicit, 2) the ways in which the Benedum Collaborative assessment study has tried to meet these challenges, and 3) the impact of the results of doing assessment that is reflective of the reform it is assessing by sharing findings from a cross-site analysis of the data gathered from students in the five original PDS sites.

Challenging the Structure and Culture of Teaching and Assessment

Traditional professional development, better known as staff development or inservice training, is predicated on the belief that learning about teaching and decision making about curriculum can take place outside the real contexts of schools and the lives of teachers and their students. This view of professional development assumes that these experiences, divorced as they are from real application and beyond the control of teachers, will automatically translate into improved learning opportunities for students. The professional development schools initiative challenges this set of beliefs by investing in opportunities for teachers to engage in learning experiences that are a part of a school-based agenda for the improvement of student learning experiences. By relocating control of teacher learning experiences and the resources that support those experiences, the PDS initiative acknowledges that the source of teacher professionalism lies, as Dempsey notes in Chapter 1, in the social context of teaching. Professional development schools are aimed at providing "what everyone appears to want for students, a wide array of learning opportunities that engage students in experiencing, creating and solving real problems, using their own experiences and working with others" (Lieberman 1995, 591). The goal is for professional development schools to become places where such learning opportunities are a seamless part of teachers' and students' lives in schools and where these opportunities are ongoing and self-renewing. Part of this goal, due to their unique connection with universities and colleges of education, is for PDSs to become places where preservice teachers engage in those learning opportunities and learn how to create them for their own students and where both public school and University teachers work and learn together.

These learning opportunities for teachers, their students and preservice teacher education students—and continual reflection on them—lay the groundwork for creating a profession of teaching, making PDSs places where this profession is most likely to develop.

Grounding the development of the professionalization of teaching in the real worlds of schools and the real lives of teachers and students rests on an acknowledgment that there is no one best way for teachers and students to learn and therefore no one best path to becoming a professional development school. This recognition of the contextual nature of teaching, learning, and school reform underlies the diversity of the change efforts the five original professional development schools in the Benedum Collaborative have engaged in. These change efforts were undertaken to best serve the students each of the schools serves based on the understandings their teachers held about their educational needs. Those understandings in turn became the frame for teachers' learning opportunities. While the schools' chosen reforms may not be radical or unique in and of themselves, the underlying belief that engaging in them will increase learning opportunities for students and provide opportunities for teachers to redefine the structural nature of their work and come to know themselves as learners is a radical departure from tradition.

Restructuring and reculturing teaching as learning in schools is a complex undertaking. The difficulties of such undertakings are well documented (Murphy and Hallinger 1993; Sarason 1990). The difficulties of assessing the impact of such broad reform efforts are most evident in what is missing from that documentation. Traditional evaluation research on school reform efforts has been dominated by implementation studies that document attempts to change adult attitudes and behaviors but neglect to address the underlying impetus for such changes—the improvement of the educational experiences of students (Webb, Wilson, and Corbett 1993). These studies, like most of the restructuring efforts they attempt to examine, typically rest on the assumptions that underlie traditional staff development or teacher training activities, that such experiences will automatically change the attitudes and behaviors of teachers, which will then change the learning conditions and experiences of students for the better. As Wilson, Webb, and Corbett (1994) note:

> To the extent that research has discussed the impact of adult change on students, the descriptions have been limited to gross but narrow measures of the artifacts of student participation in school, student perceptions of changes in school climate, or adults' perceptions of changes in how students are acting as students. No studies establish a convincing thread of logic that connects adult implementation to the kinds of changes in the daily lives of students that could reasonably account for these outcomes. Restructuring can only be assessed in terms of student results, and a

compelling argument needs to be made that adult changes really make a
difference for students. (176)

A fundamental challenge to the assessment of the impact of PDS is the need to
address the leap of faith required to connect adult and student learning
experiences. This is not merely a theoretical challenge, as Dempsey notes in
Chapter 1. The problem faced by efforts to restructure schooling, teaching, and
learning is that we must come to grips with the connection between professionalism and better education for children if we expect these efforts to be supported. Even efforts that have been explicitly about changing the experiences of
teachers are eventually held to the same bottom line—the improvement of
learning opportunities for students. This raises another critical challenge to the
assessment of PDS; while there is no one best way to engage in reform, many
stakeholders and audiences are convinced that there is one best way to measure
results, regardless of the nature of the change effort. Merely recording changes
in standard student performance indicators will not capture the authentic results
PDS was intended to be about, nor will it help us explain those results. The
challenge is to begin to change the nature of the bottom line to reflect the real
changes occurring in PDSs.

Relying primarily on standardized measures to evaluate the impact of
change efforts that are intended to do anything other than teach the material
covered by the tests will provide a limited and relatively superficial view of
broader changes (Wiggins 1993). This reliance ignores the complexity and
multiplicity of goals such as those set by PDS initiatives, as reflected in the
Belief Statements (see Chapter 3) designed to guide the development of the
Benedum Collaborative PDSs. Further, allowing assessment to be tied solely to
standardized measures sends the message that what is valued is what is embedded in the tests, and vice versa. As Corbett and Wilson (1991) reveal in their
study of the impact of statewide testing, what gets measured drives practices in
schools. When we set "better results" as our goal, without attaching them to
different forms of teaching and learning, we can expect to get traditional forms
of teaching and learning. Assessment of new forms of practice should instead
create possibilities to sustain both new practices and new assessments. Balancing
the need to consider stakeholders and audiences who have an expectation for,
and are more secure with, traditional measures and assessments with the need to
create these possibilities is yet another challenge to the assessment of PDS.

A final challenge is inherent in the changes the PDS initiative supports for
teachers. Just as teachers in PDSs are encouraged to take on new roles with
respect to schooling, teaching, and learning, they should also be encouraged to
take on new roles with respect to evaluation and the assessment of the impact of
changes they initiate and sustain. In describing the "pitfalls" of the evaluation of
school programs, Herman and Winters (1992) describe the traditional role

educators are encouraged to assume in evaluation, in part due to an over-reliance on standardized measures. As they explain:

> Tests have been used to satisfy legislators and administrators at the federal, state, and even local levels who wished to know how mandated and other special programs were working and whether schools were effective. Until recently, school people—teachers and administrators— have been used primarily as data providers rather than data users and as implements of reforms rather than initiators of such efforts. (12)

Restructuring has moved decision making about school programs and resources into schools and the hands of teachers; decision making about the evaluation of those programs and the allocation of resources should not be far behind. Just as restructuring requires opportunities for teachers to learn, to reflect, and to take action based on their growing understandings, restructuring assessment to include teachers as meaningful participants requires making opportunities for them to learn about assessment, to reflect on the results of assessment and to make changes based on the understandings they develop from that reflection. The final challenge is then to create an assessment that offers those opportunities in order to build the capacity for teachers to be both critical consumers of evaluation results and active participants in decisions about how the impact of their efforts can best be assessed.

Reconsidering Assessment

Although individual change efforts enacted by the five original sites in West Virginia under the umbrella of PDS initiative had been the topics of research during the early years of the Collaborative, little had been done to look across the schools to examine the impact of PDS itself. The first phase of the assessment was conceived by University faculty as a means to document and describe the impact of PDS on the experiences of teachers, enhance the work in the schools, gather information that would assist in the development of new professional development schools, and provide an improved knowledge base for field-based activities within the College of Human Resources and Education. The thrust of this work was a blend of formative assessment and scholarly research, and while the Claude Worthington Benedum Foundation provided funding for the endeavor, it was in response to a grant request. The results of the initial teacher assessment work created a demand for more information—both from the participating schools and from the Benedum Foundation. The first of the challenges confronted by the assessment of the Benedum Collaborative PDS initiative was the need to negotiate ways to serve both the needs of our funding agent, who essentially commissioned the second phase of the assessment in order to determine "what they had paid for," and those of Collaborative participants who wanted information about the impact on their students. Audiences external to the Collaborative are invested in "the bottom line" drawn by standardized measures of student achievement and school performance, while internal audiences are skeptical of the explanatory power of such measures. Additionally, the process of becoming a PDS was never envisioned to be about raising scores on standardized measures but rather to be about changing learning opportunities for teachers and students—changes that may or may not be related to any standardized measure. Additionally, while the funding agent was most interested in the potentially summative aspects of assessment, such as the ability to compare student performance of PDS sites with that of non-PDS schools, Collaborative participants were willing to participate in an assessment because it had the potential to formatively support their ongoing efforts. These tensions were compounded by the need to begin to build the capacity of school-based participants to be critical consumers of evaluation information and to increasingly shift the primary responsibility for assessing the impact of cross-site and site-specific reforms from its traditional location—the University research community—to a shared and collaborative location—the partnership between the University and the public schools. This capacity-building was not a goal for the funding agency, and so the time and energy required to create and carry out a collaborative study had to be creatively packaged and sustained. Finally, the scope of the assessment broadened significantly to include the experiences of public school and teacher education students at roughly the same time that the Collaborative grew to include eight new PDS sites, more than doubling the needs for information.

The research activities for the assessment came from multiple research methodologies and multiple perspectives within those methodologies. One of our primary philosophical positions has been to come at our work from the standpoint of "blurred genres" (Geertz 1973). The study team, including members of both the first and second phases of the assessment, attempted to pull strategies from many different perspectives, including anthropology, history, psychology, and sociology. These perspectives were represented in the expertise and training of the faculty members on the team, who came from Educational Psychology, Special Education, Curriculum and Instruction, Speech Pathology and Audiology, and Social and Cultural Foundations of Education. The assessment was conceived as a way to develop a set of emergent understandings— understandings that would "emerge" in the collection and analysis of the data. This emergent strategy serves two purposes. One, little work had been done to assess the school restructuring movement when this work began, so we had little to fall back on in terms of research precedent. We were very much in the same boat as colleagues across the country who were in the thick of attempts to look at the same general phenomena, but had little at that point to share. Two, we were working from the standpoint of "grounded theory" (Glaser and Strauss 1967), where we take what we can know about previous experience in school reform and let those generalizations guide our early research strategies and framework. We intended, as we spent more time in the schools and came to know each site's contexts more deeply, to allow the emerging data to begin to guide the work in lieu of the early generalization-driven framework. Careful consideration of the data, and an intricate strategy for articulating the context for each school and for the PDS initiative as a whole, would give us not only a narrative for describing the story of each school, but also an overall strategy for coming to know the work of the schools collectively.

The design of the second phase of the assessment was intended to serve several purposes; these include: to continue to document the impact of PDS involvement for teachers, to establish a basis for documenting the impact of PDS on the learning experiences of University students and public school students, to develop an ongoing system for assessing changes connected to PDS—the changes connected both to the cross-site initiative and to the site-specific changes implemented as part of each PDS's strategic plan—to build the capacity of PDS faculties to participate in ongoing assessment activities, and to build an awareness of the need to include school-based assessment strategies as part of future school reform efforts. The first consideration in accomplishing these goals was the composition of the study team. Including the perspectives of the University faculty described above, the team includes researchers with expertise in the area of PDS and in both qualitative and quantitative research methods. University faculty were joined by Benedum Collaborative staff, graduate assistants, and representatives from each of the thirteen PDSs. The teacher representatives from each of the PDS sites were provided release time through the assessment budget to periodically participate as study team members and to inform the design and the development of instruments. To facilitate communications about the assessment, each school also had a study team liaison—a study team member who handled the majority of the arrangements for data collection and other communication tasks and who spent time "hanging around" the school to get a sense of the context for the data from that school. School representatives to the study team also helped facilitate communications; however, their most valuable role was in helping to translate research questions into the language of their students and assisting in the development of meaningful and appropriate indicators of the PDS belief statements from students' perspectives. Faculty in each of the sites were made aware of their school's study team liaison and participated in nominating their school representative so that they would have "familiar faces" to go to with their concerns throughout the assessment. For the five original sites, this was a continuation of the precedent set during the first phase of teacher assessment data collection; for new sites, these practices began to lay the groundwork to accomplish the purposes described above.

Prior to beginning to operationalize the design of the second phase of the assessment study, the Director of the PDS Impact Assessment Study Team attended at least one meeting with faculty in each of the thirteen sites. These meetings ranged from PDS site steering committee meetings or steering sub-committee meetings to full faculty meetings. In each of the five original sites the Director and other study team members attended both site steering committee meetings and one full faculty meeting to outline the study, address concerns about the assessment, and gather general input concerning the design and specific input about which of the school's reform efforts to focus data collection on. Few of the new sites had begun to implement changes, most were still in the process of beginning to develop their strategic plans, and so input was solicited in these schools to identify areas where these sites would like to have baseline data gathered. These meetings served several purposes: they informed the study design, they began the process of building local capacity, and they began the process of establishing collaborative relationships between the study team and PDS participants that reflect the nature of the PDS initiative. These purposes continued to be considered throughout the assessment process.

In addition to tapping the expertise of the school representatives, an advisory board was created to inform the study team's activities from an external perspective. This Board includes representatives from critical stakeholding groups—the five PDS district Superintendents, a representative of the West Virginia teachers' union, a representative from the West Virginia State Department of Education, the West Virginia Education Fund, the Governor's Center for Professional Development, the Appalachian Education Lab (the regional federal education lab serving West Virginia), WVU's teacher education program, and the College of Arts and Sciences. The Board was asked to review the design for the assessment and the instruments. This group made suggestions for additional data collection from administrators involved in the PDS initiative, including superintendents and principals, and from parents and community members. Board members were also able to help clarify some of the issues the groups they represented would be most interested in. The broad-based representation of the Board was also intended to serve to create a supportive network of individuals and agencies involved in the PDS initiative and the improvement of education throughout the state of West Virginia. This network was seen as a means of beginning to access and inform state and local educational policy systems.

The comprehensive design included gathering both interview and survey data from teachers, students, and preservice teacher education students. The bulk of the second phase of the work has initially centered around data collection with the public school students being served in PDS sites. Members of the study team spent a day in each of the twelve participating PDSs (one of the new sites was undergoing an accreditation review and asked to delay data collection) interviewing students. Elementary and middle school students were interviewed individually during thirty to forty-five-minute semi-structured, open-ended interviews. These individual interviews were fieldnote scripted and interviewers then transcribed their notes. Secondary students and students in one of the elementary schools were interviewed in focus groups of three to five members. Focus group interviews typically lasted between sixty and ninety minutes and were also semi-structured and open-ended, audio taped and transcribed. A set of core questions, intended to elicit general discussions of students' perceptions of their learning opportunities and specific descriptions of their school experiences as they related to the guiding PDS belief statements, was asked across all the interviews. These questions were deliberately framed to reflect the kinds of experiences students were anticipated to be having if PDS were embedded in the schools' cultures. The study team started with the five guiding PDS Belief Statements, described in Chapter 3, to build the core questions. The core included:

- How do you feel you learn best? How do you know that is how you learn best? Do you have opportunities that encourage you to learn that way in school?
- What do you like to learn about in school? What's the best way for you to learn about that? Do you have opportunities to learn that way in school?
- What do you do that makes you feel successful? Do you have opportunities to feel successful in school? What happens in school to make others feel successful?
- What kinds of decisions/choices do you make about your learning? What kinds of decisions/choices are you involved in at your school?
- How are people in your school different from one another? Are students treated differently because of their differences, if so, how? Are people's differences respected?
- Is there anything about your experiences at school that I haven't asked you about that you think I should know?

Questions generated to either gather data about the school's specific reform efforts or baseline data about possible areas for reform were added at the end of the core protocol. These core and site-specific questions also guided the development of items for student surveys.

To date, interviews have been conducted with more than 400 PDS students; approximately ten percent of the total PDS student population. Samples of students to be interviewed were chosen to represent the population of each school with respect to gender, ethnicity, academic ability, and indicators of socio-economic status. Surveys have been collected from more than 3,000 students in kindergarten through twelfth grades. Surveys were administered by PDS teachers, with the exception of those collected from kindergarten and first graders, where study team members recorded responses for students. West

Virginia State Department of Education School Report Card data was also gathered and organized for each PDS site. Where appropriate, given the nature of the schools' change efforts, this data was used to provide additional information about those efforts. For example, one of the elementary schools targeted its math and science curricula as areas for improvement—it was appropriate to look at their CTBS scores in these areas.

Impact of the Results

The most compelling result of the manner in which the assessment was designed and carried out was the impact of the feedback of findings in each of the schools. As findings were shared with site steering committees and other faculty groups, both during meetings and through written reports, without exception they began to consider how to address the implications of what the data said about their school as a PDS for students and what the data said about learning opportunities as they related to their site-specific reform efforts. For example, an area where students typically expressed concern was peer interactions. Elementary school students in particular described how "playground behaviors" such as "name-calling," "teasing," and having "cliques" worked against feelings of mutual respect and acceptance. When these findings were shared, schools whose students had expressed such concerns barely got to the end of their initial feedback session before they began to strategize about how to begin to foster more positive student interactions. They were also able to connect this area of concern to areas of strength indicated by their findings— linking the need to foster mutually respectful student interactions with strong and influential (from students' perspectives) parent involvement and beginning to explore how a parent group might be able to examine interactions during recess and other non-instructional time and propose strategies for decreasing the opportunity for negative behaviors.

There were also examples where initial feedback raised flags, indicating a need to gather additional data. These instances provide a natural next step in local capacity building by inviting broader participation in future assessment activities. In one elementary school, African-American students were found to be less positive about themselves as successful students than other groups. This finding motivated the teachers in the school to begin to plan how they might look more closely at the experiences of these students, both in the current data set and in future data collection efforts. The responses of vocational track students and the perspectives college prep track students held of "Vo-tech" students in one of the high schools were consistently negative. Here again, teachers not only claimed ownership of the findings, they immediately began to plan how to gather additional data to better inform their understandings of the experiences of these students and to inform their efforts to improve them.

Beyond the site-specific findings related to each school's efforts to become a PDS and each school's particular reform initiatives, a set of findings was generated out of an analysis looking across the data sets. These findings are being shared at a variety of cross-site meetings in order to help new PDS sites consider the implications of student perspectives as they complete their first round of strategic planning and to encourage original sites to reflect on their efforts with respect to what the data implies about what strengthens the "PDS-ness" of school and learning experiences for students. These findings are reported here around the five belief statements intended to guide the development of the PDSs and the assessment.

All in a Professional Development School are learners.

A clear finding in the student interview and survey data is that just as there is no "one best way" to become a PDS or to assess what the impact of PDS might be, there is no one best way for all students to learn. Students describe a wide range of instructional approaches that they believe help them learn best—ranging from direct instruction coupled with note taking, to hands-on activities and cooperative work groups. The implication is that the greater the variety of instructional approaches teachers use, the greater the likelihood that students believe they have sufficient and appropriate opportunities to learn. Relying primarily on one approach or another means that some students will believe they are left out. While they might not be able to articulate their understandings of themselves as learners in "educational jargon," student responses about learning indicate an awareness of their individual needs and abilities, and of how the teaching strategies employed in their classrooms either match their needs and abilities or not. Students are critical of putting their effort into activities that do not contribute either to their learning or understanding or to their feelings of success. A high school student described a situation she did not feel was serving her well, underscoring this connection:

> My [class] I really don't like because it's like . . . she doesn't explain the theory. She doesn't really, she's just like, "This is how it goes and all you have to do is plug in the numbers and it's really easy." But it's not like, it's not gonna challenge me and I know I'm gonna regret taking that class with her. And I'm not gonna learn what I need to do . . . I can't learn like that.

The two most frequently cited instructional approaches that emerged across all responses about experiences that students believe help them learn best are "one-on-one" individualized instructional time with their teachers and "hands-on" learning. "One-on-one" with their teachers not only supports learning by allowing teachers to customize instruction to fit a student's needs, it also indicates a more personal relationship between teachers and students. "Hands-on" learning activities are valued by students because they are engaging, because they make abstract concepts concrete, because they typically allow students to make choices or have some control over the activity, and because they provide increased opportunities for "one-on-one" with their teachers. A third grader shares the kind of engagement "hands-on" experiences encourages:

> I learn best when we're doing it. Hands-on. Up close. For example, in "A is for Arts," [visiting artist] brought in a bag of clay and we looked at it. We looked at a locust skin. This stuff is not in books. I know I learn best this way because I get the idea of what it really is rather than it being "cleaned up" for books. We try to have opportunities to do that in school. We try to do lots of active things in third grade.

Another elementary student describes the concrete power of these experiences:

> I like to do hands-on. It's easier for some reason. In science a WVU student asked us, "Who can change the shape of a bubble?" She gave us a bubble blower and we blew bubbles. The only way I could make it different was when they stuck together. I call that hands-on because you use your hands a lot.

During a focus-group interview, a group of fifth and sixth grade students explained why they believed a hands-on approach enhanced learning, illustrating how these experiences make learning concrete and offer opportunities for interaction with teachers:

> [How do you feel you learn best?] Student 5: Using manipulatives. [What do you mean by manipulatives?] Student 5: They are objects that help you learn. [How do you know manipulatives help you learn?] Student 5: With manipulatives you can see what the problem is and correct it. Like we do in science. There are lots of hands-on materials there. [And what about you?] Student 4: Hands-on stuff. Instead of talking about the projects in the books [this student had raised this as a critique of the school he had previously attended] it helps when they do it with us.

A sixth grader who described learning best in science because it was "hands-on" also shared that this offered opportunities to make choices:

> Sometimes the teacher sets up choices on the table in science and you get to choose. There are different projects and you get to choose.

Another sixth grader made a direct connection between "hands-on" activities and "one-on-one":

> I learn best when teachers interact with students. [Can you tell me what interacting with students means?] When they work with you doing hands-on activities. [What about that helps you learn?] The teachers discuss it more with you, it helps me better than just a lecture.

Interestingly, when direct instruction, such as lecturing, is interesting, content-rich, and students believe that their teacher cares about the subject and students, students define what are traditionally described as "passive" learning opportunities as "active," even "hands-on." An eleventh grader's description of how he learns best illustrates this:

> Well, if it's not really interesting, like if it's something I'm not really interested in then I'll have to . . . just like run it through my mind a bunch of times, like I have to do a lot of work at home, like trying to memorize stuff. It's more memorizing, it's like something I don't really care about, but something I really like and I'm interested in, I really learn it, it just stays in my mind. I don't have to worry. [What kinds of opportunities do you have to learn that way?] Well, classes where the teachers like lecture, it's not like they, you know, lecture; it's not like a boring monotone thing you know. It's just like something where they're excited about it and they want to talk about it and it's something that sounds pretty neat to me . . . some of them [teachers] are really excited about what they're talking about and, and they use different things, like visuals, and stuff like hands-on. Really just them being excited about it is the only thing that really catches my attention, that I really care about.

Neither the interview protocol nor the student survey instruments included a question directly asking students to describe the opportunities they had to be active learners, making the numerous instances where students in some schools offered descriptions of learning experiences that encouraged active participation, the kinds of experiences that one elementary school student described as "when real things happen," all the more powerful. An elementary school student displayed the two most frequently cited reasons that students liked active experiences, because they are engaging and because students believe they enhance learning, when he explained that his favorite things in school were "doing crafts and experiments and computers" because "they are fun and you could learn new things from them; doing things helps you learn." Students' perceptions that experiences are fun are important because they appear to lay a foundation for students actively participating in learning activities, for their belief that learning is a worthwhile activity, and for their learning experiences being memorable—all of which make retention of skills and content more likely. This retention was evident in the descriptions of content that accompanied discussions of active learning experiences. For example, a third grader described a unit on endangered species that included a variety of instructional approaches and opportunities for student choice as one of the "fun things like you do here to help you learn" and then displayed his understanding of the content of the unit:

> I want to learn about how the earth was once. [Have you had opportunities to learn about that?] Yes, such as like maybe the Dodo bird, we learned about the Dodo bird when we learned about endangered animals. I feel sorry for extinct animals. People are responsible for this, like the Dodo birds, the passenger pigeons. Not the dinosaurs, but I think men are responsible maybe for the woolly mammoths, because they killed too many, more than they ate. [How did you learn about these things?] Doing exciting and fun stuff. I learn about them in school here, I'm learning more here.

Another student's description of favorite learning experiences also illustrates the impact of active learning on content acquisition:

> Student 7: I like science, just the way you get to learn about the way everything works. It just inspires me... one of the special lessons was about clouds — what they did and what they meant. We did pictures— how high they would be and what they would bring. Student 2: If we're in science, my favorite unit was how they were building bridges. [Student describes in detail, with contributions by others in the focus group, how to place the beams and support poles in the water and how a special pump pushes the water aside so that the beam can be laid—including a discussion of how air had to be pumped down constantly.]

All in a Professional Development School have the opportunity for success.

The expectations for student experiences that reflect this belief statement are that students will have opportunities to be successful in school and that they will believe they are successful, exhibiting positive self-esteem. Students were asked to respond to several survey items and a direct interview question about their opportunities for success and their feelings of success. Student beliefs about what it means to be successful in their schools vary dramatically from school to school. When asked to describe a successful student or what made them personally feel successful, the most frequent categories of response to both survey and interview questions reflected students' understandings of what is valued in their school cultures. Most frequent categories ranged from "grades" and "learning" at one elementary school to "working hard" and "helping others" at another, and "grades" and "sports involvement" at one high school to "learning for college" and "grades" at another. These beliefs are greatly influenced by the explicit reward, recognition, and discipline structures in each school and by the more subtle, but powerful, messages implicit in teachers' and parents' attitudes and behaviors. A college-bound high school senior described one of those subtle messages:

> It's not an academic atmosphere at all. It is all extracurriculars . . . see we have a newspaper and very seldom do you ever see any people that do well in academics in the paper, but every sports team is in there.

Schools that reward, recognize, and encourage positive social outcomes and personal effort in addition to academic outcomes and reward, are more likely to promote positive self-esteem for a greater range of students. When positive social outcomes and personal effort are a viable part of what it means to be successful in school, the broader characteristics that parents, employers, and educators often include as important goals for schooling are more likely to be fostered. For example, in their discussions of what makes them feel successful students in one of the elementary schools frequently mentioned helping other students. This school serves a significant number of international students who come to the school to learn English as their second language. A sixth grader from Indonesia explained what she believes makes international students feel successful, illustrating the power of the tutoring and informal "helping" opportunities encouraged by teachers in this school:

> They [international students] learn from others and must be part of the class after being helped by others, they then must help others learn.

Students who come to believe that getting along with others, helping others, and being able to work cooperatively are characteristics of successful students are more likely to strive to develop these characteristics. One astute sixth grader, in describing what made her feel successful, made a recommendation along these lines:

> There are not a whole lot of opportunities to be successful other than just grades. Kids should be commended for being a good friend and for being willing to lend a hand to other people. Even little things like the teacher saying, "You did a good job on something," or "Thank you for doing that," that's important.

It also follows that when students believe that making an effort contributes to success, and is rewarded and/or recognized as one of the characteristics of a successful student they are more likely to believe trying is valuable. During an interview at an elementary school, a sixth grader shared her definition of success connecting success and effort:

> To me it isn't about getting good grades, its trying your hardest. [Is trying your hardest recognized by others?] Our teacher does a good job of recognizing us not just for how we do on a test, but how we know and how we work interactively, what we talk about in class. She knows because of that.

It is important to note that definitions of success that are most reflective of PDS are those that include learning. When students believe that learning, in and of itself, contributes to success and is valued in their school and home lives they make connections between other indicators of success and learning. Grades may or may not be a measure of learning for children, as they often associate getting good grades with appropriate behavior or personal effort, rather than learning. In schools where learning is not explicitly valued, students often miss the connection between indicators such as grades and learning. In schools where learning is celebrated as the ultimate outcome, rather than some form of achievement or effort, student's responses about success and what they believe is valuable center around learning. A third grader's response to an interviewer's question about what happened that made her feel successful illustrates how students make this connection:

> [Grades] they help me very much. Grades tell me that I learn a lot. They tell me what I haven't learned.

Another elementary student was more critical of grades as an indicator for learning:

> Mostly I like to learn language. I like to learn to improve my reading, reading is my weakness. [How do you know reading is your weakness? What lets you know that?] . . . Not really grades, because you can do other work for extra credit. It shows up when I do the test—my weakness on the test is reading.

A sixth grader explained that while she enjoyed learning about "things I know [how to do] already," like "music and art," she believed that it is most important to work on skills that will enable her to learn, such as "reading," because "that naturally leads to learning." In schools where learning was a critical component of students' definitions of success, the standard against which students measure themselves may be more likely to be themselves—rather than the grades and achievements of others. A third grader who had been described by his teachers as having struggled in school shared that the thing that made him feel good about himself was "learning how to do stuff," because, "just that I learned it and I can know it for the rest of my life."

The organization of a Professional Development School encourages all to be empowered.

While shared governance is one of the hallmarks of teacher empowerment, the indicators of student empowerment are often less formal. Teachers report increased commitment to their work as a result of increased autonomy and involvement in what they believe are key decisions about schooling, teaching, and learning. Students report increased engagement when they are given opportunities to make choices about their learning and about other aspects of their lives in school. Making these choices also promotes students' ability to make other decisions and to become critical consumers of their learning experiences. A first grader shared how having opportunities to make choices about learning activities promotes engagement in response to an interview question about what he liked to do in school:

Writing. [What is it about writing that you like?] I like writing stories about what I like, that's what I like about writing.

Students who have opportunities to contribute to the learning of others—helping other students as tutors or in groups, being encouraged to share their ideas and new understandings with their teachers, peers, and parents—believe learning is important. Further, these opportunities are as empowering for students as opportunities to learn together and contribute ideas and new understandings are for teachers in restructuring schools. Just as it is empowering for teachers to believe that they produce knowledge and that they have expertise to contribute, students are also empowered when they have opportunities to come to believe they produce knowledge and can contribute expertise—rather than simply acquiring or consuming knowledge. Cooperative student work groups provide these opportunities, as a high school student shared:

I think that group projects are good because, um, you learn from different people their knowledge so that you can put it all together and benefit from everybody's knowledge on the subject.

Working in groups also increases opportunities for students to develop more tolerant attitudes toward peers who are culturally "different" and to recognize the "knowledge" of others. An elementary school student explains:

> I learn best when I'm in small groups. [How does that help you learn?]
> Well, different people know different things and you learn all kinds of
> different things when you work with them. . . . I like helping a student
> from Africa because we can give each other good tips.

Beyond an appreciation for their own abilities and the abilities of others,
cooperative groups provide students with opportunities they believe will
translate into success beyond school. A high school senior's response to a
question about how he learned best illustrates the power of being a critical
consumer of learning experiences and the power of believing that school
learning experiences are enabling:

> I work well in groups. I don't prefer to work in groups. I prefer to work by
> myself, but I have lots of opportunities to work with groups and I feel in
> order to be a successful student you have to learn how to work in groups
> even if you don't like it . . . [also] it's something you have to do to work in
> the real world.

A Professional Development School fosters an environment of mutual respect.

Compelling patterns emerge across student beliefs about teacher respect
for students. Student definitions of teacher respect most frequently reflect
dimensions of "caring." Teacher respect is defined by "taking care" of students,
by teachers protecting students' opportunities to learn and to be safe in school.
Older students recognize respect as reciprocal—they believe they make decisions about whether or not to show respect for teachers based on whether or not
they believe teachers exhibit an appropriate level of respect for them. A high
school junior explains this reciprocity:

> I'm kind of straight-laced, right down the line. I will give my teachers
> respect until they don't [give me respect] and when that point comes they
> will have problems with me. I have got to see respect in how they treat
> me. If they treat me like a person, they look me in the eyes when they talk
> to me, that's respect.

Teacher respect is also tied to caring about whether or not students learn.
Students consistently described knowing that their teachers respected them,
regardless of how "strict" they might be, when they also knew their teachers
cared about their learning. Students believe that teachers that don't respect them
don't care whether or not they learn. In a discussion of how he knew his teachers
respected students, a high school sophomore described:

Most of my teachers pretty much take charge of a class . . . whenever they're taking charge they bring you up to their level enough that you can understand them. I know I've had [names teachers] my hard, my hardest teachers were like two very strict teachers but they were excellent teachers. I learned more in their classes than I have in any other classes I've ever had. [What made them excellent?] . . . if you talked to them, like whenever they aren't trying to teach or something, then they're the best people that you'll ever get to know. It's just they want you to learn and they don't want you [just] being there . . . they don't want you playing around. They want you there to learn.

Students were also asked to discuss student respect for other students. A general intolerance for one group of students permeated the data across PDS sites—students who interfere with learning opportunities for others due to inappropriate behaviors are typically scorned. The most frequently cited barrier to learning was the behavior of other students. A core elementary survey item asked students to complete the statement, "Things that happen in school that do not help me learn are . . . "; the most frequent response to this item across this data had to do with inappropriate student behavior, "when teachers have to spend all their time on kids who are being bad." The majority of students who discussed this barrier to learning did so with a high degree of frustration—indicating that opportunities to learn are important to them.

To be able to understand how students in each school defined diversity, whether it had to do with cultural or racial differences or something else altogether, students were asked a very broad open-ended question: "Can you describe how people in your school are different from one another?" Definitions of "difference" varied as much as definitions of success from school to school. Not surprisingly, students attending the elementary school serving the large population of international students included cultural diversity in their definitions. Surprisingly, students attending an elementary school serving the highest number of African-American students did not include cultural or racial diversity in their definitions; instead they perceived behavior, students being "good" or "bad" or "nice" or "mean," as the defining characteristics that made people in their school different from one another. Students also described school practices and learning opportunities that contributed to their understandings of difference. A second grader described learning about the historical mistreatment of African-Americans in this country during a unit on the black artist Romare Bearden and how that influenced her treatment of others:

[How are people in your school different from one another?] Some are taller or some of them can do things better or some of them talk more than others and some stay real quiet. [Are students treated differently because of those differences?] Yeah, like if we're playing and another girl likes to play and some people don't let them play, I let her play with us. Learning about the African-Americans and thinking about how it's not fair how they were treated makes a difference.

Opportunities to learn about cultural diversity also have an impact on student self-awareness and self-respect. An African-American third grader reflected on what kinds of things she would choose to learn about:

I would like to know more about social studies and English. In first grade in social studies we had this big book. We learned about black people and white people, about this lady who wanted to ride a bus and they tried to make her move and she wouldn't. Have you heard about her? [Yes. That was Rosa Parks. . . . Did you get to learn about black and white people this year?] Not much. In third grade we read *Meet Addy*. It was about slaves and how they escaped but they had to leave their family behind.

Working in small groups or partner arrangements and celebrating students' unique capabilities and cultures also provide opportunities for fostering an appreciation for diversity. These opportunities can encourage students to see students who are "different" as resources for learning. During his discussion of diversity in his school, a second grader explained:

Some are from different countries, four are deaf. No one gets different treatment. The teacher talks about their country, and then they talk about what they did in their country and how they lived. We get to talk about different cultures here.

A fourth grader from the same school described that something that made her feel good about school was, "the many different cultures," because, "I can learn from those students, I can learn many facts about other countries." Having opportunities to help students who are "different" also fosters self-esteem, as shared by a fourth grader:

A Chinese girl needed help, she didn't understand words. I helped her, sometimes you don't know who your friends are when you can't speak English. She learned more English and made more friends. Another friend [also from China], she asked lots of questions in the lunch line when she first came here. I told her about colors, food, she could only say, "Hi" and "Bye." Another boy, he didn't know any English. He is learning good. Sometimes he didn't want to learn. He is stubborn. One time [he] refused to say anything in English . . . a fifth grader came to persuade him to talk in English. [Writing teacher] is very helpful, she gave me a box of cards with pictures to help my friends learn English. [She] talks about different ways to help kids learn English.

A Professional Development School promotes curriculum and instruction that evolves from continual review and that reflects the school's vision.

Each of the five original PDS sites has engaged in reforms intended to yield enriched and engaging learning experiences for students. These are the initiatives that can be tied most directly to their involvement as PDSs; they have provided the agenda for teachers' professional development experiences. These reform efforts can also be connected to the support schools and faculties have received from the Benedum Collaborative in the form of training, release time to collaborate with one another and with WVU faculty, and the intangible resource of teacher empowerment. It is significant to note that the majority of student discussions of these initiatives were unsolicited—students were typically not asked survey or interview questions designed to directly elicit data about specific reform efforts. Instead, descriptions of these initiatives emerged in students' general discussions of learning and school life. While these discussions were more frequent in smaller schools with a tighter reform agenda, they were also common in larger schools where all students had access to a central reform. The belief that their school is a special or unique place to learn because of these initiatives helps connect students to the same sense of mission or vision that educators often adopt to help frame their efforts to improved learning conditions for their students. A great deal of time was spent in the early days of the Benedum Collaborative PDS initiative trying to come to consensus about what it meant to be a PDS amd what the defining characteristics of a PDS were—how would you know a PDS if you saw one. Adult commitment to reform is enhanced by a clear and understandable mission or vision for change. Extending that mission or vision to students enhances their ability to participate in the reform, to recognize it and understand its intended outcomes. Student awareness of the impact of reforms is enhanced when they can simply identify the effort in their school experiences and make a connection between it and their opportunities to learn.

One of the elementary schools has created a "Students as Authors" program to help meet the literacy needs of their students. Numerous unsolicited references to writing and the "Students as Authors" program were made throughout student responses to questions about what makes them feel good about themselves and what kinds of choices they get to make in their school. A fifth grader described the writing process:

We have a teacher who comes in and helps us make books. We write them and then check them to see if everything is spelled right. She publishes them and then we get money for them. I have one, The Christmas Party, that I just published, that makes me feel good . . . it makes me feel good just writing a book. Some schools you don't get that opportunity. With the first, second and third grades she helps them write their books as a group. They tell her the story and she helps write it down.

A fourth grader explained what kinds of writing she likes to do, describing the development of the writing process:

> In third grade [writing teacher] did stories with kids. We made books. We would think about a story and put it on paper. . . . In fourth grade I finally finished my book. The name of the story was Itching Down. I rewrote it and turned it into a poem, I put it on tape, published it, illustrated it on white paper. . . . In third grade we did it as a whole group. Now, in fourth grade, we do single writing and publish it. Now I am finished!

A sixth grader, preparing to move on to junior high, shared her powerful understanding of herself as an author and her role of critical consumer of her educational experiences:

> I write books, that's what authors do. They write books and get paid . . . we write books and we illustrate them. Now in the sixth grade we're writing poems. I want to know what we will be able to do about writing at [the junior high school.]

The reform of the writing curriculum appears to provide the vision or mission for many students in this school. A third grader illustrates the power of this kind of "vision":

> This school is different. You learn a lot more here. It's more active—we do more activities. Like we write books for the world to have! Did you know that we do our own books? We can make our own books. Have you heard about it?

Students in other schools with a central reform also expressed an awareness of the impact of their reforms and illustrated the way they become embedded in their understandings of what their school experiences are about. Faculty in one of the elementary schools have invested in professional development in 4MAT learning styles training and have "4MATed" their curriculum, creating units that integrate across the disciplines. These units provide students with a variety of ways to engage in learning, and students not only displayed an awareness of the "units," they also displayed a belief that this approach helps them learn. When asked what he had learned that was his "favorite thing," a student replied:

> That's hard to answer because I liked everything we did. Well, we're doing a mystery unit now, we did the body, plants, dinosaurs, a whole bunch of units. Doing things in units helps me learn.

A second grader in the school exhibited a sophisticated understanding of curriculum integration in her description of what she likes to do best to learn in school:

> I like writing stories. I'm writing a story about jello now . . . writing goes with reading. I like when we combine subjects—like doing math problems in science. Computers help me learn math . . . I don't like to learn out of a book. . . . There is a writing and publishing center on the computer where we write newsletters about what we learn. All third grade did a newsletter. We can write our spelling words there. [One of the newsletters] was the Holocaust unit. My grandpa fought the Nazis, so that's neat. We read *Number the Stars* on our own. [My teacher] read other stories about this. We made portfolios on this.

Students also displayed an awareness of the opportunities to learn in ways that fit their individual needs and interests with the 4MAT approach:

> [What is the best way for you to learn?] Sometimes I like improvisation, you know, acting out. [Do you have those opportunities here?] Yeah, we work together in a group and then act out what we read in front of class. [How do you know that is the best way for you to learn?] Well, usually I can act out and it helps me remember. Its easier. I still remember things we did a couple of months ago.

Another student, when asked at the close of her interview if there was anything she wanted to add, shared the engagement of this curriculum approach in an unprompted testimonial:

> I love this school. I will be sad to leave it. It's so fun! We don't do normal work. We don't use textbooks that often. We do English in different ways. We did a "Watery World" activity where we danced to the Little Mermaid music. We made a big poem book. It was so fun! Everyone in third grade made one. I still have the book.

A third elementary school established a Science, Math and Technology (SMT) Lab early on in their development as a PDS to enrich and integrate student experiences in these areas. Students most frequently mentioned the SMT Lab in response to questions about what they liked to learn about and how they believed they learned best. When asked what they liked to learn about a typical response was:

> Nature, animals, what's going to happen in the future. [How do you learn these things?] . . . the science lab helps you study about those things.

During a focus group interview a group of fifth graders shared their perception of what made their school unique:

> Student 6: The technology is different. Student 8: We're like the computer school. Student 2: We got some computers by selling candy bars . . . we have the Internet. Student 4: Now we have clusters and all the clusters have computers, everything is computers. Student 6: It's the main thing about this school. Student 8: You could call this the school of the future.

One of the high schools made a major structural change by moving to a ninety-minute "block" schedule in order to facilitate efforts in order to offer students more cooperative learning and critical thinking learning experiences. The schools' students offered overwhelming support for the change, for the very reasons teachers implemented the restructured schedule. Students typically chose to discuss block scheduling when asked to talk about changes in their school in general. Those who discussed the change all "like it better this way." At the top of their list of reasons for this opinion were that the longer periods provided more time for active learning experiences and for one-on-one with their teachers. Students shared that the new schedule offers: "more time to discuss and talk with your teachers and figure out the problems," and "more time to work with people." A "special needs" student made a connection between the school's move to the block schedule and her opportunities to learn in the way she believed best addresses her needs and abilities:

> The best way for me to learn is in groups and I'm also auditory. I don't see. I'm diagnosed with attention deficit disorder and dyslexia so it's hard for me to just sit down and do things by myself. It's easier for me to work in groups and we do a lot of that since we have the ninety-minute classes. We have a lot more time than we did before.

Just as a central reform brings coherence to a school's reform and professional development agendas and gives teachers a common mission and shared experiences, a central reform helps students define their school experiences. When that central reform is related to increased learning opportunities it has a powerful impact on school culture for students. Being a student in a school that is identified as "better" because of increased opportunities to learn reinforces the value of learning and moves that school closer to becoming a place where "all are learners."

Conclusions

Designing and implementing assessment that is reflective of the reform it is intended to document and describe is a challenging and risky undertaking. Attempting to change the "bottom-line" for some stakeholders in order to better serve the informational needs of others is a constant balancing act that requires continual negotiation and consideration. As assessment of professional development schools initiatives and other school reform efforts continues to struggle to build support for such work while informing the work itself, the possibility of creating new forms of assessment becomes that much more real. The assessment described here is ongoing and will build on the lessons learned not only about the impact of the reform on the learning experiences of PDS students, but also those lessons learned about doing reflective assessment.

References

Corbett, H. D. and Wilson, B. (1991). *Testing, reform and rebellion.* Norwood, N.J.: Ablex Publishing.

Geertz, C. (1973). *The interpretation of cultures.* New York: Basic Books.

Glaser, B. S. and Strauss, A. L. (1967). *The discovery of grounded theory: Strategies for qualitative research.* New York: Aldine Publishing.

Herman, L. and Winters, K. (1992). *Tracking your school's success: A sensible guide to evaluation.* Beverly Hills: Sage.

Lieberman, A., ed. (1995). *The work of restructuring schools: Building from the ground up.* New York: Teachers College Press.

Murphy, J. and Hallinger, P., eds. (1993). *Restructuring schooling: Learning from ongoing efforts.* Newbury Park, Cal.: Corwin Press.

Sarason, S. (1990). *The predictable failure of educational reform: Can we change course before it's too late?* San Francisco: Jossey-Bass.

Webb, J., Wilson, B., and Corbett, H. D. (1993). Restructuring systemically for students. Is it just talk? In J. Murphy and P. Hallinger, eds., *Restructuring schooling: Learning from ongoing efforts.* Newbury Park, Cal.: Corwin Press.

Wiggins, G. P. (1993). *Assessing student performance: Exploring the purpose and limits of testing*. San Francisco: Jossey-Bass.

Wilson, B., Webb, J., and Corbett, H. D. (1994). Locally initiated reform. In W. Pink and G. Noblit, eds., *The ways we were: The pasts of the sociology of education*. Cresskill, N.J.: Hampton Press.

13

IMPACT ON COLLEGES OF EDUCATION

RICHARD D. HAWTHORNE

A central purpose of the Benedum Collaborative has been to stimulate and sustain fundamental reforms in the education of teachers and other education professionals. Thus far, the primary focus of this book has been the professional development activities of experienced PDS teachers, how they have engaged in the reform of their schools, and the collaborative relationship they have evolved with university faculty as they have pursued both of these activities. It is the belief of the Benedum Collaborative, among many other school-university collaboratives nationwide, that these combined efforts form the most desirable contexts for the preparation of a generation of exceptional teachers and the renewal of experienced educators who in turn construct the best pedagogical experiences for children. This cycle of renewal and reform is the essence of a vital and reflective education profession. While recognizing that these renewal and reform activities are simultaneously at play in each of the sites and that they involve many of the same people, this chapter is restricted in focus to a consideration of the impact of these reform activities on the culture, programs, and practices of faculty (primarily teacher educators but also involving the other professional preparation programs associated with schooling) housed within a college of education (COE) and the several related units within the college and across the university.

The Holmes Group (1995) and others have set out in clear and compelling terms the need for a fundamental reform of teacher education programs, the cultures in which they function, and the emerging changes in the role of the faculty. The next section of this chapter identifies and elaborates several clusters of those expected reforms.

Following the discussion of expectations and indicators of professional education, attention turns to how the desired reforms in the life and work of the COE might be assessed. The organizing questions of this section are: How might we describe the beliefs, programs, policies, and practices that are present in the culture of the college, how do they reflect the desired features and qualities of best professional education practice and inquiry, and how are they internalized and enacted by professional education students? How will we know if substantive and consequential reform has indeed occurred?

This discussion is followed by a description of key principles, processes, and events that define the first six years of the reform efforts and some of the indicators of sustaining change that are emerging in the professional education programs, culture, and roles of the College of Human Resources and Education faculty and their arts and science and professional development school partners at West Virginia University.

The final section sets out some tentative understandings, cautions, and recommendations about reform in a COE and university working collaboratively with colleagues in associated schools.

Expected Impact on Colleges of Education

The expectations for change in colleges of education discussed in this chapter are largely those set forth by the Holmes Group in its most recent publication, *Tomorrow's Schools of Education* (1995); Clifford and Guthrie's *Ed School* (1988); Howey and Zimpher's *Profiles of Preservice Teacher Education* (1989); Goodlad, Soder, and Sirotnik's book, *Places Where Teachers Are Taught* (1990); and the experiences we have had in the Benedum Collaborative.

Of the many expectations set out in these works, six interrelated clusters seem to organize the majority of them. As will become evident, the expected changes are much more than matters of technique or organizational structure. Indeed, the changes expected in the faculty and cultures of teacher education programs are very much the same as those reform expectations laid out for schools. That is, the expectations represent the substantive rethinking and redirecting of core beliefs, constructs, and roles that have dominated the way things have been done in COEs for decades. They call for the reallocation of power across a new mix of participants as decisions are made and resources are distributed through a collaborative arrangement. They seek no less than a new set of norms to guide and discipline our judgments and actions.

First Expectation: A New Centering of Colleges of Education

The core expectation for change in a college of education is framed in moral terms; namely that the work of faculty in COEs must be centered by a commitment to being an active partner in dramatically improving the quality of life and educational experiences of all children and youth. This represents a commitment both to democratic values and to principles of pedagogy. Such a democratic commitment strives to include parents, community members, teachers, and administrators in the deliberation and decision-making activities about the conduct of schooling. It means acknowledging and incorporating the strengths of cultural and human diversity as policies, programs, and practices are formed and enacted. It seeks to enable all to be well-informed, critical, and imaginative participants in the conduct of their individual and collective lives. It assures no political, economic, or cultural entity will have dominance over inquiry or the search for meaning.

Regarding the pedagogical centering, Van Manen (1992) writes that "To have a sense of pedagogy implies that one is capable of perceptive insights into the child's being or character. It also implies that one has a grasp of what is good for children and for their healthy development" (4). Maxine Greene (1986) advocates pedagogical centering through these words:

> I would like to think of teachers moving the young into their own inter-
> pretations of their lives and their lived worlds, opening wider and wider
> perspectives as they do so. . . . I would like to see teachers tapping the
> spectrum of intelligences, encouraging multiple readings of written texts
> and readings of the world. . . . Such a project demands the capacity to
> unveil and disclose. It demands the exercise of imagination, enlivened by
> works of art, by situations of speaking and making. (441)

A corollary commitment is to the continuous examination of the college's own policies and practices; critical reflection on what those policies and practices mean in relation to the commitment to be involved in the improvement of life and educational opportunities for children; and, in Eisner's (1994) terms, engagement in educationally imaginative action.

In its third book, *Tomorrow's Schools of Education* (1995), the Holmes Group issues a blunt challenge:

> We begin this brief with a radical premise: institutions preparing educators
> should either adopt reforms along the lines proposed in these pages or
> surrender their franchise. . . . We assume this drastic stance precisely
> because we believe that the country needs university-based education
> schools and that they can make a difference in the teaching and learning of
> children. . . . Schools of education that exercise introspection and refocus
> their mission accordingly can, indeed, must help solve the problems that
> afflict the public schools. . . . Within these education schools and the
> universities that house them resides a vast, mostly untapped potential that
> can be unleashed in the service of better public education if only the
> faculty members and administrators implement changes of the sort we
> envision. . . . developing sensible strategies, making sound contributions,
> and setting standards of accountability. (3).

Soder and Sirotnik (1990) frame the commitment this way:

[T]he reconstruction of schools of education is at least twofold: First, they must rediscover their mission as professional schools, built around the moral and ethical responsibilities of teaching and preparing to teach and all the scholarly and service activities that would be expected to support, nurture, and sustain this central purpose. (400)

This set of commitments to equity, pedagogy, and reflective practice grounds all of the work of the faculty associated with educator preparation programs and research in a COE. For many colleges of education, these commitments reflect a major shift from an arts and science knowledge production and transmission, from a use of schools in the region as places for practice teaching and other educator roles, and from research and classroom content disconnected from the policies and practices of educators in the region and beyond.

The proposed centering is not that of impassive scholars examining and reporting on the techniques, contexts, politics, or effects of particular pedagogical practices. It is characterized by passionate and well-reasoned inquiry into, preparation of, and advocacy for excellence in professional preparation programs, pedagogical practices, and quality of life in the school context. It is expected that the tools of inquiry, ethical interrogation, deliberation, and imaginative problem solving be applied actively to the day-to-day problematics of pedagogy in partner schools.

The second commitment is to continuous analysis, reflection, and action as a way of professional life. The critical eye is directed toward theory and practice as they intertwine and are enacted in the contexts of the schools and universities. Beneath the surface of this commitment is an acknowledgment of the uncertain, messy, and problematic nature of educational activity. It places at the center of professional education practice well-reasoned, ethical, and contextually informed judgments and decision making. It replaces technical rationality as the primary justification of professional work with democratic, scholarly, and pedagogical values as the grounding for educational judgments and actions (Henderson and Hawthorne 1995). Accordingly, the recursive cycle of analysis, reflection, and action asks not only what is happening in university and school classrooms and what the effects of those educational activities are, they ask what the effects—both intended and unintended—mean and if they are good and right for children in a pluralistic and participatory democracy.

In a pluralistic, participatory democracy, equity is a key value. In the context of a COE, equity is associated with the preparation of educators who understand and have the capacity to promote the education of ALL children. It means the deliberate formation of a student body and faculty that represents human and cultural diversity because it is believed that a diverse student body and faculty provide a good and right context in which to prepare educators.

Equity is one of the values Gidionese (1995) identifies as the glue that holds the profession of teaching together.

Centering the programs and practices of college of education faculty on pedagogical values and critical reflection provides a powerful model for those in the process of becoming professional educators. It makes clear that the COE faculty are full partners in the complex and imaginative problem solving that must permeate the conduct of schools. And it brings into proper relationship the joint sources of thoughtful professional education activity; pedagogical values (van Manen 1992) and examined actions and their meanings.

Second Expectation: Connection to the Real Worlds of Students and
Professional Practice

It is expected that COE faculty will contribute demonstrably to the quality of the lives and work of students and professionals in schools through (1) furthering understandings of the complex social and cultural forces that influence those same students, parents, and educators; and (2) creating even more meaningful and engaging forms of teaching and learning about matters of consequence. In *Tomorrow's Schools of Education* (Holmes Group 1995), the authors cast the need for such connections this way; "How can schools of education stand by in good conscience and watch the public schools confine themselves to practices and policies that any school professional ought to recognize as hopelessly dated?" (6).

Perhaps the single most promising vehicle for forging deep and sustaining connections between the roles of teacher education faculty and the lives of teachers and students is the professional development school (PDS). As has been described through several case studies in the previous chapters, professional development schools have enormous capacity for developing pedagogical judgments, imaginative planning, and a repertoire of pedagogical understandings and actions on the part of novice and experienced educators. These professional capacities develop through experiences with and reflections on the lives of "real" children, the complex cultures of schools, the aspirations and challenges of parents, the politics of schooling, and the constraints of time, resources, and personal energy. It is in these schools that experienced educators model the pedagogical mind at work in the hallways and classrooms. It is in these contexts that teacher education students and experienced educators have the opportunities to talk in depth about the otherwise hidden reasoning and judgments of teaching and schooling. Through modelling, trying on various approaches to teaching, coaching, and mentoring and talking and reflecting, teacher education students are provided opportunities to construct complexly layered perspectives and understandings of teaching and schooling.

A bit more needs to be said about the value of story as a text for both novice and experienced educators. As teachers share their personal-professional stories, delve into the pedagogical assumptions and principles that form their conceptual frameworks of teaching (Connelly and Clandinin 1988; Elbaz 1983; Holly 1989), and jointly engage the natural problematics of teaching and schooling, they develop a community of reflective and imaginative practice (see McDonald 1994 for an extensive treatment). A basic belief of the Holmes Group is that when COE and other university faculty become part of the professional practice reflection process they will become trusted and valued partners in the democratic problem solving and professional development way of life which defines a PDS.

The potential power of PDSs to provide connections between practice and the important principles, concepts, and research on teaching and learning can not be overly stated. In addition to the advances in understandings of teaching and learning and teachers' learning and development is the growing understanding of the influence of the culture of the school on the ways teachers believe, think, and act (Kennedy 1991; Pajares 1992). While many principles and concepts about the culture of the school can be articulated in college classrooms, the contextual meanings of teaching, learning, and schooling are found in the day-to-day negotiations of students, teachers, and others through the ethos of the school. Accordingly, clear and deep connections of research and theory on teaching, learning, and schooling with the context and conduct of pedagogical practice serve as strong indicators of reform in teacher education curriculum. Making these connections authentic requires extensive collaboration between COE, Arts and Science, and PDS faculties; a matter to which I now turn.

Third Expectation: Collaboration Within and Across Contexts

Across the sources examined, the expectation for collaboration with colleagues across the university campus and with colleagues in schools and human resource agencies is a commonplace. Such collaboration may take the form of teacher (or principal, counselor, supervisor, and other professional roles) education curriculum development, enactment, and assessment. As will be described later, this has been a jointly conducted activity in the Benedum Collaborative. Collaboration may also be expressed through the design and conduct of action research or program assessment by people from different departments, schools, and other sites and roles. This kind of joint activity is congruent with the commitment to inquiry on practice and is a wonderful opportunity for university people to learn to frame questions of inquiry on practice in relation to specific school contexts and connect those with the larger research agendas of other educators in other settings. Or it may involve bringing together limited resources to address matters of common interest to school and university partners. A fundamental assumption is that the framing of problems to be examined, the creation of exciting and contextually appropriate learning activities or assessment strategies, or the mixing of funds and other resources to ensure ongoing professional development is more imaginatively and powerfully done through the synthesis of multiple perspectives than is realized when the problem solving is limited to one source.

In Chapter 2, Shive reviews the multiple uses of the term collaborative, sets out an array of alternative meanings, and suggests strongly that we be quite clear about just what we mean when we commit to a collaborative relationship. Hargreaves (1994) underscores the need to be clear about what we mean by the term collaboration as he distinguishes between contrived collegiality and collaborative cultures:

> [C]ollaborative cultures can extend into joint work, mutual observation, and focused reflective inquiry in ways that extend practice critically, searching for better alternatives in the continuous quest for improvement. In these cases, collaborative cultures are not cozy, complacent and politically quiescent. (195).

Hargreaves defines collaborative cultures in terms of working relationships characterized as spontaneous (they emerge from the group, are not administratively imposed), voluntary, development-oriented (initiate their own changes rather than primarily responsive to others' agendas for change), pervasive across time and space, and unpredictable (in an uncertain, perplexing context, political control does not provide the appearance of predictablity) (192–193). These indicators were developed with schools as the primary referent; however, they seem most appropriate to the university and the university-school collaborative efforts as well.

It is worth underscoring that the transition to a collaborative culture within and between institutions requires the evolution of a new ethos—a new set of values and ways of doing things which re-center and justify the relationships and rewards of the institution. This takes on special meaning in the university setting when it becomes apparent that many (often the majority) of the prime movers in the change to a collaborative culture are junior faculty without tenure. It is not sufficient for the Dean to declare collaboration to be of value in the work of a professor, it must be a shared belief held by a critical mass of colleagues who in turn mentor junior faculty accordingly. The rewards of an individualistically oriented model of productivity for a professor can not be transferred to the work of a professor in a collaborative culture. Indeed, one significant indicator of serious change in the culture of a COE will be clear expectations about how quality collaborative work in schools and with colleagues across the campus will be defined and rewarded at tenure and promotion time (see Henderson and Hawthorne 1995b for a more fully developed discussion of this matter).

Collaboration is a necessary condition and element of change in the life of a COE that is invested in the types of reform this book describes. If collaboration is to be of consequence, it must represent open and meaningful deliberations about matters central to the way curriculum work is done; how university, college, and school resources are allocated jointly to support practices of benefit to all; and how personnel are recognized and rewarded for this time-consuming and difficult work.

Fourth Expectation: Practice Related Research

The authors of the Holmes Group's *Tomorrow's Schools of Education* (1995) chide COEs and universities for a lack of research on matters of peda-gogical consequence: "Universities are accustomed to conducting research and development activities in behalf of other fields, but they give short shrift to the study of teaching and learning as it is carried out in the public schools" (7). There is an expectation, indeed a plea, that the measure of worthwhile educa-tional inquiry be that of fostering greater understanding of the complexities of educational practice, of describing and supporting even more imaginative and effective practices, and of providing powerful and useful means for engaging in the critical appraisal of various practices and policies. In such cases, the research conducted by many (not all) COE faculty, school practitioners, and graduate students would be defined by school and university faculty based on persistent and systemic problems and issues of policy, programs, and practice.

In PDSs, that might look like a series of action research projects that address the development or adaptation of a curriculum and the extent to which the faculty are in fact enacting it and the effects it appears to have on student engagement and learning. The direct and sustained involvement of university faculty as partners, not directors, in the research is expected. Reference to the research in university courses, public reporting at conferences or through publications, and dissemination through professional development activities are all expectations of action researchers.

At the university, we might expect to see three or four clusters of inquiry focused on a rich body of practice or policy problems that draw faculty from different departments and PDSs together. As collaborative inquiry groups, they might critically analyze related theories and research, conduct several series of connected studies (rather than relatively isolated pieces of inquiry done by individual faculty or doctoral students), spawn multiple perspectives, generate more effective tools of data collection and analysis, and support and stretch each other as the problems are examined in depth through multiple lenses. For example, one group of faculty might come together around the problems of motivation, attention span, and diverse modes of learning present in virtually any classroom. Further, they may wish to examine a host of the motivation, attention, learning modes, and learning problematics and questions in relation to various forms of instructional design and instructional technologies. How children with different learning styles react to and learn through the use of different instructional technologies has in fact been a focus of several of our doctoral students under the mentorship of faculty (Reed et al. 1995).

Another line of inquiry might be the analysis of how people in education leadership roles in a region conceptualize how teachers in different school levels, content areas, and settings make decisions in the day-to-dayness of the classroom and how the culture and climate of the schools influence teachers' judgments and decision-making processes. What do they think supports and inhibits best practice by teachers? How do they understand their role in providing support and reducing inhibitors?

It is through studies of these and a host of other similar persistent problems and issues that research by COE faculty leads to new policies, more appropriate programs, and more imaginative and meaningful practices.

The four clusters of reform in professional educator preparation efforts could be set forth as six or eight and include many more specific changes deemed essential to fundamental reform. The position taken here is that these four and other desired changes reflect a basic examination and reformulation of the beliefs and policies at the core of the culture and practices toward the improvement of the quality of life and learning for children through improving the quality of professional life and learning of professionals in the schools. The clusters are clear in their call for the development of new relationships with colleagues in PDSs and across the university. New lines of inquiry, which are connected in direct ways to the quality of life and learning in schools, must be established with the input of practitioners who are the consumers of such knowledge. And best pedagogical practice connects the concepts and perspectives engaged in the university classroom with the best practices and contexts of schools.

And if such reform were undertaken, how might the changes be identified and described and how might the impact of the changes on the culture, faculty, and professional education students be assessed?

Describing and Analyzing the Reforms and Their Impact

The first section of this chapter identified changes in the policies, programs, organizational culture, and professional practices that could be expected in a COE that had acted on the reform agenda. The organizing question posed in this section is; how might the manifestations and impacts of such expected changes be identified, described, analyzed, and interpreted? In short, how might we determine if reforms have occurred, what they "look like," how they interact with each other, and to what extent they are sound, sustainable, and effective changes. Do the professionals prepared through reformed programs and contexts think and act more complexly, imaginatively, and consequentially and are the insights gained through inquiry having an impact on policy and practice?

Before the evaluation design is presented, it is helpful to keep several matters in mind. First, it is assumed that complex reform is a matter of changing belief systems and ways of thinking about and acting on, in this case, the preparation and continuous development of education professionals, and not a matter of changing an element or two or changing simple relationships between two or more elements. Therefore, the evaluation of complex reforms in COEs must also be complex and delve beneath the taken for granted. Most of the changes in belief systems, curriculum design, and relationships between PDS and university faculty are intertwined and multi-layered. Expressions of shared power, open communication, reflective practice, trust, joint problem solving, equity, and pedagogical centering are not made evident through the "eye" of simple measures. To "see" manifestations of COE reform and to interpret the meanings embedded within requires that we try to view and understand them from several vantage points.

Some forms of assessment may be directed toward describing the ways teacher education faculty, arts and science faculty, PDS faculty, and teacher education students think about such central matters as learning, teaching, knowing, and who should have access to what ideas or skills (Howey and Zimpher 1989). Such inquiry is premised on the assumption that centering teacher education programs on pedagogical, equity, and reflective practice values and concepts should reflect the development of cognitive frameworks that foster professional judgments and actions that are congruent with such beliefs and understandings. Other forms of assessment may critically analyze the power relations of different roles; for example, to what extent are PDS teachers, arts and science teachers, and other key players genuinely involved in the deliberations and decisions that form, evaluate, and revise teacher education programs and related policies?

Accordingly, the second consideration is that multiple forms of data gathering which enable descriptive and critical analyses of the markers of change are essential if a holistic understanding of the work and life of a COE is to be obtained. To describe and analyze the nature and impact of reform in a COE is complex, incomplete, and always messy work. If it were otherwise, we would have hundreds of evaluation studies and a substantial body of knowledge about the reform of COEs at our disposal.

Third, while the new centering and related policy, program, and practice changes will be expressed in many dimensions in the life of a COE, it may be helpful to conceptualize them as critical aspects of three overlapping clusters: (1) the culture of the COE (i.e., the way we do things, (Deal 1989); (2) the design, development, enactment, and evaluation of the curriculum (Henderson and Hawthorne 1995); and, (3) the conduct of inquiry by faculty and students. The clustering of many activities and conditions into three overlapping entities represents a commitment to the principle of parsimony on the one hand and the use of a systems approach to conceptualizing reform on the other. More bluntly, the principle of parsimony suggests that if we attempt to obtain data on all or even many possible aspects of the reform of a COE, we are more likely to have a very thick report than a deep understanding of the essence of the reform.

The systems perspective recognizes that a change in key aspects of the culture, say the way power is shared or how quality work is recognized, necessarily has an impact on other aspects within the culture cluster and on the curriculum and inquiry areas. Accordingly, a change in what is deemed to be the priorities of the COE accompanied by the reallocation of resources to areas most supportive of those priorities will have an impact on activities in the curriculum cluster and in the focus of the inquiry cluster.

At the nexus of the three intersecting clusters of reform in a COE is the development of the pedagogical mind. That is, the ultimate expression of centering on pedagogical virtues, democratic values, and reflective practice is the development of the pedagogical minds in novice and experienced teachers. By pedagogical mind is meant the system of personal-professional beliefs, conceptions, skills, and judgments an educator holds and acts upon. Professional educator preparation and development programs are about learning how to value, think, and act pedagogically, democratically, and reflectively. Simultaneously, inquiry on pre-K–12 educational policy and practice is about understanding more fully or creating more imaginatively and ethically meaningful and effective pedagogical events and experiences.

The fourth consideration is that the evaluation design must be contextually appropriate. The particular perspective and conduct of the assessment of the impact and quality of reform must be established by those engaged in the reform if the information is to be used with respect and passion. Because programs and practices are defined by transactions between what is envisioned and the political, social, and economic context in which they are enacted, the evaluation design must acknowledge those contextual forces. This does not mean that such forces are immutable or that they have disproportionate power in the design of the evaluation activities. Indeed, some of the evaluation focus needs to be on the impact the COE has on its larger context and vice versa.

With these considerations in mind, along with the reminders that complex reform takes more time than anyone is willing to accept and accordingly requires more substantial resource allocation or re-allocation than anyone wants to underwrite, the design for describing and evaluating the reform of a COE can be entertained. The central issues in the construction of the evaluation design are classic:

1. Who needs to know what and why?
2. How might the information best be obtained and shared and by whom?
3. How and by whom is the information to be analyzed and interpreted and used?

It has been suggested that three overlapping and transacting clusters of activities, roles, and relationships serve as major conceptual organizers of the evaluation design: the culture of the COE, the curriculum (design, development, enactment, and impact of the learners), and the research/scholarly activities of the faculty and students, A set of illustrative questions is presented in relation to each of the clusters along with ways of collecting and analyzing data appropriate to each question.

The culture of the COE. Getting inside the culture of a COE means being able to identify and understand the ethos of the place. Deal's (1989) powerfully simple definition of culture as "the way we do things here" is a place to begin. Some would hasten to add "and why" to his definition. Feiman-Nemser and Floden (1986), in their chapter "The Cultures of Teaching" in *The Handbook of Research on Teaching*, provide a discussion of perspectives and means for understanding the culture of teaching in schools that seems very useful to seeking understandings of the culture of teaching and scholarship of those who work in COEs:

> Teaching cultures are embodied in the work-related beliefs and knowledge teachers share—beliefs about appropriate ways of acting on the job and rewarding aspects of teaching, and knowledge that enables teachers to do their work. (508)

Changing a COE from a knowledge production and educator training centered undertaking to one centered on pedagogy, equity, and reflective practice suggests differences in work-related beliefs, relationships, rewards, communication patterns, and ways of doing things in the hallways and classrooms of COEs and PDSs. Ferreting out of the day-to-day life of a COE the beliefs, relationships, norms, communication patterns, modes of teaching and student engagement, problem framing and solving strategies, and the various power arrangements requires attending to life in the hallways, classrooms, and offices as portrayed by students, faculty, and others.

The questions proposed to guide these analyses are derived in part from the work of Howey and Zimpher (1989) and in part from Henderson and Hawthorne (1995).

1. What is the demographic profile of the student body and faculty? What cognitive, motivational, and life history do they bring to the culture of the COE? (Howey and Zimpher 1989)
2. What is the professional climate of the COE? How are students regarded by one another and by the faculty? How do faculty across specialties interact with each other? How do PDS and COE faculty interact? How are policies

and curriculum design features known? How comfortable are students and faculty with one another? How enthusiastic are students and faculty about their programs?

3. What qualities and features characterize what it means to be a student in the program? a professor?
4. Who makes decisions (or influences decisions) about the programs, the quality of life and learning in the COE, key policies, about what is important in the professorship, about what/who gets resources and rewards?
5. What do data about all of the above mean in relation to pedagogical centering, equity, reflective practice?

The curriculum. To assess and understand the curriculum (in this case, the teacher education programs) requires examination of the design of the curriculum, how the curriculum is developed and enacted, and what the impact of the accumulative curriculum experiences are on teacher education students' cognitive structures and strategies, values, and skill mix.

The curriculum design sets out the goals, key assumptions, dominant features, and general flow of experiences over time that, when woven together in a conceptual framework, provide faculty and students a common language, criteria for the selection and organization of content, key organizing centers, and scenarios of possible experiences to guide development, enactment, and assessment (see Henderson and Hawthorne 1995 for a full discussion of these dimensions). When the design is clear, coherent, comprehensive, and compact it provides a powerful image and grounding for the ways faculty and students think about and organize their planning and decision making during their curriculum development and enactment activities. More specifically, the cognitive constructs and beliefs the faculty have about students, content, teaching, and how people learn to think and act pedagogically are fundamental to the curriculum design they construct.

Curriculum development and enactment have a reciprocal relationship as planning decisions and classroom actions are constantly being informed by the design on the one hand and the contextual realities of the lived interactions of students, faculty, and settings on the other. Design and development activities, which are often matters of the individual mind and thus difficult to render observable, are also made public through the verbal deliberations among faculty as they consider options, make claims, justify proposals, and ultimately make curriculum decisions (Walker 1970; Hawthorne 1993). Curriculum enactment can be described and examined through multiple lenses through observation and analysis of classroom and hallway transactions between faculty and students and ideas.

The impact of the curriculum experiences, intended and unintended, on the constructs and perspectives of teacher education students and subsequently on the quality of life and learning in their classrooms when they become certified and experienced educators, is for many the ultimate focus of the evaluation design. Based on the works of Kennedy (1991) and Schulman (1986), it is clear that the problematic nature of teaching and the complex understandings, judgments, and imaginative actions that define it as professional practice require equally complex and imaginative assessments. The work of the Board of Professional Teaching Standards provides a rich basis for identifying the most salient dimensions and collecting samples of information about the cognitions, problem framing and solving strategies, the depth of understanding of content, children, pedagogy, and schooling, and the array of skills associated with teaching. Accordingly, the assessment of how teacher education students think, make decisions and judgments, and act out their repertoire of skills will include multiple indicators of performance.

The following organizing questions are offered as points of departure in the complex task of describing, understanding, and critically considering the meanings and consequences of the teacher education curriculum:

1. How do the students and faculty conceptualize the design of the teacher education curriculum? What do students and faculty understand the expectations and outcomes of the curriculum to be? What do they mean by teaching, learning, learning how to teach, etc.?
2. How is the design connected to best practice, to research, and to pedagogical, democratic, and reflective values?
3. In what ways are the students and faculty nurtured and intellectually challenged? (Howey and Zimpher 1989).
4. Is the design reflected in the syllabi, the materials selected and used, the organizers, the content, and the activities intended and experienced?
5. In what ways are faculty from the various university and school partner sites actively involved in curriculum development and enactment activities? Are the clinical activities clearly related to the course work?
6. What forms of student cognitive engagement, clinical experiences, involvements with children of diverse cultural backgrounds and of handicapping conditions, and use of a range of instructional technologies are evident?
7. In what ways are faculty modelling best pedagogical practice?
8. To what extent do the teacher education students evidence:
    a. a deep understanding of content areas, pedagogical content, human development and learning, curriculum and teaching, schooling, assessment of teaching and learning, and the meaning of education in a democratic society;
    b. an ability to "read" students and the dynamics of the classroom;
    c. an ability to develop learning activities that are appropriate for specific learners, invite sustained student attention and engagement, and are congruent with the curriculum design; and

d. an ability to construct assessment activities and measures that provide feedback to the students and inform the teacher and others about the quality of student understanding and the need for additional or different activities.

The work of Howey and Zimpher (1989) and Goodlad, Soder, and Sirotnik (1990) illustrate in some depth the value of focus group interviews, artifact analysis, and individual interviews across diverse populations in the university and school contexts in obtaining a rich data base on the success of teacher education students. Add to that examples of several diverse university student portfolios, which they have developed over their experience with the curriculum and COE and PDS cultures, performance indicators similar to those used in the National Master Teacher Board assessments (responses to problem-solving situations that elicit depth and breadth of conceptual understandings of students, learning, teaching, social contexts, assessment, diversity). Additional assessments of the abilities of novice educators to frame and solve typical but complex classroom problems can be conducted through the combined efforts and judgments of practitioner and researcher panels where each candidate for certification presents their best understanding of the situation, sets forth a proposed series of actions and evaluations, and offers a coherent and informed rationale for their position. Other facets include performance tests of classroom management understandings and skills, the use of curriculum-grounded instructional technologies, the development of student assessment activities and measures, communication and team building skills, and ability to explain programs and student assessments to parents and other educators.

Comprehensive and systemic assessment designs which gather and interpret the full complex of professional knowledge and skills must be developed and implemented if responsible and responsive curriculum evaluation is to be obtained. Funds and special professional development of teacher education faculty are basic to conceptualizing and conducting such in-depth and complex assessments. The assessment effort can not be left to external accreditation reviews or to the assumption that the graduates will learn the rest on the job.

Patterns of inquiry. What are the foci and impact of the research and scholarly efforts of students and faculty in a COE? In what ways do these efforts contribute to understanding and improving the quality of life and learning in schools and COE's? To what extent does the scholarship contribute to the deliberations of policy makers at district and state levels? If no more research was done by the COE, how would it change the conduct of teaching and schooling in the area and beyond?

Describing the focal points and patterns of faculty and graduate student inquiry is a matter of doing a content analysis of dissertation abstracts, articles, grants, and refereed presentations. What are the primary areas of inquiry? Are there patterns of inquiry? In what ways are the patterns connected to the problems and issues of policy and practice in the schools and COE? In what ways are the patterns of inquiry informed by research reported by others across the nation?

Assessing the quality and impact of the inquiry is a much more complex task. The guiding questions will range from the more technical (Do the forms of inquiry reflect current research methodologies and standards?) to the value of the problems and issues engaged (Are they central to the conduct of teaching and schooling?), to the critical queries about the ideological soundness, biases, and interests represented in framing and conducting the inquiry.

The assessment activities could include the establishment of a panel of external reviewers including researchers from other institutions and practitioners in the service area. Following appropriate preparation, their task would be to examine the primary research efforts conducted over a five or more year period and to deliberate the value of the questions and problems addressed, the means employed, and the apparent utility and meaning of the findings, and to make recommendations for policy and practice.

Focus groups of teachers and other educators in the service area could be interviewed to indirectly and directly ascertain the extent to which they as potential users of the research were part of framing the problem or contributing to the data collection and analysis, are aware of and have read/heard about the research, use the research on a regular basis, seek out the faculty/college to work with them to do research related to significant problems of policy and practice, and perceive the college to be a useful source of information and problem-solving processes.

While not all the research and scholarly activity of a COE needs to focus on teaching, learning, and schooling in the service area of the college, a significant (i.e., makes a difference) amount must be. The new measure of appropriate and consequential research and scholarship by COE faculty and students must become its impact on practice and policy work in the area served and thus becomes a contribution to a larger profession-wide accumulation of inquiry. While the conventions of publishing and presenting in contexts that involve professional criticism by others should be continued as standards of quality scholarship, in professions such as those represented in COEs, the impact on practice and policy can no longer be left to hope.

Instances of Impact on One College of Education

It is difficult to describe and thus understand in any comprehensive sense a culture that is in transition. The transformation of the College of Human Resources and Education at West Virginia University is, from this writer's perspective, real and progressing incrementally on a day-to-day basis. I will describe selected aspects of the HR&E experience which illustrate the transformation of core beliefs and actions: a major curriculum change in teacher education, a new collaborative governance approach, and the evolution of the liaison role connecting PDSs and the college.

The Redesigned Teacher Education Curriculum

The reconceptualization of the elementary and secondary teacher education programs represents the long term efforts of more than one hundred arts and science, PDS, and HR&E faculty. Grounded by a thorough review of teacher education-related research and practice, extensive deliberations by the participants, and a national context of teacher education reform led by the Holmes Group, the curriculum design for the new program took form. Organized into interdisciplinary teams, the faculty designed new core courses and program strands for the pedagogical content, established criteria for and initiated prototypes of the related clinical and field-based experiences, identified appropriate liberal studies clusters, and reconfigured the teaching discipline clusters.

The direction and substance of the curriculum design work was based on a set of beliefs and research about the characteristics of good and effective novice teachers. The characteristics include professional, moral, and ethical grounding of practice; a strong liberal (liberating) education; a reflective posture using a variety of analytic and critical perspectives, in-depth understanding of best pedagogical practice and subject matter content; and in-depth understanding and respect for human and cultural diversity and the facilitation of learning for *all* students. With these characteristics in mind, the goals were formed and the new curriculum design was developed. The curriculum design for the new elementary and secondary teacher education program is now characterized by:

- a close collaboration with the PDS sites
- a five-year program leading to a bachelor's degree in a teaching discipline and a master's degree in education
- academically exceptional students who proceed through the carefully sequenced programs in cohort groupings with continuous mentoring from WVU and PDS faculty
- a generous segment of coursework committed to liberal studies
- well-planned field experiences throughout the program based in PDS sites
- an integration of liberal studies, subject matter, and professional education courses
- a full semester Professional Internship
- a final semester of advanced course work featuring action research.

The first cohort of students began their journey through the new program in the Fall Semester of 1995. As has been described in previous chapters, the development of the PDS sites as professional communities which model and foster best pedagogical practice has been ongoing. Many of the PDSs have served as field sites for the current teacher education program and have created extensive and challenging clinical experiences for teacher education students that will serve the new program well. An evaluation design is also being developed to gather baseline data to provide feedback to the faculty as they enact and continuously revise the new curriculum and to enable groups to assess the quality and impact of the new program.

Translating the design into fully developed courses and classroom experiences is challenge enough for any faculty. Functioning in the three curriculum worlds of (1) the high enrollment current teacher education program, which is being phased out over a four-year period, (2) the continuous curriculum development, recruitment, admission, mentoring, and teaching associated with the new program, and (3) maintaining large master's and doctoral programs has stretched the College's teacher education faculty to the limit.

In addition to the normal challenges accompanying change there is the realization that the Collaborative's commitment to the program calls for a substantive reconsideration of the professorial and classroom teacher roles and how they are defined and rewarded. All members of the Collaborative are confronting the reality that the Benedum Foundation will not continue to support the evolution of this reform effort for many more years. It is becoming evident to all that internalization of the new curriculum and the associated policies and new practices will require the reallocation of internal resources—both human and fiscal. The College and University are entering a period of very tight fiscal conditions. As the implications of this condition are acknowledged by administrators and faculty, the impact of the commitment to the new program on the entire College is being even more fully realized. These concerns, along with lingering reservations held by some faculty about the radical changes embodied in the new program, are to be expected in such a reform effort. It is one aspect of the impact such a major change in a basic program and the related policies and practices has on the faculty and culture of a COE.

In spite of these and other concerns, there is a core group of the HR&E faculty who have a high commitment to the program and the newly developed relations with PDS and Arts and Science colleagues. New faculty have been recruited and employed in HR&E with the key qualifications including high interest in working in the newly designed program and experience and commitment to working closely with colleagues in HR&E, Arts and Science, and PDSs. In addition, standards for renewal, tenure, and promotion are being reconsidered and means for assessing the quality of work in a newly defined professorial role are being developed.

While much more curriculum development and evaluation work will be done over the coming years, it is already evident that the impact of the new curriculum has affected the assumptions and conceptual frameworks undergirding the work of the faculty. For example, other non-teacher education curriculum development efforts and project proposals are beginning to reflect greater cross-departmental involvement. There is also evidence of even greater working relationships with school and non-school professionals in the review, revision, and teaching of new courses and programs in non-teacher education areas. Still other non-teacher education faculty are recognizing the need for their work to be connected with the efforts of their colleagues engaged in the reform of teacher education and schooling. Finally, the deliberative and decision-making structure and processes and membership of the governance body of the Collaborative and thus of the teacher education program are radically different and are beginning to make an impact on the culture of the College.

The Governance of the Collaborative and Teacher Education Program

During the developmental stage of the reform work, the governance structure was the PDS Cross-Site Steering Committee. This group included the Site Steering Committee Chairs, the principals, and University faculty members working with each of the original six PDS sites. The director and other members of the Benedum Management Team were also part of the structure. Teams of PDS teachers and administrators, Arts and Science faculty members, and HR&E teacher education faculty worked in teams to develop both the overall design of the new teacher education program and specific courses and clinical activities. Communication was frequent between sites and the Management Team and between the various members of the curriculum design and development teams.

For a period of two or more years, the design and development of the new curriculum and the reform efforts at the PDS sites were disconnected. That is, while the proposed design was being reviewed and subsequently approved by University and State bodies little other teacher education curriculum work took place. Subsequently, most of the energy of the staff was directed toward PDS reform work and the selection and orientation of eight new sites. Due to these shifts in focus, the pressure to implement a complex and comprehensive assessment program and changes in the leadership of the reform efforts, communications among all parties were strained and in some cases halted. It became clear that the Cross-Site Steering Committee and Management Team could no longer meet all of the needs for assistance, full involvement, and emotional support of the thirteen PDSs' faculty, Arts and Science faculty, and HR&E faculty. In short, the work of the Benedum Collaborative could no longer be done by one community-wide body.

In an attempt to meet these needs and do the more and more complex work of the Collaborative, a new governance structure was constructed.

Recognizing that the Collaborative's work resides in the domains of teacher education, school and professional development reform, assessment, and policy and change leadership, several councils were formed. Each has membership from the PDS, Arts and Science, and HR&E faculties to underscore the centrality of the Collaborative ethic and process.

The Teacher Education Coordinating Council represents nearly 200 members of the teacher education faculty. The teacher education faculty is made up of PDS faculty and administrators, Arts and Science faculty from teacher education-related departments, faculty from Physical Education, Creative Arts, and Agricultural Education units, and faculty from most of the HR&E units. The Council establishes the standards for admission to the program, policies and procedures for recruitment, course review and revision, and will have ultimate responsibility for the evaluation of the program.

The PDS Cross-Site Steering Committee (now Council) continues to function with a primary focus on the school reform efforts and related curriculum and professional development problems and issues. The meetings provide important time for sharing information and feelings, for supporting mutual risk taking in an uncertain venture, and participating in the decision making process of the Collaborative. In addition to the liaisons who are all HR&E faculty, the Council is made up of the chair of the site steering committee at each PDS, and the principal of each PDS. A University representative and two PDS faculty serve as the three co-chairs of the Council. In the past, faculty from Arts and Science have also been part of the Council and Management Team.

A newly formed Leadership Council includes representatives of PDS and district administrators, PDS teachers, faculty from the HR&E Department of Educational Leadership Studies, participating Boards of Education, State Department of Education, and members of participating communities. This Council came into being in response to the PDS superintendents and principals expressing a need to meet on a regular basis to develop their own team building, conflict resolution, and community communication skills so that they would be effective players in the reform efforts. Community representatives, Board of Education members, and State Department of Education representatives were included to enhance communication and institutionalization of the reforms. Teachers are part of the Council to reinforce their critical leadership roles and to assure direct communication between the classroom and the policy world. The Department of Educational Leadership Studies also wanted to have an advisory group to react to and make recommendations about their school administrator preparation programs.

An Assessment Advisory Board also functions both to advise the Coordinator of Assessment and to communicate to other interested parties the quality and impact of the Collaborative's efforts.

To maintain the connections between the Councils and the faculties, an overarching Governing Board has been formed. Representatives from each of the Councils make up the membership of the Board, with the Director of the Collaborative serving in an ad hoc status. The responsibilities of the Governing Board include setting policies and making Collaborative-wide decisions about goals and priorities, strategic planning, funding, use of assessment data, institutionalizing the work of the Collaborative within the participating institutions and beyond, publicly promoting the work of the Collaborative, addressing Collaborative-wide problems and issues, reviewing the work of the Benedum Collaborative director, and advising the Dean of the College.

The significance of the new governance structure is its high involvement of people from schools and units not typically part of a COE's decision-making framework and the sharing of power across the institutions and faculties. The intent is to assure a voice for all participants in the varied but connected domains of the Collaborative and thus the College. How well it will work is yet to be seen. That such a shared decision-making structure and process is in existence is a statement of impact on the ways things will be done in the College. As it matures the structure may be revised to fewer units, perhaps back to a single body representing all dimensions of the reforms in teacher education, administrator education, PDSs, and policy formation at district and state levels.

PDS and University Liaisons

Connecting the worlds of schools and the University requires strong, ongoing personal relationships between the faculty of both. Personal relationships formed the key building blocks during the initial years of the reform work in both settings. Old wounds and expectations about the University telling the schools what was wrong and how they should change had to heal and change. Trust and mutual regard had to be fostered and the risk taking and changes had to be shared if the Collaborative was to be collaborative. With thirteen PDSs, multiple Arts and Science units, and several units in HR&E involved, the need for continuous and accurate communication, for maintaining a focus on the vision and key processes of this reform effort, and for addressing the multitude of problems that naturally emerge in such an effort requires a concerted effort to renew and extend the connections. The role of liaisons, largely HR&E faculty members, has been given more attention in recent years in an attempt to forge strong connections among the parts of the Collaborative. The liaison role is becoming particularly critical as we approach the placement of the first cohort students in the PDSs.

The role of the liaison is conceptualized currently to include the following functions:

- becoming a participant in the site's reform efforts by assisting with strategic planning and action research at the PDS site

- facilitating communication and collaboration between faculty and administrators at WVU and at each PDS
- being an advocate for the new teacher education program in the PDS context and an advocate for the PDS reforms at the University
- assisting with the design of site-based assessment and action research, serving as a broker connecting University faculty with particular expertise to PDS needs and vice versa
- providing advice and training in the development of skills central to functioning as a PDS (e.g., communication skills, team building, action research, strategic planning, etc.)

The thirteen liaisons meet every month to talk about the role, share experiences and concerns, and develop new insights and skills related to the role. Each person involved in the liaison role tends to have personal and contextual variations on the meaning of the role. Each site has involved the liaison to differing degrees in the week-to-week functions of the site so that some liaisons are involved on an in-depth basis for as much time as they can spend at the site, while others attend the site steering committee meetings on a regular basis While up to $2000 per faculty member per year has been dedicated to supporting the time and functions of the liaisons, their teaching loads have not been altered significantly. It will take yet more time and sustained developmental efforts for the faculty and department chairs to internalize the liaison role and its critical linkage function.

Those who appear to have integrated and internalized many of the liaison functions seem to have a personal history of close working relations with colleagues in school settings. They already had a trusting and supportive relationship established with their PDS colleagues. Once a person has been mutually agreed upon by the PDS faculty, the University department chair, and the faculty member to serve in the role of liaison, the development of the relationship begins. For most it is a halting, incremental, and time-consuming undertaking. For several of the faculty, particularly junior and untenured faculty, there is considerable anxiety about how much time to spend in such work, whether or not it will be acknowledged and rewarded when done well, and how it will affect their scholarly productivity.

The impact of the liaison role is only beginning to be felt. All recognize the importance of the role in linking PDSs and University units, in gluing the teacher education clinical parts to the University classroom components to form a program, in identifying problems and issues, and in enabling action research and the development of solutions.

The degree of impact that these and other curriculum and organizational changes in HR&E have or will have on the culture of the College and the roles of faculty is known in part only. Clearly, the curriculum design changes in the teacher education program are significant. The extent to which the new design becomes the conceptual framework the faculty and students use as they think and talk about the teacher education program will be the measure of the impact of the new design. The extent to which the new governance structure and processes reflect a full exchange of perspectives and program ideas that meet the standards of best practice across PDS, Arts and Science and other content units, and HR&E faculty will be the measures of the quality of its impact. The impact of liaison role will be known by the extent to which liaisons feel comfortable working in the two worlds, are engaged in facilitating the reform efforts, and are able to effectively communicate the perspectives, concerns, and visions of PDS and university faculty to each other. Finally, the practica are promising in their potential to provide a safe yet challenging context for sharing and examining the actual practices of PDS faculty and of university faculty. Out of the collective networks of reflection will come proposals and actions that signal the ongoing learning community the Collaborative has sought to create over the past six years.

Summary and Cautions about Reform and COEs

The purposes and qualities of good and consequential colleges of education of the future as articulated by an array of scholars and professional groups reviewed in the first section of this chapter set forth a challenging set of expectations. The first represents a shift from training competent and effective educational practitioners based on idealized models of teaching and effective teaching research to the design of teacher education programs centered by pedagogical and democratic values and informed by accumulated research across time and place and research conducted in the context of the schools and universities involved. Clearly, the very best of research and the best of practice are critically important referents in the development of teacher education programs. However, without clear and compelling values about what constitutes good teaching, good learning, and thus good education, the research and evaluation results are of little worth (see Brad Macdonald's [1995] edited book of his father's [James B. Macdonald] development of these and related curriculum matters). If teacher education, administrator education, and counselor education programs lack a pedagogical and democratic centering, they will make little impact on the professional lives of novice educators or the personal lives of children. A commitment to thoughtful action in the interest of educating human beings toward liberation from ignorance and narrowness of perspective, toward full exploration of their talents and human possibilities, and toward full participation in democratic deliberation and action must center the work of the COE. Other reform expectations include creating strong and sustaining connections with the day-to-day home and school lives of children and professional educators, collaboration with colleagues across the university and COE and throughout the field of professional practice, and framing and conducting research that contributes to the quality of life and learning of students. The message to COEs from the public and the profession is clear: get directly involved in dealing with the problems and issues of schooling and professional education—help make a difference or get out of the way!

The second set of reform activities addressed in this chapter was that of describing, analyzing, and evaluating the quality and impact of the reform of a COE. Bold new curriculum designs are necessary, but not sufficient indicators of substantive reform in a COE. How might we go about assessing the curriculum—its value base, its conceptual framework, its depth and breadth, its perspective on learners and learning—teachers and teaching, whether or not it engages students in imaginative construction of teaching events and the critical interrogation of policies, programs, and practices? Similarly, a case was set out for assessing the impact of the reforms on the culture of the college (role definitions, mores, power allocations, expectations for quality work and subsequent recognitions and rewards, communication patterns) and on the forms and consequence of the research and scholarship engaged in by the faculty and graduate students. Any attempt to engage in systemic reform of a COE must have a comprehensive assessment design in place and a staff of qualified people engaged in doing assessment work. Without it, statements about the impact of the reforms are speculative at best and self-serving at worst.

Finally, three aspects of reform and their apparent impact on the College of Human Resources and Education at West Virginia University were described. The complete revision of the teacher education curriculum, the construction of a collaborative and deliberative governance structure, and the evolution of the liaison role were discussed to illustrate how one COE is attempting to re-center its work on matters of consequence in the lives and learning of children and professional educators. It also illustrates the extensive amount of time, interpersonal work, and organizational openness needed if the programs and practices of a teacher education faculty are to be connected simultaneously to the realities of schooling, the insights of research, and the critical eye of theory. Finally, the Benedum Collaborative experiences illustrate the messiness of organizational change, particularly when it is done collaboratively.

From our work in progress we are learning several lessons. I will frame them as lessons I am learning, since the assessment data are not in on how my colleagues react to and make sense of the changes.

1.   Make a commitment to the vision and each other. Many faculty apparently believed this was just another one of those externally funded projects. A nice idea, but it will bite the dust as have so many before it. As one colleague, with only some tongue in cheek, put it, "This project wasn't

supposed to last this long! Nobody thought the funding would last or that we would be expected to actually act on the plans!"

Obtaining a long-term commitment to such a major and systemic reform as is expected in COEs is a matter of fostering daily the vision and its potential. The vision must be clear, believable, and shared by as many as possible. Fostering a shared vision is a key responsibility of the Collaborative leaders.

2. Allocate internal resources early and continuously to underscore the importance of the reforms to the College. If external funds are viewed as the basic resources for change, the minute those funds are gone, the changes are on their way out. Reallocation of faculty loads, assignment of graduate assistants, distribution of travel funds for national presentations, and annual reviews and tenure and promotion decisions all signal the value of the changes to the faculty of the College and the University.

3. Share the changes with others often—let others know that the COE is serious about reforming its programs and its relationships with the affairs of schools and those who work in them. The Benedum Foundation President, Paul Jenkins, has helped us acknowledge this lesson by providing the expertise of a journalist who is helping us tell our story in terms that are readily understandable and exciting to State-level policy makers.

4. Continuously revisit the expected indicators of impact on the preparation of a new generation and genre of educators, new forms of teaching and schooling, and new forms of partnerships between the faculties of schools and university departments. While it is essential to keep the vision out in front of all, it is equally vital that potential indicators of how the vision is being translated into lived experiences and conditions be kept in mind.

5. Money from external sources, while absolutely critical to support the time and develop the capacities of very busy people to think, argue, plan, try on, assess, and reflect on the meanings of the reforms, cannot be expected to sustain the continuing operational work of the reform of a COE. To sustain the new approaches of professional preparation and continuous development, of the new forms of schooling, and of the partnership and the collaborative principles that glue the entire entity together, calls for the commitment of the leadership of each institution to reallocate its own funding. While this is a point that is difficult to sell, it is perhaps the most telling indicator of institutionalization of the reforms in a COE.

In closing this examination of the impact that simultaneous reform might have on a college of education, I suggest the following indicators of how we will know when the conceptualizations, principles, and journeys partly taken have had lasting impact on the life and work of a COE:

- The teacher education and non-teacher education faculty are able to articulate in their own words what the reform work is about and why it is vital that the COE be committed to it.
- Teacher education faculty (and others such as faculty in Arts and Science, education administration, counselling, foundations, and educational psychology) roles have clear expectations for a significant allocation of time and energy in working collaboratively with each other and with colleagues in PDSs and similar agencies that serve children and their families.
- Promotion and tenure expectations and standards reflect in clear terms the quality of work desired and the support such quality will accrue.
- The COE budget reflects a clear investment in sustaining liaison roles, research directed toward problems and issues encountered in the day-to-day conduct of schooling, and PDS-based professional experiences.
- University and PDS colleagues speak highly of the quality and significance of the reform work and convey such support to students and the community at large.
- The State legislature and Department of Education personnel recognize the quality and impact of the reform work and seek out the expertise of the faculty in addressing policy issues associated with school reform, educator preparation, and the assessment of such work.
- The collaborative governance structure and processes for the simultaneous reform work become permanent in the culture of the COE and its relationships with colleagues from the partner sites and units.
- Clusters of faculty and graduate student research about matters related to the simultaneous reforms have been developed, are used by all in the Collaborative, and are sought out by other educators across the nation and beyond.

While others might be added, we in the Benedum Collaborative and the College of Human Resources and Education at West Virginia University will use these as markers for our own reform journey.

References

Clifford, G. J. and Guthrie, J. W. (1988). *Ed school: A brief for professional education.* Chicago: University of Chicago Press.

Connelly, F. M. and Clandinin, D. J. (1988). *Teachers as curriculum planners: Narratives of experience.* New York: Teachers College Press.

Deal T. E. (1989). The culture of schools. In L. T. Scheive and M. B. Schoenheit, eds., *Leadership: Examining the elusive.* Alexandria, Va.: Association for Supervision and Curriculum Development.

Eisner, E. W. (1994). *The educational imagination: On the design and evaluation of school programs* (3rd ed.). New York: Macmillan.

Elbaz, F. (1983). *Teacher thinking: A study of practical knowledge.* London: Croom Helm.

Feiman-Nemser, S. and Floden, R. E. (1986). The cultures of teaching. In M. C. Wittrock, ed., *Handbook of research on teaching.* (3rd. ed.), New York: Macmillan.

Goodlad, J. I., Soder, R., Sirotnik, K. A., eds. (1990). *Places where teachers are taught.* San Francisco: Jossey-Bass.

Goodlad, J. I. (1991). *Teachers for our nation's schools.* San Francisco: Jossey-Bass.

Greene, M. (1986). Philosophy and teaching. In M. C. Wittrock, ed., *Handbook of research on teaching* (3rd. ed,), New York: Macmillan.

Hargreaves, A. (1994). *Changing teachers, changing time: teachers' work and culture in the postmodern age.* New York: Teachers College Press.

Hawthorne, R. D. (1990). Analyzing school-based collaborative curriculum decision making. *Journal of Curriculum and Supervision 5*(3): 279–286.

Henderson, J. G. & Hawthorne, R. D. (1995). *Transformative curriculum leadership.* Columbus, Ohio: Merrill/Prentice Hall.

Henderson, J. G. and Hawthorne, R. D. (1995). The dialectics of creating Professional Development Schools: Reflections on work in progress. In H. G. Petrie, ed., *Professionalization, partnership, and power: Building Professional Development Schools.* Albany: State University of New York Press.

Holly, M. L. (1989). *Writing to grow.* Portsmouth, N.H.: Heinemann.

Holmes Group (1995). *Tomorrow's schools of education: A report of the Holmes group.* East Lansing, Mich.: Holmes Group.

Howey, K. R. and Zimpher, N. L. (1989). *Profiles of preservice teacher education.* Albany: State University of New York Press.

Kennedy, M. M. (1991). *An agenda for research on teacher learning.* East Lansing, Mich.: National Center for Research on Teacher Learning Special Report.

Macdonald, B., ed. (1995). *Theory as a prayerful act: The collected essays of James B. Macdonald.* New York: Peter Lang Publishing Inc.

Pajares, M. F. (1992). Teachers' beliefs and educational research: Cleaning up a messy construct. *Review of Educational Research 62*(3): 307–332.

Shulman, L. S. (1986). Paradigms and research programs in the study of teaching: A contemporary perspective. In M. C. Wittrock, ed., *Handbook of research on teaching* (3rd. ed.). New York: Macmillan.

Soder, R. and Sirotnik, K. A. (1990). Beyond reinventing the past: The politics of teacher education. In J. I. Goodlad, R. Soder, and K. S. Sirotnik, eds., *Places where teachers are taught*. San Francisco:Jossey- Bass.

van Manen, M. (1992). *On pedagogy as virtue*. Paper presented at the AERA annual conference in San Francisco.

Walker, D. F. (1971). A study of deliberation in three curriculum projects. *Curriculum Theory Network 7*(4): 118–134.

Author Index